AUTHORED, EDITED, OR COEDITED BOOKS BY DAVID LaROCCA

On Emerson

Emerson's Transcendental Etudes by Stanley Cavell

The Philosophy of Charlie Kaufman

Estimating Emerson: An Anthology of Criticism from Carlyle to Cavell

Emerson's English Traits and the Natural History of Metaphor

The Philosophy of War Films

A Power to Translate the World: New Essays on Emerson and International Culture

The Bloomsbury Anthology of Transcendental Thought: From Antiquity to the Anthropocene

The Philosophy of Documentary Film: Image, Sound, Fiction, Truth

The Thought of Stanley Cavell and Cinema: Turning Anew to the Ontology of Film a Half-Century after The World Viewed

Inheriting Stanley Cavell: Memories, Dreams, Reflections

Movies with Stanley Cavell in Mind

Metacinema: The Form and Content of Filmic Reference and Reflexivity

The Geschlecht Complex: Addressing Untranslatable Aspects of Gender, Genre, and Ontology

GUEST EDITED

Conversations: The Journal of Cavellian Studies No.7: Acknowledging Stanley Cavell

Praise for *The Thought of Stanley Cavell and Cinema: Turning Anew to the Ontology of Film a Half-Century after* The World Viewed

A brilliant collection of original essays by major figures in the field. The genius of Cavell's writings on film is in sharp focus throughout—likewise the continued provocation of *The World Viewed* and its successor books and essays.

> MICHAEL FRIED, J. R. Herbert Boone Emeritus Professor of
> Humanities and the History of Art, Johns Hopkins University, USA

Stanley Cavell argued that film exists in a state of philosophy. Part of what he meant by this was that thinking about a film is a way of doing philosophy. That has been his influential and most controversial claim. The authors in this collection explore what he might have meant in ways more variegated, thoughtful, original, and illuminating than anything I have seen before. *The Thought of Stanley Cavell and Cinema*, exemplary in its clarity and carefulness, is a watershed both in our understanding of Cavell and of film itself.

> ROBERT PIPPIN, Evelyn Stefansson Nef Distinguished Service Professor,
> University of Chicago, USA

Now for a new audience comes David LaRocca's edited collection *The Thought of Stanley Cavell and Cinema*. [...] The expertise of its contributors speaks for itself, and it will undoubtedly become [...] the definitive record of the scholars of Cavell and what they had to say about *The World Viewed* at the time of Cavell's death. [...T]he collection will serve as further evidence of the canonization of *The World Viewed* and its centrality to the discipline of film-philosophy or the philosophy of film (*Screening the Past*, no. 45).

> REX BUTLER, Professor of Art History & Theory, Monash University,
> Australia

Praise for *Movies with Stanley Cavell in Mind*

This volume pushes Cavellian scholarship forward, showing that the value of Cavell's work lies not simply in understanding it but in applying it. By extending the philosopher's methods to an exciting range of international and contemporary films, the chapters compose a timely consideration of what it is to read a film, and to read a film generously.

> KYLE STEVENS, Assistant Professor of Film Studies, Appalachian State
> University, USA

Stanley Cavell is, to my mind, the best thinker for helping us account for the power of the film experience, and the fourteen chapters collected here provide ample reason for understanding the importance of Cavell for the study of film. All of the contributors to this wonderful, collective enterprise—brought together by David LaRocca—have in a similar way encountered him and his work. Whether they are revisiting films Cavell loved or taking up the invitation to explore new films, they reveal the importance of Cavell's writing and method."

> SANDRA LAUGIER, Professor of Philosophy, Université Paris 1
> Panthéon-Sorbonne, France

Praise for *Inheriting Stanley Cavell: Memories, Dreams, Reflections*

Inheriting Stanley Cavell, beautifully edited by David LaRocca, is so much more than a gathering of reminiscences and testimonials. So many of the pieces in the volume prove gripping, and they cumulatively transformed my sense of what Cavell had accomplished. This volume makes a strong case for the revolution that Cavell's extraordinary philosophic sensibility, powerful presence as a teacher, and wide-range of concerns brought about in North American philosophy. For many of the contributors, Cavell not only revived their faith in philosophy, but showed them what it meant to be alive in their feelings and thinking. He demonstrated, not only in *The Claim of Reason* but in his astonishing exploration of films, Shakespearean tragedies, and Wittgenstein, Emerson, and Thoreau, that the road back to ordinary language criticism was open, and our best hope for restoring value to humanistic study. The collection is also impressive for its decision to include dissenting voices.

>GEORGE TOLES, Distinguished Professor of English, Theatre, Film & Media, University of Manitoba, Canada

In moods ranging from the elegiac to the exuberant to the contentious, the essays collected here remember Cavell and his work, put it to further use, and engage with it critically. Together their authors compose a conversation that amounts to what Cavell once described philosophy as being—an education for grownups—in which accomplished, mature thinkers continually seek their better selves, amidst the plights and possibilities of culture.

>RICHARD ELDRIDGE, Charles and Harriett Cox McDowell Professor of Philosophy, Swarthmore College, USA

The welcoming tone rightly identified by the editor as one genius of Stanley Cavell's exacting style has demonstrably been answered by this timely volume—and in just the right blend of reminiscence, reflection, and fresh testing. The intellectual heritage proposed, and so luminously proven, across these pages—convening a lineage of distinguished readers in their role, as always, of interlocutors—honors the balance of intimacy and reach in Cavell's influential philosophical writing: a style of thought inseparable from the searching prose that gave, that gives, it shape.

>GARRETT STEWART, James O. Freedman Professor of Letters, University of Iowa, USA

The voices gathered in this collection, each finding a different balance between the claims of memory, sympathy, and critique, together illuminate the relation between Stanley Cavell's life and his writings, and disclose an unattained but attainable future for philosophy to which we all might be attracted.

>STEPHEN MULHALL, Fellow and Tutor in Philosophy, New College, University of Oxford, UK

David LaRocca has gathered together some of the world's foremost scholars of Stanley Cavell's work for this terrific volume of essays responding to Cavell's philosophy. Collating reprints of groundbreaking essays and original contributions, the book offers wonderful insight into the breadth and depth of Cavell's influence and features a beautifully detailed and lucid introduction by LaRocca that interweaves the various strands of Cavell's philosophy and their legacies. This is without doubt a definitive body of responses to Cavell's work: a must-read for anyone interested in Cavell's work, whatever discipline they are approaching from, and whatever their level of specialism.

>CATHERINE WHEATLEY, Reader in Film and Visual Culture, King's College London, UK

The Thought of Stanley Cavell and Cinema

Turning Anew to the Ontology of Film a Half-Century after The World Viewed

Edited by
David LaRocca

BLOOMSBURY ACADEMIC
NEW YORK · LONDON · OXFORD · NEW DELHI · SYDNEY

BLOOMSBURY ACADEMIC
Bloomsbury Publishing Inc
1385 Broadway, New York, NY 10018, USA
50 Bedford Square, London, WC1B 3DP, UK
29 Earlsfort Terrace, Dublin 2, Ireland

BLOOMSBURY, BLOOMSBURY ACADEMIC and the Diana logo are
trademarks of Bloomsbury Publishing Plc

First published in the United States of America 2020
This paperback edition published in 2022

Volume Editor's Part of the Work © David LaRocca

Each chapter © of Contributors

For legal purposes the Acknowledgments on pp. 291-295 constitute an extension
of this copyright page.

Cover design by Eleanor Rose
Cover photograph © Getty Images

All rights reserved. No part of this publication may be reproduced or transmitted
in any form or by any means, electronic or mechanical, including photocopying,
recording, or any information storage or retrieval system, without prior
permission in writing from the publishers.

Bloomsbury Publishing Inc does not have any control over, or responsibility for, any
third-party websites referred to or in this book. All internet addresses given in this
book were correct at the time of going to press. The author and publisher regret any
inconvenience caused if addresses have changed or sites have ceased to exist, but can
accept no responsibility for any such changes.

Library of Congress Cataloging-in-Publication Data
Names: LaRocca, David, 1975- editor.
Title: The thought of Stanley Cavell and cinema: turning anew to the ontology of film
a half-century after the world viewed / edited by David LaRocca.
Description: New York: Bloomsbury Academic, 2020. | Includes
bibliographical references and index.
Identifiers: LCCN 2019025889 (print) | LCCN 2019025888 (ebook) |
ISBN 9781501349164 (hardback) | ISBN 9781501349171 (epub) |
ISBN 9781501349188 (pdf) | ISBN 9781501349188 (pdf) |
ISBN 9781501349171 (epub) | ISBN 9781501349164 (hardback)
Subjects: LCSH: Cavell, Stanley, 1926–2018–Criticism and interpretation.
Classification: LCC PN1998.3.C416 T48 2019 (ebook) | LCC PN1998.3.C416 (print)
| DDC 791.43092–dc23
LC record available at https://lccn.loc.gov/2019025889

ISBN: HB: 978-1-5013-4916-4
PB: 978-1-5013-8407-3
ePDF: 978-1-5013-4918-8
eBook: 978-1-5013-4917-1

Typeset by Deanta Global Publishing Services, Chennai, India

To find out more about our authors and books visit www.bloomsbury.com and sign
up for our newsletters.

Cavell was not interested in theory but in thought.
—CHARLES BERNSTEIN

CONTENTS

Foreword: Stanley Cavell and Cinema
    THOMAS ELSAESSER   xi

Introduction: Philosophy's Claim to Film, Film's
   Claim to Philosophy
    DAVID LAROCCA   1

**I Underwriting and Overhearing: Reconceiving
Cinematic Ontology and Genre**   21

  1 "Assertions in Technique": Tracking the Medial
     "Thread" in Cavell's Filmic Ontology
     GARRETT STEWART   23

  2 Revisiting *The World Viewed*
     NOËL CARROLL   41

  3 The World Heard
     KYLE STEVENS   63

  4 What a Genre of Film Might Be: Medium,
     Myth, and Morality
     STEPHEN MULHALL   88

II Interlude: Temperaments for Film   105

  5 My Troubled Relationship with Stanley Cavell:
     In Pursuit of a Truly Cinematic Conversation
     SCOTT MACDONALD   107

  6 *Film as Film* and the Personal
     WILLIAM ROTHMAN   121

III Philosophy, As If Made for Film 127

7 Between Skepticism and Moral Perfectionism: On Cavell's Melodrama of the Unknown Woman
ROBERT SINNERBRINK 129

8 Overcoming Skepticism in *Casablanca*
THOMAS E. WARTENBERG 152

9 A Skeptic's Reprieve: Cavell on Comedy in Shakespeare and the Movies
LAWRENCE F. RHU 170

IV Film, As If Made for Philosophy 189

10 Film Exists in a State of Philosophy: Two Contemporary Cavellian Views
SHAWN LOHT 191

11 The Conception of Film for the Subject of Television: Moral Education of the Public and a Return to an Aesthetics of the Ordinary
SANDRA LAUGIER 210

12 On Film in Reality: Cavellian Reflections on Skepticism, Belief, and Documentary
MATHEW ABBOTT 228

13 On the Aesthetics of Amateur Filmmaking in Narrative Cinema: Negotiating Home Movies after *Adam's Rib*
DAVID LaROCCA 245

Acknowledgments 291
Contributors 296
Index 302

FOREWORD

Stanley Cavell and Cinema

Thomas Elsaesser

THERE IS AN OLD JOKE that, in the days before television, the English music hall comedian Max Miller used to tell:

> When I was a lad, I wanted to marry the girl across the road. So I says to my Dad: "Dad, I fancy marrying that girl across the road." And my father says, "Son, I have a confession to make. When I was a young lad I used to get around, and I'm sorry to have to tell you this, but you can't marry her because she is really your sister." So, I get a little depressed, but then I pick myself up again. I get on the bus and when I get home I says: "Dad, I want to get married to the girl that lives three streets away." And my dad starts looking glum and says: "Son, I've got something to tell you. When I was your age, we didn't have buses, but I had a bike, and to make a long story short, that girl's your sister." Now I'm getting desperate. I go and buy myself a railway ticket and when I come back, I make straight for my father: "Dad, I bet you've never been to Birmingham!" And dad replies: "Oh yes, I have!" So, quite crushed, I go off to the kitchen to talk to my mother. "Looks like I'm never gonna get married, Mum!"—"Why's that?" she says—"Well, it seems every girl I fancy turns out to be my sister!" And Mum says: "You go right ahead and marry whoever you want, my lad. *He's* not your father."[1]

I could now go on and ruin the joke by starting to explain it, or worse still by starting to explain what pertinence it has for Stanley Cavell's philosophical project. Instead, I want to come to this project, at least as it has a bearing on the cinema, by briefly characterizing another project—the "philosophical turn" in university film studies.

Film studies, ever since it entered the academy in the 1970s, and especially in the United States and Great Britain, has not only been in response to but also a symptom of, the general "crisis in the humanities." While this crisis takes many forms, one manifestation is surely connected with the momentous transformations of a culture of the word, of written evidence and material proof, to a culture of sounds and images, where the materiality of evidence relies, for its production as well as for its reproduction, on complex electronic technologies, and for its reception on the transitory sense-impressions of the eye and ear. Living this paradigm shift in culture, students have become almost peremptory in demanding of their teachers that they enable them to learn (note that I do not say: "to teach them'") about cinema, about the media, about image culture and visuality, about music and noise. But if this reflects their awareness of the "now," their acute participation in the several revolutions taking place (which we rarely name as such, fearing that the word itself has been appropriated by the advertising copy-writer for start-ups and high-tech "disrupters"), it also testifies to a certain continuity. Students, I would surmise, probably seek in cinema what they once sought (and occasionally still seek) in literature: confirmation and a validation of self-doubt and self-exploration, as well as those moments of self-fulfillment which, in childhood, were also moments of self-oblivion, and—among the most precociously acute of unhappy adolescents—moments of intense self-alienation.

These pressures from students, combined with constraints emanating from the university institution, have within a very short space of time given the subject of film studies not only canonical texts, genres, and authors—witness the extraordinary rise of Hitchcock as the canonical author *par excellence*, or of "film noir" and "horror" as canonical genres—but also traditions of hermeneutics and interpretation. Many of the textual strategies elaborated around these conjunctures have until recently—perhaps surprisingly in light of what I have just said about a cultural paradigm shift—not been fundamentally different from those in contemporary literary theory and cultural studies. The discipline thus reflects only partially some ultimate (ontological) truth about the cinema, but responds to a more generally felt need to find for the humanities ways of talking about authors, texts, and audiences that break with the modernist credo of the autonomous and self-sufficient artifact no less than with the concept of authorship as self-expression.

In respect of both "author" and "work," the study of Hollywood films has a special significance, obliging the student of cinema to come up with, but also come up against, new conditions of textual production, of aesthetic reception, and of attributing cultural and political meanings to the products of an unapologetically commercial culture. For instance, "we" the spectators, who in sociologically inspired mass media studies had traditionally been discussed as passive consumers, as victims of visual rhetoric (e.g., montage versus the long take), of propaganda (e.g., Nazi cinema) and of commodification strategies (e.g., the Frankfurt School's dictum of mass entertainment as mass deception)—these spectators have greatly benefited, at least as theoretical objects, from linguistic, psychoanalytic, cognitive, and phenomenological theory. Reader-response, narrative comprehension, and the study of affect and emotion have widened the scope of what used to be a choice between the "textually constructed subject" (of psychoanalysis) and the various types of "negotiated readings" (in cultural studies). In this respect, feminist theory has perhaps been one of the most successful, and certainly the most influential interventions, trying to unify a field of research, by programmatically transgressing the academic boundaries of literature, art history, and film studies.

It is here that I see Stanley Cavell's work, and his eminent standing as a philosopher, to have at once opened up possibilities of continuation, as well as introduced certain ruptures, obliging or, rather, *inviting* this by now no longer quite-so-young discipline of film studies to become once more reflexive, though perhaps not self-reflexive (which it has been, and often painfully so), but to become more dialogical, conversational: one might even say, more gregarious and convivial.

Cavell, for the film student, is the author of four books on film (*The World Viewed*, *Pursuits of Happiness*, *Contesting Tears*, and *Cities of Words*). His interest in the cinema is a complex one, and he seems to enjoy the status of his work as not confined to or defined by the dominant critical doxa of the discipline, but he also sometimes—as in the preface to *Contesting Tears*—publicly worries about his standing in the film studies community. If he is not unduly concerned with the debates in past decades over the "cinematic apparatus," and if his interest in the cinema is different from that of, say, Roland Barthes who diffidently pondered films as our culture's last manifestations of "*le romaneseque*" (defined as the experience of time charged with meaning because of exemplifying a destiny), Cavell's passion for films has at once the gravity and the diary informality of the thinkers he is most drawn to. Wittgenstein's *Philosophical Investigations*, Heidegger's *What is Called Thinking*, and Sigmund Freud's debt to Kant furnish important signposts that frame Cavell's discussion of Hollywood movies. In *Pursuits of Happiness*, a study of what used to be called "screwball comedies," but which Cavell has illuminatingly renamed "The Hollywood Comedy of Remarriage," Cavell weaves his reflections, observations, and close readings around two paradigms: one is the philosophical crux of "the existence of other minds," and the other is "repetition," glossed with a quote from Freud's *Three Essays on the Theory of Sexuality*: "the finding of the object is in fact the refinding of it," but as we know, a notion also central to both Jacques Derrida and Gilles Deleuze.

Cavell's other major study of cinema, *Contesting Tears*, explicitly takes up the same motifs, to sketch the outlines of another genre, "The Melodrama of the Unknown Woman," comprising such classics of the woman's film (or "weepie") as Max Ophüls' *Letter from an Unknown Woman*, King Vidor's *Stella Dallas*, George Cukor's *Gaslight*, and Irving Rapper's *Now, Voyager*. Elsewhere, he has added Michael Curtiz's *Mildred Pierce*, Mervyn LeRoy's

Random Harvest, and Josef von Sternberg's *Blonde Venus* to the list, as well as Heinrich von Kleist's novella, *Die Marquise von O.*—made into a film by Eric Rohmer, and Henrik Ibsen's *Nora*, adapted for the screen by Joseph Losey.

The "Melodramas of the Unknown Woman" are structurally related to the "Comedies of Remarriage" insofar as they involve a woman establishing her right to existence across a number of *im*possibilities, chief among which is "men" or (in Emerson's phrase, "nonchalant boys who are sure of a dinner"). The tragedy of these women, or, indeed, of "the woman," is that she needs "man" to be "created," but man is a creature who is himself in all relevant respects incomplete, unformed, with an irresponsibility that spans from the "nonchalant" to the "villainous." The woman's right to existence, then, takes the form of a metamorphosis in both the genres Cavell has fashioned, but in melodrama it entails a traumatic use of language (the eloquent muteness of the unknown woman inverting symmetrically the love of dialogue and the "high embattled wit" of the couples in the comedies of remarriage). Clearly, Cavell is only partly interested in new readings of these films, and certainly not in canonical readings. Rather, in a move typical of the post-structuralist mode of thinking, he makes the reading process itself the essential part of the "reading" he proposes (with an elegant theory of transference and counter-transference).

Interrogating his own unusual combination of disciplines, Cavell discovers in the films he has singled out an unexpected connection, not only among the two bodies of texts. Operating with yet another bold inversion of habitual perspectives, and still taking his cue from Hollywood, Cavell discovers that psychoanalysis, philosophy, and cinema are all spoken from the same (male) perspective, because they share the same implied addressee: woman. They all ask "what she knows, how she knows, and how she escapes doubt about what she knows."

Skepticism, the philosophical issue that attracted Cavell to Wittgenstein and ordinary language philosophy, turns out to be a problem—as well as the displacement of a problem—constitutive of the male. Cavell traces it back to the Renaissance, to the break up of the feudal order, tied to legitimacy and inheritance, grounded in the doubts expressed most poignantly in Shakespearean tragedy, such as in *Othello* or *King Lear*, and articulated most nakedly in *The Winter's Tale*, which explicitly turns on the question whether men can ever really know that their children are theirs. With this formulation, Cavell seeks to rephrase not only the problem of the existence of other minds, but also the issue of recognition, the search for the lost object and its mis-cognition, which he sees enacted in the Hollywood melodramas of the unknown woman.

Returning once more to our own modernity and the cinema, I take Cavell to suggest that after Nietzsche, it is psychoanalysis and the cinema that most plausibly furnish an answer to the "death of God" and to "radical skepticism." For if philosophy is, indeed, crucially concerned with what we can know, then psychoanalysis does make a contribution to philosophy, and, indeed, can be considered as a displacement of philosophy in this respect, since the question that skepticism puts to philosophy receives in psychoanalysis a name: that of The Unconscious. Cavell has some admirably concise pages on this, and I hope I will be forgiven for not attempting to paraphrase them.

Considering the near-contemporaneity of psychoanalysis and the cinema, does this suggest that they are the *recto* and *verso* of each other? Each quite distinct (we know that Freud had little interest in or patience for the moving image), but nonetheless conjoined by the fact that both are, as it were, answers to a question they were not altogether aware that it was being asked of them? Or, taking the thought one step further, could the cinema be regarded as in some sense the "limit" of psychoanalysis, more specifically voiced in a passage from *Contesting Tears* where Cavell writes that his readings of a particular film come to an end when he feels that psychoanalysis is called for?

What is more certain is the task that Cavell assigns to the cinema: to "gender" both these displacements, putting the woman at the center of the burden or in the "path" of skepticism, but also as both origin and riddle of psychoanalysis; the "feminization" of skepticism, so to speak, as well as of the talking cure. Might it be that instead of Oedipus encountering the Sphinx, it is the Sphinx that not only "knows" about Oedipus' lack of knowledge, but also knows that he knows that she knows . . .? This knowledge, in melodrama, unlike tragedy, does not produce *anagnorisis*, or recognition. The woman's role in melodrama is "to be consumed by the longing for creation, the affirmation of her unknownness."

Repetition and Melodrama: Is this the conjunction of symmetry and asymmetry displaced in time, forever non-aligned, and thus a special instance of the Derridean *différance*, deferral? Or is it closer to the Freudian *Unheimliche*, the Uncanny, the all too familiar made strange by returning, unexpectedly, at the wrong moment, which is, of course, for Freud and Lacan at least, invariably the right moment? Melodrama is all about time, about timing, *bad* timing. Or in Cavell's brilliant formulation *apropos* of *Letter from an Unknown Woman* (as well as of *Hamlet*): melodrama is about appointments, missed appointments, dis-appointments.

But melodrama also differentiates, especially in its temporalities, and not along the binaries of *chronos* and *kairos* so typical of the classical literary and dramatic genres. This makes it so modern: melodrama knows the temporality of "too late" and the modality of "if only"—both conditions of repetition, but both marking crucially the gaps that open up between an event and its return in the constitution of the subject. Melodrama knows and speaks about this repetition, but from the vantage point of a barrier, a limit. What exactly this limit is—the blockage to exchange, or to "conversation" in Cavell's terms—is something on which feminists and Cavell might agree to disagree. "Female subjectivity" versus "the woman's insistence on unknownness": I tend to hope that Cavell is right, because in his version, paradoxical as it may sound, the default value is dialogue, communication, not the withdrawal into radical otherness, essential difference, the blackness of the screen, the tain/foil of the mirror (as it tended to be in the first, "radical" phase of feminist contestation).

Why this default value of dialogue in Cavell? Precisely because of skepticism, the (poisoned) bait laid out for the male—but as it happens, this poison, this *Gift* is also a gift—and if I understand Cavell right, a gift for both genders. The issue on which Cavell and feminists will agree is that these temporalities and modalities of melodrama can also go under the name of "nostalgia," the male's time of loss and mourning that is so useless to women, and which in turn, represents perhaps the cinema's most common currency, its own particular sweet poison of postmodernity (nostalgia, which is defined by Cavell as "parody" or "avoidance").

* * *

A question this raises, and on which I want to end, is one I am not sure whether Cavell has given us his views on: What is it that makes the cinema so profoundly American? And what does the cinema have to do with Cavell's other preoccupation, so eloquently put before us in the opening chapter of *A Pitch of Philosophy*: Jewish religion, Jewish ritual, and the history of Jewish secular emancipation in the modern epoch?

Let me hazard a wild speculation. Wittgenstein, Freud, Stefan Zweig, the author of the novella on which *Letter from an Unknown Woman* is based—what do they have in common? Vienna, 1900: the Vienna that was the capital of the multicultural Habsburg Empire, up to the First World War, the Vienna of Jewish cultural and intellectual assimilation, but also of Hitler's anti-Semitism. And one might add: the Vienna of Otto Weininger, author of *Geschlecht und Charakter*, a book so radical in its anti-feminism that it can serve as feminism's negative foil.

So my question is: Has Cavell reflected publicly on his debt to Vienna? Or put differently: Why stop the series of displacements where Cavell locates them? Is it not incumbent upon him, within the terms of the argument his writings imply, to operate other displacements, say, from woman and melodrama, to such additional moves as from feminism to Jewish emancipation, from popular culture to Jewish identity, from Hollywood to Jewish assimilation, from the Vienna of Wittgenstein, Freud, and Stefan Zweig to the Hollywood of Carl Laemmle, Adolf Zukor, and Max Ophüls? And beyond that (I am thinking of such by no means unproblematic, but stimulating, books as Neal Gabler's *An Empire of their Own: How The Jews Invented Hollywood*, or Michael Rogin's *Blackface, White Noise*) from the founding fathers of Hollywood, almost all Jewish, almost all central European immigrants, to the invention of the American Dream. By "inventing" Middle America, were the founding fathers of Hollywood compensating for their own cultural insecurity? When inventing America for the Americans, were they not also (re-)inventing an idea of childhood and "home" that has persuaded the rest of the world? Rogin's *Blackface, White Noise*, on the other hand, tries to document the extraordinary contortions, reversals, negations, and disavowals undertaken by Jewish entertainers, in the fields of music, dance, movies, in order to enter the mainstream by systematically mimicking, parodying, and—dare one say—even appropriating the cultural languages of those other outsiders, black Americans.

Does the cinema arise in the late nineteenth century in order to console us for radical skepticism or does it teach us to learn to live with its consequences? For me, as a male, the joke of Max Miller's joke is, of course, that what is offered as consolation by the maternal instance, the affirmation of my freedom, my right to choose, is no consolation at all. Her "Son, you go right ahead—*he*'s not your father!" cements my most absolute insecurity, for it confirms my own redundancy, my being caught in the eternal recurrence, burdened with the dead weight of repetition. Worse: as soon as I follow my mother's advice and "go right ahead," I shall be meeting my father, coming toward me on the road back from Birmingham. In this particular (tragi-)comedy of a marriage, then, the couple does not talk to each other at all, except, fatally, across the son.

Is this a lesson I can pass on to my students, keen to learn about sounds and images, as the sensory supports of their ways of being in the world? As we learn to *trust the cinema*, by recognizing in it the new "irony" of skepticism, or of Richard Rorty's version of anti-metaphysical, anti-foundational pragmatism, we should also bear in mind the Lacanian lesson of *les non-dupes errent / les noms du père*: fools are those who think themselves too clever to be fooled, (for they will be caught by) the name of the Father. Does such "trust" beyond/in the full knowledge of skepticism mean popular culture need not necessarily, not inevitably be tantamount to "mass-deception," as Adorno and Horkheimer saw it in their Southern Californian exile? Let us just say, that to learn about repetition and difference not only from Deleuze and Derrida, but also from Katherine Hepburn and Spencer Tracy, Joan Crawford and Joan Fontaine is a lesson I gladly pass on, with special thanks to Stanley Cavell.

Note

1 The Max Miller joke is perhaps more familiar from a song by Trini Lopez, also made famous by the Kingston Trio, "Shame and Scandal in the Family."

INTRODUCTION

Philosophy's Claim to Film, Film's Claim to Philosophy

David LaRocca

A HALF-CENTURY HAS ELAPSED since Stanley Cavell published his seminal work of film theory, *The World Viewed: Reflections on the Ontology of Film* (1971), a book that was as much an intervention into the prevailing landscape of thought on film as it was an invention of the philosophical treatment of film. Indeed, as Charles Bernstein's epigraph to this volume attests—in a fitting refrain to and reflexive comment upon its title—it may be better to call Cavell's intrepid book something other than "theory," but such are the categories we have grown accustomed to. Suddenly, all those years ago, and not without causing some measure of alarm among the custodians of both fields (as well as a dose of productive frisson for the rest), "film was as if made for philosophy"—and in the same breath, philosophy, despite its ancient precedence, was as if made for film.[1] Plato's cave, at last, was clearly protocinematic, and the history of philosophy became an active picture of skepticism (a picture realized at the movies).

In the present volume, a roster of considerable talent, laboring creatively in the now-familiar field of film-philosophy takes up anew Stanley Cavell's work on film, and at this auspicious juncture—nearly fifty years on, in the aftermath of his recent death—to continue the conversation Cavell inaugurated. Along with *The World Viewed* (issued in an expanded edition in 1979), scholars have Cavell's other landmark works to explore—such as *Pursuits of Happiness: The Hollywood Comedy of Remarriage* (1981), *Contesting Tears: The Hollywood Melodrama of the Unknown Woman* (1996), and *Cities of Words: Pedagogical Letters on a Register of the Moral Life* (2004) among a bevy of articles, chapters, reviews, lectures, and occasional pieces. In the collected work here, contributors test the virtues and durability of Cavell's deft thinking about film even as they dauntlessly address emergent limits and lacunae; in both cases, they aim to tease out undeveloped potential and unrealized insight while acknowledging his unmatched contributions to this field and others. In these compellingly written, starkly original, newly composed contributions, our scholars provide a collective shudder to our thinking about cinematic ontology and film aesthetics. Settled thoughts are here given a thorough vetting—enriched and enlivened by these innovative reconceptions—so that new proposals take up company with the best of the tradition.

In these pages, we are returning to a thinking about or a rethinking of film ontology. We arrive asking, "What can we say now about the ontology of film?"—not just in the light of decades of debate in film-philosophy, but even more specifically, and to the occasion of the present gathering, in the company of Cavell's substantive contribution to these fields of inquiry. Secondly, is there something like a consensus among critics about the things Cavell writes on film, including, principally the ontology of cinema, but also in matters of genre, medium, cycles, character, actors, and related topics and issues in the aesthetics and phenomenology of film? And if there is a consensus, does Cavell's work align with it or depart from it? Similar questions were raised about twenty years ago by William Rothman and Marian Keane in their *Reading Cavell's* The World Viewed: *A Philosophical Perspective*. While their task was (as they say) "to present a consecutive reading" of the book, our project here, and our object here, is something more like understanding Cavell on film in order to revisit and renew our thinking about what he has offered us on this subject, that is, as we begin the long, no doubt still gratifying, if lonely, task of doing this work without his gracious company and peerless companionship.[2]

Given the intellectual horsepower marshaled to critique Cavell's work over this past half-century, it is a marvel (isn't it?) that *anything* one writes could hold up to such scrutiny? Our book offers an example of such pressure and the results of its application (its *impression*, we might say), as we approach dynamic, inventive readings of Cavell's *The World Viewed* (and related relevant writing on film by Cavell) by some of the finest minds working in film-philosophy today, and moreover, with nearly five decades worth of primary and secondary scholarship at their disposal. And yet, what is the result? For all the interrogation, Cavell's book—his second, arriving between *Must We Mean What We Say?* and *The Senses of Walden*—holds its own, with grace, while its many favorable and influential attributes are vaunted, and its faults, shortcomings, elisions, and moments of exasperation or calling for necessary revision are duly noted. More to the point, Cavell's book provides the foundation for the present volume, for in that book, written in the late sixties and then revised over the course of the seventies (in an era when the academic study of film was taking shape, no doubt in part because of Cavell's initiative), we find sufficient fortitude and insight to provoke us to think at the dawn of the third decade of the twenty-first century. *The World Viewed* is not perfect, is not a last statement on the subject, nor did it aspire to be such; it is, however, without doubt, uniquely generative (and in the spirit of its author, generous) enough to propel this entire experiment, to set the terms and conditions for this conversation about what it means to think and write philosophically about cinema—and, indeed, to further advance by individual efforts our collective understanding of what it is we mean when we speak of "the thought of movies."[3]

The title—*The Thought of Stanley Cavell and Cinema*—makes a substantive and intentional allusion to "The Thought of Movies," a piece Cavell published in 1983, and later collected in the intellectually capacious, "extracurricular" collection fittingly titled *Themes Out of School: Effects and Causes* (1984). Moreover, though the verb tense is different, one can also hear clear echoes of Cavell's pivotal, self-correcting chapter "Thinking of Emerson" (first published in 1979, and then appearing in the expanded edition of *The Senses of Walden*, in 1981, and later in what Cavell called his "book about Emerson, . . . the only one, or kind, it is given to me to write about Emerson's work," *Emerson's Transcendental Etudes*).[4] As the phrase signals a productive and meaningful double entendre in Cavell's usage, so it does here. We are interested in "how films think" and also how Cavell has thought about film. Is it too much to say that in his writings "on film," Cavell not only created a new genre (or subgenre) of philosophy, but also inspired, or at least enabled one in, from, or for others—from *Thinking on Screen* (Wartenberg) to *Filmed Thought* (Pippin), from *Thinking in the Dark* (ed. Pomerance and Palmer) to "How Movies Think" (Eldridge), and scores more, which seem to ask perpetually: What *is* the thought of movies?[5]

Drawing from Garrett Stewart's chapter for this collection, in which he glosses the subtitle of Cavell's book—*Reflections on the Ontology of Film*—we are reminded how "that benchmark philosophical term"—*reflections*—"suggests, in its usual doubleness, both the being of film and the study thereof, say its technology and its science" as well as its art.[6] To study film with an awareness of this doubleness means to allow, and even encourage, the fact that we are reflecting on reflections. "Turning anew to the ontology of film" in the midst of an ever-expanding digital era entails that what we mean by "film" (and by extension, "cinema") has changed—and will continue to change—from its emergence in the nineteenth century (and especially since the first lights of prehistory captured our attention—the moon, the stars, fire, and the shadows we cast along with the pinhole images whose fidelity we were startled by). "Film" may seem, to some readers, a quaint anachronism—so we are surely in need of recovering our understanding of its origins as celluloid, and its development as an art form thereafter, even as we continue to think ourselves into a contemporary, critical, and compellingly relevant understanding of our almost ubiquitously digital (and thus nearly film-free) lives, now and into the future.

Our reflections on this reflective medium—what it was, what it is, what it may become—benefit immensely from the model of "reading film" that characterized Cavell's relationship to the form. As Rothman and Keane account for it, the pursuit of a philosophical investigation of film means embracing "the methodological principle that we can find out what kind of object a thing is by investigating expressions which show the kinds of thing that can be said about it . . . by appealing philosophically to what we ordinarily say and mean."[7] So much, we might add, can be claimed for what we can say about *Cavell*'s study of film—since the exemplarity of his remarks on film remains undeniable, even if also, for many of us, at once intriguing and illuminating, and also at times, perplexing and disorienting (if provocatively and productively so). As D. N. Rodowick remarked not long ago, *The World Viewed* is "still one of the most misunderstood books, both conceptually and historically, in writing on the cinema."[8] Even in this undeserved double state, we can take heed from a wonderfully liberating observation, one among many granted by Rothman and Keane, that "*The World Viewed* is one kind of thing that can be said about film." Note how the qualification is not presented as a cause for circumvention or dismissal, but, instead, an invitation to closer inspection: "By investigating, philosophically, the obscure promptings of this expression, the motivations of its own writing, *The World Viewed* enables us to know something about the kind of object film is, and something about what philosophy is, as well."[9] In this way, Cavell has written a book that offers a model for the investigation we might adopt or transform in trying to better understand *The World Viewed*'s conceptual and historical import.

In cases of interpretation (of specific films or genres, of discrete philosophical notions), but also more generally in *The World Viewed*, Cavell confides: "I was counting on having earned the right to expect my reader to take these expressions symbolically, as mythological descriptions of the state of someone in the grip of a movie."[10] Here, in this (captivating) image of the "grip," I would say, the metaphysics of the medium *and* of movie-watching overlap—a position in which Platonic resonances blend with Wittgensteinian ones to show how we are "held captive by a picture."[11] Still, Cavell has cautioned that "it is wrong to think of movies in terms of dreams and hallucinations," so his suggestion of symbol and myth provides a path forward—indeed, a methodology to navigate the phenomenology of film.[12] And part of that offering entailed putting himself, and his work, on trial before the profession he entered, or found himself within. As Lawrence Rhu has remarked: he "had a lover's quarrel with philosophy's professionalization as a discipline because he was in love with what philosophy is in love with and he found it at the movies, among other places where academic philosophy was disinclined to venture seriously."[13] The intensity of the personal stakes of these claims recurs—namely, that we are not, for example, bearing witness to a philosopher's insistence on reasons, or the logic of his program, etc.; or, rather, that the personal advances its own reasons and logic that philosophy has grown, somehow, deaf to or ignorant of. As Cavell puts such matters: "Film is an interest of mine, or say a love, not separate from my interest in, or love of, philosophy. So, when I am drawn to think through a film, I do not regard the reading that results as over, even provisionally, until I have said how it bears on the nature of film generally and on philosophy."[14]

And yet that "saying" (of how it bears on film and philosophy) is, as Cavell notes in a reading of *North by Northwest* (1959, dir. Alfred Hitchcock), something that gets "said" by the cinematic medium itself: "What I found in turning to think about film was a medium which seemed simultaneously to be free of the imperative to philosophy and at the same time inevitably to reflect upon itself—as though the condition of philosophy were its natural condition." When William Rothman glosses these lines in his contribution to this collection, he sees *The World Viewed* (as a book, as a project) making a sustained case for the entire tradition of film as "being under its own question."[15] To wit, all cinema is metacinematic and thus all cinema is philosophical. Yet, these qualities may demand qualifications as much as they call for readers to discern them.

At the outset of his remarkable public airing of the foregoing kinds of questions and concerns, "The Thought of Movies"—composed in the decade after *The World Viewed* and trailing *Pursuits of Happiness*—Cavell conjectured: "It must be the nature of American academic philosophy (or of its reputation), together with the nature of American movies (or of their notoriety), that makes someone who writes about both, in the same breath, subject to questions, not to say suspicious."[16] For his own part, Cavell admits that this conjugation of realms—in the era in which he experienced them—led him to grow defensive (his word).[17] Perhaps we can mark as one among many gifts of Cavell's impact and legacy that we are no longer forced to feel that way when thinking about movies in a philosophical vein.

Despite the maturation of film studies as a bona fide academic field, indeed, one that philosophers can now specialize in without apology or shame (and, indeed, in some cases, with a measure of celebrity), we may keep in mind how cultures—inside and outside of the academy—were not always so amenable to "the use or uses of film" for philosophy and related fields. Richard Rorty, a philosopher of renown—and a risk-taker—in his own time, wrote in the *New Republic*: "Cavell is among professors of philosophy what Harold Bloom is among the professors of English: the least defended, the gutsiest, the most vulnerable. He sticks his neck out farther than any of the rest of us."[18] Indeed, Cavell has remarked that writing about film, about "the movies," from within the Department of Philosophy at Harvard, in Emerson Hall, while colleague Willard Van Orman Quine, a logician and analytical philosopher, worked just a few doors away, "caused me a certain amount of grief."[19] And criticism of Cavell's work, or his approach to philosophy, was not limited to his study of film (from within philosophy). As a philosophical peer, Anthony Kenny once said: Cavell's *The Claim of Reason* is a "misshapen, undisciplined amalgam of ill-assorted parts."[20] Closer to home, Cavell's peers at Harvard once called a sampling of his writings "deleterious to the future of philosophy." If one has studied the fates of other iconoclasts, such as Emerson, Thoreau, Kierkegaard, Nietzsche, and Wittgenstein, one finds that none found homes (or happy ones) in the academy. They wrote philosophy "for the future," for "tomorrow and the day after tomorrow." Anticipation and belatedness define their contributions. Much the same holds for Cavell.

Cavell did not question why he himself was interested in film—an interest, we might say, that would be difficult to defend or prove in a logical sense—but, rather, "why, since everyone is interested in film (one supposes throughout the world), why don't philosophers write about it? That was the question that, perhaps, more than anything, puzzled, bothered, even provoked me."[21] Depending on one's frames of reference, a reader in the present day may wonder if we have overcorrected for an earlier, inherited sense of the limitedness of legitimate philosophical exploration, as when we encounter any one of innumerable instances of the philosophy of popular culture with ready-made titles to situate the latest trend or otherwise until-now neglected topic (e.g., something *and Philosophy*, or *The Philosophy of* [insert here]). Perhaps one's estimation of the current state of affairs on this front comes down to whether one believes more is more—or not.

But back in the sixties and seventies, there was not an abundance, much less an overabundance of work being done on the philosophy of film and popular culture (if mainstream [American] movies are, by definition, among the principal constituents of popular culture, we can remember that many unpopular cultures, such as avant-garde, documentary, and experimental cinema, along with the expansive field of global, non-Hollywood works, are *also* part of the story told and to be told). We should treat the gestational period for *The World Viewed* capaciously so it includes Cavell's youthful experience of films as well as his expanding repertoire of viewership in the 1930s, 1940s, and 1950s, along with an emergent training in philosophy, and reading work by James Agee and Robert Warshow (among a select few others whose receptivity from film and responsiveness to it attracted his attention)—as he says at the commencement of the project: "Memories of movies are strand over strand with memories of my life."[22] Cavell's acutely developed sensibility *for* or *toward* film should be noted as figuring into an understanding of his general orientation to human experience as such. Cavell proposed "learn[ing] to think undistractedly about things that ordinary human beings cannot help thinking about, or anyway cannot help having occur to them, sometimes in fantasy, sometimes as a flash across a landscape."[23] Readers of Emerson, as Cavell was, cannot help but wonder about such flashes—"gleams of light"—that make themselves known, if fleetingly. And movie-lovers will appreciate that such flashes and gleams of light are yet further irresistible figures for our experience of motion picture projection. "Philosophers after my own heart," Cavell attested, provide us the license to attend to, and to account for, such brief but potent instances, adding "that while there may be no satisfying answers to such questions *in certain forms*, there are, so to speak, directions to answers, *ways to think*, that are worth the time of your life to discover."[24] It may be safe to say that those who find themselves writing—or wanting to write—about Cavell already believe that such "directions to answers" are part and parcel of the experiment underway: that philosophy, at its best, is a practice of desire focused and deployed. In this way, a movie-lover cannot help but be philosophical about film. And yet, the quality of such insights separates the vast majority of hearty, fan-based impressions from the artful articulations of a masterful mind such as Cavell's.

While conjuring the intellectual, cultural, academic, and cinematic scenario in which *The World Viewed* appeared in the early seventies, and in which it served as a field-defining, genre-bending/-blending, disciplinary provocation, we may be at a loss; one could study the popular book- and journal article-titles of the time to catch a measure of the prevailing trends and authorized territories (again, as analytic philosophy ruled most top departments). Such a glimpse can be sobering for the way it makes Cavell's work on film—at *that* time—seem not just foreign but extraterrestrial. In the years since *The World Viewed* was published, it has influenced generations of readers, filmmakers, and philosophers. Yet, even with the existence of many important studies of "Cavell on film"—both in a titular, topical sense and in a below-the-surface, his-influence-has-been-digested-and-incorporated sense—the domain has become ripe for a robust review and reassessment. Given the depth and extent of his influence on how we think about film (and, indeed, in those moments when he is strangely left out or otherwise marginalized), there is a need—one this book aims to help fulfill—to have critical accounts *of* that influence (and its many permutations).

We are, in this collection, primarily exploring film ontology, yet to borrow from Cavell's old job title, we are (also) engaging the broader domain of "aesthetics and the general theory of value" as it pertains to film as such. Since, as Wittgenstein attested, "ethics and aesthetics are one," and since film ontology is so very much entwined with domains beyond it, the newly commissioned chapters gathered here offer commentary of radiating significance. Thus, what film ontology is and what it might mean for us today—questions of the immediacy of the medium—are coupled, by turns, with a sense of how we might judge it and what we might do with it. In what follows, the multi- and interdisciplinary spirit of the investigation creates "volatile transfer points" (about prevailing debates) that signal potential transdisciplinary insight.[25] That Cavell's appointed topic—"the ontology of film"—may seem, to some readers, limited, even hermetic, and worse, antiquated, vestigial, irrelevant, a relic of late modernism, we are here to attest to the contrary: that Cavell's innovative approach to a century-old debate remains a dynamic arena for discovery and advancement in present-day film studies, and for audiovisual experience in whatever vivifying future form it might take.

Each of the contributors to this volume—under the auspices of an invitation to revisit Cavell's approach to cinema—had to confront the question of how an inheritance of film, philosophy, *and* the hybrid film-philosophy, might be expressed. We can think about the duty, the ambition, the challenges involved in articulating the stakes and implications of such research. As these fields evolve, they accumulate new texts, traditions, and techniques. A multiplicity of material announces itself at every turn—not least the staggering number of new films, articles, and books that bear relevance to our continuing conversation. With Barbara Cassin's *Dictionary of Untranslatables* in mind, and by analogizing from her "philosophizing in languages," we could consider how these individual works are invested in and constituted by "languages" (or, if one prefers, discourses).[26] Introductory texts in film studies assume fluency in "film language" or the "grammar of cinema"—that is, how to navigate *speaking* and *writing* about the audiovisual realm. This is, no doubt, a bold translation, often unconsciously adopted and thereafter perpetuated without further interrogation. Film itself is often regarded (sentimentally?) as a "universal language"—as if subtitles or the content of what is said is less vital than an invigorating encounter with *mise-en-scène* and the suggestive force of editing. As the contributors have, the reader may now consider the strains and styles and substances at issue: Cavell's written texts, the films he addresses, the films he doesn't address, the medium (of film), the media he doesn't (or couldn't) address, the films he has seen and hasn't, the written texts he has read and hasn't. All of these call to us for translation—across languages, across media, across time and space. The volume in hand is one dispatch from this ongoing, shared endeavor.

Part of a community of inquiry—adding here another chapter to a decentralized, burgeoning project of enduring significance—we are eager to acknowledge the many fine things that have been said on this subject. Indeed, among the articles, chapters, and books that complement the research in this collection, many of those works were written by contributors to this volume. These essential pieces regularly percolate to the top of any discussion of Cavell and film, among them, books by William Rothman (*Reading Cavell's* The World Viewed, *Cavell on Film, Must We Kill What We Love?, Tuitions and Intuitions*), Robert B. Pippin (*Filmed Thought, The Philosophical Hitchcock, Fatalism in American Film Noir, Hollywood Westerns and American Myth*), D. N. Rodowick (*The Virtual Life of Film, Elegy for Theory, Philosophy's Artful Conversation, What Philosophy Wants from Images*), Garrett Stewart (*Between Film and Screen, Framed Time: Toward a Postfilmic Cinema, Closed*

Circuits, Transmedium), Lawrence F. Rhu (*Stanley Cavell's American Dream*), and the collections *Film as Philosophy: Essays in Cinema after Wittgenstein and Cavell*, edited by Rupert Read and Jerry Goodenough; *Philosophy and Film*, edited by Cynthia Freeland and Thomas E. Wartenberg; *Film as Philosophy*, edited by Bernd Herzogenrath; as well as Hugo Clémot's French counterpart to Rothman and Keane's book—*Philosophy After Cinema: A Reading of Stanley Cavell's* The World Viewed (*La philosophie d'après le cinéma: une lecture de La projection du monde de Stanley Cavell*) and many volumes by Sandra Laugier.[27] (Catherine Wheatley's *Stanley Cavell and Film: Scepticism and Self-Reliance at the Cinema*, Rex Butler's *Stanley Cavell and the Arts*, and Daniel Shaw's *Stanley Cavell and the Magic of Hollywood Films* arrive after our session here has concluded.) Since so many worthy works must be left out of this quick reference library, the best place to find company in the currents of these tumultuous thoughts is, no doubt, in the contributors' endnotes and bibliographies, since those citations confirm the texts that have commandeered their attention and propelled them forward; as we must, the present scholars exhibit their indebtedness to such works by offering critical readings of them—and perhaps more importantly, make that acknowledgment (even of their own, earlier work) meaningful by *going on* from it to test new thoughts; to explore new films, new phrasing; to push back from settled opinion and push beyond the comforts of rehearsal; and on occasion, with familiar, trusted works coursing vigorously in the veins, they dart straight for the wilds, thereby pointing us to new terrain worthy of further exploration.

Sustaining Rorty's praise above, Cavell's contributions to thought, full stop, are unique—truly one of a kind—yet are especially pronounced in the history of philosophy and film studies from the past few decades. Arthur Danto once said of him, having just finished reading *Pursuits of Happiness*: "This is a voice like no other in philosophy, today or ever."[28] With the voice of his prose still intact in his books, and the particular register of that distinctive sound part of the permanent landscape and language of thought about film, he is, in these respects, still very much alive. As this volume attests, it is by the modeling of that voice, his cadence of thought, his attunement to problems and his distinctive replies to them, that he remains fecund for us—as if we have been charged with the task of continuing a conversation in his absence, and now, to be sure, ever after, in his stead.

As If: The More Perfect Union of Film and Philosophy

Stanley Cavell may be the first philosopher in history to say "film was as if made for philosophy."[29] Pointing it out is one thing (and no small thing, given the time and context of its proclamation), but illustrating, articulating, and defending why it is the case, quite another. And for more than half a century he did just that.

The chiasma of the Introduction's subtitle is deployed as a means for appreciating the *interaction* between film and philosophy. Given cinema's predominance and continuing digital evolution and endless expansion via the internet—and by contrast, some may argue, philosophy's perpetual cultural diminishment and accelerating, widespread neglect—it is worth remembering that philosophy as a practice has been around for thousands of years and across global cultures.

Meanwhile, cinema sprang up in the middle of the nineteenth century. That the upstart technology and art form may have eclipsed the popular appeal of philosophy (much less its academic one) is worthy of debate. Using Cavell's phrasing ("film . . . as if . . .") and then flipping the predicates—"philosophy . . . as if made for film" (while admittedly an *avant la lettre* sentiment)—underscores how the interactivity of thinking in philosophy and film are mutually supporting, interdependent phenomena. The turning we do between them—the turning over, turning anew, returning (in a gesture at once Wittgensteinian and Cavellian)—only intensifies and enriches the ineluctable braid. To wit, if one begins with a philosophical text or question or problem and looks to cinema for insight, cinema will provide it; and turned the other way, if one begins in cinema and looks to philosophy for counsel, philosophy, in its depth of traditions, will have something significant to offer.

Philosophy and literature, no doubt, have a longer—if still fraught—relationship than do philosophy and film, drawing us back to antiquity in order to source the strains. Yet, the parallel is apt, since even with a head start of a couple of millennia, philosophy does not seem entirely clear or forthcoming about ready and reliable answers to questions such as "What is fiction for?" or parsing the differences between (classical) realism and idealism, words and concepts, and suchlike.[30] As a measure of therapeutic guidance, let me repurpose a few lines from Stephen Mulhall's transformative study of these subjects by swapping out the word "literature" and replacing it with the word "film": "We might be better served by thinking more in terms of a dialogue, in which philosophy and [film] participate as each other's other—as autonomous but internally related. One might say: their distinctness is constituted by the very distance that not only allows but requires that they address one another. I am not suggesting that philosophy can or should become [film], or [film] philosophy; but I am suggesting that for each properly to acknowledge the other would require both to confront the challenge of reconceiving their self-images, and so their defining aspirations."[31] The Cavellian pedigree of such a passage is gratifyingly evident, but we can simply underline the notion of two parties who are distinct and yet come in for enhanced self- and other-understanding by means of a "dialogue"—call it a conversation. Whether film and philosophy achieve a "meet and happy conversation" or a crisis is a subject for us to debate and discern.[32]

Drawing on Cavell's significant work on the nature of marriage (as a conversation between opposing, if not opposite parties—hence the need for "remarriage"), and his attunement to the way national identity and politics play a role in the making up of a person's and a people's "constitution" (the "pursuit of happiness" was Jefferson's before it was applied to the Hollywood comedy of remarriage), we may adopt the further notion of a "more perfect union" to summarize the ambitions for the country and a couple, and moreover, for the aspirational relationship between film and philosophy. The "more perfect union" doubtless encodes an (Emersonian) moral perfectionism that Cavell recovered and conceptualized—that is, conversation that proceeds ever onward to some refinement of purpose, most especially the hope for an ever-ameliorating mutual intelligibility. And so also for philosophy and film, not from the start quarreling lovers, so much as distant strangers that need to be shown their shared preoccupations. These two disciplines, these two regions of mind and experience, that, in Cavell's early years were thoroughly quarantined demanded someone speak to their *constitutional* intimacy. Cavell, who in his own work, did so much to bring these realms together—and whose achievements in this regard have been invoked for decades—has helped us see, and then search for and then savor, the uncanny connections that make them so essentially entwined, so mutually compatible. For those who come to film and philosophy after Cavell, the match seems so erotically charged that it generates a kind of delirium—the ecstasy of insight, the solicitation of a humanistic sublime.[33] Hence the sustaining sentiment—"film, as if made for philosophy"—that underwrites the entire volume.

The purpose of an introduction is self-contained—namely, a brief letter to the prospective reader concerning the agenda of the given volume and the contours of its contents—and yet it must make claims about what lies beyond its perimeter. If it is a map, an introduction is also a promissory note. In some cases, such a dispatch does its best service by remaining brief—by getting out of the way for the exceptional remarks that surround it. Gratefully squeezed as this one is, between three titans of film-philosophical thought, Thomas Elsaesser, Garrett Stewart, and Noël Carroll (whose work does so much to establish the tone and caliber of the proceedings while laying out its topography), I feel eager myself to bypass any belaboring excurses, and painful attempts at condensing carefully wrought prose into quippy retreads and blasé repetitions, and move as quickly as possible to the chapters themselves—full as they are of the nuance and critical acumen suggested by the chapter titles and the many published works of these emerging and celebrated thinkers. In this way, the labor of "explaining" each chapter is self-delegated by its independent author—recognizable, I hope, as a Cavellian virtue, namely, that we remain committed to the weight of the specific words and phrasing we use, ordinary and otherwise. And no doubt, a virtue, one among many, of a multiauthored volume such as this— since we do not presume to arrogate one another's voice even as we gladly benefit from one another's research and admit that these varied postulations and positions are worthy of our attention, here and elsewhere. In short, group work ratifies (or corrects, as the case may be) one's solitary work. The midrash is here *and* to come. As each of these dedicated bees has taken up his or her hexagon of concern, we may, at last, look up to see the collective labors of the hive—the pressure and presumptions of isolated research, in time, giving way to a season of sharing, in which we make ourselves (and our work) accountable to the invested group and its community of readers. It is just this mood of approach, or atmosphere of encounter, that meaningfully conveys *Cavell*'s appraisal of what it is we are all working at. Early in *The World Viewed*, Cavell established what he called the "first fact" of his labor there by asking "Why are movies important?"—and replying: "I take it for granted in various obvious senses they are."[34] Has a first-class mind ever belabored a crucial point less?

To be sure, though, things are more complicated: "The first fact is paired with a second," Cavell tells us: "The movie seems naturally to exist in a state in which its highest and its most ordinary instances attract the same audience (anyway until recently)."[35] This observation causes Cavell to digress in some fascinating ways about how that parenthetical betokens a "necessary region of indiscriminateness" that "creates three separable nightmares."[36] I leave aside the account of such "nightmares" to focus on the way this art form conjures its audience, and why *that* fact prevails as a signal for the significance of film as art and artifact (i.e., as aesthetic object), as ethical guide (part of film's interactivity with its audience), and as a still-beguiling phenomenological region of human experience (one that often defies comprehension, leaving us somewhere between memories and dreams and "reflections"—call them thoughts). "Now that there is an audience," Cavell notes, "a claim is made upon my privacy; so it matters to me that our responses to the film are not really shared. At the same time that the mere fact of an audience makes this claim upon me, it feels as if the old casualness of moviegoing has been replaced by a casualness of movie-viewing, which I interpret as an inability to tolerate our own fantasies, let alone those of others—an attitude that equally I cannot share."[37] If we (an audience of individuals) do not share a film, how do we come to share its "world," or the world beyond it that we return to upon leaving the movie theater? Secondly, if we *do* share the film, but are not equipped to "read" it—to make it intelligible, for example, in terms of my own private fantasies as well as yours (and moreover, of those fantasies we may be said to share, in part, *because* we share a world)—what, in fact, are movies *for*? The bland, binary retort—"education or entertainment"—fails to get the import of the question, as if the purpose of a film were discovered by its effect on us instead of our effect on it.

The World Viewed, like its predecessor *The Immediate Experience* (by Robert Warshow), could be said to offer a summons to readers: calling them forth from the privacy of their viewing and listening to the project of attesting to the meaning of what has come to pass on screen (in sight, sound, and motion). Such an injunction leads to at least two significant outcomes: that we take specific movies seriously (and so assume the mantle of reading them well) and that we take seriously the specificity of movies-as-such (the ontology of the medium, say, or the aesthetics and phenomenology of its attributes). Contributors to the present volume marshal the first outcome—take it for granted—in pursuit of the second. How they do this is, again, shown in the evidence of their prose, the best picture we have for their casts of mind.

As part of our deliberation on the "marriage" of film and philosophy, the volume has two main ambitions: to offer new readings of canonical issues in Cavellian thinking about film; and, more extensively, to address Cavell's relevance to the wide-ranging and far-reaching debates in film and media studies (including some awareness of how those studies interact with literary and cultural studies). It is worth noting that some among the gathered crowd of critics are not merely friends and acolytes of Cavell's, aiming, after the fact, to reinforce and defend an already lustrous legacy (though a few, no doubt, are justifiably invested in providing the reasonable *ground* for it). We may say, instead, that there is a continual *fort da* at work here—where the effort to support Cavell's ideas invariably requires that they be challenged, pushed in new directions given the evolution of film and of the study of film and transmedia; consider, for example, Scott MacDonald's probing reconsideration of otherwise canonical, indeed, liturgical aspects of Cavell's work on the genre of remarriage comedies; or Noël Carroll's scintillating and unflinching "re-viewing" of *The World Viewed*. As befits a project on Cavell's work, there is a wonderfully rich metacritical layering of preoccupations—where our contributors investigate the investigators. Meanwhile, most of the contributors are analysts coming to texts and films on their own terms, while concomitantly seeking their own way to Cavell—that is, with him and beyond him. Thus, the collection is not a generic review or rehearsal of Cavell's thoughts about film, as if in paraphrase; still, as one would hope, it *does contain* competent orientation to his thought in its richness of style and diversity of content. The contributors therefore offer us at once a reliable *resource* for this mode of inquiry and a *model* for what future research might aspire to be.

Ideally, in addition to offering an original and apposite program of research, the volume will spur and support new conversations, while also serving as a candidate for easy and effective course adoption. All of the contributors to this book are some version of esteemed and celebrated film scholar or philosopher of film; key contributor to the work and legacy of Stanley Cavell; or luminous emerging talent in film-philosophy. Several of the contributors have stand-alone monographs dedicated to Cavell's work, and everyone has published or taught it. The volume should be of immediate and thereafter long-standing use to graduate students and professional academics working in philosophy (aesthetics, philosophy of art, philosophy of film); media, literary, adaptation, and translation studies; art history, anthropology, communications, comparative literature, and many other kindred fields and subfields. Readers familiar with Cavell's work will know it, in part, for its distinctive and expansive contact with disparate domains of scholarship and types of media; and since the contributors know this feature intimately (and themselves arrive from many divergent precincts of intellectual inquiry and pedagogical practice), the book is written in a way that at once achieves the mandate of careful, rigorous scholarship in film-philosophy and also makes itself available to a wide and ever-broadening band of academic interests—as well as "themes out of school."

In the Foreword and in Part I, our contributors aim at a thoroughgoing assessment of Cavellian film ontology, and for that involve crucial, necessary forays into the nature of cinema's media, and thus subsets of form and its affiliate concepts (e.g., inscription, indexicality, genre, sound, etc.). Not to be missed, Elsaesser begins his serious remarks with a joke—a gesture Cavell had ears to appreciate. ("Intimacy, commonality, parabolic point and [intellectual and emotional] dominance are all achieved in these so-called jokes."[38]) For a joke is a kind of story and the "human craving for narration is about as primitive a wish or form of interaction as exists."[39] How our experience of film takes flight from existential longing and the need for others yields yet another lesson in Cavell's protean reading of the human condition. Likewise, these authors, drawing from their own unique points of reference and inspiration, are very much fulfilling the promise of the book's subtitle by turning anew to the ontology of film a half-century after Cavell's *The World Viewed*. It is a special feature—and fortune—of this collection that the contributors whose work is placed in the opening segment of this volume have written chapters of such decisive clarity and impact on the way film ontology and film genre make themselves known in Cavell's work in *The World Viewed* and the relevant, radiating remarks we find in his subsequent books, articles, and lectures. Each in his or her own characteristically probing way, these philosopher-film critics *par excellence* provide a cascade of crucial annotations on our chosen subject and Cavell's signature film text.

In Part II, the tone is decidedly and deliberately personal. Scott MacDonald and William Rothman pick up on their relationships to film and specifically to Cavell's work on film. MacDonald, a leading historian of American art cinema (especially in its experimental and avant-garde traditions), addresses with sincerity and good humor what may be called Cavell's blind spot—"cinemas" that, despite their proximity to his home campus (or on it!), nevertheless, lay beyond his purview: documentarians and avant-garde filmmakers, as well as the films of Ernst Lubitsch. We are left to wonder (to worry about) the extent to which, "for Cavell, commercial narrative cinema *is* cinema—all else is peripheral."[40] In another octave of the personal, Rothman meditates on the relationships and differences between two canonical works—*The World Viewed* and *Film as Film* (1972)—in the wake of their authors' deaths. A friend to both Cavell and Victor Perkins, Rothman explores the temperaments and preoccupations of these indelible thinkers and, in turn, their profound, perspicacious, and enduring thoughts on film. Part II, therefore, offers something of an informal interlude, if still rigorously rendered—a space in which the *manner* of writing about cinema activates our thinking about authors and authorship. The texture and tone of the "voice" of such writing (along with what preoccupies its authors as worthy of concern) may put us in mind of the way that (all?) film criticism belies its status as "metaphysical memoir"—a genre Cavell invokes (or invents) to account for the kind of writing he manifests in *The World Viewed*.[41]

If a certain diagnostic framing of, or definitional foundation for, the topic (and its questions) is provided by the first half-dozen contributions (viz., the Foreword, Introduction, and Part I), and Part II invites us to a fittingly personal recalibration to the medium and its effects, the book's remaining entries take up, we might say, the application and inheritance of Cavellian cinematic ontology and its correlated notions. These chapters present us with instances of interpreting films by means of Cavell's conceptual grammar (meaningful portions of which having been outlined and attended to in the opening phases of the book). The variations on the theme of skepticism (that comprise Part III and are reengaged in chapter 12) offer a uniquely sustained arbitration of issues that remained at the core of Cavell's broader philosophical project for more than fifty years, and are here honed and hewed to the specific contours of criticism about film genres and our readings of the movies that constitute them—or, even more interestingly, have thus far exceeded or eluded them, or, in fascinating ways, may productively problematize them. I have in mind here the way Robert Sinnerbrink draws on Todd Haynes' *Carol* and Thomas E. Wartenberg returns to *Casablanca* to reevaluate the standard bearers of the comedies of remarriage and the melodramas of the unknown woman.

Moreover, the chapters that form the second half of the volume reveal a sensitivity to the registration of Cavell's work—its potency and potential—in the writing of contemporary film-thinkers influenced by Cavell (e.g., as seen when Shawn Loht looks to the development of the field in research by fellow contributors Mulhall and Sinnerbrink). Not only are Cavell's landmark contributions explicated in constructive and satisfying ways, they are also amplified by readings of films (and genres and theories) beyond his familiar list—indeed, beyond film as a discrete object of study, as when Sandra

Laugier extends and updates our understanding of film by tethering it to the prevalence and increasing dominance of television serials in the twenty-first century. As befits a succession of generations and the trends that go with them, we can notice that while Cavell was caught up in the maelstrom of Hollywood's golden age of studio productions, so his elder son, Benjamin, has found his way to the propitious energies of present-day television.[42] In consequence of the experimental nature of such well-researched, field-stretching forays, a certain tact is required for reading specific films (along with their theoretical analogs, artistic heirs, and adjacent modes, such as television), and by its achievement we are treated to further elucidation of problems native to our ongoing thinking about film-as-such (whether in the form of a high-end studio confection, avant-garde installation, home movie, or, indeed, a streaming serial). In this mood of receptivity, we are happily returned to the scene of our encounter with these varied works of art—how they are presented to us, and how we make ourselves available to them. In our relationship with art, we are then given to remember that, as Rothman and Keane put it: "The kind of understanding Cavell seeks by reading a film is not only an understanding about the film, but an understanding, we might say, *with* the film—an understanding that acknowledges the film's understanding of itself. We cannot understand a film's worth, its meaning, by applying a theory that dictates what we are to say, but only by entering into a conversation with the film."[43] As readers, then, we are ever-poised between making interventions on behalf of theory (call them, after Emerson, "manipular attempts to realize the world of thought"[44]) and being responsive to and responsible for our experience of film, which may, despite our aspirations for coherency, result in divergent outcomes and the deferral of conclusions.

The two-stage chiastic structure of Parts III and IV trades on a phrase of Cavell's, now familiar to readers of this introduction, that "film was as if made for philosophy."[45] The labor of thinking about the relationship between these two "fields" (or forms or discourses) alerts us, yet again, to what might be called the work of *translation* (and thus also the fact or factor of untranslatability). We can say, without hesitation or embarrassment, that philosophy has been very good for film and, likewise, film for philosophy. They are a couple, or coupling, with decidedly generative results—the conversation that has come, in some quarters, to be called, with knowing alliteration, the *philosophy of film* or *film-philosophy*, or, indeed, *film-as-philosophy*. The "of" commends possession, even intimacy, while the all-important hyphen bespeaks union, hybridity, and yet the cautious retention of a distance, of an acknowledged in(ter)dependence; the "as" invites and challenges our thinking of film's identity and essential nature since it stops short of *is*. Again translatability—and the specter of untranslatability—looms. We are not suggesting in these borrowed, now-familiar phrases, then, the reduction of one field to the other, but, rather, the interrelatedness of their rich histories and the unique characteristics that make their union that much more puissant. My invocation of "claim" in the title for these opening remarks can signal a clear (and clearly Cavellian) instantiation of the picture being drawn: namely, that these are domains of human experience that *call to* one another, *call upon* one another (perhaps now and again arrogating the voice or power of the other when needed—as, indeed, any writer writing on Cavell must contend with). Meanwhile, film's call upon us or to us—its provocation, its seduction—feels as real, as abiding, and as vexing as ever. Though some attribute to Jean-Luc Godard the notion that film criticism itself is a form of moviemaking, it is fine to say that the two realms benefit from the integrity of independent identities even while (as we do emphasize especially in Parts III and IV) these identities—and their meanings—are expanded and illuminated by means of mutually attuned commentaries on one another.

Occasionally, we step headlong into a lover's quarrel, but wherever we look and listen, there is an unmistakable and enduring romance. Contest and conversation prove elucidating. As we speak of lovers—in their mutual attraction, in the complementarity of their characteristics, and even in the *agon* of their aversion—as being "made for one another," let us apply the same sentiment (no doubt a Cavellian sentiment) to film and philosophy.

Notes

1 Stanley Cavell, *Contesting Tears: The Hollywood Melodrama of the Unknown Woman* (Cambridge: Harvard University Press, 1996), epigraph and vii. See also "Reflections on a Life of Philosophy: Interview with Stanley Cavell," *Harvard Journal of Philosophy* VII (1999): 25.

2 William Rothman and Marian Keane, *Reading Cavell's* The World Viewed: *A Philosophical Perspective* (Detroit: Wayne State University Press, 2000), 9.

3 The phrase is drawn from the first chapter—"The Thought of Movies"—in Stanley Cavell, *Themes Out of School: Effects and Causes* (San Francisco: North Point Press, 1984).

4 Stanley Cavell, *Emerson's Transcendental Etudes*, ed. David Justin Hodge (Stanford: Stanford University Press, 2003), 4; *The Senses of Walden* (New York: Viking, 1972); *The Senses of Walden, An Expanded Edition* (San Francisco: North Point Press, 1981); the Expanded Edition was taken over by the University of Chicago Press in 1992.

5 Thomas E. Wartenberg, *Thinking on Screen: Film as Philosophy* (New York: Routledge, 2007); Robert B. Pippin, *Filmed Thought: Cinema as Reflective Form* (Chicago: The University of Chicago Press, 2019); *Thinking in the Dark: Cinema, Theory, Practice*, ed. Murray Pomerance and R. Barton Palmer (Rutgers: Rutgers University Press, 2015); and Richard Eldridge, "How Movies Think: Cavell on Film as a Medium of Art," *Estetika: The Central European Journal of Aesthetics* LI/VII, no. 1 (2014): 3–20.

6 See in this volume, Stewart (chapter 1), 27.
7 Rothman and Keane, *Reading Cavell's* The World Viewed, 36.
8 D. N. Rodowick, *Elegy for Theory* (Cambridge: Harvard University Press, 2014), 73–74.
9 Ibid.
10 Stanley Cavell, *The World Viewed: Reflections on the Ontology of Film* (Cambridge: Harvard University Press, 1971; enlarged edition, 1979), 211.
11 While alluding to Plato's allegory of the cave, of course, I have in mind: "Here they live, from earliest childhood, with their legs and necks in chains, so that they have to stay where they are, looking only ahead of them, prevented by chains from turning their heads." Plato, *The Republic*, ed. G. R. F. Ferrari, trans. Tom Griffith (Cambridge: Cambridge University Press, 2000), 220.

Bracketing the troubling sense of bondage, I mean to emphasize their positions as viewers—as those kinds of beings who are (however coerced) addressed by the play of flickering light and dancing shadows before them. The paraphrase from Wittgenstein is drawn from his remark: "A *picture* held us captive. And we could not get outside it, for it lay in our language and language seemed to repeat it to us inexorably." *Philosophical Investigations*, trans. G. E. M. Anscombe, P. M. S. Hacker, and Joachim Schulte; revised fourth edition by Hacker and Schulte (Oxford: Blackwell, 2009), §115.
12 Cavell, *The World Viewed*, 211.
13 Lawrence F. Rhu, "Three Cheers for Stanley Cavell," *Forma de Vida*, no. 15 (2018). Direct link: https://formadevida.org/lrhufdv15.
14 These lines are drawn from the beginning of an earlier version of "Naughty Orators,"—entitled "Naughty Narrators"—that Cavell later revised and expanded as the opening chapter of *Contesting Tears*. See Stanley Cavell, "Naughty Narrators: Negation of Voice in Gaslight," in *Languages of the Unsayable*, ed. Sanford Budick and Wolfgang Iser (New York: Columbia University Press, 1989), 340.
15 See in this volume, Rothman (chapter 6), 122.
16 Cavell, "The Thought of Movies," 3.
17 Ibid., 4.
18 Richard Rorty's assessment of—and praise for—Cavell was part of his review of *In Quest of the Ordinary: Lines of Skepticism and Romanticism* (The University of Chicago Press, 1988), "The Philosophy of the Oddball," *New Republic* 200, no. 25 (1989): 38–41. Rorty continues: "Who touches this book touches a fleshy, ambitious, anxious, self-involved, self-doubting mortal."
19 Harrison Smith, "Stanley Cavell," *Washington Post* (June 21, 2018). washingtonpost.com
20 Ibid.
21 Ibid.
22 Cavell, *The World Viewed*, xix.
23 Cavell, "The Thought of Movies," 9.

24 Cavell, "The Thought of Movies," 9; italics in original. See also, Smith, "Stanley Cavell."

25 Donald E. Pease, "Re-mapping the Transnational Turn," *Re-framing the Transnational Turn in American Studies*, ed. Winfried Fluck, Donald Pease, and John Carlos Rowe (Hanover: Dartmouth College Press of the University Press of New England, 2011), 4.

26 *Dictionary of Untranslatables: A Philosophical Lexicon*, ed. Barbara Cassin, trans. and ed. Emily Apter, Jacques Lezra, and Michael Wood (Princeton: Princeton University Press, 2014), ix. See also Stanley Cavell, "Beginning to Read Barbara Cassin," *Hypatia* 15, no. 4 (Fall 2000): 102–21.

27 Hugo Clémot, *Philosophy after Cinema: A Reading of Stanley Cavell's* The World Viewed; *La philosophie d'après le cinéma: une lecture de La projection du monde de Stanley Cavell* (Rennes: Presses Universitaires de Rennes, 2014).

28 Arthur C. Danto, "Philosophy and/as Film and/as if Philosophy," *October* 23 (Winter 1982): 13–15.

29 Cavell, *Contesting Tears*, vii. See also, the section "Film, As If Made for Philosophy," in my "Representative Qualities and Questions of Documentary Film," in *The Philosophy of Documentary Film: Image, Sound, Fiction, Truth*, ed. David LaRocca (Lanham: Lexington Books of Rowman & Littlefield, 2017), 3–7.

30 For clarification on these topics and questions, see, for example, Bernard Harrison, *What Is Fiction For? Literary Humanism Restored* (Bloomington: Indiana University Press, 2014) and K. L. Evans, *One Foot in the Finite: Melville's Realism Reclaimed* (Evanston: Northwestern University Press, 2018).

31 Stephen Mulhall, *The Wounded Animal: J. M. Coetzee and the Difficulty of Reality in Literature and Philosophy* (Princeton: Princeton University Press, 2008), 3.

32 Cavell writes: "the genres [of philosophy and literature, or in our case, philosophy and film] occur simultaneously, and perhaps work to deepen their differences, even to bring them to a crisis." Stanley Cavell, "The *Investigations'* Everyday Aesthetics of Itself," *The Cavell Reader*, ed. Stephen Mulhall (Oxford: Blackwell, 1996), 373.

33 For more on the humanistic sublime, see my "'Profoundly Unreconciled to Nature': Ecstatic Truth and the Humanistic Sublime in Werner Herzog's War Films," in *The Philosophy of War Films*, ed. David LaRocca (Lexington: The University Press of Kentucky, 2014), 437–82.

34 Cavell, *The World Viewed*, 4.

35 Ibid., 5.

36 Ibid., 6.

37 Ibid., 11.

38 "What Becomes of Thinking on Film?" (Stanley Cavell in conversation with Andrew Klevan), *Film as Philosophy: Essays in Cinema after Wittgenstein and Cavell* (New York: Palgrave Macmillan, 2005), 173.

39 Ibid.
40 LaRocca-MacDonald correspondence, March 10, 2019.
41 Cavell, *The World Viewed*, xix. See also Rothman and Keane, "Preface: A Metaphysical Memoir," *Reading Cavell's* The World Viewed, 35–41.
42 Benjamin Cavell has written for and worked as a producer on *Justified*, *Homeland*, *Sneaky Pete*, and *SEAL Team*.
43 Rothman and Keane, *Reading Cavell's* The World Viewed, 11. Italics added.
44 Ralph Waldo Emerson, "Experience," *The Complete Works of Ralph Waldo Emerson*, Vol. III, ed. E. W. Emerson (Boston: Houghton, Mifflin and Company, 1904), 85. See also David LaRocca, *Emerson's English Traits and the Natural History of Metaphor* (New York: Bloomsbury, 2013), 279 and Cavell, *Emerson's Transcendental Etudes*, 136, 221, 245.
45 Cavell, *Contesting Tears*, vii.

PART I

Underwriting and Overhearing: Reconceiving Cinematic Ontology and Genre

1

"Assertions in Technique": Tracking the Medial "Thread" in Cavell's Filmic Ontology

Garrett Stewart

CELEBRATION—AND FURTHER SPURRED CEREBRATION—is the business at hand. Little room, or even occasion, for lament. Yet, in my exactly half-century's engagement with the work of Stanley Cavell (since 1969's *Must We Mean What We Say?*), there are two decisive crests of passing regret, early and late, that can actually propel us forward. With this new volume attesting, prima facie, to the longevity and grip of Cavell's film work, there is no reason to revisit early resistances on their own terms. Yet, it is strangely the case that, in his searching account of film, what seemed missing for some of Cavell's early detractors has gone underattended by partisans as well: namely, his engagement with the medium's material support, his attuned feel for the aberrant wrinkles and quirks of cinematographic transmission as, in fact, the medium's disclosed quintessence—if not by *definition*, at least in sensed operation. That seldom mapped zone of his attention is the crux of what follows.

Though Cavell is increasingly explored and debated within those crossover circles predisposed to his ethical and ontological vocabularies, bridges remain more often burned than rebuilt between a thriving film-philosophy of this stamp and the previous disciplinary enclaves of moving image analysis, first film studies, then cinema studies, then screen studies. From the 1971 appearance of *The World Viewed* forward, Cavell was never, as they say, "trending" in these domains. At first, for the semioticians, he had too little to offer about signs and syntagma, then for the suture theorists too little to note about transferential identification with the camera. He seemed to received opinion, if one may put it this way, a philosopher of film with no "theory" of it. For the historians of Hollywood as institution, he had too little to say about production, distribution, and exhibition practices, while for the feminists too much to say about women, and then for the Deleuzians, zilch. That last is, for me, the second regret in "Cavell's uptake" (both senses) over the decades: not just of his own work by an entrenched media studies academy, but of Deleuze by Cavell himself (and of course, vice versa). Among the missed chances of rapport and debate, and often concerning some of the same classic films they took a shared interest in, there might have been ground laid for a clarifying triangulation, as well, with the philosophical film writing of Jean Epstein—as attempted briefly below—with whose ontological skepticism Cavell's project might otherwise seem merely and blankly at odds.

The very logic of this volume's title, *The Thought of Stanley Cavell and Cinema*, thus puts me in mind, as it were, not just of Cavell's thought, but of cinema's own, as registered by Cavell—and this in ways that bear on Epstein's *The Intelligence of a Machine* (1946). If a machine can think, it can also assert itself, which immediately directs us to a chapter in *The World Viewed* that has been too little scrutinized in subsequent commentary, "Assertions in Technique." Earlier in that volume, one encounters Cavell's open-ended definition of cinema as "an automated succession of world projections"[1]—a characterization cast up with an abstract generality calculated to leave cold the practitioners of academic film scholarship at the time. For semiotic or psychoanalytic cinema theory, for materialist and ideological attention alike, this definition might seem to beg four vexed questions at once. Succession where? Real on the strip—or as perceived motion on screen? Automated how? As sprocket advance or in the viewer's ultimate perception? When thereby delivered to the screen, what or whose "world"? And "projections" in what sense other than tautological, as thrown images? It isn't that each of these questions doesn't find answers in Cavell—ramified and refaceted time and again in the pages of *The World Viewed* and later works. But they remain rovingly philosophical rather than technical answers, evocative rather than "scientific," and therefore elude the enthusiasm of the film studies academy at its most "disciplinary" rather than speculative. In pursuing them, we will no doubt see why—and also at what cost—they were thought too loose to come to grips with.

Here is one place where the link to Deleuze might have been richly elucidating over the years. The French philosopher neared the finish of his two-volume cinema study, just before his death, by wondering what the coming of "numerical" (digital) imaging would do not just to cinema at large but to his favored manifestation of the time-image[2]—a foundational postwar category many of whose instances, so we'll see, magnetize Cavell's discussion as well under the sign of assertive "technique" and its skewed temporalities. Released early in the next decade, during the earliest computerization of Hollywood editing, one of the handful of contemporary films Cavell was to remark upon in print was, in fact, an oddball fable of the time-image: the comic fantasy *Groundhog Day* (1993, dir. Harold Ramis). His enthusiasm seems mostly thematic, attracted to the time-loop plot of human perfectability. But a return to the film in more detail, in light of untapped resources in *The World Viewed*, will smooth our transition, in the same terms, to the high-tech narrative experience two decades later in *Billy Lynn's Long Halftime Walk* (2016), from Ang Lee, a film whose accelerated "automatisms," as Cavell would put it, afford a whole new degree of world viewing on screen, an almost palpable feel for embodied duration itself. In concentrating on these two films—*Groundhog Day* and *Billy Lynn's Long Halftime Walk*—at opposite ends of the digital spectrum, the effort is hardly to drag Cavell, let alone Deleuze, into the electronic era. Rather, the instinct is to reanimate in Cavell's pages a latent analytic of particular use, beyond any application of it on his own part, in the medial transition from filmic to digital cinema, from photogram to pixel. Though the "picture element" of image momentum on screen (originally the single celluloid frame, later the pic-el) is granted only to be minimized in the variant screen phenomenologies of both Cavell and Deleuze, its inherence in their most rudimentary definitions of cinema—as well as its disruptive cameo appearance at times, at least by inference—offers an immediately revealing axis of comparison between philosophical orientations. For what the founding condition of image-motion "asserts," we will find, is the engrained force of a *techné* beneath the flourishes of technique.

Let me turn first, then, to an appropriate recent occasion for this return to Cavell's first film book: an explicitly pedagogical venue. For one abiding issue is what viewing the screen world Cavell's way might still have to teach us about a process now so differently automatized and successional—with the screen view composed in postfilmic cinema by a perpendicular gridwork of algorithm-driven image tiles rather than by the discrete celluloid increments of a photo-mechanical series (or "succession"). To borrow one of Cavell's titles, *Themes Out of School: Effects and Causes*, I turn, therefore, to the schoolroom utility of distinguishing screen effects from their own material causes.

At a winter symposium at the University of Chicago Center for Teaching, focused on the conjoined pedagogy of film and philosophy, a circulated paper by philosopher James Conant based on a 2012 seed lecture for a forthcoming book on the subject—"The Ontology of the Cinematographic Image" (adjusting Bazin's famous position paper on "The Ontology of the Photographic Image")[3]—pursued its argument in a way that was actually less insistent than Bazin on the material valence of the indexical imprint. Conant and fellow-presenter Robert Pippin, in line with Cavell, would both seem to agree that the pertinent medial determination of cinema, as aesthetic form, is only the force that a given technical aspect exerts in a given case: a realized potential of its means that is only to be estimated by its aesthetic ends. Though their point is readily taken, there is another place to take it—as I wanted to show in my own presentation at that seminar on classroom approaches. Putting aesthetics aside for the moment, we might isolate a philosophy of the medium that concerns, instead, the discovery, case by case, of the ways in which narrative is caught up in the general premises rather than the immediately achieved possibilities of its own material conditions, whether plastic underlay or digital array. That's what Cavell shows, even if not quite what he means, by his glance at "Assertions in Technique," which thus deserves a close second look.

Now, and fair enough, Conant's understandable purpose, as preceded in print by Victor Perkins (a writer also important for Cavell[4]), is the effort to separate—within what Conant calls "photographic narrative film"—the medium as such, or more to the point, the medium qua aesthetic vehicle, from its sheer "material substrate."[5] Here, Conant is certainly right to stress how, photographic though it is, a movie, "in order for it to become a movie," must employ "further means for defeating this default ontology of the photographic image, in order to introduce the requisite ontological divide between the world of the viewer of the movie"—the signaled Cavellian vocabulary—"and the world of the movie." The essential means of "defeat," however, begin in precisely the transfer of photographic imprint to transparent back-lit photogram in the underlying plastic matter at work in any transmission of the projected image: the serial infrastructure of motion itself. The defeat of this is crucial, but not total, I would add, not invulnerable to resurgence: always liable, varying Cavell, to re-assertion—as if by way of a return of the optical suppressed. We may say, or might eventually be prepared to, that such technological functions come to recognition as something like the ontological unconscious of machinic "intelligence" in Epstein's sense (still pending).

When Cavell famously defines the movies as a "succession of automatic world projections," his main claim, in the play between automatism and world, is clear enough—at least once all initial allergic resistance is cleared away. Re-state his assumption, perhaps, as manifestation via machination. But "succession," the more problematical term, happens at two levels: the first minimized by Cavell (as by Deleuze at this same period, though in neither case excluded). On the material level, there is the tracked path by which mere stills *succeed in making motion pictures*. Which is to say making movies by the moving of pictures. Gone but not always forgotten on screen, the pieced-out service of these single photo-cells is brought to the surface of narrative in certain filmic moments that, at the phenomenal level, can thus be found to philosophize their own process, whether, just for example, by overt freeze-frame disclosure or by tampered frame rates.

Freeze frames (masterfully in Truffaut), along with slow motion (legendarily in Kurosawa) come in for the bulk of comment in "Assertions in Technique," splendidly discriminated in their aesthetic force from film to film. For Cavell, though, neither strip nor its rotary activation as image track locates the "automatism," still less the "succession," at the relevant level indicated by his subtitle, *Reflections on the Ontology of Film*, where that benchmark philosophical term suggests, in its usual doubleness, both the being of film and the study thereof, say its technology and its science. In Cavell's usage, "succession" points, not so much back to the plastic spool of traced frame captures, as to the potential captivation of a viewer before the screen's displayed kinetic world. In "More of *The World Viewed*," appended in 1979 to the enlarged edition of his 1971 philosophical meditation, Cavell wants to make it further clear that cinema (he could still call it film), though based in photography, is not a projected record but rather a projection all told, wherein "any role reality has played is *not* that of having been recorded"—but rather of having been evoked by the configuration of camera angles and montage.[6] In Conant's terms again: the "defeat" of record by construction. Film does not transcribe a space or event in the world whose site you can revisit, and thereby trust in that way, take on faith; it doesn't capture a segment of *the* world in space or time, but rather projects *a* world (itself sliced up, fundamentally intermittent) whose nature, to put it crudely, you take on faith.

Since Cavell wrote, and long since the films that counted for him, the fact that cinema is not a recording but a projection may seem all the clearer when it is no longer film at all, especially (and markedly) when infiltrated by so-called computer-generated imagery (CGI): in semiotic terms, the irruption of pure icon without indexed photochemical trace. If, according to Cavell's deepest logic, this digital turn might be said only to enhance cinema's anti-skeptical exercise in conviction for the invested viewer, one is still moved to ask whether the screen image's former photographic basis— when cinema was still film—served to constitute, or at least locate, the movies' onetime *medium,* and if not, why not? Are the instrumentations on which the "machines of magic" depend, and precisely in connection with their "technique," not rightly the place to anchor any definition of the medium?[7] In unpacking a sense of cinema as *"The World Viewed,"* Cavell does allow that "succession" is a factor that "includes the various degrees of motion in moving pictures": both "the motion depicted" and "the current of successive frames in depicting it"—the "current," the immanent optic currency, as it were, that makes for the screen "present."[8] By contrast, in clarification of "automatic," he has gone back before the reeling strip to photochemical origins, since this term for him "emphasizes the mechanical fact of photography, in particular the absence of the human hand in forming these objects." But not any absent hand in the sequencing of these cumulative *objectifs*. And even before editing, it is the already second-degree automatism of succession itself that is the crux of "world projections" (plural) on screen. Never is Cavell inclined to deny this, of course, but the question remains whether this crux is medial or just mechanical: "One necessity of movies is that the thread of film itself be drawn across light."[9] If by that very phrasing we are led to infer the animation effect of a "drawing" with light and shadow, the suggestion is incidental. The main point, in regard to this plastic "thread," emerges in a question of Cavell's immediately following, and ours from it: "Is this a possibility of some medium of film?" Of *some* medium? One among several? Or, rather, of something we might want to call *the* medium of film?

Cavell actually thinks the latter, at least in certain cases, or seems to, as when shots of immobility in the "epilogue" of Antonioni's *Eclipse* (*L'Eclisse*, 1962), for instance, elicited as among the film's technical "assertions," put us in mind of the "patience" required of succession itself on the track, frame after frame, to automatize such fixity. This is a striking moment in Cavell's account, where the narrative thread sends us directly back to the "thread of film" in its felt alternative (such is his point) to the sheer iterations of a freeze frame.[10] For "depicted motionlessness feels and looks different from motionless depiction."[11] One need only add to such classic examples of technical extrusions in *The World Viewed*, the capping relevance of the freeze-cut from remarriage altar to presumed newsprint archive at the end of *The Philadelphia Story* (1940, dir. George Cukor), as discussed in *Pursuits of Happiness*, to note the ongoing purchase Cavell finds in such medial reflexes.[12] In that closural transition from wedding ceremony to *Spy* magazine's paparazzi capture of it, with invaded privacy translated to tabloid circulation while its victims enter again, in some sense, upon their coveted (anti-filmic) freedom from publicity, one dialectic of the remarriage genre—between sociality and intimacy—is secured by technique alone.

However pointedly thematic and loaded an irony of image culture this match cut from event to its record may inscribe, it returns us more generally to something like medial "acknowledgment," one of Cavell's key terms across many philosophical registers, from Shakespeare to screwball comedy. Like much else in this engrossing chapter on "Assertions in Technique," however, its title powerfully (whether or not intentionally) equivocates. With its choice of preposition, it seems to evoke what might be asserted *about* the filmic medium by such exertions (and expressions) of its technical basis—as opposed, say, to mere "assertions *of* technique" for their own signifying sake, or sense. Yet, it's no accident that six chapters separate this late one from the earlier "The Medium and Media of Film." Nothing about mediation can finally, for Cavell, be reduced, whether "assertive" or not, to the technological substrate of spooled celluloid and its edited "succession." To vary the intervening chapter title, "The Camera's Implication," with its own double sense of inference and complicity, there is no notion in Cavell that the medium should depend necessarily on the strip's implication instead, whether passively entailed or by active intimation. In all its abstraction as such, the "camera" is his encompassing metonymy for filmic immanence and succession.

In Cavell's claim about the nature of mediation authorizing the screen's "world view," he is responding initially to Panofsky's isolation, for the art of cinema, of certain "unique and specific possibilities of the new medium."[13] These "possibilities" are not necessarily technical ingredients, in their gradient linear form as celluloid frames, and in any case are summed too quickly, according to Cavell's paraphrase, "as the dynamization of space and the spatialization of time."[14] Realizing that more "specificity" will be required, Cavell concentrates at this point on the plural noun instead. Such "possibilities" are factored in only if they *count* aesthetically, from case to case. And what would "give significance" in a particular narrative case is not a given. So "possibilities," in a view similar to Pippin's, cannot be comprehended in advance, but only glimpsed in emergence from film to film.[15] This may seem hard to argue with, but the point is pressed further. Insisting that the full "possibilities" of a medium cannot be known ahead of its local achievements may seem to suggest that the medium is realized, or actualized, differently from film to film, rather than just manipulated differently. Again the slippery logic of the genitive seems pertinent. The "possibilities of the medium" is a concept as well as a phrase (originally Panofsky's) that can take medium as its object, waiting for various potentiations (as in a grammar like "the elements of film"). Alternatively, the suggestion may be that the medium can be defined (the so-called equative genitive) only by its own possibilities (as in "the power of film") whenever a technical condition is made to signify, is given significance.

This isn't circular reasoning, but it separates Panofsky's "unique and specific," not just from the category of manifest properties, but from that of underlying components made present to representation even when not visibly implemented by it. To cast the point up in an expanded and necessarily wordy paraphrase, this might seem the rough gist of Cavell's logic: medial conditions, however defined, make possible whatever potential assertions of specific properties can be made significant as technique. But Cavell's terminological point is narrower and more surprising yet. Rather than media creating possibilities, possibilities create media. This is a truly extreme claim: "The discovery of a new possibility is the discovery of a new medium"—by which, one assumes, he must intend a new and specific means of communication.[16] Luckily, helpfully, his insights mostly tack well this side of a position so hard to implement for analysis in any material terms. It is the counter-premise of this chapter, then, that there must be something short of the open standard of "possibility"—in locating mediality—that would have to do with the inbred potential of the filmic system. Or call it the difference between aesthetic possibility and medial (because it is technical) *provision*. And it is here, in such a liminal zone, that two of Cavell's key terms—"automatism" and "succession"—have achieved, as if in the etymological sense, an *ostentatious* recent enhancement in the work of Ang Lee.

But, with Cukor also in view from later writing in this volume[17], let us make the leap from instances in *The World Viewed* lifted from Antonioni, Truffaut, and Kurosawa—not accidentally, with the fixed frame, the freeze frame, and slow motion, respectively, three signal avatars of Deleuze's time-image—to Ang Lee's high-speed digital innovation via a modest transitional work, certainly in technical terms, singled out by Cavell within the subgenre of time-loop cinema. For this is a film that closes another loop as well: by discovering its particular iterative "medium," risen from the level of apparatus to plot, in the foreordained conditions of narrative film itself. This, as promised, is the 1993 "screwball" comedy *Groundhog Day*, about which Cavell remarks with brief enthusiasm when asked in a 1996 *New York Times Magazine* feature about movies he's been impressed by since his earlier favorites.[18] He clearly likes the wit and uplift of this comedy's guiding idea: betterment through repetition, a variant (unspoken) of his theme of bested skepticism in the service of human perfectability. But there is more to say, here and in general. Cinematographically as well as thematically, it is in the spirit of Cavell's continuing provocations for screen thinking that we might find technique, tapped at the level of plastic substrate as well as filmic codes, operating to inflect movies discussed by him in other terms, as well as many a film since. This would be a matter of picking up, while very much in his own terms, where Cavell leaves off. Case in point. The softly piled cloudscape behind the end-titles of *Groundhog Day*, signaling a better day begun for the TV weatherman hero—after his allegorical ordeal of being stuck in a rut and only slowly learning how to master the inexplicable magic of a time warp that launches him into the same day over and over at 6 a.m.—was bookended in the opening credit sequence in the altered form of a time-lapse rush of billows. This was an effect cryptic enough—or say merely atmospheric—at that point: the primal special effect of cinema in the alteration of space-time ratios. Kurosawa in reverse. Epstein: film thinking for us (time-lapse being one of his decisive instances) about a temporal progression otherwise invisible to the naked eye.

Inexplicable magic, yes, no sci-fi premise in sight—only the work of cinema's "machines of magic" (Cavell's phrase again).[19] Other reflexive in-jokes fall in line with this tampering of image tempo at the start, including the blue screen (for subsequent digital backfill) across which the hero's empty gestures will eventually track, in live broadcast, the illustrated satellite-scanned weather fronts: the "world viewed" a mere studio composite. That's, of course, just a localized visual clue via a routine broadcast trick. The deeper trick of "world projection" does, however, seem even more "assertive" in the very structure of this film. In what we might term its metaplot, one day relates to the already next (what dialogue plays on as "the same old same old") in a way that renders each superseded version like on out-take on Hollywood's cutting room floor—so that watching the film in feature-length time may feel like sequencing through a pastiche of deleted scenes retrieved via DVD menu in standard-issue releases since that time. As we are "schooled" in the plot's thematic logic (Cavell's title phrase in mind again), "cause" is put forward as anomalous "effect." The differential iteration is unmistakably more like staged duration on a movie set than like the routinization of daily life. Knowing the scene he's yet again in, for instance, the hero, halting before an anticipated risk, can quip under his breath: "Cue the truck." Existence is entirely subsumed to scenario.

It is easy to see how Cavell would have been drawn, well short of any such "acknowledgment" of the medium's possibilities, to this exponential version of an unusually sentimental "remarriage" comedy, where only love—after the always and already failed efforts with the heroine, one after another—allows the protagonist to break out of this vicious circle for a genuinely fresh start. The fact that time has been, until now, out of joint, spun round as if on an ontological carousel, trapped on an artificial treadmill, what have you, running in place to nowhere, is precisely what was captured in anticipation by fast-forwarding that opening sky of clouds: time itself made visible in its passing, adapted for analysis rather than depicted experience. That this would have been, by the mid-1990s—comparable to the binary rather than analog clock whose radio alarm wakes him into diurnal recurrence—an effect of digital (in this case, *video*) rather than filmic cinema is, as it were, a secondary "assertion" (like the blue screen in the opening sequence) of technique in media-historical evolution. All told, via the optics and edits of his virtually purgatorial recurrence, the hero, in this encounter with a "world" perpetually *re*-"viewed," must first submit to the generative premises of cinema—the doctored *mise-en-scène* and adjusted dialogue within the whole temporal re-thread (or retread)—in order to come fully alive. In this aberrant case, assertions in and of technique have thus grown coercive in their ingrown figuration. In limbo between character and subject, the protagonist has been forced to live under the conditions of iterative montage. Yet at the same time he becomes the spectator of his own moves. In the end, he must recover his status as a character *in* rather than *at* the movie.

The merest hints of digital technique here give way to what has become a full-blown digital breakthrough in the other film, two decades later yet, on which I wish to test Cavell's sense of the difference between what we might call cinematographic *means* and their cinematic *medium*. Nothing could be farther from the fantastic diurnal suspension of *Groundhog Day* than the distended interval known by title as *Billy Lynn's Long Halftime Walk* (2016, dir. Ang Lee). Yet it is perhaps no coincidence, given certain notable traumas of recurrence in contemporary American culture, that the recent film most directly indebted to the iterative template of *Groundhog Day*—the sci-fi thriller *Source Code* (2013, dir. Duncan Jones), about a downed American war pilot whose brain is kept alive long enough for computer-driven synaptic mapping onto the POV of a slain bomb victim in order to surveil the scene in retrospect for clues to the identity of the domestic terrorist—would ironize its far-fetched plot ordeal as serial tours of duty: "Isn't one life enough," asks our wired hero, "to give for your country?" Remove the sci-fi element of nefarious CIA technology that distinguishes this premise from that of *Groundhog Day*, together with the battery of confessed digital effects referred back to causes in the plot's metacinematic flair—and transitional flare-ups—and the film may seem to figure by allusion, almost to allegorize, the same kind of stop-loss program that will return Billy Lynn to the killing fields of Iraq. If cinematic conditions, short of any digital showiness, were thematized to a fare-thee-well in the "retakes" of *Groundhog Day*, how does one think through the implications of technique when it avoids any marked salience, let alone comic disclosure, by a sheer saturation of effect?

How, that is, to read the *lack* of any obvious "assertion" in the very throes of innovation? I ask in connection with the most digitally compressed, elision-smooth, flicker-fused, and vividly virtual-presence film in the annals of cinema—barely enshrined at all in contemporary media history and lost (at least so far) to any chance of a recovered first-hand experience. The question again, then, rephrased: how to read a cinemachinic experiment, if in a seamlessly new digital mode, that asserts nothing in particular about camera or lab-work except the astonishing, luminous clarity of its own self-successive chain of accelerated "world projections"? If not thereby "asserted," what is nonetheless averred about the process of technical mediation in such a film?—namely, *Billy Lynn's Long Halftime Walk*—a little-seen box-office disaster that, worse yet, was almost never seen as intended. For it was available in the year of its US release in only two public venues, in Los Angeles and New York, that were equipped to project it in its intended 4K ultra-high-definition 3D—with its "succession of world pictures" whipping past at five times the normal frame rate, 120 fps, and thus more closely approximating the way the compressive structures of human vision sample the world itself in normal eyesight. To my eye, there at the AMC Lincoln Square Theater in Manhattan, the film was in every sense an event: a technical revelation and an adventure of eerie presence, of things happening before one's eyes at a new level of unimpeded interface. With no optical allusion to an electronic matrix until halfway through its Super Bowl halftime centerpiece, Ang Lee's privatized psychological extravaganza of the image per se, rather than its spectacle, stuns us from the first frames forward with the power of the unprecedented, which never lets up.

If *Billy Lynn* was massively underseen, it has also been quite systematically underappreciated in the spotty press as well. Dismissive critics repeatedly found it an ill-matched wedding between low-keyed psychological drama and a hyper-technology whose capacity for spectacle was by turns wasted on a raft of talky close-ups, undersold in routine Iraq War flashbacks, and squandered in a pyrotechnical Super Bowl show whose own digital grandstanding was beneath the film's pay grade. But this threefold division of labor was precisely the nub of its experimental venture, which unfolds as its own metacommentary on the epitomizing cinematic affect of the close-up (newly effected at super high-speed "attention"), on the suspended distinction between present (presence) and past in the traumatic flashback, and on the electronic gimmickry and showmanship of arena pageants against which this screen breakthrough is, in fact, meant to avow its own more engrossing technology as counter-display in the realm of big-screen spectacle. On all three fronts, the ungodly clarity of the image—or is godly more like the right idiom here?—reaches to unprecedented levels of medial immersion. Which is to say that, in its entirely realist scenography of mostly bland interior locations or familiar bleacher seats, the film nonetheless takes us, as cliché might have it, to places—by bringing their details so vehemently forward—where cinema has never before been. And emplaces us there. In ways impossible finally to describe unless you've, in fact, "been there" (may the technology take hold again somewhere!), suffice it to say that the viewer sits face-to-face with a peopled world seen with the clarity one associates with a very clean mirror.

In just these ways, *Billy Lynn* induces a rare experience in either photogrammic or digital cinema: a completely knowing participation in projection's more than ever invisible basis. Where possible, one sought out the movie precisely to see the retooled cinemachine at work: recorded bodies standing and moving before the viewer with a nonetheless preternatural im-mediacy. Defying the routines of screen spectacle in its normal panoramic ambitions, the eerie hyperrealist—and thus less naturalistic than preternatural—immediacy of the image in Ang Lee's approach is focused repeatedly on the human close-up. This venture in specular intimacy—including its risky commercial wager—comes across as an implicitly media-historical gloss on the prominence of the close-up, the actor's face per se, as cinematic touchstone: from Bela Balázs through Eisenstein to Epstein and on to both Cavell and Deleuze. And in the maximal sharpness of the image, in all its riveting perspicuity, the avowed cinema-specificity of the canonical close-up seems at the same time to dissolve—across the crispness of its own resolution—into a quasi-direct somatic engagement with the viewer as well. What results is the further sensorial quotient of actually being there—and often too close for comfort at that. Activated by such means are all the tributary affects this is likely to trigger, both in prolonged scenes of tearful intimacy and their occasional punctuation by assaulting memory flashes from Iraq firefights. Much of the time, to put it in a corporeal paradox, we find ourselves as if staring into the eyes of subjectivity itself. Which is why the introvert performance of the hero, together with the film's frequent lack of any notable dynamism in camerawork, is both so marked and so cogently motivated. In the immediacy of the image per se, the enhanced medial apparatus—though its optical innovation is never far from mind—goes into suspension as such. At this interface of an almost inhabited fidelity, you are *there* because it is here before you.

In the process—which is to say in this high-velocity procession of separately indecipherable frames, digital now rather than photogrammic—we may well be reminded that there was, after all, something centrally underspecified in Cavell's definition of film as a "succession of automatic world projections"—rather than just world *pictures*. At least from the vantage of Ang Lee's cinematographic upgrade, Cavell's formulation may seem latent with a Bazinian teleology that would take us, within the ambit of "projections" (in the sense of participatory investment as well as thrown light) from standard screen formats through 3D to virtual reality—with *The World Viewed* being less and less comprised of mere pictures of itself in succession, and more and more felt as its tangible (photogenic, now electrogenetic) approximation. Here, then, in the asymptotic achievement of *Billy Lynn*, is automaticity found disappearing into ontology on the cusp of full illusionism, rather than just given over to the normative effects of framed representation. If, according again to Conant's Cavellian emphasis, standard film must, in a war of optical wills, "defeat" photography's documentary offices in order to bridge the gap between our world, faithfully recorded, and the screen's cinematic fiction, then Ang Lee's extraordinary initiative has—more decisively than ever before—served to defeat the single resolved image-cell altogether, sweeping the field by whisking the individual digital frame (and its own thousandfold composite) into a faster-than-ever effacement of itself.

But what about the plot of this film, in its widely assumed mismatch with technique? Or ask: how does the new cinematography achieve—or abort—its narratographic potential? To answer, even tentatively, requires addressing again, in more detail, those leading and blanket objections to the film, mentioned above: the matter of the close-up first; then the backing off in time rather than space to underdeveloped memory inserts; then the tacky splendors of the halftime extravaganza and its computerized stadium backdrop. Building on canonical thinking about the close-up in Balázs, its place in Deleuze's "affection-image" is only one conceptual pressure point in the Deleuzian system that *Billy Lynn*'s hypertrophic vividness can serve to highlight. Deleuze derives his entire system from Bergson, of course, only by first forgiving him his resistance to film, which Bergson distrusted as the mechanical simulation of the world as image, one discrete capture after another, split second by split second. For Bergson, it is clear, this abets the mistaken way in which the mind betrays memory, as well as perception itself, by conceiving of it as separate slices of time rather than as inseparable moments in the continuous medium of duration (an illusory continuum according to Epstein, as we'll see, that machinic intelligence thinks differently, differentially).[20]

With the camera scrutinizing Billy Lynn's watery-eyed features with such determination (and high-definition) that it seems to screen even his tear ducts, not just the occasional welling up of tears, the halftime hiatus of the plot pulls the protagonist two ways from center. Its titular duration sketches, at twin levels, not just the interregnum between quasi-gladiatorial gridiron encounters at the Super Bowl, where Billy's heroic squad from Iraq is literally paraded in a turn of political theater and patriotic dazzle, but also the entire length of the film between "tours" of duty in the Iraq "theater" of war[21]: between, that is, Billy's furlough and his planned redeployment, an interregnum in this more literal, martial sense. In this middle space of plot, the whole sense of an ongoing narrative is almost forestalled by a Las Vegas money-man bidding for film rights on the heroic saga of Billy and his squad, as if their story were a closed one, ready for Hollywood repackaging. With Billy already on show at the stadium for his heroics, this backstage bid for a further narrativization strikes him as a bridge too far. So back he goes into the militarized fray, as if for a reality check.

In the mounting (and middling) meantime, the logic of suspended action is sustained across all those uncanny close-ups on the faces of his crew, lined up in stadium seats for whole low-keyed scenes at a time. And this premium on faciality is further thrown into relief when, as part of the halftime "walk," they take their assigned, stagey places—Billy front and center—before a digitally generated LED display of their own features magnified to stadium scale in the Pop graphics that conclude the halftime extravaganza. With the "grounding" image (rather than its background) sharper than any filmic or digital moving image has ever been—jutting out in 3D in front of a 2D blur of oversized and pulsing bulb-like digital blips clustering in pointillist exaggeration of Billy's battle-tested stature—here is an "assertion in technique" at two scales of digital presentation, where 4K hi-def comes into further definition by immanent contrast. The result is a computerized version of Slavoj Žižek's "interface effect," as described in his punning commentary "Back to the Suture," where he considers the facial image and its own doubling in the same frame—not by cutting, say, between body and mirror image, but by secondary representation (Charles Foster Kane dwarfed by his own campaign poster, for instance).[22] Putting the very concept of editing and montage under analysis by suspension, such a conflation of interface can seem to suggest that the screen's own technological plane of duplication is absorbing its original into the same optic field.

With Billy standing at fragile, patriotic attention before his own broadcast real-time publicity image, with its inflated and frail approximation of seen reality, it is here, as fireworks go off, that sonic free-association triggers the first flashback from playing field to the gun bursts of the Iraqi killing fields. In a second iteration of the so-called interface effect, and against a thematized limit case of digital HD and 3D alike, the parched earth and its distant sniper targets are dramatically reflected in the battle goggles of Billy and his squad leader. In Žižek's terms again, it is as if shot and its reverse shot are held in focus in the elided distance of imminent firing lines: the very ground of carnage made present to their vision—and, by reflection, ours as well—across the immediacy both of technical close-up and transferred adrenaline rush. As plot then reverts to the halftime hoopla breached by this narrative return of the repressed, the vapid and humiliating parade of star heroics is soon over. But in the backstage subplot, in Billy's final rejection of the movie deal—and its metacinematic dealing-out of the film's own overarching ontological irony—Billy explodes at the would-be producer after being patronized and low-balled in the offer: "You can't make a movie of this. . . . It's our life." But, of course, Ang Lee has done just that, in a mode of machination whose life-likeness, in the final spiraling of an implied technological paradox, is the exception that proves Billy's rule.

In the process, *Billy Lynn's Long Halftime Walk* reads almost like the self-conscious tailing off of the Mideast war film after its many commercial disappointments—in all their metafilmic re-mediations through helmet cams, infrared gun-sights, and drone transmits.[23] In this halftime as interregnum, the plot (despite flashbacks and a pending stop-loss return to the war) leaves all that wired violence behind in an aesthetic of the up-front (albeit hypermedial) 3D close-up. What is here "asserted in technique"—lambent and unmistakable in every superrealist frame—is a radical five-fold increase in (to vary Cavell) the automaticities of "succession," together with a resulting new depth of "projection" into a credibly dimensioned 3D space. Ang Lee's newly engineered shift rate, of course, disappears the optic subunits (encoded digital frames rather than indexed photograms) faster than ever before—in the history of "world projections"—into the all the more nearly "realized" scene. We don't see this increased pixel differentiation "phenomenally," but we sense the result as a new phenomenon: metacinematic as well as technical. Here is a streamlined "defeat" of the fixed frame that Conant would recognize, one assumes, as all the more quintessentially Cavellian. In this way we are affected by the conditioning genius (Epstein's "intelligence") of this one film's unique approximation to nothing less than the synaptic rate of human perception itself. A neo-Bazinian teleology of realism has brought us to the brink not of a reproduced world, but of a surrogate human vision. At this level, *Billy Lynn's* uncanny counterpart to—or interlock with—the brain's own perceptual engineering offers itself as yet another subliminal parable of time (on screen as well as off) as no more than the abstract derivative of subliminal change per se, graphed in the now-reigning apparatus by pixel shifts.

Here is where the synchromeshed speed of imprint and optic impression in Ang Lee's experiment invites the triangulation of philosophical paradigms I anticipated at the start. Epstein's sense of film's defining rudiments—slow motion, acceleration, close-up, and montage—enlists projection to show us views of the world we wouldn't otherwise see, even as they relativize what we take to be normal vision. For him "cinematographic reality is . . . essentially the idea of a complete mode of location," but, as such, and with his italics, it is "*a kind of trick or special effect*. Nonetheless, this trick [*truquage*] is extremely close to the process by which the human mind itself conjures up an ideal reality for itself."[24] No film has ever come closer to narrowing the gap between human sight and constructed image than *Billy Lynn*. For Epstein, it is out of intermittence that cognition, too, not just cinema, *invents* continuity. As in Bergson, the world is all and only image, but entirely compromised as such (for Epstein) in any sense of its *durée* or continuity. The machine whose thinking is done in spurts, in bits and pieces, from the ground up, works to approximate the mind's own operation in constructing—or, in a more radical sense than Cavell's, in "projecting"—the world, and our temporal and spatial orientation in *regard* to it. Even Deleuze, in his allegiance to Bergsonian *durée*—and his lone major departure from his French philosophical predecessor on the score of the earlier thinker's distrust of film as fabricated motion—still needed to admit the piecemeal increments separated only by framelines on what Cavell calls the "thread of film."[25] More like an optic enchainment than a continuous thread, such for Deleuze is a "zeroness" of visual registration whose uncongealed molecular units suggest the "gaseous state" of a sensory-motor optic, the realm of the "engramme"—or "photogramme"—before its bundling and binding as kinetic image.[26] As Deleuze clarifies in the glossary to Volume 1: "not to be confused with a photo."[27] At the same scale of recognition, it is the aggregation of such optic data-cells that constitutes, for Epstein, the fundamental (and fertile) deception of filmic imageering—as it disabuses us regarding all supposed ontological continuities of both matter and perception. The mission of cinema is to expose the universal fabric of intermittence itself.

How far this is from Cavell (as well as Deleuze at key moments) on a faith in the world exercised, or a skepticism therapized, by cinema becomes unmistakable when Epstein speaks of the way cinematic images "bear a subtle venom" that he insists has been given "little attention" in regard to its "corrupting" force.[28] This is a toxin whose power it is—in precisely the medium's best "philosophical" use—to poison reality's facile assumptions for us. Thus, "having taught us the unreality of both continuity and discontinuity, the cinematograph rather abruptly ushers us into the unreality of space-time"—when any such localized temporality is, in fact, merely a function of discrete images in their timed spacings.[29] Effect to this cause, mirage of this machination, *all cinema*—like all supposed reality—is, again, a "special effect" of perception. It is an effect placed under further dissection and analysis when "asserted" anomalously in the likes of slow motion and looped superimposition, as recruited famously by Epstein himself for his film version of Poe's *The Fall of the House of Usher* (1928, *La Chute de la maison Usher*). This is exactly the heuristic "irrealism" of cinema (the title of Epstein's closing chapter) that *Billy Lynn* approaches from the near side of the virtual rather than the far side of the fantastic.

In sum, powerful thinking about media tends to survive the latter's ongoing inventions, even in their most radical forms. So it is that, beyond any regrets about the failed conversation between the two greatest postwar philosophers of film, Cavell and Deleuze, the photochemical threshold at which their texts separately held firm, in the filmic moment, provides a tantalizing yardstick for innovations since. In moving from what can only be called Ang Lee's hyperphonemenality to the all-but-immanent sci-fi parable of interactivity in Steven Spielberg's 3D *Ready Player One* (2018), for instance, in respect both to the latter's own digital technique and to the electronic virtualities it narrativizes, we have come to the point where we can track Deleuze's thinking about screen temporality, altered perhaps irrevocably by the "numeric image," alongside a transformation in the fictive World Viewed en route to the new limit case of the Virtual World inhabited: all "time-image" relegated now to that of performance rather than depiction. At which point Cavell's resonant point about an unfolding world "present to me" by photographic dispensation, even though "I am not present to it" (delimiting the very essence of the cinematic medium in whatever mutation) has been obliterated by retinal subterfuge—and a new cyberoptic transference.[30] At the very least, Cavell joins Deleuze in giving us residual terms to measure just how far we've come—and how much, by way of aesthetic contemplation, may soon be altogether behind us in the process.

Notes

1 Stanley Cavell, *The World Viewed: Reflections on the Ontology of Film*, Enlarged ed. (Cambridge: Harvard University Press, 1979), 72; definition repeated, 146.

2 See Gilles Deleuze, *Cinema 2: The Time-Image*, trans. Hugh Tomlinson and Barbara Habberjam (Minneapolis: University of Minnesota Press, 1989), on whether the "numerical image" is destined to "transform cinema or to replace it" (265).

3 Available in an earlier incarnation through the Duke University Center for Philosophy, Literature, and Film (PAL): https://dukepal.org/2012/04/05/philosophy-literature-and-film-two-lectures-by-james-conant-and-cora-diamond/.

4 See in this volume, Chapter 6, William Rothman on Cavell and Perkins.

5 Conant's general acknowledgment is to V. F. Perkins, *Film as Film: Understanding and Judging Movies* (New York: Penguin, 1972), in a title that, like Conant's paper, places a less materialist emphasis on the specifying phrase "as film" than, to say the least, does the present chapter.

6 Cavell, *The World Viewed*, 183; emphasis added.

7   Ibid., 145.
8   Ibid., 72–73.
9   Ibid., 142.
10 Ibid.
11 Ibid.
12 See Cavell, *Pursuits of Happiness: The Hollywood Comedy of Remarriage* (Cambridge: Harvard University Press, 1981), 159–69, where, without examining the immediate technical feat of the match-cut freeze in its "assertion" of the strip itself as such, Cavell's subtle discussion goes so far as to allow that our presumed presence in real narrative time at the wedding—canceled by this retrospective pair of (what?) production stills, album photos, magazine images (equivocation is all)—has never been anything but our presence to a photographic space, though until now a moving one.
13 Cavell, *The World Viewed*, 31.
14 Ibid.
15 Cavell suggests here, in the evolution of a particular genre, that a moviemaker would discover the "possibilities" of some technical feature only when seeing "that certain established forms would give point to certain properties of film"—whether or not they are "unique properties" of its *medium* (31). It is important to see the logical turnabout this involves. Instead of a traditional notice of the way, say, "technique enhances meaning," Cavell stresses how only "meaning can give point to technical properties"—as the local potential of a medium otherwise not (and so never fully) determined in advance.
16 Cavell, *The World Viewed*, 32.
17 See Chapter 13 where David LaRocca addresses *Adam's Rib* (1949, dir. George Cukor).
18 In the third of three short sentences on *Groundhog Day*, in the September 29, 1996, issue of *The New York Times Magazine*, there is this signature Cavellian turn: "Its vision is to ask how, surrounded by conventions we do not exactly believe in, we sometimes find it in ourselves to enter into what Emerson thought of as a new day."
19 Cavell, *The World Viewed*, 145.
20 See my discussion of Deleuze's demurral from Bergson in *Between Film and Screen: Modernism's Photo Synthesis* (Chicago: The University of Chicago Press, 1999), 86–87.
21 For more on the home front and the "theater" of war, see my "War Pictures: Digital Surveillance from Foreign Theater to Homeland Security Front," in *The Philosophy of War Films*, ed. David LaRocca (Lexington: The University Press of Kentucky, 2014), 107–32.
22 See Slavoj Žižek, *The Fright of Real Tears: Krzysztof Kieślowski between Theory and Post-Theory*. (London: BFI, 2001), 39.
23 See again "War Pictures," my treatment of this wired war aesthetic, in David LaRocca, ed., *The Philosophy of War Films* (Lexington: The University Press of Kentucky, 2014).

24 Jean Epstein, *The Intelligence of a Machine*, trans. Christophe Wall-Romana (Minneapolis, MN: Univocal, 2015), 104 (originally published as *L'Intelligence d'une machine* [Paris: Jacques Melot, 1946]).
25 Cavell, *The World Viewed*, 142.
26 Deleuze, *Cinema 2: The Time-Image*, 32.
27 Deleuze, *Cinema 1: The Movement-Image*, trans. Hugh Tomlinson and Barbara Habberjam (Minneapolis: University of Minnesota Press, 1986).
28 Epstein, *The Intelligence of a Machine*, 7.
29 Ibid., 25.
30 Cavell, *The World Viewed*, 23.

2

Revisiting *The World Viewed*

Noël Carroll

Introduction

STANLEY CAVELL'S *The World Viewed: Reflections on the Ontology of Film*, first published in 1971 and then reissued in an expanded version in 1979, was immensely important for the rise of the field of the philosophy of film—or, as I prefer to call it, the philosophy of the moving image—in contemporary Anglophone philosophy.[1] For it was the first book by a major, living Anglo-American philosopher on cinema and, as such, it secured a measure of legitimacy for those of us, emerging from the movie-crazy 1960s, who wished to philosophize about motion pictures.

In the United States in the 1960s, film was suddenly taken seriously, due to the influence of the Art Cinema—including the films of Bergman, Bresson, Fellini, Antonioni, Kurosawa, Ozu, and the New Wave—on the one hand, and the re-evaluation of the Hollywood cinema by the so-called "auteur theory," on the other hand. Cinema was being considered as an established art form and, as such, it called for a philosophy of its own. And *The World Viewed* pioneered the way.

The book, I think, it is fair to say, is not an easy read. Part of the reason is that Cavell is involved in doing a number of things at the same time: proposing a philosophy of film, distilling philosophical insights from individual films, doing film criticism, and doing traditional philosophy, including political philosophy, outright. These concerns interweave in ways that can seem digressive. Moreover, this difficultly is often compounded by Cavell's own self-acknowledged insistence on saying things his own way.[2] However, though the book may have a reputation, in some quarters, for obscurity, I think it possesses a reasonably continuous, through-argument, despite the apparent digressions. So, the first order of business in this chapter will be to trace what I take that argument to be by way of an extended commentary. Only after that commentary will I review the argument critically, highlighting what I see as potential problems.

Commentary

I would like to begin my interpretation of *The World Viewed* in a somewhat linear fashion, starting with the section "An Autobiography of Companions." There are two points in this section to which I wish to call attention. One point is more or less methodological. The other concerns the object of Cavell's inquiry.

First to the methodological point: Appearances notwithstanding, *The World Viewed* is dedicated to answering two perennial questions of film theory: (1) Is film art? and (2) if it is an art, is it a unique art, that is, an art form in its own right? Both of these questions arose because of the provenance of film in photography, a medium to which many denied art status on the grounds that it is nothing but the sheer, slavish, mechanical recording of reality, thereby allowing no space for the intervention of artistic expression or imagination, formal or otherwise. Photography, and by extension cinema, were virtually equivalent to holding up a mindless mirror to reality, to use a Platonic metaphor.

Thus, classical film theorists set out to show that film was an art. However, even if it was art, the question arose as to whether it was a unique art form unto itself or merely theater in a can. Again, the problem was the photographic provenance of cinematography. Is there an art of cinema or is cinema merely the sheer, slavish, mechanical recording of theatrical spectacles staged before the camera, as *The Cabinet of Dr. Caligari* was said to be. Cavell's answers to these questions organize a great deal of *The World Viewed*.

In order to answer the question of whether film is an art, Cavell develops a definition of film—an answer to the question "What is Film?" However, he opens "An Autobiography of Companions," with a very distinctive methodological move. He announces that just as Tolstoy required of his definition of art that it make clear why art is important to human life, so Cavell requires that any acceptable answer to the question "What is film?" must account for the human importance of film.[3] In fact, Cavell does not think that the questions "What is film?" and "Why is film important?" are separate questions. Thus, in identifying film as a succession of automatic world projections, it will be incumbent on Cavell to explain why this is important—that is, what human desires are satisfied by an automatic succession of world projections, something that I will argue is not fully explained until the final paragraph of the section "The Acknowledgement of Silence," though it is suggested several times throughout the text.

So methodologically, "An Autobiography of Companions" introduces the constraint that however one answers the question "What is film?" if it is to be an account of film art, it must simultaneously explain why film is important to human life.

But, in addition, this section, among other things, also clarifies how Cavell understands the object of his inquiry. He remarks that film attracts the same audience for its highest and most ordinary efforts.[4] What this indicates is that there is something that movies *tout court* (i.e., the highest and most ordinary) share that will account for their importance. That this is so is further putatively supported by the film-going practice of yesteryear whereby one entered the movies at any time, even if it was in the middle of a feature, and then sitting through the cartoons, newsreels, coming attractions, and the second feature until one was back to the scene in the film that was playing when one entered. For Cavell, this practice suggests that we had some interest in just going to the movies, over and above an interest in seeing the feature film itself. In other words, going-to-the-movies is an experience with its own attractions. Just as nowadays, when asked what I am doing tonight, I might say "Watching television" with no particular program in mind, in the old days, I might have said "I'm going to the movies," which suggests that there is the promise of value in the experience of movie going simpliciter.

Cavell thinks that the experience of movies is patently important since "all care about movies, await them, respond to them, remember them, talk about them, hate some of them, are grateful for some of them".[5] In this, movies, he believes, have escaped the plight of the other modern arts insofar as, *ex hypothesi*, everyone is interested in movies, whereas only specialized audiences care about the art forms that have entered the advanced stage of modernism. It is the task of *The World Viewed* to explain which seemingly ubiquitous human desires film could be satisfying.[6]

In the next section, "Sights and Sounds," Cavell pursues the question "What is film?" as past film theorists have done by drawing a contrast between film and neighboring art, forms—in this case between film and painting which distinction is also meant to explain the grounds for considering cinema to be an art, albeit a historically novel one. Cavell's approach, here as elsewhere, is especially influenced by the French film theorist André Bazin, and others, such as the art historian Erwin Panofsky. Like them, Cavell thinks of cinema as crucially a photographic medium. Unlike earlier film theorists, like Sergei Eisenstein, Cavell does not underplay the relevance of photography to film art but embraces it as central.

Moreover, he approaches its centrality through a contrast with painting. He maintains that what a photograph presents is ontologically different from what a painting presents. A painting presents us with a likeness of what it is a painting of. David's *Death of Marat* presents us with an image that resembles the assassinated revolutionist. A photograph, on the other hand, is allegedly transparent—we see through it as we might see through a pair of binoculars—across time rather than space—to behold the very subject of the photo, for instance, Hitler saluting his followers. That is, in some sense, photographs enable us to see what they are photographs of, whereas paintings only afford imitations of what they represent. Cavell says, "A photograph does not present us with 'likenesses' of things; it presents us, we want to say, with the things themselves".[7] This is not to say that the things themselves are co-present with us. But, rather, that with photographs we putatively see things that are not present. We see the things themselves.

Cavell argues for this counterintuitive conclusion by drawing a contrast between sound recording and photographic recording. With sound recording there are two things—the object, say the drum, and the sound of beating the drum. But, there is not a parallel situation with photography, because with photography there is not anything like the distinction between the object and its sound. You might question this by claiming that there is a distinction between the object and the sight of the object that parallels the object/sound distinction. But Cavell rejects this on the grounds that there are no such things as sights as distinct from objects. Why not? Cavell advances several considerations:

1. In ordinary language sights are places we visit like Mt. Rushmore. Talk of Mt. Rushmore having a sight sounds strained. Rather, it is a sight.
2. Sights cannot be assimilated to the philosopher's sense data for all the reasons that theory has been rejected.
3. Sights unlike sounds are not from somewhere. We can "sight" something from everywhere. That is, there are an infinite number of positions from which an object can be viewed and hence an infinite number of sights. Thus, there is no single sight for the photographic recording to reproduce in the way that a sound recording can reproduce the sound. Indeed, there are too many "sights" to be ontologically feasible.[8]

Furthermore, these insights can be worked into an argument:

1. A photograph presents us with either the sight of an object or the object itself.
2. Objects don't have sights.
3. Therefore, photographs present us with the object of itself.

So what we see when we see a photograph is the object itself. Moreover, Cavell rejects the retort that what we see are photographs on the grounds that what is involved in his argument is the attempt to ascertain exactly what a photograph is.

A second contrast Cavell draws between photography and painting in "Sights and Sounds" is that photography is an automatic process, whereas painting is the result of intentionality. That is, a camera is a machine; once it is set in motion, if set properly, it will record whatever stands before it, whether or not the cameraperson intended it. If there is an unwanted fly on Aunt Sadie's nose, the camera will capture it. In contrast, everything that is in the painting is there because the artist intended it to be there. Thus, Cavell agrees with Bazin that not only is the photograph "of reality" but that, in a certain sense, it is also "objective." Moreover, both these features of photography/cinematography will figure in explaining why film is important.

So far Cavell has argued that films are automatic projections of reality in terms of objects. In the section "Photograph and Screen" he wants to expand the notion of the projection of objects to projecting the *world*. (Note how freely Cavell moves from "reality" to "world.") Cavell argues for this expansion by once again contrasting photography, as the determinant feature of film, to painting. Cavell writes:

> You can always ask, pointing to an object in a photograph—a building say—what lies behind it, totally obscured by it. This only accidentally makes sense when asked of an object in a painting. You can always ask, of an area photographed, what lies adjacent to that area, beyond the frame. This generally makes no sense asked of a painting. You can ask these questions of objects in photographs because they have answers in reality. The world of the painting is not continuous with the world of its frame; at its frame, a world finds its limits. We might say: A painting *is* a world; a photograph is *of* the world.[9]

Moreover, for Cavell, since the photograph frame is basically just a bracket that circumscribes a portion of the world, screening off the rest, the photographic/cinematographic image implies the presence of the rest of the world, a world past, a world viewed by us, but a world from which we are absent.[10]

The idea that Cavell is getting at is reminiscent of the notion of lateral-depth of field that Bazin discussed in relation to Renoir's use of irregular panning. According to Bazin, Renoir favored this strategy in order to defeat the impression of the action being bounded on a theatrical stage, thereby affirming the spontaneity of the acting in a continuous, open environment. Bazin thought emphasizing the continuity of on-screen and off-screen space heightened the realistic effect. Cavell thinks that the photographic frame itself, in contrast to the frame of a painting, somehow makes us aware that it is part of something that the screen screens from us—the rest of the world. So in the viewing of the world photographically framed, we are viewing a slice of the continuum of the world automatically projected.

In the next section, "Audience, Actor, and Star," Cavell continues probing the nature of film as a distinct art, this time by contrasting it with theater. Specifically, he compares acting in film with acting on the stage. Basically, Cavell appropriates the often-repeated claim that the stage actor plays a character whereas on film the character is absorbed into the actor[11] as in "Clint Eastwood is Dirty Harry." That is, onstage many actors play Hamlet; many actors interpret that role. But in film, stars supposedly play themselves, their characters swallowed up by their star personae. Paul Robeson, Orson Welles, Lawrence Olivier, James Earl Jones, and many others have played Othello, but Clark Gable *is* Rhett Butler, or so the story goes. Perhaps needless to say, this view of film acting fits neatly with Cavell's conviction that film has a special connection to reality in that the characters portrayed on screen are rooted in the actual behavioral comportment of the stars who represent them.

Cavell does not explain why he thinks film characters fuse in this way with their stars; he seems to accept this as an established truism. However, some of the reasons commonly given for this alleged phenomenon are very consistent with Cavell's view of *The World Viewed*.

In his *Film Technique and Film Acting*, the Soviet film theorist V. I. Pudovkin observed that "the first desideratum of the [stage] actor is that he must be distinctly seen and heard."[12] In order to ensure this, typically the stage actor has to speak at a higher volume and make larger movements than normal so that she will not only get her character across not only to the audience in the orchestra section but to those in the balcony as well. Thus, gestures onstage will not be of their ordinary scale but will be exaggerated or enlarged. The everyday idiosyncrasies of tone and movement of the actor will be subjected to the discipline of technique. The actor's interpretation of the character has to be writ large, so to speak, in voice and movement. Think, for example, of the exaggerated crookedness of Kevin Spacey's Richard III. So, putatively, the technique of stage acting, given the demands of projection, will distract attention away from the actor's smaller, natural mannerisms, thereby effacing her personality and submerging her in the magnified artifice of her character.

But in cinema, there is no need to augment the scale of the performer. The screen itself is already larger than life. Kim Basinger's head may occupy a screen space as large as a tank, and a close-up can record every twitch of her lips. There is no need to enlarge gestures in cinema. Indeed, to enlarge them is often to be criticized pejoratively as "theatrical." The camera works as a telescope, casting the actor's natural comportment—like John Wayne's swagger—into view so that it appears to become an indissoluble property of the character.

The performer on film is under a relentless microscope through which personal mannerisms are captured and made large. One's everyday behaviors—how one stands, or walks unselfconsciously is recorded and enlarged by the camera—behaviors such as Katherine Hepburn's briskness, Jimmy Stewart's hesitancy, James Cagney's clipped diction, and Bruce Lee's sideways glance. All these real-world ticks of the stars become incorporated in the mode of being of the characters portrayed on screen, putatively as a result of the relation of photography/cinematography to reality. The screen character, in a certain way of speaking, is *of reality*. Perhaps this is why when we recount movie plots, we typically say things like "then Matt Damon did that" rather than "then Jason Bourne did that." Moreover, we also watch stars age from film to film which further reinforces our sense that films are connected to reality, to *The World Viewed*, albeit a world from which we are absent.

In the next section, "Types: Cycles and Genres," Cavell continues the discussion of film acting but links it to a long-standing debate in film theory, namely, the notion of medium specificity. This issue arises almost naturally in the process of differentiating art forms. Once it is conjectured that one art form in virtue of its medium can represent a certain content more efficiently than some other—as Lessing claimed poetry can represent events better than painting—the temptation arises to legislate—to say that an art form should only pursue those effects it discharges best and should be limited to just those possibilities. Film should not pursue what theater does better and theater should not attempt what film does best. Siegfried Kracauer, for example, thought film was essentially photographic. Furthermore, he believed photography had a special affinity to reality and that reality itself is marked by open-endedness. From this he surmised that the film narratives that best realized the potential of the film medium were open-ended narratives like those of Italian neo-realist film such as *Paisan* (1946, dir. Roberto Rossellini). On the other hand, closed narrative structures like tragedies, and, for our purposes, thrillers such as those of Hitchcock are allegedly ill-suited to the medium.

Cavell, rightly I believe, rejects this approach, arguing, instead, that the medium does not predetermine the range of its aesthetic possibilities, but, rather, that the achievement of significance creates the medium by giving significance to specific possibilities of its productive resources. That is, the possibilities of a medium are discovered by using it to convey significance. Georges Méliès discovered the possibility of using stop-action photography for representing magic and fantasy, fairy tales, and science fiction. It is not as though these possibilities were dictated by the camera/projection mechanism.[13] Cavell writes:

> ... the aesthetic possibilities of a medium are not givens. You can no more tell what will give significance to the unique and specific photographic images by thinking about them or seeing some, than you can tell what will give significance to the possibilities of paint by thinking about paint or looking some over. You have to think about painting and paintings; you

have to think about motion pictures. What does this "thinking about them" consist in? Whatever the useful criticism of an art consists in.[14]

And in what does the useful criticism of an art form consist? Presumably in the identification of the significance of an artwork and the particular way in which the significance in question gets made.

But how does significance get made in film? Cavell argues that one of the major ways in which significance is made in film is by means of genres. Genres discover how to make sense in film and thereby reveal the possibilities of the medium for making meaning. Contra Kracauer, it is not by analyzing, the nature of the medium that you identify what genres are suitable to the medium. It is through genres that the medium is forged.

But where do genres come from? Here we return to Cavell's discussion of film acting and star personalities. On Cavell's account, successful genres emerge as vehicles for certain star personalities who *are*, so to say, their characters. For example, in the silent period Westerns developed as a major genre to accommodate W. S. Hart and Tom Mix; silent comedy provided a vehicle for Charlie Chaplin, Buster Keaton, Harry Langdon, Harold Lloyd, Laurel and Hardy, among others. The swashbuckler epic was called forth by the athleticism of Douglas Fairbanks Senior, to be carried on in the 1930s and 1940s by Errol Flynn. Romance sprouted from the foreheads of Rudolph Valentino, Greta Garbo, John Gilbert, Gloria Swanson, among others, while the genre of the grotesque was born around Lon Chaney Senior, the Man of a Thousand Faces.

The correlation of the emergence of successful genres with star personalities continued into the thirties. Gangster films were associated with figures like Edward G. Robinson, James Cagney, George Raft, and the early Bogart, just as in the 1940s Bogart emerged as the epitome of the hard-boiled detective, a role that undoubtedly profited, as Cavell astutely notes, from his earlier screen identity as an outlaw. The horror film of the 1930s owes a great deal of its success to the star personalities of Lugosi and Karloff; the musical to Fred Astaire and Ginger Rogers, and to Gordon McCrae and Jeanette MacDonald; the screwball comedy to Carey Grant and Katherine Hepburn; and the western to John Wayne and Randolph Scott.

By identifying genres as *a* way of making significance in movies, albeit a way of major importance, *and* by linking genres to star personalities, Cavell grounds this major way of making meaning in films in photography's connection to reality—to the world—because the star himself/herself is a product of photography's in-many-ways-unselective assimilation of the actor's everyday behavioral comportment as properties of the characters around whom genres are built. In this way, genres and cycles emerge, on Cavell's account, through photography/cinematography's connection with reality. Thus, genres remain tethered to reality—to the world—through photography.

Of course, stars are not the only sort of recurring factors that make successful genres possible. There are antagonists as well as protagonists as well as supporting characters. Erich von Stroheim, the man people loved to hate, was an example of both. But like the star, his characters grew out of his everyday mien, as do the products of such appropriately called "character actors" as Roy Jenkins and Kathy Bates.

Genres emerge not only from the personalities of stars but also from the character actors who surround them as exemplified by the recurring repertory of actors in films by Preston Sturges, on the one hand, and John Ford, on the other. Character actors like stars are types, marked by their physiognomic and behavioral singularity as captured by the camera (and sound recording), and from such types genres emerge as *a* primary means for creating significance in cinema.

Cavell pursues this theme starting in section seven, "Baudelaire and the Myths of Film." Using Baudelaire's figures of the Military Man, the Woman, and the Dandy, sometimes somewhat fancifully, as his extension of the idea of the military man to those who do the work of the world, Cavell reviews, often with penetrating insight, how a parade of star personae have imbued their films and the genres they inhabit with significance. He also spends quite a bit of time worrying about whether what he is calling the New Hollywood—the Hollywood of the 1960s—will be able to sustain the rich repertoire of types—stars and character actors—that populated the films that he loved in his youth. In retrospect, his anxieties here strike me as generational. After all, by now we think that actors like Dustin Hoffman, Robert De Niro, Clint Eastwood, Al Pacino, Jack Nicholson, Julie Christi, Faye Dunaway, Vanessa Redgrave, Diane Keaton, and the like are just as iconic as the stars of Cavell's memory.

From discussing actors and genres as modes of creating significance, Cavell in section thirteen—"The World as a Whole: Color"—reviews, somewhat unsystematically but with great sensitivity, a variety of ways in which in individual films—like *Vertigo, The Wizard of Oz, Rosemary's Baby*, and *Red Desert*, color has been used to create significance in film—a process that he seems to regard as a means of unifying the world of the film (although it pays to note that "world" in this case seems to refer to "the world of the work of art" rather than to "the world" as a synonym for "reality" as that notion is typically used throughout the rest of the book).

After discussion of color as a way of producing significance in film, one might expect sections sixteen, seventeen, and eighteen to follow naturally— for these sections continue to canvas ways of making significance in film, including strategies of self-reference, the camera's implication of its presence, and assertions of technique. But they don't. So the question arises: Why not?

My hypothesis is that these sections are placed where they are because they do double-duty for Cavell. They are not merely part of the continuing inventory of devices by which cinema makes meaning—and thereby creates the medium; they are also meant to show that certain cinematic strategies that might appear to be reflexive, modernist gestures are not really such, but, rather, have better explanations when seen in the context of the films in which they occur.

So, I conjecture that the reason the sections in question do not appear immediately after the section on color is that in between the issue of modernism and film's relation to modernism, which has popped up here and there throughout the text, comes to the fore in sections fourteen and fifteen. And sections sixteen, seventeen, and eighteen must wait until the issue of modernism has been introduced thoroughly.

What exactly is the issue of the relation of film to modernism? There are various ways of framing it. One might ask whether film—or the movies—are or can be a modernist art. Cavell appears to have stronger and weaker attitudes toward the issue. In a weaker mood, he seems to admit that film, the last traditional art, may be on the brink of modernism; at other times, he seems to adopt a strong stance, seeing film as a traditional art, one that has avoided modernism. And at still other times, he maintains that the concept of modernism has no clear application to film.

Film is a modern art form; sometimes it is said to be *the* modern art form. Michael Fried claimed that it escapes the condition of modernism.[15] This is a claim that Cavell, with modification, accepts and wants to defend. Why?

Recall the emphasis that Cavell earlier placed on the notion that everyone is interested in film. That motivates his search for some generic human desires that film satisfies as a basis for the human importance of film. But also recall that Cavell maintains that the other modern arts have signed on to the reflexive agenda—the interrogation of their own conditions of possibility—and that this has severed their relation with a general audience. The modernist arts, in other words, attract self-selected audiences with special interests. So, if Cavell is to discover some general human importance for cinema, it would appear that it will be possible only because film has escaped the condition of modernism.

But what does this mean? Indeed, what does modernism mean in this context?

Here is my interpretation. Following Fried, Cavell agrees, notably with reference to painting, that the modernist artwork must establish its presentness to and of the world.

What does that mean? I think it means that the modernist painting has to establish its objecthood—it has to establish that it is an object in the world (and, in that sense, is *of* the world). That is, it is an object among all the other objects and, therefore, present to them (and us). As Frank Stella said, his paintings were like any other objects—like radiators, for example. In other words, the modernist painting is not an illusion; it does not refer us to something elsewhere. It is present to us, the way any other object is present to us, or, in Cavell's idiom, it is present to the world.

According to Cavell, it is the task of the modernist artist—her absolute condemnation to seriousness, he says[16]—that she establish the presentness of the artworks *to* the world by being *of* the world.

Why is the modernist so committed? Continuing my interpretation, here is my suggestion. For centuries, Western art had an overriding commitment to capturing the appearances of things; call this realism. This quest to capture the real, so to speak, by the nineteenth century, led to the recognition that the representation of real things by way of resemblance was still at one remove—to appropriate Platonic lingo—from reality and that, instead of making simulacra, the commitment to the real required them to make artworks that were real things—real painted things, things that foregrounded their nature as painted objects, as Pollock drip paintings declare themselves to be things constituted of line, color, and canvas. That is, the modernist painter strives to acknowledge the objecthood of her painting by saliently affirming the kind of object it is—a painted object rather than a window onto the other objects of the world.

What does this have to do with film? Cavell argues:

Movies from their beginning avoided (I do not say answered) modernism's perplexities of consciousness, its absolute condemnation to seriousness. Media based on automatic world projections do not, for example, have to establish presentness to and of the world: the world is there.[17]

That is, film's causal relations with coexisting objects establishes its "of the worldness" automatically. Film doesn't have to establish its objecthood; its mechanical-physical provenance secures it. Likewise, its presentness to us is also secured for us because we are screened from the world on film in that we are not a part of that world—it is separate from us; we encounter it as an alien presence. Nor is the artist's presence at issue because supposedly, due to the automatic, causal nature of photography, what is on screen is, in a certain sense, out of her hands.

Cavell then supplements this argument with a number of further considerations.

The first involves the three sections—sixteen, seventeen, and eighteen—that I have already mentioned. Here Cavell examines cinematic strategies, like self-reference and assertive technique that might look like examples of modernist reflexivity, but he argues that they have better alternative explanations when viewed in context.

For example, the extended reflexivity in Keaton's *Sherlock Jr.* (1924), Olsen and Johnson's *Hellzapoppin'* (1941), and Fields' *Never Give a Sucker an Even Break* (1941) are transgressions of the mechanical or conventional conditions of cinematic narration for the purposes of comedy.[18] That is, such candidate examples for modernist reflexivity through self-reference and assertions of technique can be explained away as potential counterexamples by means of better explanations or interpretations in terms of the significance they make in the films in which they occur.

In the section on assertions of technique—section eighteen—he goes through a catalogue of techniques—like freeze frames, slow motion, split-screens, flash-insets and so on—that might be thought of as acknowledgments of cinematic objecthood but which when interpreted in terms of the films in which they appear can be shown to have a nonreflexive significance. For example, the freeze frame in *Butch Cassidy and the Sundance Kid* (1969, dir. George Roy Hill) is meant to signify their immortality and not to bare the cinematic device.

As Cavell notes, "If the camera is to be known, it has to be acknowledged in the works that it does".[19] That work, he shows, in case after case is involved with advancing themes within specific narratives, not in disclosing the conditions of possibility of cinema. Thus, at the same time that he continues his review of the ways in which film forges significance in sections sixteen, seventeen, and eighteen, he simultaneously dispels the notion that well-known examples of self-referencing and assertive strategies are best interpreted in terms of modernist reflexivity.

Another way in which Cavell attempts to undermine the claims of film as a modernist art is to draw a distinction between modernist art and avant-garde art.[20] Again, this move is an attempt to show that certain examples that might look like evidence of cinematic modernism are really something else. What? Avant-garde films.

But what are avant-garde films in Cavell's sense?

Here it perhaps is helpful to think about the phrase "experimental film." Just as drug companies experiment with various chemical concoctions in order to discover the ones worth putting forward for general use, one way of thinking of experimental filmmakers is as pioneering various techniques that can then be taken up as contributions to what might be called "the vocabulary of cinema"—that is, new ways of making significance. One might think of Buñuel's and Dali's use of disjunctive editing in *Un Chien Andalou* (1929) or Clair's *Entr'acte* (1924) this way. Moreover, this is how Cavell appears to view people like Eisenstein.[21] He is not a modernist, but a modernizer.

Eisenstein, and what Cavell is calling the avant-garde tradition, is experimenting in an effort to discover new techniques for cinematic significance making. Thus, something that looks like a modernist exploration of the nature of cinema, like Vertov's *Man with a Movie Camera* (1929), might better be classified as an avant-garde film in the experiment-sense. (The example here is mine, not Cavell's, although I think it does show how the modernist/avant-garde distinction is meant to function in Cavell's overall argument.)

Cavell also challenges what he takes to be the best evidence for modernist film.

He writes:

> The declaration of film's essence I heard most frequently was that it consisted of "light and movement." That seems the natural, the only, answer to the isolated question: "What is the essence of the medium of film?" Since the answer seems to me more or less empty, I take the question to be more or less the wrong question to ask. In particular I have seen no objects consisting essentially of light and movement (and nothing else) that have struck me as having the force of art. And since the objects of film I have seen which do strike me as having the force of art all incontestably use moving pictures of live people and real things in actual spaces, I begin my investigation of film by asking what *role* reality plays in this art.[22]

So, these considerations all support the contention that film is not a modernist art, which means, among other things, that film is still an object of interest for people in general.

What is the basis of that interest? What desires does film satisfy? Why is film important, to return to the language of the first section of the book? Specifically why is it that automatic world projections are important?

Here are four variously interrelated answers that Cavell offers:

1. Film relieves us from the burden of response because we are screened from *The World Viewed*. We can never help or hinder whatever is going on in *The World Viewed*. We can plunge into the screen and stop the film from being projected, but we cannot save the virgin from Dracula.[23]
2. Film fulfills the wish for invisibility. We can view the world unseen. This satisfies a desire for anonymity of modern privacy.[24]
3. In virtue of being automatic—in virtue of photography's casual provenance—film, in some sense, enables us to penetrate the doxastic cocoon of subjectivity that emerges with developments like Cartesian skepticism. Cavell writes: "So far as photography satisfied a wish, it satisfied a wish not confined to painters, but a human wish, intensifying in the West since the Reformation, to escape subjectivity and metaphysical isolation—a wish for the power to reach this world".[25] How exactly does photography accomplish this? Recall that it is automatic in the sense that once its casual mechanism is set in motion it will imprint whatever is in front of the lens, no matter what the photographer's subjective intention is. It is in this sense that photography escapes subjectivity and, in that sense perhaps reinforces the hope that such an escape is possible.

Of course, the issue of subjectivity raises the question of skepticism, one of Cavell's most enduring themes. For Cavell, skepticism is part of the human condition; it is not something we can defeat. But neither is it something to which we can surrender. This tension is embodied in cinema.

On the side of skepticism, film withholds the existence of the world from us. But is there also some way in which film gives us the resources to resist skepticism? This is the fourth, and for Cavell I think the most significant, way in which film is important.

4. For film as such may satisfy the desire to resist one particular form of skepticism, namely solipsism, the suspicion that I alone exist and everything else is my subjective imagining. How does film as such stoke this desire? It is an automatic world projection—a world viewed—a world past from which I am absent. Symbolically this confirms experientially the possibility of a world without me. This does not logically defeat skeptical solipsism conclusively. But it does give us something to hold onto in the face of skeptical doubt.[26]

Cavell intends his ruminations on the ontology of film to be taken symbolically, as "mythological descriptions of the state of someone in the grip of a movie".[27] Here, I think that it is helpful to think of what Cavell is doing in light of Kant's notion that beauty is the symbol of morality. For Kant, we require intuitions to ground our confidence in the possibility of certain rational ideas, like morality. Beauty can function in this way because, among other things, it illustrates experientially the possibility of disinterestedness. Likewise, I want to suggest that Cavell thinks that film as such is a symbol of a world without me, a world beyond solipsism.

Moreover, this symbol also suggests the promise of a certain form of immortality, which is more Shakespearean than Bazin's "mummy theory" of cinema. In the last paragraph of the first edition of *The World Viewed* Cavell writes:

> A world complete without me which is present to me is the world of my immortality. This is an importance of film and a danger. It takes my life as my haunting of the world, either because I left it unloved (the Flying Dutchman) or because I left unfinished business (Hamlet). So there is reason for me to want the camera to deny the coherence of the world, its coherence as past: to deny that the world is complete without me. But there is equal reason to want it affirmed that the world is coherent without me. That is essential to what I want of immortality: nature's survival of me. It will mean that the present judgment on me is not yet the last.[28]

In contrast to solipsism, where nothing would survive me, film symbolizes the possibility that I can at least live on in memory, a promise of immortality, quite different than the one Bazin identified, but which offers, nevertheless, consolation. That is, in viewing a world past from which I am absent my desire that there be a world apart in which I may be remembered symbolizes a way in which the human desire for immortality might be satisfied. Film as such does not prove this. Rather, it is a powerful—and for that reason—welcome symbol of it.

Critical Review

So far, I have been offering you my interpretation of *The World Viewed*. Now I would like to raise certain potential problems with it for the purposes of discussion.

Early on, Cavell defends the notion that film is of reality, by arguing that in photography and film, we see the object the image is of. The argument used to demonstrate this is:

1. With photography/cinematography we see either the object itself or the sight of the object.
2. Objects do not have sights.
3. Therefore, we see the object itself.

This is an argument by elimination. Thus it is important that the first premise set out all the alternatives to be eliminated. But it is not clear that it does.

One alternative that Cavell himself mentions is that the image is an impression or a visual mold, like a death mask. Cavell rejects this possibility by saying: "My dissatisfaction with that idea is, I think that physical molds and impressions and imprints have clear procedures for getting *rid* of their originals, whereas in a photograph, the original is as present as it ever was."[29]

This is pretty obscure and not obviously true. The body is still there after the death mask is taken, and you can destroy the object after you take a photograph of it. Is there a non-question-begging way to say that the original is still present in the photograph in a way that cannot be gotten rid of as supposedly it can be with visual impressions?

Until that is shown, Cavell's argument is inconclusive. In addition, there are alternatives that Cavell has not even countenanced: for instance, that the photograph is a tree or a natural recognitional prompt.[30] Of course, this does not settle the matter. There may be other arguments for photographic transparency—like those of Patrick Maynard and Kendall Walton—that will secure the conclusion that Cavell wants. But as it stands in *The World Viewed*, Cavell has not established the transparency thesis.

Next, Cavell attempts to move from the notion that we see objects in photography to the idea that we are viewing the world, of reality as a whole. One wonders whether this expansion is an equivocation. The various arguments that Cavell uses in its behalf are suspect. Most of them rely on comparisons between photographs and painting that serve as intuition pumps. For example, Cavell says you can always ask, of an area photographed, what lies adjacent, beyond the frame. Putatively, this generally makes no sense with a painting.[31] But there are paintings that cut figures in half at the edge of the frame, like Degas' *Pauline and Virginia Conversing with Admirers* and Manet's *At the Café*. Surely it makes sense to ask where the rest of their bodies are. Some paintings like Velasquez's *Les Meinas* have mirrors that refer to what is outside the painting. Cavell maintains that you cannot ask what is behind an object in a painting, but the mirror behind the couple in Jan van Eyck's *Arnolfini Portrait* shows us their backs. And a great many paintings, like such innumerable battle scenes, refer to activities beyond the frame, as does William Holmes Sullivan's *Battle of Waterloo*.

Cavell thinks you can ask questions about what is adjacent to or behind photographic/cinematic images because there are answers in the world. But aren't there answers in the world with regard to pictorial maps, like those of Hartman Schedel's *Nurnberg Chronicle*, which contains pictures of the cityscapes of Prague and other towns with recognizable rows of buildings? Surely there were answers in the world with respect to their buildings and rivers about what was adjacent to them.

Another complication that Cavell does not consider is whether the kind of optical aids and mirrors used by artists like Durer and Vermeer do not make their pictures by tracing in a way that converges on photography.

But perhaps Cavell's biggest problem regarding the claim that photography, and by extension cinematography, imply the rest of the world is that it is so at odds with the phenomenology of viewing a movie. When I watch *The Martian*, I am not thinking about where in the nation of Jordan it is that Matt Damon is standing or what is next to the Wadi Rum location site. Phenomenologically I imagine the action is occurring on Mars. I do not think about where the movie's exteriors are being shot nor am I supposed to.

Moreover, this problem with the phenomenology cannot be dismissed, for if I am utterly inattentive to the place of the actual location of the action in the world, how can the alleged consequences of viewing *the world* take hold? This is a problem that will obtain with most fictional films. Nor is it clear how Cavell will solve it, since he appears to confess that "I do not know what the particular artifice of fiction is."[32]

From the contrasts with painting, Cavell moves to comparing theater with film, especially in terms of the stage actor versus the movie star. Supposedly, where the stage actor takes on a role and the movie star plays herself. Although this formula is virtually a commonplace, it at best signals a tendency rather than a categorical distinction. There are stage actors who seem to play themselves—for example, Nathan Lane, Zero Mostel, Maria

Callas, Mary Martin, and others. And there are film actors who disappear into their parts, like Daniel Day-Lewis and Meryl Streep. There is some truth to the notion that stage acting and film acting typically operate on different scales and with different requirements. But this is very variable; some theaters are very intimate, making the performers' everyday mannerisms more noticeable, thereby investing the character with them in a way that shapes the character. Indeed, one suspects that James Dean's performances in the Actor's Studio differed not at all with his performance in *Rebel Without a Cause* (1955, dir. Nicholas Ray). Thus, the difference between stage acting and movie acting that Cavell seems to assume is ontological is really more a matter of degree, contingent upon context.

Cavell seems to make three major claims in his discussion of film genres:

1. That the possibilities of a medium are discovered in the process of making sense (where making sense is very broadly constrained as "particular ways of getting through to someone.") Thus, in contrast to Kracauer, Cavell denies that certain genres are questionable in virtue of the nature of the medium. Rather, genres discover or create the medium.
2. That genres are a (not the) primary way of making sense in cinema.

    Cavell must hold this view because he goes on to identify other ways of making sense in cinema.
3. Star personalities generate genres or, at least, the ones that take hold.

I tend to think that the first two theses are solid. But I have a number of reservations about the third. Here are a few:

1. Genres and cycles are not always generated by stars. Méliès invented the science fiction/fantasy film, but even though he was in those films, it was not his personality that generated the genre. Indeed, the star system was not even discovered yet. Moreover, one of the genres Méliès inspired—the trick film—required no stars.
2. Many genres are generated from sources independent of star personalities—James Bond films, Sherlock Holmes films, Tarzan films and so on. You may say these genres rest on types. But they are types that pre-exist the film genres in question.
3. There are film genres without stars like the 1950s horror/science fiction films such as *The Creature from the Black Lagoon* (1954, dir. Jack Arnold). These films employ actors like Richard Carlson, Peter Graves, Rex Reasoner, and Richard Denning who were not stars, not to mention the actresses who played the many damsels in distress. You may say these guys were of a type—nice looking/brainy/straight arrows—and the ladies were what were called bombshells—but they

were pretty interchangeable (both the males and the females). Again, it was the genre that called for certain sorts of actors, not the actors who called for the genres.

4. In a number of cases, technical innovations seem to have made the prominence of certain genres possible. The genres found actors who could exploit these possibilities but it was the technical innovation that really got the genre going. For example, the introduction of sound made the detective genre and the horror far more feasible than they had been in the silent period. Both profited from the fact that sound allowed more fluid dialogue than intertitles as the detective reasoned his way through the mystery and the mad scientist rehearsed the rationale for his experiment. The detective genre found stars like William Powell and Myrna Loy, but their fast repartee would never have survived intertitling. Moreover, the horror genre not only benefited from acquiring a voice; it also inherited an arsenal of sound effects: off-screen howls and rattling chains, thunderclaps and the crackling electrodes of Dr. Frankenstein's laboratory. And in our own day the comic book blockbusters like Marvel's *Avengers* owe more to computer imaging than stars. They have stars but the genre selects the stars rather than the stars mandating the genre.

Before turning to Cavell's conjectures about the importance of cinema, I would briefly like to consider his reasons for questioning whether film has avoided modernism or that the concept of modernism is not applicable to it.

First, it should be noted that even if Cavell can show that many apparent cinematic claimants to the mantle of modernism—due to their employment of self-reference, assertive camera work, and other forms of demonstrative technique—are not modernist, that, as a matter of logic, cannot establish that there are not or cannot be other films that are modernist for those very reasons. Arguably, there is a tradition of modernist filmmaking stretching back to works like Ferdinand Léger's *Ballet Mécanique* (1923–24), which would appear to be a work of modernist metacinema reflexively declaring movement—mechanical movement as its title broadcasts—to be the sine qua non of cinema.

Nor does it seem that Cavell can marshal the distinction between modernism and the avant-garde to block cases like this insofar as the best explanation of a film like *Ballet Mécanique* is that it is attempting to explore the nature of film rather than test-driving novel techniques for later use by the more traditional movies.

Furthermore, there is not just one counterexample in this neighborhood. The movement called structural film—which Cavell certainly knew of by the time "More of *The World Viewed*" was published—produced many metacinematic critiques. Works by Andy Warhol, Ernie Gehr, Michael Snow,

Owen Land, and Hollis Frampton were inspired by the same reflexive concerns that were driving invention in contemporary painting and sculpture. Frampton's *(nostalgia)* (1971) is a cinematic investigation, for example, of linguistic description, visual depiction, photography, and cinematography that creatively acknowledges the putative essential differences between these media by calling attention to them. That is the best interpretation of Frampton's film as opposed to the speculation that it is an attempt to pioneer new techniques for traditional cinema.

Cavell charges that films in this tradition that declare that cinema is a matter of light and movement do not strike him as having the force of art. But that is something to be proven, not merely asserted. And, in order to do that, Cavell would have to show why some specific films of this sort fail and not simply discard the unnamed lot of them. It is incumbent on Cavell to show why films, such as Stan Brakhage's *The Text of Light* (1974) lacks the so-called force of art.

At this point, it might be argued that the counterexamples that I have recruited are irrelevant because they are not modernist because they are not committed to establishing their presence to the world. They are not involved with the problematic of objecthood. I am not completely convinced that is true across the board. I am thinking especially of Warhol's *Empire* (1964).

However, even if that were true, it would only be true that film has avoided modernism *à la* Fried. The examples I have cited are modernist under a less specific understanding of modernism—one that regards as modernist simply the reflexive exploration of the art form. Fried's version of modernism was highly exclusionary, cashiering Minimalism from the corpus because of its theatricality. Showing that cinema is not modernist under Fried's dispensation might not be enough to get Cavell what he wants—that film, or, at least, certain movements in it, have eluded the sort of self-consciousness that compromises its claims to being traditional. A further complication is that in his more recent work, Fried has claimed that photography has embraced the modernist problematic.[33] Does that entail that photographic film may do so as well? Cavell has said that film is not compelled to accept the burden of self-consciousness. But that does not preclude film's acceptance of it anyway.

We have been probing Cavell's analyses of film. Now, finally, let's take a look at his conjectures about the human importance of film that he draws from these analyses of film.

The first human desire that film addresses is to release us from the burden of response. We are not called upon to relieve the trials and tribulations we witness on screen because it is impossible to do so. That seems true enough. But it does not appear to differentiate film from theater.

Film is said to enable us to view unseen, at least by those on-screen. This satisfies a human desire for anonymity, which is presumably connected in some ways to the alleviation of our sense of responsibility, since this appears to enable us to witness all sorts of things, like lovers' intimate moments and the death throes of strangers, that we would never watch without guilt in everyday life. We would turn away in embarrassment.

This is perhaps accurate, but it raises a problem that runs through all of Cavell's conjectures about the importance of film, namely, that they are equally applicable to home movies and surveillance footage as they are of the kind of films that Cavell is discussing throughout the book—what, for want of a better term, we might call the artistic films. The kind of anonymity Cavell is talking about is available from films as such. It is available from documentary out-takes that are never woven into a narrative. But films as such are not something that everyone is interested in—that is not the sort of film whose generic human importance Cavell set out to elucidate.

A similar problem bedevils Cavell's claim that film facilitates the escape from subjectivity. Maybe there is a sense in which film as such is not swathed in an epistemic cocoon in virtue of engaging a sheerly casual process, rather than an intentional one. But the films Cavell cares about are intentional through and through. If something appears in the image that the filmmaker does not want to be there due to the mechanical-chemical operation of the camera, she will do another take if she can. The films we encounter in movie theaters are predominantly the product of intentional choice. The fact that mechanical factors are part of the process is no more significant with respect to artistic films, than the fact that a piano is a machine makes Andras Schiff's performance on one any less expressive of his artistic temperament. Photographs as such may be objective in Cavell's sense but the photographs of Eugène Atget, Diane Arbus, and Nan Goldin bear the personal imprint of their creators. And since the appreciation of that is apt to be the focus of the normal viewer, it is unlikely that she would glean from them the intimation of the escape from subjectivity putatively implied by a photograph considered as such.

Lastly, what can we say about the claim that film—*The World Viewed*—can serve as a symbol of the possibility of defeating solipsism? Again were this significance available from film, it would be available from any kind of image on film, since all the considerations from photography on behalf of "*The World Viewed* Hypothesis" would apply to everything on film, whether amateur home-movies or artistic films. But I doubt that most home movies interest everyone or satisfy a basic human desire. I question that that captures our basic phenomenological response when we experience films as such. I would go so far as to claim that I bet it crosses almost no one's mind. It is just an inference beyond the ken of virtually every viewer. And if it is an unlikely thought to be derived from the viewer of the film as such, it is even more unlikely to be suggested by the artistic film, since that viewer will be preoccupied with attending to the fictional narrative rather than ruminating upon possible associations regarding its photographic provenance. Thus, even if "*The World Viewed* Hypothesis" were compelling for film as such, a proposition I question, I think it does not shed understanding on the importance of the artistic film which is what I think one naturally takes to be the topic of Cavell's book, since few, if any, are interested in films-as-such. Thus, the ambiguity that I highlighted earlier in this chapter in the question, "What is film?" between the film-as-such and the film-as-art plagues *The World Viewed* to the very end.

Notes

1 Stanley Cavell, *The World Viewed: Reflections on the Ontology of Film* in this article will be to the Enlarged Edition (Cambridge: Harvard University Press, 1979).
2 Ibid., xxv.
3 Ibid., 4–5.
4 Ibid., 5.
5 Ibid.
6 It should be noted that in the section entitled "An Autobiography of Companions" when Cavell asks "What is film?" he seems to be asking "What is film art?" rather than "What is film as such?," which would include not only feature films but advertisements, instructional films, home movies, and the like.
7 Cavell, *The World Viewed*, 17.
8 Ibid., 18.
9 Ibid., 23–24.
10 Ibid., 24.
11 Ibid., 27.
12 Vsevolod I. Pudovkin, *Film Acting and Film Technique*, trans. Ivor Montague (London: Vision Press, 1954), 232.
13 Indeed, it is claimed that Méliès discovered the phenomenon of stop-action by accident when his camera jammed and then he figured out how to exploit it. Stop-action was originally a glitch, rather than an essential feature of the medium.
14 Cavell, *The World Viewed*, 31.
15 Michael Fried wrote: "It is the overcoming of theater which modernist sensibility finds most exalting and which it experiences as the hallmark of high art in our time. There is, however, one art which, by its very nature, escapes theater entirely—the movies." Fried, *Art and Objecthood* (Chicago: The University of Chicago Press, 1998), 21. Rosalind Krauss says that Fried regards this "escape" as an impediment to cinema achieving the status of a modernist artform. See Rosalind Krauss, *Perpetual Inventory* (Cambridge: MIT Press, 2010), 280.
16 Cavell, *The World Viewed*, 118.

17 Ibid.
18 Ibid., 126.
19 Ibid.
20 Ibid., 217–18.
21 Ibid., 217.
22 Ibid., 164–65.
23 Ibid., 40.
24 Ibid., 40–41.
25 Ibid., 21.
26 Ibid., 23, 160.
27 Ibid., 211.
28 Ibid., 160.
29 Ibid., 20.
30 See Noël Carroll, *Philosophy of Motion Pictures* (Malden: Blackwell Publishers, 2006).
31 Cavell, *The World Viewed*, 23–24.
32 Ibid., 210.
33 Michael Fried, *Why Photography Matters as Never Before* (Chicago: The University of Chicago Press, 2008).

3

The World Heard

Kyle Stevens

THE WORLD VIEWED: Reflections on the Ontology of Film. The world *viewed*. The title seems so clear. And when followed by the subtitle the implication is plain: this is a book that will ask what film is and that will answer in terms of vision and the world. Moreover, it is *the* world, not *a* world. The book will not be about some indefinite fictional world but the definite one. Its answer will then likely have to do with reality, too. And, accordingly, for almost fifty years, Stanley Cavell's book has functioned as part of "classical film theory," because it has been read as offering a view of the filmic medium rooted in indexical realism in visual terms.[1] *The World Viewed*, though, is anything but plain. I want to disrupt the ubiquitous understanding that Cavell conceptualizes cinema as a visual art form, even if he devotes the majority of his pages to such visual matters as the import of film's photographic roots and the aesthetic legacies of painting. Tracing where the concepts of sound, dialogue, and silence hold on to, and let go of, one another in *The World Viewed* clarifies Cavell's idea of cinema, and the limits that cinema must explore if it is to achieve the modernist aims he endorses. It also unearths connections that allow us to see that the meanings of "world" and "viewed" change over the course of the book, that they undergo a process—that the book is itself cinematic in its unfolding. Furthermore, accounting for the importance of the sound of speech generates an important link between *The World Viewed* and Cavell's broader Wittgensteinian body of work, in which we cannot claim to know the world without wording it.[2]

Yet my interest in Cavell's discussion of sound arises not simply from the desire to understand an important work of film theory, and to redress readings that run the fool's errand of partitioning ontology and epistemology. The study of film sound has grown in popularity in recent decades, yet it is often in the grip of a theoretical picture that attending to *The World Viewed* loosens. First of all, contemporary scholars tend to emphasize continuities between silent and sound cinema, considering how the *addition* of a sonic register affected editing patterns, performance styles, audience reception, and so forth. Secondly, and relatedly, they focus on the *relation* of sound and image.[3] (That this scholarship concentrates on noise, music, and voice surely contributes to the penchant for treating the elements as somehow beside each other.[4]) In doing so, they attest that sonic aesthetics model ways of apprehending the world akin to visual aesthetics, and insist that sonic representation's neglect is a result of bias in a field whose history encourages readers to conceptualize the medium as primarily, even properly, visual. Through Cavell, I want to ask whether this analogization of cinematic sights and sounds is adequate, for even if one *can* theorize (as Gilles Deleuze does) that a sound is like an image in that we register it sensorily, we do not, say, experience speech as we do music, although there are aspects of musicality to it. Instead, I want to suggest that how sights and sounds hang together is a condition of the medium, and to thereby resist the usual impulse in film theory to consider these elements in relation but as nonetheless discrete. That is, I want to argue for the value of leaving a film intact, for acknowledging cinema as audiovisual. This approach departs from the typical critical-analytical impulse to isolate constituent components, but it is nevertheless philosophical, one that seeks to explain things as they are.[5] It also demonstrates that the advent of the talkie is far more than a simple technological advance for Cavell, and opens up a way of connecting his film historiography to his philosophical project.

Ontological Peace

The judgment that *The World Viewed* is chiefly concerned with visual matters stems from the book's first chapter. Cavell begins by asking what art is. He praises painting for furnishing "more ways of responding" than other arts at the time of his writing in the late 1960s and early 1970s, thereby establishing his experience-based approach.[6] For him, art is measured by the intellectual and affective possibilities it creates, possibilities that do not inhere in the artwork but in its audience. Cavell then turns to the further question of what film is. To answer it, he builds on the writings of Erwin Panofsky and André Bazin, seeming to adopt their premise that film is a fundamentally and photographically realist medium. We must ask, he ventures: "What happens to [physical] reality when it is projected and screened?"[7] In posing this question this way, Cavell moves quickly from a position of Bazinian curiosity about the relation of image to reality to one of doubt about the image's veridicality. (Throughout Cavell's body of work, doubt is essential to being a decent person. His widely circulated concept of acknowledgment, through which he connects epistemology and ethics, manages the problem of doubting one's ability to know the content of other minds.[8]) Film's solicitation of doubt provides the conceptual distance needed to undermine too-pat assumptions, such as that we apprehend the idea of reality operating in this aesthetic context. Cavell makes clear that an easy answer of "'physical reality' as such, taken literally, is not correct" and goes on to explain how we might understand the distinction he has in mind by reminding us of something that might seem obvious: that "an immediate fact about the medium of the photograph (still or in motion) is that it is not painting."[9] The force of this assertion is that it might tempt one to assert that "a photograph does not present us with 'likenesses of things'; it presents us, we want to say, with the things themselves."[10] And from this follows the rub on which much of the book lies: "But wanting to say that may well make us ontologically restless."[11] Cavell explicates this restlessness through a paradox that emerges: a photograph of an earthquake or Greta Garbo is not an earthquake or Garbo, and yet, at the same time, it is also "false to hold up a photograph of Garbo and say, 'This is not Garbo,' if all you mean is that the object you are holding up is not a human creature."[12] "The image is not a likeness; it is not exactly a replica, or a relic, or a shadow, or an apparition," frets Cavell.[13]

Significantly, and in a move not found in Panofsky or Bazin, the first step Cavell takes toward alleviating this ontological anxiety is to "wonder that similar questions do not arise about recordings of sound."[14] I take it to be of enormous significance that the first chapter of *The World Viewed* solely concerned with cinematic ontology is entitled "Sights and Sounds." Cavell must immediately address, and then marginalize, sound if he is to succeed in articulating a theory of film as offering a view of the world. But before I describe the Venn diagram Cavell draws between cinematic sights and sounds, I want to pause on his use in this chapter of the word "sound" as metaphor for understanding: "[Statements like] 'Photographs present us with things themselves' sound, and ought to sound, false or paradoxical."[15] For Cavell, how a claim lands on our imaginary ear is a key measure—in fact, the key measure—for the correctness of an ontological claim. This sort of sound, which is not a sound at all, and not just the imagination of sound, but the imagination of experiencing that sound-as-word, either said by one's self or imagining one's self saying it as the voice of another, is vital to Cavell's method. In this way, sound never really vanishes as a concern. Even when discussing the image, he is talking about how our conceptualizations of the image sound to us. Cavell will confront this dual meaning of "sound" (cinematic sound and our hearing of words) at the end of the book, when he acknowledges the advent of speech to cinema. In doing so, as I will show, his method informs his model of cinema, and, in turn, his model of cinema informs his model of mind and language. But we can already see that conceptualizing inner voices as sonic, and so, as bearing an aesthetic that is historically and culturally conditioned (and in ways that we are often not conscious of) is integral to Cavell's version of ordinary language philosophy on display in *The World Viewed*.

Now, I want to proceed carefully through Cavell's contrast of visual and aural experiences at the cinema. He tests a direct parallel: "I mean, on the whole we would be hard put to find it false or paradoxical to say, listening to a record, 'That's an English horn'; there is no trace of temptation to add (as it were, to oneself), 'But I know it's really only a recording.'"[16] There is something about the photograph, according to Cavell, that *tempts* us to question its nature, something which a recorded sound lacks. This is precisely the sentiment that scholars of film sound bemoan (that sound is somehow too obvious to be theoretically interesting), but before we object, I want to—rather than rejecting this premise in order to justify sound's study in the same terms as the visual image's—ask what it might mean if we do *not* register ontological anxiety about sound. What might it mean that we are not restless but calm? And given the centrality of doubt to Cavell, what might it mean that we lack doubt as listeners?

To understand the absence of ontological restlessness that accompanies sound recording, Cavell asks: "Is the difference between auditory and visual transcription a function of the fact that we are fully accustomed to hearing things that are invisible, not present to us, not present with us?"[17] Cavell accepts this "because it is in the nature of hearing that what is heard comes *from* somewhere, whereas what you can see you can look *at*."[18] This is, for Cavell, why "sounds are warnings" and why "a man can be spoken to by God and survive, but not if he sees God."[19] Despite the urgency attached to these sonic examples, Cavell suggests that since we are accustomed to hearing things that are invisible, the restlessness follows from the unusual version of seeing we perform when confronted with a photograph, where "we see things that are not present."[20] Although nothing turns on this analogy, it is worth noting that it is imperfect. We are well accustomed to seeing things that are inaudible (such as a person in the distance), though it would be weird to hear things not readily available to vision (such as an insect's footsteps).

Cavell elaborates his contrast between sight and sound in a passage that is more complex than it may at first appear, so I quote it in full:

> Suppose one tried accounting for the familiarity of recordings by saying, "when I say, listening to a record, 'That's an English horn,' what I really mean is, 'That's the *sound* of an English horn'; moreover, when I am in the presence of an English horn playing, I still don't literally hear the horn, I hear the sound of the horn. So I don't worry about hearing a horn when the horn is not present, because *what* I hear is exactly the same (ontologically the same, and if my equipment is good enough, empirically the same) whether the thing is present or not." What this rigmarole calls

attention to is that sounds can be perfectly copied, and that we have various interests in copying them. (For example, if they couldn't be copied, people would never learn to talk.)[21]

For a philosopher of language this parenthetical is striking, and not just because he shifts so quickly from music to speech. Comparing language learners to recording and replaying devices seems strange: if a child hears and reproduces sounds, and so does not yet *mean* these sounds as words, then the child ought not really be said to be talking. Moreover, linguistic replay is necessarily imperfect, occurring in the voice of the learner and not of the voice heard, and beyond this, there is the gap between the learner's words-in-thought and how the learner's voice sounds uttering them. But this picture of language acquisition suggests something important: *how* words sound—including all the expressive force bestowed by the speaker—is inseparable from the learning of the word. This is vital to a philosophy of (ordinary) language that departs from traditional philosophical accounts that emphasize language acquisition as the amassing of referential vocabulary. If an expressive register is engrained into one's language, then the ordinary language philosopher's method of measuring the rightness of *how* a claim lands on one's imaginary ear makes sense. Learning to think in language, to speak, and to word the world, emerges as, at least in part, a matter of sounds, and of what it *sounds* like to mean words in particular contexts, not merely a matter of reproducing the pitch and grain of the voices that one hears utter them. This view also implies that learning language via performances in such media as film and television is crucial to the development of thought (not just the development of vocabulary but thought).

But let me return to the subject at hand in this lengthy quotation. That the sonic copy may be indistinguishable from its source is a strong claim, and Cavell underlines it: "the record reproduces [a] sound, but we cannot say that a photograph reproduces a sight."[22] This disanalogy is a hermeneutic tool to explain that "even if a photograph were a copy of an object, so to speak, it would not bear the relation to its object that a recording bears to the sound it copies."[23] According to Cavell, we need not, and perhaps cannot, distinguish between a recording of the object's sound and the object, whereas we can, even must, distinguish between a photograph of an object's sight and the object: "A sight *is* an object . . . and what you see, when you sight something, is an object—anyway, not the sight of an object. Nor will the epistemologist's 'sense-data' or 'surfaces' provide correct descriptions here."[24] In this way, Cavell means to reinforce Bazin's proclamation that the photographic image "[satisfies], once and for all and in its very essence, our obsession with realism," since there is simply no escaping "the fact that objects don't *make* sights, or *have* sights."[25] (Of course, other conditions are necessary for a sight to be an object, such as light.)

Realism, Limits, and Conditions

This ends Cavell's initial treatment of sound. Given that it was precisely against the perfection of sound recording's capture of sonic reality that Cavell measures the photograph's unclear relation to visible reality, his assertion that it is the photographic image that satisfies our obsession with realism is surprising. In this section, I want to look closely at why this account of sight and sound's differences renders sound unavailable to his ideas of realist and modernist aesthetics, and so, to the categories of the cinematic and art. For Cavell, art and realism coincide, because it is in art's proximity to reality (even as we do not fully grasp that contiguity) that it affords us the experience of being present to the world. We need such experiences, because "at some point, the unhinging of our consciousness from the world interposed our subjectivity between us and our presentness to the world. Then our subjectivity became what is present to us, individuality became isolation."[26] Aesthetic movements offer different responses to our anxiety over this isolation. And, after the first chapter, and up until the last, *The World Viewed* is a sustained argument for the value of modernist cinema's mode of self-scrutiny as a model of subjective reflection in strictly visual terms. Cavell writes: "In modernism, a medium is explored by discovering possibilities that declare its necessary conditions, its limits."[27] Or, to put it another way, Cavell insists that a movie "must acknowledge, what is always to be acknowledged, its own limits: in this case, its outsideness to its world, and my absence from it."[28] It is, then, part of modernist cinema's built-in task to ask what cinema is. He looks to the medium's material in order to ponder its ontology, and the answer to the further question "What conditions of movie-making are to be explored?" turns out to be "*a succession of automatic world projections*."[29] This underpins Cavell's assertion that "the physical basis of movies, being irreducibly photographic, necessitates or makes possible the meaningful use of human reality and of nature as such."[30] Cavell thus, and unequivocally, excludes the sonority he felt it necessary to first address.[31]

Cavell's rationale, that sound comes *from* while we look *at* sights, sets up a further contrast: between the viewer's differing relations to a painting and to a photograph. Cavell argues that painting learned to "[give] up the idea that 'connection with reality' is to be understood as 'provision of likeness.'"[32] "A painting *is* a world," Cavell clarifies, while "a photograph is *of* the world," a point underscored by our differing experience of the frames of each form (a film's frame suggests the world extends in a way a painting's does not).[33] That filmic images are "not *hand*-made" but manufactured leads to "the inescapable fact of mechanism or automatism" in their making, which is vital to the realism they may access.[34] The automatism of photography can return a sense of presentness *to*; it can function similarly to Wittgenstein's investigations into "what our pictures of phenomena are, in order to wrest the world from our possessions so that we may possess it again."[35] Photography "[overcomes] subjectivity in a way undreamed of by painting," and so, "photography maintains the presentness of the world by accepting our absence from it."[36]

This allows Cavell to elaborate that modernist films work precisely to undermine the presentness of the world which the medium seemingly guarantees: "The world's presence to me is no longer assured by my mechanical absence from it, for the screen no longer naturally holds a coherent world *from* which I am absent."[37] Acknowledging my absence from the world of the film, as well as its own separateness from its world, is, we see, fundamentally the same gesture. In encountering a modernist film exploring its own limits, I also see that I am outside, too, and am made aware of its presence to me. The *film* is made present. This is not a contradiction of his earlier claim about film's photographically realist nature but a means of explaining the achievements of modernist cinema. His explanation is also praise, praise for the "loss of conviction in the film's capacity to carry the world's presence," praise, that is, for inculcating doubt. Doubt is now compounded as film works "against its nature" to suggest reality, precisely because that suggestion entails—reflects upon—the mysterious doubt that drives us to wonder about film.[38]

Now we can begin to see how his use of sound in contrast enables these conclusions. If the photograph's curious relation to reality is at the core of its realism, and if recorded sounds admit no distance between rendering and world, then they do not inspire the right sort of doubt (like the image does). Nor can film sound, as mere recording, suggest the effect of presence and concomitant experience of absence. Sounds are thus not available to realism, and, by extension, perhaps even to the aesthetic rank of the cinematic. Because, again, if we can possess sound, and there is no gap between it and the world, then through it we possess the world. Sonic representation is thus too literal, not mimetic; it does not feel *screened* to, or for, us.[39]

But surely our conviction in the fidelity of recorded sound is not so perfect that we are tempted to say that recordings *are* reality, or that recorded sounds at the cinema cannot be realist.[40] Cavell's French horn example is rather crafty in this respect. How different might it sound if it were replaced by the verbal recording of a deceased loved one? Might we not then react differently to the assertion that there is no empirical difference between the sounds?

Perhaps not, but it is far less obvious to my ear. And note the shift in grammatical subject in his rationale for contrasting sight and sound: sound comes from somewhere *to* us. It meets us, whereas *we* meet the image. Cavell's characterization of sight prioritizes the seer; his characterization of sound prioritizes the object heard.

We might also—and, indeed, we should—object that Cavell's comparison is not as parallel as he suggests. On one hand, there is an object, its sight, and a photograph of its sight. On the other hand, there is an object, its sound, and the recording of that sound. His contrast dwells upon the third element in each case; however, the relation between the first two elements is dissimilar. An object is a sight, but a sound results from an action of some sort. Sounds are *made*. A horn must be *played*. It does not, by itself, *make* or *have* sounds, either. Even when we would not want to call a sound the result of an action, our grammar invites us to treat its cause as agential, as when we ask "What was that?" and receive the reply "A branch tapping at the window."

We may also bear in mind that Cavell is in most respects a philosopher of the cinematic experience, and although sound is physical, it routinely *feels* immaterial. Jean-Luc Nancy writes: "Sound has no hidden face; it is all in front, in back, and outside inside, *inside-out* in relation to the most general logic of presence as appearing, as phenomenality or as manifestation, and thus as the visible face of a presence subsisting in self. . . . To listen is to enter that spatiality by which, *at the same time*, I am penetrated, for it opens up in me as well as around me."[41] Although far more erotic than Cavell's account of sound, Nancy's corroborates the robustness of sonic experience. Similarly, Suzanne Langer writes of the way that, despite our knowledge of frequencies and so forth, "sound, though it is propagated in space, and is variously swallowed or reflected back, i.e. echoed, by the surfaces it encounters, [is] not sufficiently modified by them to give an impression of their shapes, as light does."[42] Sonic art seems to be everywhere and nowhere. It does not make us *feel* absent or doubtful (though we can, of course, remind ourselves to be). In contrast to the model of the visual gaze that penetrates or looks *at* (which maintains the discrete Cartesian subject and is thus a more amenable metaphor for most epistemological systems), with sound the listening subject is construed as absorbed, enveloped, and even entered.

Positions and Prepositions

Looking *at*, sound coming *from*, a painting *of*, being present *to*, being absent *from*. *The World Viewed* is a jungle of prepositions and descriptions of orientations, and as it develops, an attentive reader realizes why. The book itself accords with Cavell's modernist ideals. He wants to locate the conditions and limits of what he can say, or, rather, write, about the conditions and limits of cinema. Prepositions are indeclinable, the end of the grammatical road, and, for a Wittgensteinian, the end of what we can say is the end of what we can claim to know (not necessarily of what we can know). Etymologically, "preposition" has origins both in the meaning of being before a thing *and* of the linguistic situation of being before another word. Prepositions suggest relations not only between words but also between people, aesthetic objects, and their worlds. In them, language and aesthetic theory come together.

Arriving at *The World Viewed*'s final chapter, as the book has long since moved on from sound to deliberate upon the visual aesthetic complexities of the cinema (save for the occasional comment on music or Natalie Wood's voice), sound returns as a concern, a return that may take a reader slightly aback. Paired with the opening discussion, a concern with aurality thus frames Cavell's discussion of the visual aspect of film. In this chapter, "The Acknowledgement of Silence," by way of summation, he lists four limits with which film contends and that he has delineated: silence, isolation in fantasy, the mysteries of human motion, and separateness. It is silence that he now finds most pressing. He finds it unclear why "the loss of silence was traumatic for so many who cared about film" when the industry transitioned to sound in the late 20s.[43] What, exactly, was thought to be once present and then lost? Or impossible to regain? More specifically: "What was given up in giving up the silence of film, in particular the silence of the voice? . . . For the voice has spells of its own."[44] This mystical assertion is followed by one of the most important turning points in the book. Cavell confesses, in a moment of self-discovery: "I think this issue now underlies *all the explorations* in film to which I have alluded."[45] In other words, without understanding the nature of the voice, we cannot understand the talkie, and he is now ready to admit that he was talking about the talkie all along. (Music and noise are not part of his concern here.)

So Cavell next attempts to elucidate the talkie's conditions by considering silence and speech in two different ways. One is, I think, relatively easy to comprehend. Cavell points out that dialogue is uniquely subject to time. Speeding up or slowing down cinematic speech does not render it poetic as can altering the duration of other human actions. He does not lament this technological limitation but, instead, makes the case for the kinds of dialogue that are successful at exploring the poetry of utterance, which entails exploring the poetry of silence, too. And—and this point is critical—it is only since the advent of sound that movies can explore silence. "The best film dialogue has so far been the witty and the hard-nosed," Cavell maintains, "because they provide natural occasions on which silence is broken, and in which words do not go beyond their moment of saying; hence occasions on which silence naturally reasserts itself."[46] The logic here is clear. Dialogue also must explore the conditions and limits of *human* speech, and, certain *ways* of speaking lend themselves to this task, because certain genres grant the opportunity to explore verbal rhythms in more radical fashions. And to fulfill the modernist task of exploring its possibilities, dialogue must explore silence, as silence is at once a condition and a limit of *cinematic* speech. On one level, this discussion leads us to topics like Welles' overlapping dialogue, film noir's staccato hyperbole, Eve Arden's queer inflections, etc. Indeed, this is true for much of Cavell's work on film, as in *Pursuits of*

Happiness, where the analysis of screwball comedy's rapid, subtext-laden conversations leads to some of his deepest insights about language.[47]

The other kind of silence Cavell wants to explore is more involved. It is silence as metaphor for what lies beyond that which can be expressed in ordinary language—the unsayable. He claims that sound cinema can, if not exactly provide access to this realm, point to it in two ways. The first is by indicating the limits of words. The second is by revealing the ineffable ways that bodies can mean. I'll take them in turn.

The Unsayable I: Synchronization

Cavell produces his most elevated language to indicate the meaning of the unsayable with respect to the limits of words:

> I have . . . in mind the pulsing air of incommunicability which may nudge the edge of any experience and placement: the curve of fingers that day, a mouth, the sudden rise of the body's frame as it is caught by the color and scent of flowers, laughing all afternoon mostly about nothing, the friend gone but somewhere now which starts from here—spools of history that have unwound only to me now, occasions which will not reach words for me now, and if not now, never.[48]

The unsayable is not expressed via stream-of-consciousness, which "does not show the absence of words as the time of action unwinds."[49] Cavell makes his entreaty direct: "I am asking for the ground of consciousness, upon which I cannot but move."[50] Cavell seems to be avoiding naming the Cartesian I here, yet he clearly has the condition for first personal experience in mind (which is always really second personal for him, since it entails encountering *something*, that is, to be in a relation to it).

In what may seem like a trivial step after making such a grand request, Cavell applauds the evolution of sound recording for allowing the actor to step away from the microphone, and focuses on the matter of synchronization as evidence that the talkie is essentially audiovisual: "The possibility of following an actor anywhere with both eye and ear seemed to make their binding necessary."[51] However, synchronization emerges as more than incidental, more than a technological development or a slave to the regulation of speech's temporality. It is a condition the talkie must explore, and a condition that has the power to alter the nature of the movie's sights and sounds. Synchronization is thus a more important term in *The World Viewed* than has been recognized.[52] It is Cavell's avenue to thinking about duration, and to moving away from a conception of film as fundamentally photographic. More specifically, it is an automatism that connects the time of action to words, affording film the capacity to proffer the ground of consciousness and become something to be acknowledged. Cavell ascribes synchronization to "a craving for realism, for the absolute reproduction of the world—as though we might yet be present at its beginning."[53] He continues: "But there is a further reality that film pursues, the further continuous reality in which the words we need are *not* synchronized with the occasions of their need or in which their occasions flee them."[54] He calls this realism beyond realism the "reality of the unsayable."[55]

This is another clue that "the world" is not identical to reality for Cavell, not simply *there* to be captured by photographic technology. Cavell's philosophical views build on those of Wittgenstein, who famously wrote, "The limits of my language means the limits of my world."[56] Similarly, Cavell writes that, "language could not function as it does without mutual and common agreement about *what* is being named or pointed to."[57] Language orients one to the world. How it does so is a question for philosophy. How films may do so is also a question for philosophy, with the added complication that we must understand it through natural language. (This view is controversial given the possibility that we might well reason about films through other métiers, such as the images of video essays, but I shall set that aside for now.)

Cavell next stresses that "it is the talkie itself that is now exploring the silence of movies."[58] Yet he also writes "A silent movie has never been made."[59] What he means is that the appellation "silent movie" obscures the truth of pre-synchronized cinematic experience, since it misleadingly suggests that "the actors and their world had been inaudible."[60] This is a mistake: "Actors were no more inaudible than the characters in radio were invisible."[61]

Using the example of popular radio character The Lone Ranger, he argues that the figure we believe speaks those words could never exist; it is too much a product of our imaginations. This is why, according to him, even a silent movie star who survived the transition to sound was a disappointment, as "no word we could hear could be the word spoken by that [previous] figure of silence."[62] We had supplied voices ourselves, so, on some level, when they replaced their silent selves with sonic ones we felt like we had been given up.

Cavell goes on: "The Lone Ranger was no more invisible than his horse or gun, unless you wish to say that what exists as sound is invisible."[63] This claim might strike us as disconcerting, for did he not say precisely that in the book's early pages? Recall his words: "Is the difference between auditory and visual transcription a function of the fact that we are fully accustomed to hearing things that are invisible, not present to us, not present with us?" This was the beginning of the grapple with prepositions, with what we can *say* about our experience of what we see and hear. It becomes apparent, then, that Cavell means his final chapter to revise his early one. This enjoins us not only to be generous readers—we must be willing to look deeper, rather than reject a superficial contradiction—but also to attend to one of Cavell's rhetorical methods: To be alert to the ways language can tempt us to accept vagueness or disguise wishes that appear to be common sense but which need refining. It now becomes evident why his question on page eighteen *is a question*, and why he writes "unless you wish to say that what exists as sound is invisible." The wish is not a mistake; it is a starting point.

So Cavell has traveled far over one-hundred-thirty or so pages. "Movies, before they spoke," he now writes, "projected a world of silence, as the radio beamed a world of sound."[64] Note that Cavell does not say that movies projected a world of sights, as one might expect. The following statement explains why: "A world of sound is a world of immediate conviction; a world of sight is a world of immediate intelligibility."[65] This point builds on his earlier ontological attributions to sound and sight, where the sound of a horn inspires utter belief that we do in fact hear a horn while a photograph inspires doubt even as, or because, we know precisely what we see. (We can be wrong about what we hear. Foley artists play with the conviction/intelligibility dynamic by making sound *mean* differently, and we might believe the ice cream cone cracking is the cracking of the dinosaur egg. But that is no counter-argument, since once we learn of the trick we understand our error.) By making seeing and listening avatars for conviction and intelligibility, Cavell now casts the talkie as that which is able to stage a drama involving both epistemological stances.

The Unsayable II: The Lucidity of Bodies

Concentrating on "the other half to the idea of conveying the unsayable" brings Cavell "back to the idea of acting on film."[66] Here it is up to "the body's lucidity" to show "experience beyond the reach of words."[67] Actors can do so, according to Cavell, not simply because human action always involves a degree of mystery (intentions are notoriously difficult to pin down) but because on-screen actions typically connote spontaneity. Even if we know they were rehearsed, we sense that seeing *those* actions done *that* way occurred in *that* moment before the camera and microphone. (In fact, we tend to call out something that feels practiced.) Our experience of the quality of spontaneity, the fullness of meaning that accompanies unpremeditated gestures—their apparent freedom—is an aspect that our description can never quite seize.

It may seem that Cavell thus shifts away from his concern with the talkie as sonic medium in the latter half of the chapter (which is also the book's conclusion). Interpreters of *The World Viewed* have been particularly prey to this reading, in part because he proceeds to clarify his thoughts on the performance of unsayability through a brief discussion of Wittgenstein's concept of aspect perception. Cavell writes:

We could study the issue this way: shown (a photograph of) a human face, I might, as in the case of the duck-rabbit, be struck right off with one of its possible aspects. This is unlike the case of the triangle, in which, to read it as "fallen over," I have to imagine something in connection with it, surround it with a fiction. But like the triangle and unlike the duck-rabbit, I *can* surround the face with a fiction in order to alter its aspects. And unlike the triangle and the duck-rabbit and all other optical illusions, I must surround the face with a reality—as though the seeing of a reality is the imagining of it; and it may itself either dictate or absorb the reality with which I must surround it, or fascinate me exactly because it calls incompatible realities to itself which vie for my imagination.[68]

I want to dwell on this last point for a moment. Earlier, when Cavell writes, "A world of sound is a world of immediate conviction; a world of sight is a world of immediate intelligibility," he follows with "in neither is imagination called upon."[69] But here, the filmic face *does* call upon his imagination. He must be thinking not just of a photographic face but of one filmed in the context of a talkie, a face subject to the jurisdictions of the sayable and unsayable as the battle between conviction and intelligibility wages.

Cavell's more explicit point is to steer readers away from thinking that *seeing as* is "some fancy species of seeing."[70] (For Wittgenstein, all seeing is seeing as.) "Aspects" indicates the fragility of communal uses of language, and the ever-present doubt that we do not mean the same things by our words as fellow language-users. It isn't about understanding the facial image. It has "to do with my relation to my own words and with the point at which my knowledge of others depends upon the concepts of truthfulness and interpretation."[71] Similarly, readers have been confused by Cavell's claim that "the knowledge of the unsayable is the study of what Wittgenstein means by physiognomy"—again thinking that "physiognomy" is a basically visual concept.[72] However, Wittgenstein does not use the word in its commonplace sense, whereby one ascertains truths by attending to external appearance. He writes of a physiognomy of words.[73] The *study of* physiognomy is a study about the *knowledge of* the unsayable: both are about what cannot be expressed fully in ordinary utterances.

Again, these halves—silence and the lucidity of bodies—comprise the unsayable because both gesture toward what lies beyond the reach of words. Thinking back to Cavell's initial juxtaposition of sight and sound, we see that his concern throughout has been about how we word the world when we talk about photographs or filmic images, as when we hold up a photograph and say "this is (or is not) Garbo." Now, he seems to be claiming that it is cinema that has the capacity to express ordinary language use that can *reflect* on this condition and fulfill its modernist mission. Talkies are not audio and visual, but audiovisual, and Cavell is thinking past the relational hindrance that the portmanteau suggests.

The Mimesis of the Unsayable

Bearing this in mind helps us to understand the book's enigmatic final paragraphs, and whether we might hope to transcend the confines of prepositional situatedness when theorizing how spectators encounter a film. These paragraphs return to mystical metaphors and could again be mistaken as defining film as a visual medium. In another framing gesture, Cavell begins the chapter talking about the spells of the voice and ends it worried about his own ghostly haunting. He writes:

> A world complete without me which is present to me is the world of my immortality. This is an importance of film—and a danger. It takes my life as a haunting of the world, either because I left it unloved (the Flying Dutchman) or because I left unfinished business (Hamlet). So there is reason for me to want the camera to deny the coherence of the world, its coherence as past: to deny the world is complete without me. But there is equal reason to want it affirmed that the world is coherent without me. That is essential to what I want of immortality: nature's survival of me. It will mean that the present judgment upon me is not yet the last.[74]

Cavell thus concludes with further anxiety about our orientation to the cinematic world. He earlier claims that "photography maintains the presentness of the world by accepting our absence from it," and so cannot be conceptualizing film here as a purely photographic medium.[75] Cinema seems to also depend upon the knowledge, even loyalty, of the self, summoning back the criterial specters of intelligibility and conviction. Perhaps even more mysteriously, Cavell seems to also mean *the* world, an experience of reality predicated upon the availability and affordances of language. He worries over the stakes that we may be ghosts: present *to* but not *of* the world.

In order to better understand how Cavell's concerns about selfhood and film spectatorship meet, and to clarify what world or worlds Cavell is referring to—which affects our understanding of his kind of realism, as well as the relation between cinema and philosophy he envisions—I want to dwell for a moment on his final cinematic example, an example he works through in the book's penultimate paragraph. That paragraph begins with his claim: "To satisfy the wish for the world's exhibition we must be willing to let the world as such appear."[76] Via Heidegger, Cavell explains that this wish entails anxiety about where "one's own existence begins or ends," and that it is only through such anxiety that "the world as world, into which we are thrown, can manifest itself."[77] This, in turn, propels the parallel claim: "To satisfy the wish to act without performing, to let our actions go out of our hands, we must be willing to allow the self to exhibit itself without the self's intervention."[78] This is not self-erasure, quite the contrary. He continues: "The wish for total intelligibility is a terrible one. It means that we are willing to reveal ourselves through the self's betrayal of itself," and turns to his illustration, from Alain Resnais' 1959 modernist masterwork *Hiroshima, Mon Amour*.[79] "The woman in *Hiroshima* is almost there," Cavell writes of the moment when the unnamed protagonist says "I betrayed you tonight" to her dead lover while looking at herself in the mirror.[80]

This scene arrives at an emotionally climactic point in the film, which has from its beginning been deeply concerned with material traces of the past, including photographic and filmic images, and the extent to which experiences of them can be shared. In a way, *Hiroshima, Mon Amour* echoes the arc of *The World Viewed*. It begins by contrasting sights and sounds. We see photographs of the effects of the US bombing of Hiroshima, and we cannot help but ask after the relation between the movie we see and the reality to which it refers. In addition, reenacted moments are folded into the documentary images, and we can detect this difference in historical recounting. This results in doubt about the nature and intelligibility of what we see. We desire to know—we must—whether the horrors we see are real, and whether we can claim to have *really seen* them. In voice-over, we hear claims that things are, or were, because they are, or were, seen. The effect of such assertions is to cast aspersions on taking what we see in filmic images as fact—to reinforce the doubt inherent in the filmic image. At the same time, we trust in the voices we hear to guide our understanding of what we see. Even as these speakers spar over what each does, or can, know, we believe in them (though we do not meet their sources for a full fifteen minutes into the film, at which point they are solidified into the material traces of on-screen bodies, too).

By the time we arrive at the monologue before the mirror we are primed to be sensitive to what she says *aloud* and to think about the extent to which her subjectivity can be made objective—the very problem of her absence and presence in the world. In the moment Cavell singles out, she is distraught over a lover, crooks her face under the cold-water tap of her hotel room's sink and then stands, hunched, staring into the mirror above it. The complex scene unfolds in four moments with markedly different audiovisual schemes:

1. An orchestral leitmotif is heard before her voice says, "You think you know, but no. Never." Her lips do not move during this utterance, suggesting that she is thinking these words.

2. Her lips move as she utters, "In her youth in Nevers she had a German love. We'll go to Bavaria, my love, and we'll get married. She never went to Bavaria." This speech is what is typically referred to as "thinking out loud."

3. She then talks *to* herself as she says, "Let those who never went to Bavaria dare speak to her of love!" Unlike the previous moment, here, her speech is intentionally directed to herself.

4. The orchestral leitmotif plays again, and a beam of light bisects her face, squaring her already doubled image. Her mouth does not move again for the remainder of her speech. She is not simply thinking but talking *to* her self without speaking: thinking *to* herself. It is in this moment that we hear the words "I betrayed you tonight" that Cavell cites.

There is a conspicuous sequence here: She thinks "internally," then out loud, then out loud *to* herself, then again *to* her "inner" self as the voice-over shifts to declarative statements to distinguish thinking from talking to one's self.[81] When her words are said *aloud*, it is easy to claim she is talking *to*. But those in voice-over are the words of both figurations of her self. We hear them in her voice—but also not. Crucially, the orchestral leitmotif only precedes those thoughts that she does *not* speak aloud. The music reinforces the difference between the thoughts she experiences as sonic and not-sonic, between those she voices and those she does not. (To what extent she is *aware* of the difference is ambiguous). In the "unsaid" words, we might say that the sound comes *from* her *to* her, yet traverses no distance.[82]

When Cavell writes earlier that objects do not *make* or *have* sights, but simply are sights, his implication is that this is not so with sound. Here, to the extent that we agree consciousness is sonic, we might dispute him. In this case, it would be impossible to *not* possess this sonic experience. It is basic to the ground of consciousness. There is perhaps only one object that we know to simply be sonic in the way that Cavell describes objects as sights, and it is our own consciousnesses. I want to home in on this point, because the fact that we so easily grasp her "speech" as thought reinforces the impression that there *is* a "sonic" aspect of thought, and, in turn, that there is an aesthetic quality to thinking. This prosody—the rhythms, intonations, and cadences, however private—may then affect one's own conviction in one's thoughts, and the utterances that result, and the reasons for those utterances.[83] On one level, thinking about the inner voice qua voice is a paradox, but it is also arguably a feature of the human experience of conscious thought. In her treatise on the life of the mind, Hannah Arendt writes: "The thinking activity—according to Plato, the soundless dialogue we carry on with ourselves—serves only to open the eyes of the mind, and even the Aristotelian *nous* is an organ for seeing and beholding the truth."[84] She suggests that it is the aural-conceptual realm, which includes the soundless, upon which notions of thinking as seeing or as image are predicated—that the mind's eye is oriented by its ear. The idea that the self is both singular and dual is, of course, basic to many philosophers' schemes of consciousness (though this may be changing in our physicalist age). "The sense of distance from self, or division of self" is exactly what Cavell calls "the problem of self-consciousness" in *The Senses of Walden*.[85] It is a problem to be resisted "by keeping our senses still, listening another way . . . we are to reinterpret our sense of doubleness as a relation between ourselves in the aspect of indweller, unconsciously building, and in the aspect of spectator, impartially observing. Unity between these aspects is viewed not as a mutual absorption, but as a perpetual nextness."[86] *Hiroshima, Mon Amour*, as she passes from the bracing sensations of cold water on her skin to the intense stillness of her own reflected nextness while listening to herself in a new way, provides another way of understanding Cavell's (and Thoreau's) moral.[87]

Furthermore, since Plato and reinforced by Descartes, the inner voice has been *the* primary model for possession (one cannot be without having a voice and vice versa). This takes on different valences over time, and *Hiroshima, Mon Amour*'s investigation—poised at the start of the social upheavals of the 1960s—into what it is to *have* a lover, or a national identity, and into when are our voices are culturally specific metonyms for, or of, ourselves, was certainly timely. *Hiroshima, Mon Amour* apprehends that having a voice is having *voices*, plural—ones present and absent to one's self. It is a political metaphor that is at heart aesthetic.[88]

The Coherence of Doubt

By invoking an example in which subjectivity is essentially audiovisual, and which features sound and listening but *not* identity of sound to object, at the close of his book, Cavell again revises earlier claims. For if sound *comes from* somewhere, from where does *this* paradoxical sound come? We know that it is from her mind, and yet we know that mental thoughts are inaudible. To think to one's self is not to speak at all. We are caught, as the woman in *Hiroshima, Mon Amour* seems to be, between conviction and doubt in her own cogito (she has gone mad before, so we know the stakes). *Hiroshima, Mon Amour* also recalls the therapeutic notion of art that Cavell expounded at the close of the "Sights and Sounds" chapter: That art helps us to cope with the fact that "the unhinging of our consciousness from the world interposed our subjectivity between us and our presentness to the world. Then our subjectivity became what is present to us, individuality became isolation." Isolated, she faces her subjectivity, interposed by both her words (in different ways) and emblematized by her mirror image.

Through this case, Cavell suggests that modernist cinema encourages us, too, to consider our own limits and conditions. Her self-reflection dramatizes the inability to extend our consciousness into the world but to feel that it exists in it, nonetheless. We might see it is a reflection of the threat of skepticism that preoccupies much of Cavell's work (that we cannot know the content of other minds). It's the personal register, what Richard Moran calls "passive skepticism."[89] This moment also speaks to why the sound of the conscious voice is vital to Cavell's method, because that is a large part of the subjectivity interposed between us and the world: *how* we say the words as we learned to think them. (What sounds right and wrong? Is it right or wrong that it sounds that way? From where did we get that knowledge?)

The words we think may be described as both present and absent, akin to the filmic image as Cavell has theorized it.

Hiroshima, Mon Amour elaborates this point in the next moment. She leaves the hotel and takes to the street, where the camera surges ahead of her, leaves her behind—and we suddenly no longer hear her heels clacking on the pavement. The film then erupts into a series of spaces that we are given no indication she was ever in: farm fields, palaces, parks, aged streets. Her voice accompanies the fleeting glimpses of these spaces in lyrical, and not clearly propositional, language. It is tempting to hear her voice as the string that connects the images like beads of a bracelet, or as an echolocation device explaining how they relate. But not only is it dubitable we are seeing places she has been or has imagined, we are certainly not seeing them as she would have—careening into and around trees, drifting up to high windows, down iron gates, and so forth. Whether she was in all these places or none of them, there is once more synchronization (her voice and the images) without sound and sight being *in sync*. To the extent that we still hear her thoughts once the footsteps fade, we are reminded that mental time is unlike social or worldly time. To sync up with one's world often requires effort. The return of the sound of her footsteps, which are in sync with her gait, signals the end of the sequence.

Here, again, *Hiroshima, Mon Amour* reflects upon synchronization as a condition, and, as in the alternation of mouthed and unmouthed utterances, sound and image are not contrapuntal or relational but fused.[90] Moreover, the scene again shows that audible speech is an orientation to and in the world, but thought has a temporality of its own. The movie displays the importance of temporality to the Cavellian unsayable and demonstrates its sense: that what it is to have an orientation to the world is not to have a sayable thought, and that no sayable thought is capable of capturing what it is to have an orientation to the world. We might, in fact, conceive of the unsayable as the unattainable state of prepositionlessness. When no preposition will do, we are in the realm of the unsayable. The comportment of the world and word depends on us. The concept of synchronization is a way of pointing to that comportment at the cinema. It points to the process by which things hang together, creating a new whole, one greater than the sum of its parts by diminishing the inherent intelligibility and conviction of its constituents.

None of this is to undermine *The World Viewed*'s claims about cinema's visual complexion, automatisms, and realism. Rather, synchronization conditions the silence of the unsayable, which, as we saw, Cavell values as an aspect of cinematic realism. Sounds can surmount their status as recordings and become part of the audiovisual category of the cinematic so long as they entail a dubitable relation of expression to referent. Doubt is, as ever for Cavell, and perhaps for all of us, more captivating than belief. This suggests that what we often call "cinematic" passages in film history— Scottie shadowing Madeline through the streets of San Francisco in *Vertigo* (1958, dir. Alfred Hitchcock) or the thrilling heist of *Rififi* (1955, dir. Jules Dassin), for example—are not cinematic because they are visual, or not just, but because they also actualize a particular experience of silence. Despite even the lushest musical score, we experience a kind of silence in these passages, a meta-silence against which words exist and mean.

Another way that we might make sense of cinema's presentation of silence as realist is to remember Cavell's statement that "the world *is* silent to us; the silence is merely forever broken."[91] Cavell was, of course, aware that the experiments of John Cage showed that one may never find true silence in the world. His claim is only that the world is silent *to us*. We experience certain situations as silent, particularly when noises interrupt. The silence of the linguistic register (whether speaking with others or one's self) is not the same as worldly silence, the kind of silence typically meant by the phrase "peace and quiet." Much as the talkie projects the concept of silence onto the world through imitation and synchronization, we project the concept of silence onto our minds via conscious reflection, affixing the sounds and silences of mental time to the spaces in which we live. The two-in-one nature of the audiovisual talkie mirrors the two-in-one nature of consciousness.

The silences of the unsayable are occasions to think, speak, and mean things. It is this kind of silence that brings together Cavell's meditation on the experience of selfhood and cinema in the final paragraph, where he worries about occupying a ghostly presence. Cinema models a way of being that can seem a lot like haunting. It grants an almost suicidal wish, to see unseen, to remove one's self from the world in order to gain the necessary distance with which to *view* the world. "The world viewed" comes to refer to a fantasy of subjectivity and distance, not the literal vision of a cinematic audience member. Indeed, the conclusion with which Cavell leaves his reader, a conclusion that is also the theoretical position he leaves the cinematic audience member in, is thus one of being suspended in the dynamic tension of presence and absence—and of being torn between the desire for both. And, again, it must be the talkie. It is the synchronized film that can indicate the unsayable not just as the ground of consciousness, where lightning strikes, but as the horizon, where ground meets sky, where lighting and thunder converse, and things float by until they disappear.

Notes

1 See prominent examples by Marian Keane, Andrew Klevan, Daniel Morgan, Stephen Mulhall, D. N. Rodowick, William Rothman, and Malcolm Turvey.

2 This is a philosophical position too elaborate to explain fully here, and it is most fully articulated in his books *Must We Mean What We Say?* (Cambridge: Cambridge University Press, 2002) and *The Claim of Reason* (Oxford: Oxford University Press, 1979). However, it subtends all his work, as in *The Senses of Walden* (Chicago: The University of Chicago Press, 1972), in which he writes: "A fact has two surfaces because a fact is not merely an event in the world but the assertion of an event, the wording of the world" (44).

Cavell wrote *The World Viewed* (Cambridge: Harvard University Press, 1971/1979) alongside these works, works that are more easily recognized as belonging to the discipline of philosophy, and particularly to the philosophy of language. I believe it is imperative to keep in mind that "they all seemed to [him] parts of one another" (*The Claim of Reason*, xxii). For more on the relation of word and world in Cavell, see Avner Baz, "On When Words are Called For: Cavell, McDowell, and the Wording of the World," *Inquiry* 46, no. 4 (2003): 473–500.

3   The point I want to make here is a slightly fussy one. While all manner of film scholars, perhaps even a majority, routinely address a film's sights and sounds in their readings, the dominant treatments of "the cinematic" have focused, and continue to focus, on its visual aspect. Hence, when scholars of film sound object, they do so by necessarily isolating sound as an object for consideration, resulting in atomistic rather than holistic theories. Even Michel Chion's book *Audio-Vision: Sound on Screen* (New York: Columbia University Press, 1994), which specifically sets out to consider the complete audiovisual experience, breaks apart sound and image throughout. Moreover, knowledge of the industry's history fosters the impulse to see sound as *added to* the image. Early examples include the well-known arguments of René Clair and Eisenstein, Pudovkin, and Alexandrov in favor of contrapuntal uses of sound. In the 1980s, theorists such as Rick Altman and Mary Ann Doane also considered sound in relation to the image in their own books but also helpfully collected, alongside others, in Elisabeth Weis and John Belton anthology *Film Sound: Theory and Practice* (New York: Columbia University Press, 1985). Here, Doane makes much of film's "material heterogeneity" and writes of sound as "supplement," though a supplement with the power to "transform that which is supplemented" (54). More recently, Lea Jacobs' *Film Rhythm after Sound: Technology, Music, and Performance* (Oakland: University of California Press, 2014) and Jennifer Fleeger's *Mismatched Women: The Siren's Song through the Machine* (Oxford: Oxford University Press, 2014) continue this tradition of thinking about how sounds match, enrich, or critique images. I do not mean to suggest that sound and image cannot productively be understood in relation to one another. Chion's very helpful concepts of spatial magnetization and the *acousmêtre* demonstrate how productive this approach can be. But we ought not be limited to this composite model in discussions of cinematic ontology. By way of contrast, we regard opera as its own art form, not theater with the addition of singing.

4   For a comprehensive survey of scholarship on the voice in film, and how it features within the study of film sound, see Tom Whittaker and Sarah Wright's *Locating the Voice in Film: Critical Approaches and Global Practices* (Oxford: Oxford University Press, 2016), particularly pages 6–9. It is worth noting that in this book Rey Chow argues that "any voice in film has to be recorded and edited, and thus [is] always already a special sound effect" (24).

5   In *Cities of Words* (Cambridge: The Belknap Press of Harvard University Press, 2004), Cavell endorses Wittgenstein's view that "what [philosophy] seeks is not (as in the case of science) to teach something new and to hunt out new facts to support its claims, but rather to understand what is already before us, too obvious and pervasive to be ordinarily remarked" (33).

6 Cavell, *The World Viewed*, 4.
7 Ibid., 16.
8 Acknowledgment is Cavell's prescriptive solution to the problem of living with the threat of skepticism of other minds. To very briefly sketch his rationale for how we might orient ourselves to, and for, others: I can know from experience that I express, so I have reason to believe that expressions are real and convey mindedness (they are expressions *of*). Thus, when I encounter the expressions of others, although I cannot claim to know that they express another mind I can, and ought, to choose to acknowledge that they do. Cavell thus sees the threat of skepticism not as a failure of philosophy but as a feature of the human condition.
9 Cavell, *The World Viewed*, 16–17.
10 Ibid., 17.
11 Ibid.
12 Ibid.
13 Ibid., 18.
14 Ibid.
15 Ibid., 17.
16 Ibid., 18.
17 Ibid.
18 Ibid.
19 Ibid.
20 Ibid.
21 Ibid., 19.
22 Ibid.
23 Ibid.
24 Ibid., 20. The epistemologists Cavell mentions tend to be empiricists, who base their epistemological systems on the registration of sense data or of surfaces being impinged, and we may be tempted to follow suit and fold sights and sounds into a single category. Yet in the working out of their views, visual examples dominate to the extent that the diversity of sensations becomes obscured. See, for example, W. V. Quine's "Scope and Language of Science," in *The Ways of Paradox and Other Essays* (Cambridge: Harvard University Press, 1976). This history trains us to think of subject-object relations in visual-linear directional terms, positing a discrete subject oriented visually toward one object, thereby threatening to blur differences in qualities of cognition or sense experiences. For more on Cavell's refutation of the empiricist view described, see *The Claim of Reason*, 221–25.
25 Ibid., 20.
26 Ibid., 22.
27 Ibid., 146.
28 Ibid.

29 Ibid., 72; italics in original.
30 Ibid., 68.
31 We might, as critics and scholars, want to simply agree that "the camera" includes the capture of sounds. For example, in Richard Moran's "Stanley Cavell on Recognition, Betrayal, and the Photographic Field of Expression," *The Harvard Review of Philosophy* 23 (2016): 29–40, the notion of the "camera" stands in for the entire cinematic apparatus, including the microphone. However, I would argue that the model of attention that the camera offers, and the claims it places on us, differs from that of sound recording technologies, particularly with respect to the expressivity of silence.
32 Cavell, *The World Viewed*, 21.
33 Ibid., 24.
34 Ibid., 20. For more on the importance of the concept of automatism in *The World Viewed*, see Daniel Morgan's "Stanley Cavell: The Contingencies of Film and Its Theory," in *Thinking in the Dark*, ed. Murray Pomerance and R. Barton Palmer (New Brunswick: Rutgers University Press, 2015).
35 Cavell, *The World Viewed*, 22.
36 Ibid., 23.
37 Ibid., 130.
38 Ibid., 138. Earlier, in his discussion of the importance of the material basis of movies to modernism's task of justifying its survival, he offers a definition: "'World' covers the ontological facts of photography and its subjects. 'Projection' points to the phenomenological facts of viewing, and to the continuity of the camera's motion as it ingests the world" (73). Not only is the category of "the phenomenological facts of viewing" a capacious category that changes as cinematic exhibition evolves, he later complicates the ability to even assert what the facts of a medium are, as "only an art can define its media" (107).
39 Bazin describes radio sound in similar terms, arguing that it is not artful because "the perfection of sound reproduction makes the difference between the live and the recorded virtually indiscernible." *André Bazin's New Media*, ed. and trans. Dudley Andrew (Oakland: University of California Press, 2014), 41.
40 In a follow-up essay usually published alongside the original text of *The World Viewed*, "More of *The World Viewed*," Cavell makes the point plain: "First of all, movies are not recordings" (183).
41 Jean-Luc Nancy, *Listening*, trans. Charlotte Mandel (New York: Fordham University Press, 2007), 14.
42 Susanne K. Langer, *Philosophy in a New Key: A Study in the Symbolism of Reason, Rite, and Art* (Cambridge: Harvard University Press, 2009), 108–109.
43 Cavell, *The World Viewed*, 147.
44 Ibid. This form of the question is a far cry from the bluntness of Michel Chion's description of silent cinema as *lacking* a voice in *The Voice in Cinema*, trans. Claudia Gorbman (New York: Columbia University Press, 1999).
45 Ibid.; italics added.
46 Ibid., 150.

47 Cavell, *Pursuits of Happiness: The Hollywood Comedy of Remarriage*.
48 Cavell, *The World Viewed*, 148. Cavell's discussion of silence in *The Senses of Walden* may help us to understand his sense here: "It is through words that words are to be overcome. (Silence may only be the tying of the tongue, not relinquishing words, but gagging on them. True silence is the untying of the tongue, letting its words go)" (44).
49 Ibid.
50 Ibid.
51 Ibid., 147.
52 In their book-length exposition *Reading Cavell's* The World Viewed: *A Philosophical Perspective on Film* (Detroit: Wayne State University Press, 2000), Rothman and Keane barely mention synchronization. In fact, they barely mention sound at all.
53 Cavell, *The World Viewed*, 147.
54 Ibid., 147–48.
55 Ibid., 148.
56 Wittgenstein, *Tractatus Logico-Philosophicus*, trans. C. K. Ogden (London: Routledge, 2001), 68.
57 Cavell, *The Claim of Reason*, 211.
58 Ibid., 149.
59 Ibid.
60 Ibid.
61 Ibid.
62 Ibid.
63 Ibid.
64 Ibid., 150.
65 Ibid.
66 Cavell, *The World Viewed*, 152–53.
67 Ibid.
68 Ibid., 158.
69 Ibid., 150.
70 Ibid., 157.
71 Ibid.
72 Ibid.
73 Relevant passages of Wittgenstein's discussion of the physiognomy of words can be found in *Philosophical Investigations*, trans. G. E. M. Anscombe (Malden: Blackwell, 1953), §38, 238, 294, 568.
74 Cavell, *The World Viewed*, 160.
75 Ibid., 23.
76 Ibid., 159.

77 Ibid.
78 Ibid.
79 Ibid.
80 Ibid., 159–60. Beyond her self-address, her apostrophizing a person who is irrevocably past but whose presence remains alive for her evokes Cavell's discussion of movie stars, who are captured in time onscreen for audience's affection. In *Unclaimed Experience: Trauma, Narrative and History* (Baltimore: Johns Hopkins University Press, 1996), Cathy Caruth's chapter on *Hiroshima, Mon Amour* illuminates the ethical stakes of the woman's traumatic recollections. She writes of the "profound link between the death of a loved one and the ongoing life of the survivor," which requires a "double telling" in order to constitute historical witness and to claim experience of it (8). Interestingly, Caruth also notes that Okada, the Japanese actor playing the protagonist's present-day lover, only spoke phonetically, reciting sounds. For this reason, Caruth argues that "Okada introduces a difference that he does not truly *act* through his role. The Japanese man speaking French in the story does not, that is, truly represent, in any mimetic or specular relation, the actor who plays him" (51). This would seem to contradict Cavell's earlier claim that people would not learn language if they could not imitate sounds, since here is an instance of a person imitating the sounds of words *without* learning the language. But there is surely a difference here between first and second languages, and the desire to perform versus learn to speak. I would also counter Caruth's assertion that Okada does not perform any mimetic relation, as there is more to delivering lines than meaning the words referentially. The emotional force, and the suggestion of thoughts and desires, is vital.
81 Wittgenstein observes "'Thinking' and 'inward speech'—I do not say '*to oneself*'—are different concepts" in his discussion of aspect perception (*Philosophical Investigations*, Part II, 180).
82 Laurence Olivier's 1948 *Hamlet* is a clear progenitor to this moment. The "To Be or Not to Be" soliloquy (which obviously shares concerns about how worldly time wears upon mental time) features a similar alternation of voiced and not-voiced thoughts.
83 The analytic branch of Anglo-American philosophy that was perhaps Cavell's imagined primary audience for *The World Viewed* at the time was deaf to this aspect of language use despite being fixated on statements and assertions. In *The Senses of Walden*, Cavell is deeply interested in Thoreau's distinctions between spoken and written language, between "the language heard and the language read" (15), and when one is compelled to "conjecture whether one is quite sure one hears, or knows, the sound of one's own voice" (38). His discussions here have less to do with the nature of thought, but there is a consistent interest in the experience of an "inner" voice across his work at this time. It is also worth appreciating that Cavell studied with J. L. Austin, who likewise bemoaned twentieth-century Anglophone philosophy's penchant for concentrating on factual assertions when he crafted his famous theory of performative utterances.
84 Hannah Arendt, *The Life of the Mind* (New York: Houghton Mifflin Harcourt, 1981), 6.

85 Cavell, *The Senses of Walden*, 107.
86 Ibid., 108.
87 The problem of self-consciousness is, for Cavell, not far from the problem of living with the threat of skepticism, the pain of which his concept of acknowledgment helps alleviate. In this respect, it is worth noting that his concepts of synchronization and acknowledgment share a structure. Like synchronized cinema, in which sound and image fuse, "One lesson to take away from the relational nature of 'minds that are other,'" Richard Moran explains, "is that the Active and Passive skeptical recitals form one phenomenon, and cannot be understood in isolation from each other," in "Cavell on Outsiders and Others," *Revue internationale de philosophie* 2 (2011): 239–54, 250. Prioritizing either sight or sound, or one's mind over others', can distort matters.
88 It arguably makes some sense that advances in depictions of voices accompany shifts in notions of the civic voice. In the United States, for example, the talkie emerged alongside the rise of "the New Woman" and as economic collapse profoundly reshaped the nation's self-image. Similarly, the popularization of modernist uses of the cinematic voice gained traction in the United States during the rise of second-wave feminism, the so-called sexual revolution, and the nation's changing self-image amid the Vietnam conflict. For a discussion of how Cavell's thoughts on silence in *The World Viewed* participate in a specifically late 1960s American cultural moment, see chapter two of my book *Mike Nichols: Sex, Language, and the Reinvention of Psychological Realism* (Oxford: Oxford University Press, 2015).
89 See Moran, "Cavell on Outsiders and Others."
90 One might be tempted to hear this revelation as evidence of Hollywood's privileging of intelligibility over fidelity on the soundtrack, and how images and sounds were made to "match" based on visual perspective or picture size. But that isn't quite strong enough. Cavell's view is upheld by historical accounts of the industrial transition to sound. In 1929, for instance, writer and director William DeMille, legendary producer Cecil's older brother, tells us, "One of the most interesting things I have found out is that the same sound track played with a semi-close-up, or with a close-up, sounds different, depending upon which pictures you are looking at. . . . [For example,] if [the close-up] was a little far away, you couldn't hear right because you got a different visual effect" in *The Introduction to the Photoplay: 1929: A Contemporary Account of the Transition to Sound in Film*, ed., John C. Tibbets (Shawnee, Kansas: National Film Society, 1977), 326. DeMille's point is that the face itself was seen *differently* due to the scale of the sound. Sound and image fuse at the level of experience. For more on sound-image matching, and how intelligibility became standardized in classical Hollywood, see James Lastra's *Sound Technology and the American Cinema* (New York: Columbia University Press, 2000), especially chapter five.
91 Cavell, *The World Viewed*, 150–51; italics in original.

4

What a Genre of Film Might Be: Medium, Myth, and Morality

Stephen Mulhall

AT THE HEART OF STANLEY CAVELL'S CONTRIBUTION to film studies lies his identification of two previously overlooked movie genres: comedies of remarriage (examined in his book *Pursuits of Happiness*) and melodramas of the unknown woman (discussed in *Contesting Tears*). The individual films under investigation in both books are among the most famous of those produced by Hollywood between 1930 and 1950, and have accordingly attracted much attention from theorists of film; but it was Cavell who proposed viewing them in relation to one another in this particular way, and thereby disclosed aspects of their nature and achievement that would otherwise have been missed.[1] And one reason for previous failures to apprehend these internal relationships is that the notion of generic membership Cavell employed in order to render them salient is itself original; his conception of a film genre differs significantly from those that have tended to predominate in film studies, and so have shaped perceptions of similarity and difference within the field.

Cavell called the prevailing conception "genre-as-cycle": "What is traditionally called a genre film is a movie whose membership in a group of films is no more problematic than the exemplification of a serial in one of its episodes. You can, for example, roughly see that a movie is a western, or gangster film, or horror film, or 'woman's film,' or a screwball comedy."[2] The underlying assumption here is that a genre is a form characterized by a certain range of features, as an object is characterized by its properties; membership in such a genre is established by establishing whether the relevant film possesses the requisite features (or a sufficient number of them), just as identifying an object as belonging to a particular kind is envisaged as a matter of establishing whether it has the features that all objects of that kind necessarily possess. Without contesting the coherence or applicability of this conception of film genre (although noting the extent to which, by encouraging a perception of genre membership as validated merely by a check-list of properties, it also encourages a perception of films as mechanically [re-]producible commodities), Cavell's experience of the individual remarriage comedies led him toward a different conception—one he calls "genre-as-medium." Since, however, his notion of a "medium" is as idiosyncratic as his notion of a genre specified by reference to it, the best way to approach the latter is to spend some time articulating the former.

Medium

Cavell takes the concept of a medium to be indispensable in differentiating kinds of artwork, and in understanding specific instances of those kinds; but it must be seen as referring not simply to a physical material but to a material-in-certain-characteristic-applications, and hence as having a necessarily dual sense. Sound, for example, is not the medium of music in the absence of the art of composing and playing music. Musical works of art are thus not the result of applications of a medium that is defined by its independently given possibilities; for it is only through the artist's successful production of something we are prepared to call a musical work of art that the *artistic* possibilities of that physical material are discovered, maintained, and explored. We can, of course, identify the independently given physical possibilities of sound qua sound, qua physical phenomenon; but to see in any such possibility a way of making art (to identify it as an aesthetic possibility) we must actually deploy it to make art, we must make something recognizable as a work of art from it. In general, we are inclined to think that possibility is prior to actuality—that something's being the case presupposes its being possible; but when our concern is with a medium of art, it is less misleading to say that actuality is prior to possibility—that an aesthetic possibility is only established as such, only created, by someone actualizing it. And such aesthetic possibilities of sound, without which it would not count as an artistic medium at all, are themselves media of music—ways in which various sources of sound have been applied to create specific artistic achievements, for example, in plainsong, the fugue, the aria, or sonata form. They are the strains of convention through which composers have been able to create, performers to practice, and audiences to acknowledge, specific works of art.

As this last formulation suggests, Cavell conceives of an artistic medium on analogy with a language:

> A medium is something through which or by means of which something specific gets done or said in particular ways. It provides, one might say,

particular ways to get through to someone, to make sense; in art, they are forms, like forms of speech. To discover ways of making sense is always a matter of the relation of an artist to his art, each discovering the other.[3]

On this conception, an artistic medium mediates between artist and audience member because it is a medium of communication, a vehicle of meaning; and just like linguistic meaning on a Wittgensteinian conception of it, artistic meaning is constituted by a dialectic between conventions and those employing them. Speakers inherit the norms and conventions of the preexisting public language they share with other speakers (that is, there is no such thing as a private language); but that language's continued existence depends upon the collective, and so the individual, willingness of speakers to go on with those conventions—in part by projecting them into new circumstances and contexts, some of which might invite or compel them to revise or otherwise question those conventions, disclosing new possibilities or impossibilities of sense-making in the light of the world's unpredictable yieldings and resistances, and speakers' shifting conceptions of the intelligibility of what other speakers say and do. Speakers at once exploit and extend the meanings of words, and so the medium of communication that they constitute; and apart from their continued willingness to seek and find sense in the ways individual speakers attempt to make sense to one another, there would be no language, no medium of speech. Linguistic conventions accordingly cannot ground or authorize, and thereby guarantee, the success of these attempts; on the contrary, the continued success of those attempts is what the continued viability of those conventions as ways of making sense consists in.

Three aspects of this analogy are worth noting explicitly, as part of Cavell's general background conception of an artistic medium. The first is that the primary locus of artistic sense-making is the particular communicative act, the specific artwork: this is where the continued viability of a given artistic convention, or the establishment of a new convention, is exhibited or seen to fail. Second, those at whom that communication is directed are necessarily involved in the task of interpreting or making sense of it (as something that someone might intelligibly have meant to say or do); in short, they must engage in acts of criticism. Put otherwise, works of art are inherently criticizable, and criticism is inherent in any relation to a work of art qua artwork. And third, the artistic significance of any artwork cannot be determined by, and so read off from, the possibilities of its medium: not from its physical possibilities (as we have seen), and not from its aesthetic possibilities, either (since each new attempt to exploit them *might* reveal their inability, here and now, to support artistic meaning as they stand, or at all).

Applied to the particular case of film, this general conception of an artistic medium delivers the following conclusions:

> You can no more tell what will give significance to the unique and specific aesthetic possibilities of projecting photographic images by thinking

about them or seeing some, than you can tell what will give significance to the possibilities of paint by thinking about paint or by looking some over. You have to think about painting, and paintings; you have to think about motion pictures.

The first successful movies—that is, the first moving pictures accepted as motion pictures—were not applications of a medium that was defined by given possibilities, but *the creation of a medium* by their giving significance to specific possibilities. Only the art itself can discover its possibilities, and the discovery of a new possibility is the discovery of a new medium.[4]

For Cavell, then, his discovery of the genre of remarriage comedy is the discovery of a medium of the motion picture medium—analogous to the sonata form in music. It constitutes one original form in which the artistic medium of film can be used to create specific artistic achievements, and thereby discloses a further aesthetic possibility of the material basis of that medium—another way in which others can utilize the photographic projection of reality to get through to us, make artistic sense. But since the same can be said of cinematic genres-as-cycles (insofar as they are cogent modes of artistic sense-making that have facilitated specific artistic achievements), more needs to be said about the distinctive mode of artistic sense-making that members of a cinematic genre-as-medium establish, exploit, and explore.

Myth

Having set aside the "objects with common properties" model of genre membership for the films in which he is interested, those familiar with Cavell's Wittgensteinian leanings might expect him to invoke, instead, the idea of "family resemblance" as their mode of unity. This idea is, after all, introduced in the *Philosophical Investigations* precisely when Wittgenstein contests his interlocutor's assumption that the unity of a concept *must* consist in an essence common to every instance to which it applies. Invoking the concept of a "game" as his primary example, Wittgenstein suggests, instead, that it is perfectly possible for a concept's unity to consist in a complicated network of overlapping and crisscrossing similarities in the large and the small that hold together the items which fall under it.

> I can think of no better expression to characterize these similarities than "family resemblances"; for the various resemblances between members of a family—build, features, colour of eyes, gait, temperament, and so on and so forth—overlap and criss-cross in the same way.—And I shall say: "games" form a family. . . .

How would we explain to someone what a game is? I think that we'd describe *games* to him, and we might add to the description: "This *and similar things* are called "games." And do we know any more ourselves? . . . But this is not ignorance. We don't know the boundaries because none have been drawn. . . . We can draw a boundary—for a special purpose. Does it take this to make the concept usable? Not at all! . . . No more than it took the definition 1 pace = 75 cm to make the measure of length "one pace" usable. And if you want to say "But still, before that it wasn't an exact measure of length," then I reply: all right, so it was an inexact one.— Though you still owe me a definition of exactness. . . .

"Inexact" is really a reproach, and "exact" is praise. And that is to say that what is inexact attains its goal less perfectly than does what is more exact. So it all depends on what we call "the goal." Is it inexact when I don't give our distance from the sun to the nearest metre, or tell a joiner the width of a table to the nearest thousandth of a millimetre?[5]

In fact, however, Cavell is quick to refuse this tempting alliance: although both he and Wittgenstein are seeking to break up an impoverished notion of "unity" and a coercive fantasy of exactness, his enemy's enemy is not in this case his friend. Cavell's explicit reason is as follows: "If I said of games . . . that they form a genre of human activity, I would mean not merely that they look like one another or that one gets similar impressions from them; I would mean that *they are what they are* in view of one another."[6] So phrased, this point may misrepresent Wittgenstein's conception of a family-resemblance concept, or at least show that he should have tried harder to find an apt expression to characterize the unifying similarities to which he adverts. For Wittgenstein's core thought is that games (for example) form a family, and, of course, the unity of a family is not determined by the existence of resemblances between its members; if anything, the reverse is true, since it is the genealogical interaction of nature and culture constitutive of a family as a historical unit that finds expression in similarities of appearance, character, and behavior in its members. So Wittgenstein does not need to deny that we can flesh out the specific affinity we see between two games, and thereby ground our impression of their being related if it is questioned by someone who happens not to share it (as he explicitly acknowledges, it might be their entertainment value, or the presence of winning and losing, or the development of a skill). All he needs to deny is that every type of game *must* be locatable on a *single* such dimension of similarity (or set of them); and he wants to remind us that as a matter of fact we rarely need to enter any such defense, since human beings naturally tend to acquire the same impressions from the same individual cases.

Nevertheless, it is clear that the family-resemblance model differs from that of Cavell's genre-as-medium model in a crucial respect. Since the former identifies a mode of unity whose strength resides in the overlapping of many distinct strands of similarity, an individual can be woven into the fabric of such a conceptual family on the basis of a direct connection with only a subset of its other members. By contrast, Cavell sees the comedies of remarriage as necessarily "being what they are in view of one another": that is, we can grasp the individuality of each only by grasping its relation to *every* other member of the genre, and what we thereby grasp is partly constituted by the view each film takes of those others, and the view those others have of it—by what one might call their opinion of each other.

Each comedy of remarriage does therefore share something with every other member of the genre; but what it shares is not a property or set of properties but an inheritance, together with a questioning or inquiring relation to that inheritance, and so to its fellow-inheritors.

> The members of a genre share the inheritance of certain conditions, procedures and subjects and goals of composition, and . . . in primary art each member of such a genre represents a study of these conditions, something I think of as bearing the responsibility of the inheritance.[7]

In those parts of the Introduction to *Pursuits of Happiness* that precede the point at which Cavell reflects explicitly on his conception of genre-as-medium, that inheritance emerges implicitly and piecemeal; but it centrally involves what he calls "a problematic of marriage established in certain segments of the history of theatre."[8] One such source is Shakespearean Romantic comedy, which typically concerns a young pair overcoming individual and social obstacles to their happiness and achieving resolution in marriage; the other is Ibsen's dramatic concern, exemplified in *A Doll's House*, with the struggle for reciprocity or equality of consciousness between a woman and a man, and more specifically with the necessity and the possibility of reconceiving marriage so that it can be a site of such mutual acknowledgment. Comedies of remarriage conjoin and remake these sources by casting a married woman as their heroine, and taking as their goal getting their central, older pair together *again*. Marriage is thus represented as inherently subject to the fact or the threat of divorce, hence as worth preserving or recovering only if both parties prove themselves willing to remarry—as if to be married just *is* to be willing to remarry, every day. The condition for that willingness is the recreation of the woman (the creation of a new woman) at the hands of the man, who has to demonstrate his worthiness for being chosen by her for that task by having undergone (or being willing to undergo) a transfiguration of his own; and a certain kind of conversation between them is at once the means for overcoming divorce and the medium through which their (re)marriage is maintained—a dramatization of Milton's characterization of marriage as a meet and happy conversation, and a synecdoche of their willingness to share a world.

When he attempts to characterize this unifying inheritance more explicitly in the light of his reflections on genre, however, Cavell does so by recasting it as a story, or, more specifically, a myth. His initial general construction of that myth goes as follows:

> A running quarrel is forcing apart a pair who recognize themselves as having known one another forever, that is from the beginning, not just in the past but in a period before there was a past, before history. This naturally presents itself as their having shared childhood together, suggesting that they are brother and sister. They have discovered their sexuality together and find themselves required to enter this realm at roughly the same time that they are required to enter the social realm, as if the sexual and the social are to legitimize one another. . . . The joining of the sexual and the social is called marriage. Something evidently internal to the task of marriage causes trouble in paradise—as if marriage, which was to be a ratification, is itself in need of ratification. So marriage has its disappointment—call this its impotence to domesticate sexuality without discouraging it, or its stupidity in the face of the riddle of intimacy, which repels where it attracts, or in the face of the puzzle of ecstasy, which is violent while it is tender, as if the leopard should lie down with the lamb.
>
> And the disappointment seeks revenge, as it were, for having made one discover one's incompleteness, one's transience, one's homelessness. Upon separation, the woman tries a regressive tack, usually that of accepting as a husband a simpler, or a mere, father-substitute, even one who brings along his own mother. This is psychologically an effort to put her desire, awakened by the original man, back to sleep.[9]

If one casts the common inheritance of the genre of remarriage comedy as a myth, then the grammar of that concept will shape the reception of that inheritance (by the films, and by us): and one immediately relevant aspect of it is that each telling of a myth is a retelling of it. The remarriage myth as Cavell tells it, for example, patently offers a psychoanalytically informed retelling of the Christian myth of the Garden of Eden, just as *The Lady Eve* offers its own retelling of that myth and just as Freud elsewhere retells what we might think of as the original Greek myth of Oedipus; but, of course, Sophocles presents his own account of Oedipus as a recounting of an ancient tale, one always already familiar to his audience and their predecessors, hence as an inherited account of the otherwise unaccountable origins of their community. Indeed, as Cavell says elsewhere, "Myths will generally deal with origins that no-one can have been present at"[10]: and if no one was or could have been present at the true beginning of the cosmos, the polis, or distinctively human life, then second-hand accounts—that is, accounts which present themselves as recountings, as new versions of an absent earlier one—are the best we could possibly have, and so aren't really second-hand at all (since it makes no sense to talk of the original or first-hand version).

Cavell applies this point in the present context in two ways: by all but declaring in his recounting of the myth of remarriage that the pair who are its concern have an essentially mythological understanding of the unaccountable origin of their own relationship (and are contesting its best interpretation), and by explicitly asserting that each member of the genre that inherits this myth constitutes a retelling of it.

> The members of a genre will be interpretations of it, or to use Thoreau's word for it, revisions of it, which will also make them interpretations of one another. The myth must be constructed, or reconstructed, from the members of the genre that inherits it, and since the genre is, as far as we know, unsaturated, the construction of the myth must remain provisional.[11]

In other words, each member of the remarriage genre embodies a way of making sense of its identifying myth's way of making sense of things (of marriage, but also—in the terms of Cavell's construction of it—of sexuality, society, desire, separateness, finitude, and so on); each such critical evaluation therefore amounts to a critical evaluation of the interpretations of all its fellow-members, a view of the myth that is also a view of all the other views of that myth. Given that all accounts of a myth are recountings of it, Cavell's construction of it is likewise an interpretation or revision: since there cannot be an unchanging essence of the relevant myth (an "original" version), Cavell's account is just as much a reconstructive version of it as are the versions embodied in any of the films. It is accordingly on exactly the same level, hermeneutically speaking, as the films it interprets—except that it is only arrived at by virtue of interpreting those films: that is, by individual acts of criticism of those individual acts of criticism.

This perception encapsulates a crucial difference between Cavell and many other theorists of film. One general tendency in film studies is to treat movies (individually and collectively) as objects to which theoretical edifices constructed elsewhere (in psychology, psychoanalysis, or politics) can simply be applied: the film becomes one further symptom of more general, underlying cultural forces by which even the finer details of its identity are wholly determined. Cavell, by contrast, has faith that films themselves (some films, sometimes) might contribute something to our understanding of them; even those produced at the heart of popular culture can contain an account of themselves, embody an understanding of why they are the way they are, and one that might also contribute to an understanding of the very issues (of perception, sexuality, power) which those theoretical edifices were built in order to help us understand. Such films are as capable of putting the assumptions of such theorizing in question as they are of being subsumed by them; they may confirm some of the theories' claims, but they may also delineate the limits of their legitimacy and even contest their basic structure. At the very least, they should be allowed a voice in their own history—an opportunity to contribute to the ongoing conversation about their particular ways of making sense of things, including themselves. And on Cavell's conception, making such a contribution is a requirement of membership of a genre-as-medium.

If, however, each such film interprets the unifying myth in its own way, and so one genre member might in principle differ in any given respect from any other, how exactly does their inheritance of the myth unify them? Cavell's response is that if a given member of the genre lacks (or appears to lack) a feature of the myth (more precisely, if it omits an apparently significant clause or provision in the story), it can maintain its claim to membership of the genre by compensating for that lack—for example, by introducing a new clause or provision to its retelling of the myth that proves to contribute to a description of the genre as a whole.[12] Take Cavell's emphasis, in his (re)construction of the myth, upon the pair's having a shared past which they understand as a shared childhood: the pair in *It Happened One Night* have no shared past, but Cavell claims that the film compensates for this absence by its emphasis upon their journeying together "on the road," which embodies a commitment to adventurousness and so to a shared future instead of a shared past. But then he finds that adventurousness in turn plays a role in each of the other films of remarriage, and that being on the road or on the way is one way of understanding the perspective every pair has to attain to overcome the threat of divorce.

> In that case, what is compensating for what? Nothing is lacking, every member incorporates every "feature" you can name, in its way. It may be helpful to say that a new member gets its distinction by investigating a particular set of features in a way that makes them, or their relation, more explicit than its companions. Then as these exercises in explicitness reflect upon one another, looping back and forth among the members, we may say that the genre is striving towards a state of absolute explicitness, of expressive saturation. At that point the genre would have nothing further to generate. This is perhaps what is sometimes called the exhaustion of conventions. There is no way to know that the state of saturation, completeness of expression, has been reached.[13]

If we can interpret a new feature that any candidate genre member incorporates as compensating for an apparently absent clause in the myth, then we can understand it as an interpretation of the same story, a way of allowing it to go on being told by developing its mode of sense-making. However, given that each new addition to a genre-as-medium (and each new critical engagement with any member of it) can revise our understanding of its founding myth, we can never regard any attempt to critically recount the central provisions of that myth as anything other than provisional. And the same is true of any judgment we are led to make (perhaps by having found no new films belonging to it for a long time) that a given genre of this kind has reached the point of expressive saturation; for all it takes to falsify that judgment is the arrival of a new film which supplies an original revision of the myth (a recurrent event in Cavell's later life with films). On the other hand, whereas the very idea of an original version of the founding myth is empty, the same cannot be said of the idea of a final version: for aesthetic media can perfectly well cease to be viable ways of making artistic sense, their conventions can become exhausted. When the relevant media take the form of genre-as-medium, this amounts to our having ceased to live the myth, no longer finding it a convincing way of making sense of ourselves and our world.

As well as cases of compensation, however, we may find that a new feature brought to the conversation by another film—for example, the man's inability to claim the woman—negates some central provision of the myth; by this we mean that it doesn't allow us to tell the same story differently, but, rather, decisively changes the story. The genre-as-medium to which this film belongs is different, and an adjacent genre is thereby identified. It turns out later in Cavell's work that it is through this kind of negating operation that the melodramas of the unknown woman are derived from, and so differentiated from, and related to, the comedies of remarriage. And since negation is an operation that can be repeatedly implemented, Cavell endorses one implication of its power:

> If genres form a system (which is part of the faith that for me keeps alive an interest in the concept), then in principle it would seem possible to be able to move by negation from one genre to adjacent genres, until all the genres of film are derived.[14]

Whether or not we share that faith (and Cavell's subsequent work doesn't go far with working it out), it is important to bear in mind that when one genre is negated, what suffers that rejection is its founding myth; and negating a myth is not the same as denying the truth of an assertion. This is not because myths are not true: as Cavell puts it, "not every way in which language fails to meet the facts is a lie" and there is such a thing as mythical truth.[15] To regard a myth as truthful is to be willing to orient one's life by it, to live in accordance with the terms it provides for making sense of (some aspect of) our common life in the world. Hence to negate a myth is to say that, for example, viewing the state as a ship or the soul as a ghost in a machine "is not merely false but mythically false. Not just untrue but destructive of truth."[16]

When the melodramas negate the comedies, they negate their myth of marriage as a meet and happy conversation: the melodramas retain the aspiration to the woman's transfiguration, but they present it as something that must take place outside the process of a mode of conversation with a man. For the women of the melodramas, the vision of such a man, and its attendant vision of the woman as needing education at his hands (however much he must submit his claim to their judgment), is not just untrue but articulates a way of making sense of the world that must be dismantled if they are to achieve and maintain their freedom and individuality. We can call the myth of the melodramas "an alternative route to integrity and possibility"[17] if we wish (and Cavell does); but we must remember that for those who inhabit one myth the other will not appear simply as another reasonable opinion for others to hold—for it helps constitute a horizon or world in which the truth of their lives is rendered inexpressible and their existence is negated. One might say that when we characterize one myth as negating another, "negation" is here being used mythologically, to conjure up the potentially coercive violence of the intelligibility-conferring and intelligibility-denying powers myths (and their believers) can wield.

At the same time, "negation," together with its kindred terms "compensation," "system," and "derivation" activate another symbolic or mythological register—that of the algorithmic; they sound like precision tools for establishing the identity and difference of genre. And this is because Cavell takes them to generate just as precise a notion of generic unity as is needed to find orientation in this aesthetic domain (as precise in its own, different way as the mode of unity conferred by family resemblance in the domains with which Wittgenstein is concerned). This connotation of precision is not in conflict with (what for Cavell is) the equally important fact that the business of judging when one film compensates for such an absent provision whereas another negates it, and so of laying out the systematic generative relation between film genres-as-medium, is itself an act of criticism; it is a further specification of the nature of such acts. To be sure, aesthetic interpretations are not in the business of constructing a proof or experimentally verifying a hypothesis: they, rather, require what all critical evaluations require—a capacity to bring the fine details of one's experience of an artwork to words, and to locate the fine details in the work to which that experience is sensitive, and a willingness to attend and respond to those whose experience differs, and who offer reasons for concluding that one's own experience isn't properly grounded in the work. They require, in short, attentive appraisals of the aesthetic significance of particular works; but such judgments demand rigor and precision in their own way (aesthetic exactness is as exacting as are its mathematical or scientific inflections).

Moral Perfectionism

But for Cavell, it is not just that his more general claims about the system of adjacent genres to which the comedies of remarriage belong are as much aesthetic judgments as are his readings of the individual films; what those individual readings reveal (however provisionally) about the situation of the pairs in those comedies provide the terms in which he characterizes the situation of the comedies themselves, understood as members of this genre-as-medium. The pairs in the comedies engage in a conversation about how best to account for the unaccountable origins of their relationship, and it is in coming to appreciate this that Cavell is enabled to appreciate how each comedy engages with the other comedies in a critical conversation about the best available account of their own founding and unifying mythological inheritance. Likewise, as the pairs in the comedies struggle to manage transfiguration, and in particular to reconceive marriage as itself a transfigurative condition—as unending remarriage, so the comedies effect compensatory transformations on one another which serve to disclose deeper reaches of shared significance in their relationship, and so disclose their individual mode of cinematic significance as itself always subject to reinterpretation in view of its present and future fellow-members of the genre. One might say: just as the mode of being of the pairs in the comedies aspires to be one of continuous becoming, so the mode of being of the members of this and all genres-as-medium stands revealed as one of continuous becoming (as its meaning unendingly unfolds in view of future developments of the genre and of its critical reception).

We might think of this willingness to regard individual genre members as if they were individual people as Cavell's methodological mythology, and it is one he draws from the films themselves—allowing them to teach him how to understand their nature. Envisioning the genre members as engaged in meet and happy conversation with one another is an enabling projection of their preoccupation with such conversations between the men and women they study, and it enables a further critical projection of the genre as itself engaged in a conversation with the wider American culture that incubated it. The point here is not that the films, on Cavell's reading, have their own perspective on matters on which psychoanalysis, religion, and politics also have perspectives, although this is plainly true; it is that the founding myth of the remarriage comedies is in conversation with the wider myths of the United States of America.

One central topic of this conversation is signaled by the title of his book on the remarriage genre, which refers to the American Declaration of Independence, according to which "life, liberty and the pursuit of happiness" are among the inalienable rights of all human beings, to the protection of which any legitimate government should be devoted. By pluralizing that last clause and depriving it of the Founders' definite article, Cavell explicitly enables it to acknowledge that happiness is to be pursued by many individual citizens, and in many different ways; but in his recounting of the remarriage myth, his emphasis upon the sexual and the social as legitimizing one another retains the idea that the couples' ability to find happiness with each other ratifies their political community's claim to their loyalty (or, of course, fails to do so). Put otherwise, these films test their primary audience's conviction that this aspect of the founding myth of the United States continues to be livable—to constitute a way of rendering membership of this political community intelligible.

One difficulty posed by these films' attempts to make us attribute national importance to the fate of their couples lies in the fact that they lead relatively privileged lives (and, indeed, must do so if those lives are to have the space to consider the questions that their marriage poses). Against the background of the Great Depression and the Second World War (when most of these films were made), such matters can seem to be of merely personal concern—even occasions for self-indulgent frivolity in the face of genuine hardship, at best, entertaining distractions from serious political issues (fairy tales for the Depression). But Cavell contests this dismissal, claiming that we can and should, rather, view these films as "taking the occasion of the Depression to ask what it is as a people we are truly depressed by, what hunger it is from which we are all faint."[18] More specifically, he suggests that these films aspire to teach us that "the achievement of human happiness requires not the perennial and fuller satisfaction of our needs as they stand but the examination and transformation of those needs."[19]

This faint echo of Thoreau's famous diagnosis of the mass of his fellow-citizens as leading lives of quiet desperation is the closest that Cavell's early book comes to touching on a theme that becomes fully explicit only through the perspective constructed by his later work, and thereby on a further dimension of this genre's critical engagement with America's myths of itself—one that is internally related to the films' incessant concern with creation, recreation, and transfiguration. In the context of *Pursuits of Happiness*, that concern leads through a new perception of genre-as-medium to a revelation of one of the cinematic medium's distinctive aesthetic possibilities: its capacity to transfigure a real human being subject to the gaze of the camera into a human *something* projected on the screen, and in some unpredictable but undeniable cases into a star. It is only later, in exactly the unpredictable but revelatory way that his model of genre-as-medium allows for, that Cavell comes to articulate an internal relation between this aspect of remarriage comedy (and of melodramas of the unknown woman, and, indeed, of the transfigurative powers of the movie camera) and what he will come to call "Emersonian moral perfectionism"—the ethical and existential vision of the American Transcendentalist tradition.[20]

According to this conception, the structure of the self is inherently self-transcending or self-overcoming, and so non-self-identical. Emersonian perfectionism understands the soul as on an upward or onward journey that begins when it finds itself lost to the world, say disoriented or unintelligible to itself, recovery from which requires a refusal of its present state in the name of some further, more cultivated or cultured, state. However, each such unattained state of the self is no sooner attained than it projects another, unattained but attainable, state, to the realization of which we might commit ourselves, or whose attractions might be eclipsed by the attained world we already inhabit. Because in that sense no state of the self is final or perfect, in another sense every attained state of the self is (that is, can present itself as, and be inhabited as) perfect—as in need of no further refinement. Hence the primary internal threat to moral perfectionism is that of regarding human individuality as harboring a specific and realizable state of perfection (even if a different one for each individual), rather than as a continuous process of self-perfecting (selfhood as unending self-improvement or self-overcoming, hence as inherently transitional, always already split or doubled, and so a matter of becoming, rather than being).

Cavell takes such issues to be especially relevant to any citizen of the United States, insofar as they understand themselves as inheritors of the Declaration of Independence; indeed, he would argue that, US citizen or not, establishing and maintaining such a perfectionist self-relation not only does not conflict with a genuine democratic concern for others, but is also, in fact, a condition of such concern. After all, if (as Kant puts it) being moral is a matter of the self's obedience to a law that it gives itself, morality presupposes and so depends upon the achievement of a genuine self from whom that law might come and to whom it can apply. Nevertheless, as the standing of the couples in the comedies attests, the question posed by moral perfectionism is especially pressing for those leading relatively privileged lives in their political community. As Cavell puts it, "There is no definitive defense, nor should there be in a democracy, against the sense of being compromised by the partiality, the imperfectness, of one's society's compliance with the principles of justice, when, that is, that partiality is one from which you gain relative advantage."[21] Even in a democracy whose basic arrangements come closest to the kind that all reasonable people would voluntarily accept, there will be some degree of existing injustice, and some extent to which certain citizens will be more materially advantaged than others. Hence, the relatively advantaged should feel that they are implicated in these arrangements, and exposed to the question of how far they can consent to a society with this degree of inequality in it. The perfectionist question is: How is one to live with this state of moral compromise? The particular threat that democratic life raises for people in their kind of position is a guilty disdain and snobbery, "a tendency to distance oneself from the cultural costs of democracy, from the leveling down of taste, the mendacity of public discourse, the intolerance of indifference. The disdain may be understood as a reaction to blunt the guilt of advantage."²² Here, Cavell's perfectionism asks his likely audience to take seriously a resentment of their own good fortune that is grounded in something other than specific failures of insufficiently just institutions—something more like a competent conviction that the existing moral ground of those institutions as such may require radical transformation. And it suggests that one reason for continuing to ratify one's society in the face of such partial compliance with justice (for judging it to be worth devoting the time and effort to helping it realize a higher state of itself) is that society's continued ability to enable its citizens to pursue their own happiness.

It is not hard to see how the comedies' reconception of marriage as diurnal remarriage more generally inherits and revises Emerson's (and Thoreau's) underlying myth of selfhood. This Transcendental background also helps account for the centrality of linguistic exchange in the comedies; for given that we are inherently language-using animals, managing the relation between one's attained and unattained states (call it one's self-relation) must involve managing one's relation to one's words. Indeed, recognizing oneself as currently disoriented with respect to one's words, and committing oneself to overcoming that settled state of unintelligibility to oneself, is exemplary of what moral perfectionism asks of its adherents—a paradigmatic instance of the kinds of struggle and self-overcoming that more broadly pervade our lives with one another. But by inflecting language in the direction of conversation, the comedies importantly emphasize the extent to which overcoming one's disorientation and recovering one's openness to one's further self is itself achievable only with the help of another, an Emersonian friend who is capable of disclosing to us the state we are in and the ways in which we might transfigure it—by aspiring to realize that friend's essentially transitional mode of self-relation rather than the particular unattained but attainable state that he or she has currently chosen to aspire to. It is this condition of active passivity, of attractively inviting another to inhabit a new world rather than enforcing entry into it, that the men of the remarriage comedies must attain if they are to show themselves worthy of the woman's choice; they must be a helpmeet rather than a scold (as Cary Grant puts it to Katharine Hepburn in *The Philadelphia Story*). And here Emersonian perfectionism realizes or revises a possibility of the material basis of cinema as Cavell defines it at the outset of his work on film—as a succession of (automatic) world projections.²³

Conclusion: Conversing with Socrates

Since the writings of Emerson and Thoreau are not recognized, either by its professional philosophers or by the wider culture, as part of the philosophical inheritance of the United States, Cavell's critical intercourse with these films amounts to the disclosure of an internal relation between them (and so between American culture at its most popular and critically disdained) and philosophy as such. And once again, this relationship is doubled or reflexive: it applies to the content of the individual films—for example, their recurrent presentation of witty, elegant, and sophisticated exchanges about concepts (identity, change, desire, selfhood, freedom) in which philosophers have always been interested; but it also applies to the medium to which these films belong, a genre whose unifying myth and interlocutory structure presents a certain kind of conversation with an enabling friend as the indispensable means of a mode of personal transfiguration that is figured as unending self-overcoming, the repeated recovery from failures of intelligibility and the reiterated aspiration to make better sense of our ways of making sense of ourselves and the world we inhabit.

This perfectionist vision is, of course, one way of describing the context and nature of conversations with Socrates, as Plato presents it; it is philosophy's founding myth, even though its original recounter presents what Socrates embodies as dependent on overcoming mythological modes of self-understanding, as exemplified in the poets and dramatists of ancient Greece. On Cavell's understanding of these mid-twentieth-century cinematic comedies, American popular art—when properly conversant with its own wider cultural inheritance—is possessed of the means to contest Plato's version of that myth. It revises his account of poetry's necessary exile from the philosophical republic, representing it as overcomeable by a certain kind of marriage between art and philosophy—one whose medium is that of a meet and happy, but critical and open-ended, conversation about every clause of philosophy's and art's mythological accounts of their own unaccountable origins and goals. Is this a myth we might live by?

Notes

1 The comedies are: *The Lady Eve* (1941, dir. Sturges); *It Happened One Night* (1934, dir. Capra); *Bringing Up Baby* (1938, dir. Hawks); *The Philadelphia Story* (1940, dir. Cukor); *His Girl Friday* (1940, dir. Hawks); *Adam's Rib* (1949, dir. Cukor); and *The Awful Truth* (1939, dir. McCarey). The melodramas are: *Gaslight* (1944, dir. Cukor); *Letter from an Unknown Woman* (1948, dir. Ophüls); *Now, Voyager* (1942, dir. Rapper); and *Stella Dallas* (1937, dir. Vidor).
2 Stanley Cavell, "The Fact of Television," in *Cavell on Film*, ed. William Rothman (Albany: State University of New York Press, 2005), 64.
3 Stanley Cavell, *The World Viewed: Reflections on the Ontology of Film*, Enlarged Edition (Cambridge: Harvard University Press, 1979), 32.
4 Ibid., 31–32.
5 Ludwig Wittgenstein, *Philosophical Investigations*, revised fourth edition, trans. G. E. M. Anscombe, P. M. S. Hacker, and J. Schulte (Oxford: Blackwell, 2009), 67, 69, 88.

6 Stanley Cavell, *Pursuits of Happiness: The Hollywood Comedy of Remarriage* (Cambridge: Harvard University Press, 1981), 29.
7 Ibid., 28.
8 Ibid.
9 Ibid., 31–32.
10 Stanley Cavell, *The Claim of Reason: Wittgenstein, Skepticism, Morality, and Tragedy* (Cambridge: Cambridge University Press, 1979), 365.
11 Cavell, *Pursuits of Happiness*, 31.
12 Ibid., 29.
13 Ibid., 29–30.
14 Cavell, "The Fact of Television," 67.
15 Cavell, *The Claim of Reason*, 365.
16 Ibid.
17 Stanley Cavell, *Contesting Tears: The Melodrama of the Unknown Woman* (Chicago: The University of Chicago Press, 1996), 7.
18 Cavell, *Pursuits of Happiness*, 6.
19 Ibid., 5.
20 Cavell's *Cities of Words: Pedagogical Lessons on a Register of the Moral Life* (Cambridge: Harvard University Press, 2004) articulates this relation most explicitly and extensively.
21 Cavell, *Cities of Words,* 181.
22 Ibid., 189.
23 See Cavell, *The World Viewed*, 72.

PART II

Interlude: Temperaments for Film

5

My Troubled Relationship with Stanley Cavell: In Pursuit of a Truly Cinematic Conversation

SCOTT MACDONALD

The hope and the wish [for the future of film culture] are based as well on the fact that films persist as natural topics of conversation; they remain events, as few books or plays now do. I would like the conversation to be as good as its topics deserve, as precise and resourceful as the participants are capable of.
—STANLEY CAVELL, *PURSUITS OF HAPPINESS*[1]

WHEN I WAS INVITED TO CONTRIBUTE to an edited collection focusing on cine-philosopher Stanley Cavell, I was torn. In recent years there are things I've thought I've wanted to say about Cavell's work, but I am very far from being a Cavell expert. I've read this and that, but mostly in the early book, *Pursuits of Happiness: The Hollywood Comedy of Remarriage*—published in 1981 by Harvard University Press. The first Cavell essay I remember reading is "Film in the University," included as an appendix to *Pursuits of Happiness*. (I was surprised to discover that the essay was originally published in *Quarterly Review of Film Studies*, vol. 2, no. 1 [Spring, 1977], as "Film in the University or Leopards in Connecticut"; one of my first essays on cinema, "The Expanding Vision of Larry Gottheim's Films," appeared, exactly one year later, in that same journal.) I didn't get around to reading "Film in the University" until many years after its publication and when I did, I thought it both brilliant and useful.

What I've found most valuable in "Film in the University" is the following assertion (part of which I include on every syllabus I design):

> Because I know that the books whose reading I teach are better than anything I say about them; and because I believe that it is one, perhaps after all the fundamental, value of a teacher to put such books before students and to show that an adult human being takes them with whatever seriousness is at his, or her disposal; and because I know, furthermore, that the gift for teaching is as rare as any other human gift; my question is this: Is film worth teaching badly? And this is meant to ask: Does one believe that there are films the viewing of which is itself an education?[2]

Of course, one hopes one teaches well, but I certainly do agree with Cavell that there are films the viewing of which *is* an education, regardless of how a teacher presents them.

Where I have disagreed with Cavell has mostly to do with which films these are, or to be more precise, which kinds of films these are and, to return to the epigraph of this chapter, how a serious conversation regarding these films, and worthy of them, is most effectively developed.

That Cavell would include "Film in the University" as an appendix in *Pursuits of Happiness* certainly suggests that the films explored in that book are, for Cavell, some of those films "the viewing of which is an education" (though, of course, it may just be, or may also be, that he wanted that essay more widely available and the publication of *Pursuits of Happiness* was the first opportunity to make it so). Seven films are discussed in *Pursuits of Happiness*; listed in the order in which they're discussed, they are *The Lady Eve* (1941, dir. Preston Sturges), *It Happened One Night* (1934, dir. Frank Capra), *Bringing Up Baby* (1938, dir. Howard Hawks), *The Philadelphia Story* (1940, dir. George Cukor), *His Girl Friday* (1940, dir. Howard Hawks), *Adam's Rib* (1949, dir. George Cukor) and *The Awful Truth* (1937, dir. Leo McCarey). That Cavell means these films to be understood as masterworks seems evident in the book's opening paragraph: "The first claim is that these seven films constitute a particular genre of Hollywood talkie, a genre I will call the comedy of remarriage. I am for myself satisfied that this group of films is the principle group of Hollywood comedies after the advent of sound and therewith one definitive achievement in the history of the art of film."[3]

Cavell's brilliance as a reader of films and his remarkable reach as a scholar of literature as well as philosophy is obvious in *Pursuits of Happiness*—for example, he is at pains to demonstrate the ways in which the "genre" of remarriage builds on Shakespeare's comedies and the various forms of British comedy that followed. Indeed, when I developed and taught a course in classic American comedy in the fall of 2017, I made Cavell's discussion of *The Philadelphia Story* available to my students in order to demonstrate how deep, complex, and wide-ranging a scholar's reading of a popular comedy, in this case a popular comedy that remains engaging, can be.

I do have misgivings both about Cavell's sense that the seven films he explores in *Pursuits of Happiness* constitute a genre and about his contention that these seven films are the principal group of comedies of the early sound era. Most cineastes recognize romantic comedy as a genre and these films are certainly romantic comedies; they are distinguished only by the fact that the final, happily-ever-after marital conclusion is reached after a previous marriage has occurred. I see them not so much as a separate genre as a series of inventive plays on the convention, necessitated in part by the Hays Office censorship guidelines of the era, that romantic comedies end in marriage.

Cavell's commitment to the particular films he explores in *Pursuits of Happiness* also seems problematic. When I developed my recent syllabus for my comedy course, I did include *The Philadelphia Story* and *His Girl Friday*. But for me the "the principal group of comedies after the advent of sound"—putting Chaplin's *City Lights* (1932) and *Modern Times* (1935) aside—must include films by Ernst Lubitsch, several of which could be understood as being in some sense about remarriage: *One Hour with You* (1932, co-directed by George Cukor) and *Trouble in Paradise* (1932), most obviously, but also *Design for Living* (1933), *Ninotchka* (1939), *The Shop around the Corner* (1940), and *To Be or Not to Be* (1942). And to include *Adam's Rib* in the vaunted "principal group" over Cukor's *Born Yesterday*, made the following year, seems peculiar to me.

Obviously, one's choices of the principal comedies of that era are in some measure a matter of personal taste, as well as a function of when one is experiencing the films—*Adam's Rib* now seems less remarkable, at least to me, than it might have seemed in 1981, while *Born Yesterday* remains fresh. And the Lubitsch films feel especially interesting now, given their often-radical assumptions about the institution of marriage itself. My suspicion is that for Cavell the seven films that are the focus of *Pursuits of Happiness* were chosen as the principal comedies because, at least at a certain moment, they were the comedies that he felt could sustain the most interesting readings. For Cavell, producing insightful readings of films was, at least when he was writing *Pursuits of Happiness*, the crucial issue. He may say the films are better than anything he can say about them, but it is what he can say about them that implicitly demonstrates their significance. In other words, the films seem to be "the principal comedies" because they instigated the readings Cavell was most excited about developing.

I do remain grateful for Cavell's readings of the seven films. And his ultimate goal of bringing a deeper, more complex intelligence to the cultural conversation about popular romantic comedies was and remains estimable. However, my own understanding of what is interesting about cinema and how a scholar should engage what in 1981 was still a new academic field developed differently from Cavell's and involved a move away—a separation—from "reading" films and toward a different form of "conversation." I hope the reader can forgive the following extended detour, which I hope will help contextualize how I have come to understand this separation. The detour involves an unusual development in American academe and two particular events that were formative for my teaching and scholarship.

My first serious academic engagement with cinema occurred as part of the unusual and, so far as I am aware, unprecedented creation of an academic field of study, less as a result of faculty interest than of a demand by students across the country that courses be offered in what has come to be called cinema studies. When it became clear to administrators and faculty at the University of Florida (where I was a graduate student in American literature, writing a Ph.D. dissertation on Hemingway's short stories)[4] that a course in film history needed to be added to the curriculum of the Humanities Department, I volunteered to teach that course (I no longer remember if others taught other sections of the course—though I assume Professor William Childers, who enlisted me, must have—and I don't remember what films our students saw).

My volunteering was based on nothing more than the fact that I had always been a moviegoer and, like so many of my contemporaries, had been impressed by the "foreign films" finding their way into American movie theaters during the mid to late 1960s and by Andrew Sarris' use of the French-inspired auteur theory to create serious interest in the films of Buster Keaton, Howard Hawks, Ernst Lubitsch, John Ford, and others. It is emblematic of this moment in the modern history of academe that my teaching this one class was instrumental in my getting my first postgraduate-school full-time teaching job, at what was then Utica College of Syracuse University (now Utica College). My teaching duties included first-year writing courses, a course in twentieth-century American literature, and a regularly offered course in "film appreciation."

I soon realized that my enthusiasm for cinema was not a form of expertise! Not only had there not been film courses in my educational history, it was also difficult to find serious, not to mention scholarly, books on cinema. And worst of all, it was still challenging to see anything but first-run films in a context that would allow for careful study (this was before the advent of VHS tapes and later, DVDs). I was reasonably confident in my classes on American literature and expository writing, but I felt at sea as a film professor. So, when I received a letter announcing a New York State "University-wide Film Symposium," to be hosted by Binghamton University (then SUNY-Binghamton), on a weekend in April of 1972, I made plans to attend.

According to the fancy announcement, the event was organized into halves: on Saturday the focus would be "films by independent film artists"; Sunday would be devoted to a lecture by Lawrence Alloway on "The Commercial Film," followed by a panel discussion on "The Role of Film in the University."[5] I wasn't entirely clear what exactly "films by independent film artists" might be and decided to attend that screening, then make a decision (in collaboration with two colleagues who had traveled to Binghamton with me) about whether to stay for what followed. But in fact, we left immediately after the Saturday afternoon screening, not even waiting until Saturday evening when a "feature film currently in production at Binghamton," directed by Hollywood legend Nicholas Ray, was scheduled.

I have written about that Saturday afternoon screening on several occasions—most recently in the introduction to *Binghamton Babylon: Voices from the Cinema Department, 1967-1977*[6]—and will not provide much detail about the experience here, except to say that the films I saw frightened me more than any horror film I'd ever seen. I remember seeing four films: Ken Jacobs' *Soft Rain* (1968), Ernie Gehr's *Serene Velocity* (1970), Larry Gottheim's *Barn Rushes* (1971), and Stan Brakhage's *The Act of Seeing with One's Own Eyes* (1972). Apparently *Happy Mother's Day*, the canonical documentary co-made by Ricky Leacock and Joyce Chopra in 1963, was shown, but I have no memory of seeing it then. The four films I do remember are better known now, at least among serious cineastes, but in April 1972, they were unlike anything I'd ever experienced in a theater.

During the twelve minutes of *Soft Rain*, the viewer sees three identical, continuous, 100-foot, silent, fixed-camera shots of a New York City street in light rain (projected at silent speed): the camera records the street from above and from a distance, across an open space that is framed on the left and right by the walls of buildings; below, by a roof, and above by a black rectangle (it gradually becomes clear that this rectangle is a piece of paper attached to the camera). For *Serene Velocity* Ernie Gehr filmed an empty SUNY-Binghamton hallway, using a zoom lens that he adjusted so that during twenty-three minutes the film takes us, multiple times per second, simultaneously closer to and further from the doorway at the end of the hallway, again in silence. *Barn Rushes* is a series of eight, three-minute, silent, multi-shot passes by the same barn, filmed from a moving car at different times of day and during different moments in the summer and fall. And *The Act of Seeing with One's Own Eyes*, the final film shown that afternoon, is a handheld, in-close, half-hour, silent exploration of autopsies in the Pittsburgh morgue (the title is a rough translation of "autopsy").

These descriptions don't provide anything like a sense of the power of the films or what I understand now as their accomplishments and implications. Their original negative impact on me had primarily to do with the fact that the first three seemed more like aggressive jokes than legitimate movies, that all (except *Happy Mother's Day*) were resolutely silent, that *The Act of Seeing* was shockingly visceral, and that the films were "edited" into what seemed like an interminable two-hour screening. When the lights came up,

I was furious. I waited for the audience to rise in rebellion and admonish Gottheim and Jacobs who were hosting the event, for their curatorial failure. But, in fact, those present gave no indication that they had seen anything unusual (I do remember that during the discussion Ricky Leacock, in his distinctive voice, said something like, "What about *boredom?*"). As a filmgoer, I was intellectually at sea in an entirely new way and, like my Utica colleagues, interested only in getting out of Binghamton.

In the days that followed, I gradually found my bearings and, at first grudgingly, then with increasing excitement, came to realize that my sense of what was possible in cinema had been challenged and transformed. Soon I was teaching *Serene Velocity*, *Barn Rushes*, *The Act of Seeing* and other films by Gehr, Gottheim, and Brakhage (along with Keaton, Welles, Ford, Buñuel, Kurosawa, and others), and finding my way into the wide world of independent cinema—"independent" of Hollywood and industrial film production in general. And in June–July of the following year, I attended another, more elaborate event (this one organized by the University Film Study Center): a three-week Summer Institute on Film and Photography hosted by Hampshire College, where I took a series of three intensive one-week courses: Ethnographic Film, taught by John Marshall; Documentary Film, taught by Alberto Cavalcanti; and Independent American Film, taught by Sheldon Renan.

At the Institute I also attended regular evening screenings of silent film classics, hosted by David Shepard, as well as a premiere of Jonas Mekas' *Reminiscences of a Journey to Lithuania* (1972), introduced by Mekas; and (here I come back, at long last, toward Stanley Cavell and *Pursuits of Happiness*) a screening of the first three sections of Hollis Frampton's seven-part *Hapax Legomena* series: *(nostalgia)* (1971), *Poetic Justice* (1972), and *Critical Mass* (1971), introduced by Peter Feinstein and Frampton ("hapax legomena" refers to words that appear only once in a language, like Latin, that is no longer spoken outside of particular institutional contexts, and therefore can never be precisely defined).

At the Frampton screening many in the audience were apparently having an experience similar to mine at Binghamton, and were becoming increasingly frustrated as the screening proceeded. *(nostalgia)* is an autobiographical film during which individual Frampton photographs are placed, one by one, on a hot plate that is then turned on. As each photograph burns and, during three minutes, transforms slowly into ash, we are hearing a verbal description of the next photograph we will see (along with an account of the social and aesthetic context within which it was made) *and* we are simultaneously trying to remember what was said earlier about the photograph—that the hot plate is continuing to transform from a representation into an abstraction. In other words, *(nostalgia)* demands a form of active viewing fundamentally different from anything I'm aware of in the earlier history of cinema.

Poetic Justice, the second film in the *Hapax Legomena* series, is Frampton's joke on a fundamental assumption of the film industry, that there must be a screenplay before there can be a film. All one sees in *Poetic Justice* (the film is silent) are the individual pages—one by one, six seconds per page—of a 240-page "screenplay" that because of the ambiguous wording of its minimal directions can, in fact, never be shot—though I expect that viewers cannot avoid mentally "shooting" imaginary films as they read the texts. *Poetic Justice* is cinematic "poetic justice" for those who accept traditional filmmaking procedures as the only way in which film art can be created. The audience endured "First Tableau," the initial 60-page section of the screenplay, but when "Second Tableau" and page 61 appeared—making clear that the film was just beginning—many in the audience left, some demonstrating their frustration by stomping up the stairs and slamming doors as they left. Very few of us remained to see the end of *Poetic Justice*, then to enjoy *Critical Mass*—a film that Steve Anker remembers Nicholas Ray calling "the funniest film since Lubitsch."[7]

Like the films Cavell discusses in *Pursuits of Happiness*, *Critical Mass* depicts an often-comic struggle between a couple—in this case, however, a struggle between lovers that does not end in marriage or remarriage, but in what we presume will ultimately be a separation—and, implicitly, an unusual kind of cinematic "divorce." The young man (played by Frank Albetta) has gone away for a weekend without telling the young woman (Barbara DiBenedetto) and is refusing to explain his absence. The resulting argument was improvised for the film and recorded in two continuous sync-sound shots.[8] Over the following months Frampton devised a complex restructuring of the argument that has two general dimensions.

At the beginning of the film, the sound of an argument is heard (there is no image as yet). Then imagery of the feuding lovers—dressed in black, standing in front of a bare white wall—becomes visible. Their arguing continues for six minutes, until the image disappears. For a time we again hear the couple without seeing them, this time during what seems like a pause in the give-and-take and perhaps a moment of make-up eroticism, then the image returns and the argument revs up again and continues until the image disappears a second time. The couple can be heard, continuing to argue, for a moment before the film ends.

The second organizational component involves the relationship of sound and image during the two extended moments when we both see and hear the couple. The first extended moment is a heavily edited, sync-sound passage during which the argument is presented in continual, looped overlap: "... when we're suppos/when we're supposedly/supposedly living together/ living together ..." During the image/sound sequence after the sound-only middle section, the presentation of the argument grows increasingly out of sync, until near the end of the film we recognize that we are re-seeing one moment of the argument while re-hearing the sound from a quite different moment.

Of course, on one level these two structural elements reflect the implicit narrative of the film. One partner in the relationship (the image) is sometimes "away," sometimes present (and Frampton offers no explanation). And the movement from sync, in the first image-sound sequence, to the increasingly out of sync second sequence reflects the slowly deteriorating relationship, which is not just boringly repetitive, but is growing more and more "out-of-sync."

How one takes Ray's comment that *Critical Mass* is "the funniest film since Lubitsch" depends, of course, on whether one does, in fact, find the film funny (obviously this is also true of the films Cavell discusses in *Pursuits of Happiness*; even *The Philadelphia Story* might not be laugh-out-loud funny for some current audiences). When I have shown the Frampton film in my classes, I have heard frequent laughter, but this is humor generated in a different way from the humor in the films discussed in *Pursuits of Happiness*. In the Cukor film, which, of course, is adapted from the Philip Barry play, it is the wit of the language (within Barry's original play and the Donald Ogden Stewart and Waldo Salt screenplay) and the actors' delivery of their lines that creates the humor. In *Critical Mass* the humor has somewhat different sources. The interchange between Barbara and Frank is often amusing; their candid language, their interrupting each other, and their references to "fucking" and "screwing" would have seemed a bit more outrageous in 1971 than they do now—though college audiences still seem to find this aspect of their dialogue engaging and funny, especially in an academic context.

The primary source of the comedy in *Critical Mass*, however, is fundamentally cinematic: a function of Frampton's witty editing of image and sound. The interruptive, looping repetition of the dialogue was, and remains, a comic surprise and it is difficult not to laugh at what this technique does to the interchange between Barbara and Frank, particularly since it confirms an aspect of real human interchange that is rarely a part of "normal" arguments in film: the fact that when real lovers or marital partners argue, they tend to confront, over and over, the same issues, repeating much the same language, while often interrupting each other. Indeed, part of the comedy of Frampton's film is that this expressionistically edited argument is far more true to the nature of real arguing than the well-written gives-and-takes of Hollywood comedies.

It is also true that *Critical Mass* isn't simply funny. From a gender-aware point of view, the basic situation seems unfair to Barbara, and it echoes the era in gender relations that preceded the new feminist awakening of the late 1960s and 1970s where men were more out-in-the-world than women and did not feel obliged to be candid about the full reality of their lives, at least with their wives. Underneath the argument between Barbara and Frank, and emphasized by the way in which Frampton expands the original improvisational interchange into a longer cine-conversation, is what we realize is Barbara's embarrassment about how she is being treated and the pain this causes. In fact, there is reason to believe that even though Frampton chose DiBenedetto and Albetta for the roles because he had been told they were the two people in the SUNY-Binghamton cinema program "most likely to fly off the handle," their passionate interchange in the film was to some degree a result of the fact that they had just finished an affair.[9]

Understanding that underneath the humor in *Critical Mass* lies the very real pain that may fuel the DiBenedetto/Albetta dialogue does not destroy the humor. After all, the humor in most comedies, ever since Chaplin began *The Kid* (1921) with the epigraph, "A picture with a smile—and perhaps, a tear," is contextualized by situations that are not necessarily all that funny (in Chaplin, of course, often abject poverty). It is unclear to me whether Frampton was fully aware of the gender inequality of the situation in *Critical Mass*, or whether this is something more obvious to audiences in the present day. But it is not unusual for classic Hollywood comedies to reveal problematic issues that seem more obvious now. Uncle Willie (Roland Young) in *The Philadelphia Story* reads differently now than he presumably did in 1940—and no longer contributes unproblematically to the film's humor.

In *Pursuits of Happiness* Cavell makes clear that he understands the comedies he discusses as "participating in . . . a conversation with their culture,"[10] and he brings his expansive sense of the history of Western culture, especially written culture and thought (literature, social theory, philosophy), to bear on the films. In his discussion of *The Philadelphia Story* he argues that the film communicates the idea that the freedom and honesty necessary for a happy marriage—happy both physically and spiritually— is a microcosm of what is necessary for a healthy nation. For Cavell the events that play out in the film, and particularly the final remarriage of Dexter (Cary Grant) and Tracy (Katharine Hepburn), ultimately represent a hoped-for unification in America of the Hellenic and Hebraic traditions, represented by Dexter and Tracy respectively, "so that American mankind can refind its object, its dedication to a more perfect union, toward the perfected human community, its right to the pursuit of happiness."[11]

Frampton understands *Critical Mass* as participating in a conversation with the very dimension of American *film* culture that Cavell explores in *Pursuits of Happiness*. Once we remember that after the advent of sound, a conventional film was completed only once the image track and the soundtrack were said to have been "married," we can see that, not only on the historical level, but also on what might be called the cine-metaphysical level, the slowly deteriorating relationship between Frank and Barbara can be understood as an emblem of the rebellion of Frampton (and other independent film artists of the late 1960s and early 1970s) against two of the traditions represented by classical Hollywood filmmaking: that all romantic comedies end in the happy marriage of the protagonists and that the particular technologies that are the basis for the cinema experience should be invisible, should remain suppressed.

To put this another way, Frampton's film is in "conversation" with the cultural and aesthetic assumptions and technological bases of the commercial film industry and the America it is understood to represent. For Cavell the comedies of remarriage confirm the idea that society is at its best when good marriages are made and/or remade. *Critical Mass* responds, confirming that romantic relationships often involve struggle (which, of course, is the source of the comedy in the remarriage films), but implicitly argues that society is truly at its best when one has the freedom to explore the nature and possibilities of relationship itself. *Critical Mass* suggests that a belief in life, liberty, and pursuit of happiness includes confronting and examining what are considered the limits of self-expression within both romantic relationships and the art of cinema—as well as within American society at large.

One might call *Critical Mass* a comedy of *de-marriage* (or at least de-"marriage," since Barbara and Frank were not formally married). Of course, divorce is usually seen as a painful experience, but those who have gone through a divorce (including some of the characters in the films Cavell explores in *Pursuits of Happiness*) know that along with the pain, anger, and frustration, there are also comic aspects to the process—and this is particularly the case, at least in retrospect, when the divorce can be said to have improved the lives of the parties involved. More to the point here, it is precisely Frampton's decision to interrupt the standard conventions of filmic conversation, then to "de-marry" the soundtrack from the image track, that is the source of the energy, and the humor, of *Critical Mass*—as well as a memorable demonstration that cinema is capable of a considerable range of powerful and transformative experiences, some of which we might not imagine if our focus is primarily on Hollywood entertainments.

There are other levels to what I see as the film-historical "conversation" between Cavell/*The Philadelphia Story* and Frampton/*Critical Mass*. Cavell recognizes that one might read the Haven family's distaste for Tracy's fiancé George (a financially self-made man who looks to unite himself with Tracy and her upper-class family) and her ultimate decision to end their engagement and remarry Dexter, as the snobbish rejection "of an upstart from a lower class, an inferior"—but argues that the "expulsion" of George is implicitly "a gesture of a promise to be rid of classes as such, and so to be rid of George as one wedded to the thoughts of class division, to the crossing rather than the overcoming of class."[12] This is a subtle distinction that may make sense within the narrative playing out in *The Philadelphia Story*. However, it ignores the fact that it is not simply these "Philadelphians" who are economically and politically privileged; the film itself is resolutely "upper class," as well. This is obvious not only in the film's subtle satire of George, but also in the box-office power of Grant, Hepburn, and Stewart, and in every dimension of the film's set-design, costuming, and presentation of itself.

Critical Mass confronts the issue of class in a different way: it demonstrates that an amusing, engaging film about a love relationship in crisis can be made entirely outside of the financial "class system" of industrial film production. All the films discussed in *Pursuits of Happiness* were big-budget enterprises produced by major studios, directed by established directors working with the participation of major stars within an established genre. The minimalist production design of *Critical Mass* and Frampton's decision to work with untrained actors improvising a simple scenario, plus the fact that this half-hour film involved only two 16mm shots made on a single day, doesn't merely suggest *a hope* that the problematic dimensions of the American class system might be overcome by a "marriage" of historical forces. *Critical Mass* is a literal democratization of the filmmaking production process, a cinematic demonstration that a filmmaker who grew up in a working-class home without substantial financial resources can make a brilliant film about a romantic relationship in crisis, and by doing so become part of the evolving conversation of American film culture.

It is not difficult to come up with a list of other independent films that simultaneously explore the terms of the institution of marriage and the institution of cinema: my choices would include Maya Deren's *Meshes of the Afternoon* (1943), Stan Brakhage's *Wedlock House: An Intercourse* (1959), Carolee Schneemann's *Fuses* (1967), William Greaves' *Symbiopsychotaxiplasm: Take One* (1971) and *Symbiopsychotaxiplasm: Take 2 ½* (2005), Martin Arnold's *Pièce Touchée* (1989), and Sarah Polley's *Stories We Tell* (2013)—as well as Alfred Guzzetti's *Family Portrait Sittings* (1975), Ed Pincus' *Diaries (1971-1976)* (1981), and Ross McElwee's *Charleen* (1977), all three of which were produced by filmmakers who were Cavell's colleagues at Harvard during the time when he was writing the essays that became *Pursuits of Happiness*.

All these films offer potentially illuminating recontextualizations of Hollywood romantic comedy (including the "Hollywood Comedy of Remarriage") and American marriage itself that are as fascinating and potentially transformative as the seven films Cavell discusses and his readings of them. Indeed, had Cavell been able to see various kinds of film in "conversation" with each other, these films might have enriched his readings.[13]

I have come to understand the approach to cinema history represented by Cavell's brilliant discussion of *The Philadelphia Story* (and by *Pursuits of Happiness* as a whole) as fundamentally an attempt to marry cinema history to literary history, to "read" cinema into the history of literature, in the sense of rendering an audiovisual medium into sophisticated literary rhetoric. And I've come to believe that this way of dealing with the history of cinema and cinematic accomplishment is detrimental to academic cinema studies.

Early on, as I was trying to find a way to function as a scholar in relation to the independent films that I had grown fascinated with, I tended to write about them as if they were pieces of written literature. When I was first showing my essays to the filmmakers I was writing about (I thought they might be excited to read them), they would explain that my written articulations, however interesting they might seem to me, had virtually nothing to do with what they understood about their filmmaking.[14] Gradually I learned that I needed to divorce myself from the ways in which I engaged the literature I wrote about, in order to do justice to the films that mattered to me. I came to believe that my best way of supporting the kinds of films that were expanding my sense of film history was to work at understanding what Stephen Colbert might call the "film-iness" of the films that fascinated me—and to put before my students (and as often as possible, before nonstudent audiences) "conversations" among films that might be expected to expand their sense of all that film has been, is, and can be.

Stanley Cavell demonstrated, as fully as anyone, that interesting literature can be written about conventional popular films. For me, however, the implicit "dialogue" within film history not only between instances of particular genres, but more importantly between different kinds of film and different approaches to filmmaking, is more interesting than any conversation within a particular film, or any "conversation" between the reader of a film (no matter how brilliant) and the film itself, or any conversation that might develop between scholarly readers writing about any one film or type of film.

The ongoing, ever-evolving conversation that is the meta-history of cinema remains my central fascination, and in my teaching, programming, and writing I work to reflect on it as best I can. The early wave of theoretical and analytical writing about cinema during its first decades within academe was probably crucial for establishing cinema studies as an academic field, but academics coming from literature (and philosophy) to cinema have generally remained wedded to verbal articulation at the expense of cinematic discourse. Within our world of constant distraction (and within the logocentric world of academe), our fundamental obligation as cinema and media scholars is to demonstrate the full range of cinema and how the myriad types of cinematic accomplishment can "speak" to each other—expanding our awareness and understanding of both cinema and the larger world within which it functions.

I offer an apology to Cavell scholars for whatever elements of my argument here might seem, or be, unfair, given the myriad writings Cavell has produced since *Pursuits of Happiness*. I wish life had given me time to explore more thoroughly both the world of cinema *and* the world of literature about cinema. My training as a literature scholar certainly tells me that I should have read far more deeply into Cavell's oeuvre before writing this chapter. But new and fascinating films continue to demand my attention, and given my obligations as a cinema scholar, I cannot turn away from these films, from the ways in which they continue to transform the cinematic dialogue, and from the opportunity to make others more fully aware of them.

Notes

1. Stanley Cavell, *Pursuits of Happiness: The Hollywood Comedy of Remarriage* (Cambridge: Harvard University Press, 1981), 38–39.
2. Ibid., 270.
3. Ibid., 1.
4. The dissertation is available here: http://ufdc.ufl.edu/UF00097727/00001/9j?search=MacDonald+%3dScott).
5. The panel: Larry Gottheim, Kenneth Jacobs, Richard Leacock, and Gerald O'Grady.
6. Scott MacDonald, *Binghamton Babylon: Voices from the Cinema Department 1967–1977 (a nonfiction novel)* (Albany: State University of New York Press, 2015).
7. MacDonald, *Binghamton Babylon*, 95. Anker, a graduate of the SUNY-Binghamton Cinema Department, recently retired after years of service as dean at the California Institute of the Arts. *Critical Mass* was shot at SUNY-Binghamton, under the auspices of the Cinema Department.
8. Thanks to Kenneth Eisenstein for this information. Eisenstein believes that the image-less middle section of *Critical Mass* occurred during the change from one 400-foot roll of 16mm film to the other—as the tape-recorder continued to run.
9. Hollis Frampton: "I asked around the film department, which was well populated by volatile personalities, for the names of the two people, the man and the woman, that by consensus were judged most likely to fly off the handle. There was virtual unanimity that Barbara DiBenedetto and Frank Albetta were my two best bets." Scott MacDonald, *A Critical Cinema* (Berkeley: University of California Press, 1988), 66.

    Steve Anker: "I was good friends with Barbara DiBenedetto at that point and the roommate of Frank Albetta, and if I remember correctly, they had just finished an affair. When Barbara saw the film, she hit the roof in a way that I still remember vividly; I thought she was going to have apoplexy. I don't agree with her reaction, but I think she was sensitive about seeing herself on screen in that histrionic way, with that voice, and so cut up in the editing and in the middle of an altercation with somebody who, on top of everything else, she probably had real feelings about. Of course, Hollis was looking for true chemistry and he got it." MacDonald, *Binghamton Babylon*, 95.
10. Cavell, *Pursuits of Happiness*, 151.

11 Ibid., 158–59.
12 Ibid., 156.
13 I have always been puzzled that Cavell did not write about the fine work being made around him, though his Harvard colleagues speak of him with great respect—apparently suppressing whatever frustration they might have felt with his decision, as a writer, to ignore their work.

   In a recent email to me (6/10/18), Ross McElwee said that Cavell "wrote a wonderful letter after seeing a work-in-progress version of *Bright Leaves* [2003].... Stanley was wonderfully supportive of my work, both as a friend and as a colleague—and, of course, as a misplaced Southerner. He and I attended a conference at the University of South Carolina, organized by Cavell scholar, Professor Larry Rhu, who, I believe, had been a student of Stanley's during his undergraduate days at Harvard. There was a side panel devoted to my films and several papers were presented. Stanley graciously attended this morning event, which touched me."

   In another email (11/27/18), Alfred Guzzetti told me: "I'm no Cavell scholar, but I've read several of his books, and a number of essays, some very carefully, have heard him speak and teach, participated in seminars with him. His range of interests was enormous, even in film. As you say, *Pursuits of Happiness* chooses movies that touched some of his interests, both in philosophy and in literature.

   "But he did, after all, spend every Tuesday evening of a whole academic year, 1971–72, coming together with a small group of us to scrutinize *2 or 3 Things I Know about Her*, in microscopic detail, image by image, sound by sound, allusion by allusion. He was intensely interested and every sentence he spoke was full of astounding insight, of things I could never have thought of. It was he who approached me about the idea of turning my seminar notes into a book and ferried it to Harvard University Press, which I doubt would have taken it seriously otherwise.

   "I remember him going over my film *Air* in detail with me. He did indeed see *Family Portrait Sittings* in 1975 and though he didn't write about it, very likely he encouraged Bill Rothman to. I remember a seminar in which the topic was *W. R. Mysteries of the Organism*, anything but a literary film, when Stanley as usual offered a stream of insights. I remember him coming to a faculty (and student?) discussion of student films, including an observational documentary about fishing made by my class working as a group, and offering comments that only he could have thought of."
14 As I remember, this happened first with J. J. Murphy, then later, with Carolee Schneemann.

6

Film as Film and the Personal

WILLIAM ROTHMAN

STANLEY CAVELL HADN'T READ A WORD of Victor Perkins' writings when he wrote *The World Viewed*, nor had Perkins read any of Cavell's writings when he wrote *Film as Film*.[1] Nonetheless, the two books have innumerable parallels. Nearly every feature of the medium Cavell cites, Perkins cites, too. Both offer virtually identical explanations of the way film, a photographic medium, can render fantasy as readily as reality. Perkins' discussion of Hitchcock's two Albert Hall sequences highlights a fact Cavell, too, ponders, that film is capable of dissolving the difference between seeing and reading, between what our eyes literally see and what we know. And so on. Are such parallels surprising? These were supremely smart men committed to finding the truth of the matter. And all it took was to trust good films to teach how to think about them—and to not let some theory blind them to their own experience.

   The theory whose grip both felt the need to loosen was what *Film as Film* calls the "orthodox theory," which defines film as a purely visual art. Both had more sympathy for Bazin's opposing theory, but distanced themselves from it, too. Both took popular movies at their best to be exemplary of the art of film and stuck to their guns when academic film study embraced a new orthodoxy and it became dogma that the kind of movies both affirmed were pernicious ideological constructs, not works of art to be valued. And both kept faith with their conviction that, as Cavell put it, the study of film can't be a worthwhile human enterprise if it isolates itself from the kind of criticism Walter Benjamin had in mind when he argued that what establishes a work *as* art is its ability to inspire criticism that seeks to articulate the work's *idea*—not a thought lying *behind* the work, but a thought it expresses, in its own way, in its own medium, the kind of criticism Perkins, like Cavell, was inspired to write.

I say this even though *Film as Film* characterizes its goal as providing a rational basis for aesthetic judgments of films. Perkins didn't write criticism as if its primary task was *judging* films or directors, in effect weighing how many Michelin stars, if any, to award them. Rather, his criticism bespeaks a conviction that its value resides in discerning what a given film is about and what it has to say about what it is about—what Cavell calls its *idea*: "Every worthwhile human enterprise, has its poetry," Cavell writes. "Film is a worthwhile human enterprise" that achieves its particular poetry when it achieves the perception that "every motion and station, in particular every human posture and gesture, however glancing, has its poetry, or you may say its lucidity." The poetry of film is open to all to perceive. We fail to perceive it only if we fail to see—truly see—those "motions and stations and postures and gestures" by which films express their ideas. The "worthwhile human enterprise" whose possibilities Perkins' and Cavell's film criticism aspires to perfect is perceiving the poetry of film and tracing its implications.

I can't honestly say, though, as many of you can, that Perkins' work taught me how to think about films. In the 1960s, I wasn't a regular reader of *Movie*. I wish I had been, for it would have been sweet, over these all too many years, to have been able to count all the *Movie* regulars, not just Perkins, as dear friends. But it was Andrew Sarris' articles in *The Village Voice*, later expanded into *The American Cinema*, that awakened me to the fact that within the popular American cinema there were directors who left personal stamps on their films. As a critic, Sarris wasn't in the same league as Perkins. Sarris *did* take his main task to be ranking films and directors. And he lacked the critical tools to justify his rankings in terms that satisfied me, or even explain what made some directors "auteurs" and others not. His claim was that the films of "auteur" directors expressed their *personalities*. I knew that couldn't be right, since directors are outside the projected world. Then what part of a director's self might a film express? That some directors' films are profoundly personal is an idea important to *Film as Film*, too. But what it *means* for a film to be profoundly personal is a question Perkins' book doesn't address. For it's a *philosophical* question that can only be addressed by writing, like *The World Viewed*, that *is* philosophy. Philosophy, for Cavell, is "any place at which the human spirit allows itself to be under its own question, indeed, that allows that questioning to happen." *The World Viewed* is a "place at which the human spirit allows itself to be under its own question." *Film as Film* is not.

In 1964, Cavell, newly arrived at Harvard, offered a graduate seminar on the aesthetics of film that he allowed me, a lowly junior, to take. In *The World Viewed* he calls this seminar a failure. It didn't fail me. But I no more learned how to think about film from Cavell than from Perkins.

What Cavell taught me was that when I think about film my way, I am doing philosophy. In many respects, my writing about film is more like Perkins' than Cavell's. It's the aspiration to philosophy that brings me into

Cavell's orbit. "Film is an interest of mine, or say a love," Cavell writes, "not separate from my interest in, or love of, philosophy. So, when I am drawn to think through a film, I do not regard the reading that results as over, even provisionally, until I have said how it bears on the nature of film generally and on philosophy." In *The World Viewed*, reflections on the historical significance of the *event* of film, its significance for Western art and philosophy, are strand over strand with reflections on film's significance for its author personally. *Film as Film* isn't concerned with such matters. Marian Keane and I argued, in our book about *The World Viewed,* that what motivates its writing is a question the entirety of the book is concerned with answering. In this "metaphysical memoir" about the period of his life when going to the movies was a regular part of his week, Cavell shares intimate confidences with the reader. In his early *Movie* articles and in *Film as Film*, Perkins does not. When Perkins writes, in his great 1963 essay on Nicholas Ray, "Almost every man acts from a position of profound uncertainty and insecurity," he leaves open the possibility that he himself—perhaps Ray, too—is an exception. But in his late book on *The Rules of the Game*—surely, there is no greater book of film criticism—he uses the phrase "like all of us" to acknowledge that he, too, acts—writes—from such a position. But he voices his confession in a tone that is anything but confessional. Cavell once observed that the need he felt in writing about film to "become evocative in capturing the moods of faces and motions and settings" left "permanent marks" on his philosophical prose. Perkins' prose tends to *avoid* becoming evocative. His assertions seem made with certainty—disinterestedly, dispassionately, from the security of an aesthetic distance. *Rationally*. And yet, surely, expressing himself in this impersonally rational voice was his *way* of being personal—a mask that revealed, revealed *by* masking, who he was. Who was he?

When Archie Leach willed himself to become Cary Grant, it was an instance of what Jean Rouch called a "fictional part of oneself being the most real part of one's self." I still say "cawffee" but little else in my native Brooklynese, but once a Brooklyn boy, always a Brooklyn boy. Perkins had his reasons, obvious and not, for willing himself to become the person for whom that voice of "impersonal rationality" was the "most real" expression of who he was. Still, once a Devonshire lad, always a Devonshire lad. The Victor Perkins he had been no longer existed, but the Victor Perkins he was, he also was not. He made his own the voice, still endemic among analytical philosophers, of those articles in philosophy journals that were a cross I had to bear on the road to my Ph.D.—a voice ideal for dismissing others as if they were social inferiors one was entitled to put down with impunity. But when Perkins, in that voice, expressed disdain for directors who stoop to "weepfests" or unsparingly criticized students, it was different. He was asserting, not his *personal* superiority, but the superiority of being rational—a path open to all.

There's a country music song that begins, "Beneath still waters, there's a strong undertow. The surface won't tell you what the deep waters know." In his Ray essay, Perkins attributes to the director's latest films a quality he calls "passionate placidity"—a perfect description of his own writing. Beneath the placid surface of his impersonally rational prose is a strong undertow of passion—his love of film, inseparable from his empathy for characters whose uncertainty and insecurity he recognized as also his own—that threatens or, better, *promises* to sweep us from the safe harbor of reason into turbulent, uncharted waters. Like Cavell, Perkins hewed to the discipline of meaning everything he says, but not to Cavell's discipline of saying everything he means—even, or especially, what seems unsayable. There are depths of emotion in films Perkins loved that he couldn't speak about in that voice of impersonal rationality—depths acknowledged only by what he consigned to silence. That silence doesn't *express*, but neither does it *deny*, his emotion. If it did, Perkins wouldn't have been the great film critic he was.

In *Film as Film*, Perkins analyses the scene in *55 Days in Peking* (1963, dir. Nicholas Ray) in which the Charlton Heston character informs a young half-Chinese girl that her American father had been killed in action. Rejecting the temptation to milk easy tears, Ray focuses not on the girl, but on the Heston character's unwillingness to deal with her emotion—or his own. But Perkins leaves it unsaid that a parallel can be drawn between the Heston character and Ray, whose decision to avoid dwelling on the girl might be seen as manifesting his own unwillingness to deal with emotion. And the same parallel can be drawn with Perkins, who praises Ray for not letting the girl distract him from his study of the Heston character—as if the director, like a scientist, is viewing the character from a secure, dispassionate position. Perkins leaves it unsaid that Ray's study—it's also a *critique*—could be of a character he sees as like himself. If the sequence didn't have a confessional dimension, what would make it profoundly personal to Ray? And what, if anything, makes Perkins' "study" of Ray's "study" profoundly personal?

Cavell writes, "What I found in turning to think about film was a medium which seemed simultaneously to be free of the imperative to philosophy and at the same time inevitably to reflect upon itself—as though the condition of philosophy were its natural condition." Painting only brought itself "under its own question" when painters like Manet couldn't make paintings they believed in without breaking with the tradition they wished to keep alive. But being "under its own question" *is* film's tradition, *The World Viewed* argues. That a film could express an idea about itself, itself *as* a film, is a possibility *Film as Film* consigns to silence. Nowhere does that silence speak more loudly than in Perkins' analysis of *Psycho*'s shower murder. He argues, brilliantly, that Marion "is destroyed by an explosion of forces existing within her own personality: the savage equation of sex and punishment, the self-comforting contempt for others' desires. Implicated as we have been in Marion's thought, we cannot entirely refuse the guilt of Mother's action." But from what position does Hitchcock express this idea? It's an idea central to *The Murderous Gaze*—an idea profoundly personal to me—that Hitchcock films are "under their own question."[2] In a Hitchcock film, the nature of love, murder, sexuality, marriage, and theater are at issue, but so is the nature of the camera, the act of viewing, and directing as a calling—what it revealed about Hitchcock, and what it made of him, that he made the role of director his own in the particular way he did, and what that way was, can't be separated from *Psycho*'s "idea." Hitchcock's films aren't dispassionate "studies." The fate of his soul was at stake, as Perkins later acknowledged in his 2000 "I Confess" essay, which ends with this strongly Cavell- (and perhaps Rothman-) inflected passage: "If, as I believe, Hitchcock's ambition was to shape this film as his own confession he was making an avowal of his riven nature, his inability to find a point of rest between the desire for recognition and the terror of being known. So he was one of us, after all."[3]

When I choke up reading my own paper at a conference—an experience I doubt Perkins ever had—I take it as a sign that I've gotten it right. I'm as American as Perkins was English. I respect his writing, and he respected mine, but I no more want to write like him than he wanted to write like me. To write in my voice, he'd have had to indulge in the sentimentality he detested. To write in his, I'd have to consign to silence what I have at heart to say about films I love, films that to me are philosophy, films that move me to write about them in a way that makes philosophy. Don't get me wrong. That *Film as Film* isn't a book of philosophy doesn't make it inferior to *The World Viewed*, much less to *The Murderous Gaze*. Philosophy isn't everyone's cup of tea. But it was Cavell's. And it is mine. I fervently believe it was Hitchcock's cup of tea, too, even if his films served it with a pinch of arsenic.

Perkins writes, "Ray's films show man as an intruder in a turbulent and indifferent, or hostile, universe. His hero often journeys into a primitive landscape like that of the Everglades in search of a lost certainty, a lost harmony between man and his environment. But he brings with him his own inner conflicts, which make that harmony unattainable." Ray himself, journeying into the primitive landscape of Hollywood, was such a hero. So was that Devonshire lad who journeyed into the turbulent and hostile or indifferent universe of the English academic world. When Perkins writes, "Ray looks toward an ideal relationship of man to nature, like that of man to man, in which the struggle for domination is resolved by the recognition of interdependence," he leaves it unsaid that Ray's dream was his own as well. It was also Cavell's, and Emerson's before him. In *The World Viewed*, it was already a theme, which he was only later to connect with Emerson's way of thinking, that human beings are *in* nature, that nature is in *us*, and that our alienation was our turning away from nature, from our own nature. If we view Ray, as Perkins' essay portrays him, from the perspective of Cavell's later writings, we can see that the achievement of Ray's last Hollywood films was to undo the repression of the Emersonian philosophy that was ascendant in American cinema, as in America, in the New Deal era. Then again, films that achieve what Cavell calls "the poetry of film" are inherently egalitarian, inherently Emersonian. Perkins ends his Ray essay on a hopeful note: "All Ray's films balance an immediate conflict against an ultimate unity, but his more recent work suggests a place for man within that unity." But Perkins didn't know then what we know now, that Ray's inner conflicts, along with Hollywood's hostility or indifference, would make the harmony he sought unattainable. Perkins attained it. That's why we're here today.

I first met Perkins in the early 1970s, when I was teaching at NYU. He had come down to New York from Boston, where he had made a pilgrimage to meet Cavell, and was on his way to see Nicholas Ray. He stayed a night with Kitty and me at our home. We talked and talked and talked, as we were to do over the next forty-five years whenever our paths crossed. Victor and Stanley had profound respect for each other, but after that first meeting, *their* paths rarely crossed. Now they've both taken that long journey to the place where the river of no return flows into the sea. I like to imagine them spending eternity watching movies together and talking, talking, talking.

Notes

1 Victor Perkins, *Film as Film: Understanding and Judging Movies* (New York: Penguin, 1972); a later edition was published by Da Capo Press in 1993.
2 William Rothman, *Hitchcock: The Murderous Gaze*, first edition (Cambridge: Harvard University Press, 1992); second edition (Albany: State University of New York Press, 2012).
3 Victor Perkins, "I Confess—Photographs of People Speaking," *CineAction*, no. 52, September 2000.

PART III

Philosophy, As If Made for Film

7

Between Skepticism and Moral Perfectionism: On Cavell's Melodrama of the Unknown Woman

Robert Sinnerbrink

STANLEY CAVELL'S UNIQUE APPROACH TO CINEMA has put the relationship between film and philosophy at the center of philosophical inquiry into film. Indeed, Cavell was the first major Anglophone philosopher of note who dedicated a major part of his work to cinema. As Cavell often remarks, the marriage between film and philosophy remains a provocation and an inspiration for both partners in this (thinking) dialogue. Indeed, cinema has the capacity to alter "everything philosophy has said about reality and its representation, about art and imitation, about greatness and conventionality, about judgment and pleasure, about skepticism and transcendence, about language and expression."[1] Although Cavell's remark has been construed as a provocation, prompting both criticisms of cinema's philosophical pretensions and defenses of cinema's philosophical contributions, it has rich implications for rethinking the relationship between cinema and ethics. As D. N. Rodowick observes, Cavell is "undoubtedly the contemporary philosopher most centrally concerned with the problem of ethics in film and philosophy, above all through his championing of an Emersonian moral perfectionism."[2] Cavell's cinematic ethics raises not only the question of skepticism and belief but also that of the relationship between cinema, ethical self-transformation, and the prevailing values within a given cultural-historical context.

In the following chapter, I consider Cavell's "ethical" contribution to film-philosophy: his claim that (Emersonian) moral perfectionism, as enacted in particular cinematic genres, offers a response to (cultural and moral) skepticism via its emphasis on open-ended, creative, as well as collective self-transformation. I explore the ethical significance of cinema as a response to skepticism, most vividly portrayed in the genres of remarriage comedy and melodrama of the unknown woman, as a film-philosophical engagement with the problem of modernity. My central concern will be to show how it is not only the successful pursuit of moral perfectionism that marks the ethical contribution of these films, but also the thwarting, breakdown, or impossibility of realizing this path, thanks to the normative context within which characters find themselves. The latter tension or ambiguity, moreover, not only finds expression in melodrama's well-known aesthetic of "excess" but also serves as a provocation to critical reflection. The limits of Cavell's moral perfectionist cinematic ethics—namely, framing moral perfectionism via its communal and democratic conditions, and thus making explicit the relation between ethics and politics—shall be addressed by way of a contemporary "melodrama of the unknown woman" that is also a queer romantic drama: Todd Haynes' *Carol* (2015).

Film as a "Moving Image of Skepticism"

Despite the evident concern with the "unethical" aspects of cinema throughout the history of film theory, it is striking how few theorists have attempted to explore the positive ethical potential of the medium.[3] Cavell is the exception proving the rule, reflecting on and elaborating, with regard to classic Hollywood genres, cinema's philosophical and ethical potential. Commencing with *The World Viewed*,[4] Cavell has placed the problem of skepticism—our loss of belief or conviction in our capacity to know the world, to understand oneself, and to acknowledge others—at the center of his philosophical engagement with cinema. Typically articulated as an epistemological problem concerning the foundations of knowledge or the relationship between belief, knowledge, and certainty, the problem of skepticism is also intimately related to our capacity for moral experience and our capacity to engage with and respond to others via the exercise of moral imagination. It is not only a paradigmatic modern concern with the problem of knowledge and the desire for certainty concerning the world, but more profoundly a concern with our capacity (or otherwise) to know others, to understand their singular perspectives, and to have conviction in the normative values that guide our intersubjective relations. These are the key ethical issues that inform Cavell's philosophical engagement with the two genres that he has reflected on the most: the remarriage comedy and the melodrama of the unknown woman.

Cavell's earlier work on film, however, focused more explicitly on the epistemic problem of skepticism. Cinema offers a way of both staging and reframing the skeptical situation of a world that remains independent of us. It offers a world that is present to us but where we are not present to it; a world that is known insofar as it can be represented and viewed as an image, but is also thereby reduced to what Heidegger called a "world-picture" (*Weltbild*), a defining feature of our historical experience of modernity.[5] If all we know of the world, however, are our representations of it, as commonly argued in modern philosophy since Descartes, then the problem of skepticism begins to loom large. Moreover, if images are the most significant mode of representation and medium of subjective experience in modernity, then a skeptical chasm opens up regarding the foundations of knowledge, the source of our conviction in a meaningful world, the veracity of our understanding of others, or the grounding for the moral-ethical norms that structure our shared forms of life. This is not just a philosophical problem but also a moral-ethical, cultural-historical one. For it is not only philosophy, according to Cavell, but also the arts—especially literature, theater, and cinema—that respond to the condition of skepticism and its philosophical, moral, and cultural-historical implications. Indeed, for Cavell, cinema is the most pervasive expression of, and productive artistic means of working through, the epistemic and moral dimensions of skepticism in the modern world; hence the cultural importance of film, and its close kinship, despite apparent differences, with modern philosophy (especially since Heidegger and Wittgenstein).[6]

To make sense of this claim we should recall the underlying realism informing Cavell's ontology of film. Following Erwin Panofsky and André Bazin, Cavell claims that the photographic basis of moving images means that they are fundamentally images of a world ("of reality or nature").[7] They are images of things that are not present, yet that have a certain presence through the images, images composed, projected, and screened as a meaningful whole (a cinematic "world") that is both a part of our world and in important ways distinct from it.[8] Moreover, the "automatism" of the moving image—its mechanical basis as a "manufactured" artifact, dependent on the relationship between an object, light, and the camera—is a defining element of its ontology and of the medium's ambiguous claims to realism. This is the case, moreover, whether realism is understood subjectively or objectively (capturing images emulating our conscious experience and also views of the world, selected and stylized aspects of reality independent of us). Photography and cinema reveal that, although the world exists independently of us, we nonetheless maintain a connection with it: reality remains present to us even if we are not present to it; we can maintain our "presentness to the world" by accepting our absence from it; and the world the cinema shows us, a world presented to me but one to which I am not present, is experienced as a world "past."[9] This inherent ambiguity of the cinematic image, as projecting and revealing a world ("of reality or nature") but also immersing us in a cinematic reality distinct from that world, lies at the basis of Cavell's claims concerning cinema, skepticism, and philosophy. The lesson of cinema is that skepticism is an ineliminable possibility of our (always partial) experience and one that can be "worked through" only by acknowledging the finitude of our knowledge.

It is in these cultural and philosophical senses that Cavell will describe film as "a moving image of scepticism"[10]: a world of moving images that both presents and dissolves skepticism. The philosophical experience of cinema, we might say, is one that both distances us from and reengages us with the world; it is an experience that makes manifest the recognition of skepticism as a condition from which we can never fully be delivered, which we can only learn to acknowledge, accept, and live with ethically in a manner that is enabling rather than destructive. From this perspective, film becomes philosophical in showing us how we can retrieve a sense of the ordinary, now transfigured and revealed in its ambiguity and contingency, reconnecting us with the world via the very medium of images that might otherwise facilitate or exacerbate our alienation from it.

Although the epistemic aspects of skepticism remain important, Cavell is more concerned in his later work on film with the moral-ethical aspects of skepticism and the manner in which cinema can respond to it. These moral-ethical dimensions, moreover, find their full expression in Cavell's work when he considers the manner in which movies can enact and explore the possibilities of (Emersonian) *moral perfectionism*. This philosophical background remains vital for understanding why Cavell turns to moral perfectionism in movies as a way of exploring culturally significant responses to skepticism. As with epistemology and metaphysics, we need to rethink ethics and morality, Cavell claims, in order to respond to the specter of skepticism, to experience how it might be acknowledged without expecting it to be dissolved, and thus find new ways, culturally and philosophically, of being no longer beholden to it. We need to "get over" skepticism (find practical release from its grip rather than overcoming it theoretically), which is where the experience of cinema becomes important, both philosophically and ethically. As we shall see, moral perfectionism, with its anti-foundational, non-metaphysical and pragmatic-existential focus is a form of ethical response to the problem of moral skepticism. Movies, as a medium for experiencing moral perfectionism and its vicissitudes, therefore provide a cultural platform for both the exploration and possible transformation of moral skepticism.

Film and Moral Perfectionism

In his more recent work elaborating cinematic responses to skepticism, Cavell focuses on the remarriage comedy and the melodrama of the unknown woman from the ethical perspective of moral perfectionism.[11] We can define the latter as a post-foundational, non-teleological conception of ethics that foregrounds the creative ethical task of individuals in shaping their conduct and composing their lives as open-ended projects. Drawing on the thought of Ralph Waldo Emerson (the American Nietzsche), Cavell suggests that narrative cinema is ideally suited for exploring characters embarking on a quest for self-knowledge or experience of creative self-transformation, the ethical process, as Nietzsche described, of "becoming who one is" independent of canonical moral rules or abstract theoretical reflection. What is distinctive about moral perfectionism, from a philosophical perspective, is its eschewal of universalist moral principles, a utilitarian calculus of consequences, or the cultivation of culturally valorized moral virtues, in favor of an individualist, experimental, "existential" commitment to freedom and autonomous self-transformation. Moral perfectionism's creative response to ethics in the absence of metaphysical foundations, rationalistic calculation, or rigid moral principles, makes it an ideal ethical response to skepticism on the moral-cultural plane.

So what is moral perfectionism? According to Cavell, it is not a distinct moral theory but, rather, a dimension of moral thinking or "register of moral life" that can be found in a variety of philosophical texts and traditions (from Plato's *Republic*, Emerson's essays and Nietzsche's aphorisms, to Heidegger's *Being and Time* and Wittgenstein's *Philosophical Investigations*).[12] We can describe it as an "anti-foundationalist" way of conceptualizing ethical experience, one that has a practical, "existential" emphasis on the importance of making oneself intelligible to others, of transforming oneself throughout one's life, and of practicing "philosophy as a way of life."[13] In this respect, moral perfectionist thinking can be found not only in certain philosophical texts but also in poetry, literature, drama, and, of course, in movies. Perhaps because of its broader cultural significance, however, moral perfectionism remains a neglected way of thinking ethics within academic philosophy compared with the dominant theories of morality (Kantian universalism, utilitarianism, and Aristotelian virtue ethics). Although it reaches back to traditions of ancient Greek thought, it also resonates with modern strands of romantic-existentialist thinking. In this respect it stands in stark contrast to the major traditions of moral philosophy and more academic forms of moral inquiry.

Of all three ethical perspectives, virtue ethics is perhaps closest to Cavell's version of moral perfectionism (despite Aristotelian ethics remaining tied to a teleological or goal-oriented conception of the good life). What they share is a focus on the singularity of moral situations and the importance of developing an ethical character as a way of being responsive to the variegated demands of the moral life. As Martha Nussbaum observes, an important domain of ethical experience concerns our responsiveness to the singularity and complexity of moral situations.[14] Being an ethical individual requires skill in the exercise of moral imagination: the exercise of imaginative sympathy, empathy, and ethical reflection in response to moral complexity. As both Nussbaum and Cavell suggest, the experience of moral sympathy, which requires emotional responsiveness to the needs of others, is better cultivated by imaginative engagement with fiction than by purely abstract reflection.

Although it is yet to be explored fully in relation to cinema, this implicit emphasis on moral imagination is a significant feature of Cavell's approach to cinematic ethics.

Cavell starts with the observation that, unlike ancient thought, modern philosophy is defined by a sense of disappointment with our knowledge of the world, or with the world in which we find ourselves.[15] The Kantian division between our sensuous world of appearances and the supersensible world of thought is a powerful expression of this division defining modern philosophy; but so too are the Hegelian, Nietzschean, or "existentialist" conceptions of the self as divided against itself, searching for ways in which to create itself, reconcile with, or discover the world anew.[16] This sense of disappointment with our limits generates a desire to transcend them, either by transforming ourselves, or the world in which we exist, in light of higher ideals. Philosophical criticism presents a vantage point from which the present state of the world can be judged and a new world envisaged in the future; or it can offer a way of evaluating our current world as preferable to future alternatives:

> The very conception of a divided self and a doubled world, providing a perspective of judgment on the world as it is, measured against the world as it may be, tends to express disappointment with the world as it is, as the scene of human activity and prospects, and perhaps to lodge the demand or desire for a reform or transfiguration of the world.[17]

This moral-existential alienation, leading to a dialectic of disappointment with the world coupled with a desire for its transformation, is the primary motivation for the development of moral perfectionism: a "register of moral life" that precedes, intervenes in, or accompanies, the more familiar forms of moral theory.[18] The moral calling of philosophy may begin with disappointment in the world, but it offers the prospect of transforming our relationship with it as well as with ourselves. This "therapeutic" dimension of modern philosophy is something Cavell finds not only in Wittgenstein and Heidegger, but also in Emerson and Nietzsche, thinkers who claim that philosophy is less about knowledge than about transforming our way of experiencing and being in the world. From this point of view, philosophy is about acknowledging our *finitude* as human beings and knowing subjects; it is about renewing our sense of being limited, mortal beings in a meaningful world, and overcoming the desire to transcend this world in favor of pure theoretical knowledge or an ideal metaphysical reality.

This is Cavell's "pragmatic" version of the perfectionist path to renewing our common being-in-the-world or to creating a meaningful form of human life.

Cavell's account of moral perfectionism thus offers an alternative perspective on prevailing moral theories, one focused on achieving self-understanding and ethical self-transformation. It advocates a creative shaping of one's own existence without recourse to pre-given moral principles, social conventions, or universal duties. In this sense it could be understood as a response to the specter of moral skepticism, cultivating a non-foundationalist way of finding meaning and value in the creative and open-ended process of self-transformation that strives to remain independent of any dogmatic reliance on rigid universalist moral principles, the utilitarian calculation of consequences, or the cultivation of moral virtues. At the same time, it does not deny the possibility of skepticism, but in responding to it strives to avoid overly speculative metaphysical commitments that dog other forms of moral thinking and ethical practice (and which in turn tend to collapse into skepticism or even nihilism).

Unlike Plato's conception of perfectionism (a teleological account of striving to attain a transcendent ideal), and recalling romanticist and existentialist conceptions of ethical choice (without overdramatizing the empty and ungrounded significance of "freedom"), Cavell's "non-teleological" moral perfectionism involves an autonomous, practical, immanent "existential" quest to become what one is, to approach, as Emerson put it, one's "unattained but attainable self":

> In Emerson and Thoreau's sense of human existence, there is no question of reaching a final state of the soul but only and endlessly taking the next step to what Emerson calls "an unattained but attainable self"—a self that is always and never ours—a step that turns us not from bad to good, or wrong to right, but from confusion and constriction toward self-knowledge and sociability.[19]

For Cavell, moral perfectionism is not only a viable alternative tradition of modern moral thinking and ethical practice, but also the mode of thinking that best defines the moral-ethical significance of the two genres of Hollywood film that he studies in *Pursuits of Happiness* and *Contesting Tears*: the remarriage comedy and the melodrama of the unknown woman. These films focus on couples seeking acknowledgment and self-education (in response to their desire), transforming themselves in a manner that can be either comic or tragic; these are films that remain related to earlier dramatic and literary traditions (Shakespearean comedy, nineteenth-century social-domestic drama) but that do not fit readily in any of the three major categories of academic moral philosophy (Kantian universalism, utilitarianism, or virtue ethics). They are films that explore the question of critical self-transformation, the characters' desire to reinvent themselves, and to explore the possibility of a transfigured world in which new ways of being with one another might be possible. In this regard, they remain closely related to Emersonian perfectionism, which neither strives for a utopian ideal, nor dismisses the existing world as inherently meaningless. Rather, in calling these films "Emersonian," Cavell suggests that they participate in the perfectionist quest for self-transformation within a world that could be itself transformed, however partially, by reinventing our relations with others within a democratic community.

Cavell explores these possibilities of transformation most comprehensively in *Cities of Words*. Based on his Harvard lecture course in moral reasoning, Cavell reveals this enduring strain of moral perfectionist thought by pairing philosophical texts by Emerson, Locke, Mill, Kant, Rawls, Nietzsche, Plato, and Aristotle with movies such as *The Philadelphia Story, Adam's Rib, Gaslight, It Happened One Night, Stella Dallas,* and *The Awful Truth*. He explores how these films and texts speak to each other about the possibilities of moral perfectionism as a way of engaging in ethical reflection in a manner that is at once imaginative and dramatic, even comic and tragic. These films explore ethical situations via narrative so as to broaden our conception of moral reasoning, attuning us to more subtle and complex registers of ethical life, thus enhancing and extending the kind of moral-aesthetic experience we can have with cinema. These are films less concerned with traditional theories of morality than with the manner in which particular characters in singular situations can transform themselves through mutual acknowledgment (or show how such transformation can be thwarted by the failure of acknowledgment). They are concerned with existential questions at the level of the ordinary, rather than the metaphysical; they explore what kind of person one is to become, rather than what the concept of a person means. As Cavell remarks:

> The issues the principal pair in these films confront each other with are formulated less well by questions concerning what they ought to do, what it would be best or right for them to do, than by the question of how they shall live their lives, what kind of persons they aspire to be. This aspect or moment of morality—in which a crisis forces an examination of one's life that calls for a transformation or reorienting of it— is the province of what I emphasize as moral perfectionism.[20]

From this point of view, moral perfectionism is an alternative perspective on the major ethical theories in modern culture. It does not displace universalism or utilitarianism (both Kant and J. S. Mill, according to Cavell, have "deep perfectionist strains in their views"), but emphasizes the therapeutic aspect of moral experience that concerns what we might otherwise call authenticity, self-knowledge, or the "care of the self" (Foucault).[21] It links up with the romanticist and existentialist ethics of authenticity, exploring how the task of self-transformation might be achieved within a democratic form of community. It is not in philosophy but in modern literature and film that moral perfectionism has found a cultural home. Indeed, academic philosophers have tended to dismiss it as "elitist" and incompatible with an egalitarian democratic ethos: a charge Cavell challenges in relation to Nietzsche and Emerson, whose moral perfectionism, he argues, does not entail a premodern, hierarchical form of society predicated on social inequality.[22]

So how does moral perfectionism relate to film? We can identify at least three strands:

(1) through cinema's egalitarian capacity to thematize and reveal the ordinary in all its rich texture of meaning; (2) through the development of narrative film and of specific genres that explore the themes of self-transformation, acknowledging others, and either reconciling with or transforming the world; and (3) through film's capacity to transfigure human figures as depicted on screen, to capture and convey emotional expression and psychological complexity through gesture and performance. All three aspects are at play in the genres of remarriage comedy and the melodrama of the unknown woman. Indeed, it is through these films' cinematic presentation of singular characters confronting the ordinary moral challenges of love and friendship, freedom and fulfillment, recognition and reinvention, that an ethical experience of moral perfectionism becomes vividly manifest.

This Emersonian aspect of Cavell's vision of moral perfectionism demands further reflection. Cavell identifies a number of themes explored in his readings of comedy and melodrama. Emersonian moral perfectionism is defined by the desire for self-knowledge: the quest for authentic self-identity through cultivation and education, the individual's striving for continuous self-transformation as a life-defining project. It interprets moral reasoning as the practice of making oneself morally intelligible, so has an intimate connection with the idea of morality as a practice of communication with others ("moral confrontation as one soul's examination of another").[23] Hence its preferred communicative form is the dialogue or conversation rather than the treatise or argument. This emphasis on conversation is directed toward the Friend, the one who will assist me in my quest, perhaps question my sincerity, acknowledge my identity, and facilitate my self-transformation. In this respect, Emersonian moral perfectionism casts itself in counterpoint with the philosophical tradition, challenging the manner in which philosophy is traditionally written, reasserting its kinship with literature, and availing itself of idioms and genres that venture outside standard argumentation. This leads to moral perfectionism's concern with moral paradoxes, its stress on the ambiguity of moral relations, the importance of careful reading, and the ideals of authenticity and ethical freedom beyond a rigid universalism, narrow utilitarianism, or dogmatic moralism.[24] These Emersonian themes will resonate strongly with the particular movies Cavell studies as exemplars of the remarriage comedy and melodrama of the unknown woman.

Moral Perfectionism and Remarriage Comedy

As remarked, two of Cavell's major philosophical works on film explore two related Hollywood genres, the remarriage comedy and the melodrama of the unknown woman. These genres transform the theme of marriage, either as a utopian possibility of mutual acknowledgment in the comedies, or as a block to the woman's quest for self-knowledge in the melodramas. In his earlier books, however, Cavell does not explicitly link either genre with Emersonian moral perfectionism, although Emerson's thought remains, as ever, a constant reference point. Rather, he draws attention to the manner in which such films thematize their condition as visual media, their inheritance of literary and dramatic traditions, their relationships with other films and constitution of a genre, and their reflection on morally relevant themes, including the Emersonian critique of conformity, and the possibility of an egalitarian relationship between the sexes. It is only in *Cities of Words* that Cavell explicitly recasts both genres as participating in the philosophical discourse of moral perfectionism present in modern culture since Shakespeare and Milton, Ibsen and Eliot, Emerson and Nietzsche.

What are remarriage comedies? Cavell addresses these films as a particular subgenre, exemplified by a selection of "seven talkies made in Hollywood between 1934 and 1949": *It Happened One Night* (1934, dir. Frank Capra), *The Awful Truth* (1937, dir. Leo McCarey), *Bringing Up Baby* (1938, dir. Howard Hawks), *His Girl Friday* (1940, dir. Hawks), *The Philadelphia Story* (1940, dir. George Cukor), and *Adam's Rib* (1944, dir. Cukor).[25] Although they share many features with other romantic comedies, these "remarriage comedies" are also distantly related to Shakespearean romances like *The Winter's Tale* and *The Tempest*. Unlike classical comedy and romance, where a young couple is shown "overcoming obstacles to their love and at the end achieving marriage," remarriage comedies commence with a mature couple, getting or threatening to get their divorce, so that "the drive of the narrative is to get the original pair together *again*."[26] They are distinguished from other versions of romantic comedy (related to what Northrop Frye called "new comedy") in which a male character pursues his beloved and battles familial and social barriers to their desired marriage. Resonating with Frye's account of "old comedy," in the remarriage comedies it is the woman who is the focus of the narrative, except that now she embarks on a "sentimental journey" to educate herself as to her desire, deciding whether the man in question is a suitable partner for her project of self-transformation. These are films that explore the concept of conversation, the ethical idea of marriage as a "meet and happy conversation" (as Milton put it in his famous tract on divorce). They explore forms of social and personal exchange in which each partner is acknowledged in his or her uniqueness, yet where each provides the other with an educative perspective as to his or her self-identity. This raises the question whether the relationship of equality between the sexes envisaged by the couple is realizable within the social, cultural, and ethical norms of the community in which the couple find themselves. The utopian aspect of these comedies thus lies not only in their exploration of a mutually transformative relationship between the sexes, but also in imagining a form of democratic community in which self-reliance and interpersonal intimacy can be mediated with social freedom and political equality.

The remarriage motif, as Cavell remarks, is prompted by the changed situation of marriage, which is "no longer assured or legitimized by church or state or sexual compatibility or children" but, rather, by the "willingness for remarriage, a way of continuing to affirm the happiness of one's initial leap."[27] Marriage, in other words, is at once a romantic and an ethical relationship sustained by an existential will to repeat one's commitment to seek happiness through mutual acknowledgment with an equal. The focus is not only on the question of marriage but also on how the latter is linked with the self-education of the woman.

Through this experience, she learns the true nature of her desire, seeking to establish her self-identity, and openness toward the future, through a process of mutual acknowledgment between her and her partner. The couple's trials are carried comically, thanks to virtuoso dialogue and artful performance; their mutual adventures take them from the city to the country (the Shakespearean "green world"), where the obstacles to self-realization through acknowledgment, hence to remarriage, are overcome. What the couple discover, finally, is that they are, indeed, "made for each other," but only after having committed themselves, through "meet and happy conversation," to educating themselves, and thus transforming and reinventing themselves, in felicitous partnership with one another.

By contrast, melodramas of the unknown woman, such as Max Ophüls' *Letter from an Unknown Woman* (1948), George Cukor's *Gaslight* (1944), Irving Rapper's *Now, Voyager* (1942), and King Vidor's *Stella Dallas* (1937), appear to negate key elements of the remarriage comedy, notably the institution of marriage itself. Within these films, the idea of marriage as a route to self-creation is "transcended and perhaps reconceived."[28] Indeed, the route to self-creation is not through marriage but involves, rather, a "metamorphosis": a radical, "melodramatic" change in the identity of the woman that takes place independently of any conversation or marital commerce with the man, and which draws its nourishment from the otherwise marginalized "world of women."[29] It is the woman's education toward self-reliance, and her subsequent rejection of marriage, that stands in sharpest contrast with the remarriage comedy. Nonetheless, both genres share an underlying commitment to (Emersonian) moral perfectionism, namely, by "working out the problematic of self-reliance and conformity, or of hope and despair," in relation to the task of individual self-transformation.[30] Indeed, Cavell insists that whatever contrasts there are between the comedies and the melodramas can be accommodated within the moral perfectionist frame, the former by offering an idealized egalitarian version of marriage, the latter by questioning traditional conceptions of marriage in relation to the task of achieving independence beyond socially allotted roles. Whereas the remarriage comedies "envisage a relation of equality between human beings" that Emerson described as "a relation of rightful attraction, of expressiveness, and of joy," the melodramas of the unknown woman envision "the phase of the problematic of self-reliance that demands this expressiveness and joy first in relation to oneself": a kind of excessive or "melodramatic" doubt, or passage through skepticism, that leads the woman beyond skeptical despair and toward a fragile recovery of herself and the world.[31] Both subgenres allegorize these aspects of skepticism and its overcoming in relation to the problem of marriage. Both traverse the possibility of skeptical doubt over our relationship to the world, our capacity for self-knowledge, our ability to know and understand one another, through comic and tragic explorations of romantic relationships, understood as expressions of the potential for acknowledgment within the everyday and the domestic. These are some of the reasons behind Cavell's otherwise surprising claim that, contrary to appearances, skepticism, understood here as "the threat to the ordinary," should show up in fiction's favorite threats to forms of marriage, namely "in forms of melodrama and of tragedy."[32]

As critics have remarked, this is one of the more questionable aspects of Cavell's reading of the melodramas and romances, particularly in regard to the question of gender relations.[33] Indeed, I would modify Cavell's claim and assert that, if melodrama is the negation of remarriage comedy, then within melodrama the moral perfectionist path is blocked or thwarted (the possibility of finding and following such an ethical path toward independence is put into question). The world within which the woman's quest for self-transformation is compromised itself becomes the object of a critical reflection; the constraints and conflicts to which she is subject, moreover, generate the hyperbolic emotionalism and aesthetic excess for which the genre is famous.

Moral Perfectionism in *Stella Dallas*

This difficulty is evident in Cavell's reading of *Stella Dallas* (1937, dir. Vidor), the subject of one of Cavell's defining presentations of a moral perfectionist approach to the melodrama of the unknown woman. His chapter in *Contesting Tears* ("Stella's Taste: Reading *Stella Dallas*") is largely reproduced in *Cities of Words*, accompanied by a reflective chapter on Henrik Ibsen's *A Doll's House*. The latter chapter substantiates Cavell's claim that Stella and her sisters are cinematic descendants of Ibsen's Nora, who famously leaves her family and husband, escaping suffocating domestic conformity in favor of an uncertain future. The relationship between Stella's struggle for independence and acknowledgment, the tension between her social aspirations and the constraints of her social class background is an ideological aspect of *Stella Dallas*—and of melodrama more generally—that Cavell's moral perfectionist approach struggles to articulate: how the conditions of a character's world shape her quest for ethical self-transformation, and, more profoundly, how the "impossible" desires that this social world stimulates yet cannot satisfy, find visual expression in an aesthetic of excess, of hyperbolic performance, and an ambivalent mood of melancholy self-affirmation. If melodramas of the unknown woman are domestic tragedies without cathartic resolution, playing out the cultural aporias of gender and class, their aesthetic presentation of the possibilities of moral perfectionism will remain conflicted, excessive, and incomplete—a "tragic" moral perfectionism that, to use Thomas Elsaesser's phrase, "doesn't quite come off."[34]

The emotional excessiveness of the film's famous concluding scene is a case in point:

Far from being sentimental tears at finally seeing her daughter happily married, Stella's silent display of emotion condenses many elements of her character and situation, not to mention conflicting features of the narrative arc, into a "private" space of viewing, emotional expression, and bodily communication: Stella's self-sacrifice, her uneasy but independent manner of relating roles of mother and of (no longer married) woman, her sense of having traversed the fantasy of marrying up—of upward social mobility achieved through romantic union—only to find that this was not for her, not to her taste, not her style, however much it remains part of her daughter Laurel's world, her romantic fantasy and desire for social status. The circular repetition of this sequence, rhyming with the earlier sequence when Stella and future husband Stephen go on their first date, Stella mesmerized by the movies and wanting Stephen to educate her into his social world, finally resolves itself through Laurel's successful achievement of social mobility through advantageous marriage. Stella's smile, while nibbling at her scarf as she did earlier with Stephen after the movies, is also an ethical rejection of this social world, of the institutions and norms that uphold it, in favor of her own unconventional mode of feminine social identity ("something else besides a mother"), however alone it leaves her on the obscured margins of this world. The "domestic sublimity" of this moment is a melodramatic expression of all the conflicting dynamics at work in Stella's divided subjectivity, her struggle to bridge estranged social worlds, dynamics that could not find direct expression in the narrative as such.

Moral melodramas such as *Stella Dallas* run up against the individualist limits of this perfectionist ethic of self-transformation within the difficult familial, social, economic, and cultural circumstances in which characters find themselves, whether as women, as mothers, or as social outsiders. Indeed, this feature of melodrama has been recognized as one of its defining features and sources of aesthetic novelty as well as ideological limitation. As Linda Williams remarks, the melodramatic mode often takes on the quality of cultural "wish-fulfilment," "acting out the narrative resolution of conflicts derived from the economic, social and political spheres in the private, emotionally primal sphere of the family."[35] This is a source of its emotional intensity but also marks a limit to what it can articulate of the broader currents shaping the domestic world of the protagonists and their interpersonal struggles.

Melodrama can delineate these background forces, but only obliquely, indirectly, suggesting them in aesthetic or dramatic ways rather than articulating them directly in narrative terms. They point, through emotional excess, to the fractures and limits of a social world that cultivates desires for selfhood, happiness, independence, and acknowledgment, particularly in women, that often cannot be fulfilled without that world itself being changed.

The challenge for Cavellian moral perfectionism, in short, is to articulate how individual self-transformation also requires recognition of how the conditions shaping one's social-cultural situation can either foster or restrict one's exercise of individual autonomy. The challenge is to make the transition from ethics to politics from within moral perfectionism's individualist framework, one that struggles to contain and explain the powerful emotional and social dynamics buffeting the female characters, who remain caught between conflicted and divided subjective and social worlds (in relation to marriage, family, and social recognition through career, sexual identity, and so on). Cavell's readings of melodramas like *Stella Dallas* tend to avoid the cultural-political question of the social conditions of the woman's desire for creative self-transformation within the conflicted social and subjective worlds of the melodrama. Stella's struggle with the entwined challenges of gender and class—to reconcile marriage, motherhood, and the "pursuit of happiness" within a social class to which she aspires but does not belong—dissolves in Cavell's affirmative reading of her self-education as a form of moral perfectionist self-transformation mediated by the cinematic exploration of feminine identity.

Romantic Love and Moral Imperfectionism: *Carol* as Melodrama of the Unknown Woman

One way to explore this claim further, and to suggest how a revised moral perfectionism might work, is to offer a Cavellian perspective on a contemporary "melodrama of the unknown woman." Todd Haynes' *Carol* (2015) is a critically acclaimed romance and melodrama based on Patricia Highsmith's novel *The Price of Salt* (published in 1952 under a pseudonym and republished in 1990 under Highsmith's name with the title *Carol*). The screenplay was written by Phyllis Nagy (who had been friends with Highsmith), who adapts the novel brilliantly for the screen. Cate Blanchett and Rooney Mara star as the romantic couple, Carol Aird is a glamorous society woman and mother undergoing a difficult divorce, and Therese Belivet is a younger woman working part-time in the toy department of Frankendale's (a department store based on Bloomingdale's) while pursuing photography. As a lesbian romance combining elements of the maternal melodrama, the film shifts focus from the perspective of the naïve Therese toward that of the sophisticated Carol, while exploring different facets of their relationship. Both women, however, are shown in their shared vulnerability, subtly articulated passion, and suppressed desire, trying to find ways to express their love within a world that refuses to recognize or legitimate it. The film's elegant visual style—its evocative use of color, décor, costume, music, and setting—provides expressive aesthetic means to articulate the emotional dynamics of a relationship that defies traditional prohibitions on permissible paths to perfectionist self-transformation through romantic love for, and between, women.

Set in New York City in 1952–53, but also venturing further afield into the Midwest (Ohio), the film explores not only the life-transforming experience of falling in love, but also the challenges of same-sex love in a world where it remains suppressed and stigmatized. The film features many elements that we can identify with Cavell's moral perfectionism, notably the quest for the characters to transform themselves, to choose how they want to live, what kind of people they aspire to be, as a romantic couple struggling to articulate their love within the conservative constraints of 1950s New York society. Chiming with Cavell's observations of the genre, both women undergo a "metamorphosis": a radical, "melodramatic" change in identity that takes place independently of any conversation or marital commerce with a male character, and which is centered on the otherwise marginalized "world of women."[36] As a melodramatic romance with a queer perspective,[37] it offers a way of exploring what we might call *moral imperfectionism*: the difficulties involved in pursuing a moral perfectionist path of self-transformation within a socially constrained, morally prejudicial, imperfect social and cultural world.

Cavell's account of the melodrama of the unknown woman acknowledges that it offers something akin to the "negative" version of moral perfectionism. A woman who is both unknown (to herself and to us) (as various aspects of her character or motivation remain concealed) undergoes a transformative experience in which she begins to explore who she is, and has to choose the kind of life she will lead, typically either rejecting the path of marriage, questioning her traditional feminine role as mother, or choosing to venture on a new way of life on her own terms, independent of marriage or the world of men. Unlike remarriage comedies, in which the woman needs to choose which partner will help educate her as to her desire, help her find her new identity, in the melodrama of the unknown woman she attempts to find a new path that might allow her to reconcile motherhood with independence, romantic relationships with family or career, personal authenticity with social acknowledgment or moral obligations. The women in these melodramas experiment with the possibilities available within their social world to become "something else besides a mother." Although Cavell identifies this genre or subgenre within classic Hollywood melodramas of the 1930s and 1940s, it remains a feature of melodramas that other critics and theorists have explored in regard to more recent European and American cinema.[38]

Many of these elements are present in Todd Haynes' *Carol*, which focuses on the passionate but thwarted romantic relationship between a wealthy and experienced New York woman trying to leave her marriage and an inexperienced young salesgirl-cum-photographer making her way in the world. The film presents its story initially from the perspective of Therese—as in Highsmith's novel—but gradually shifts perspective toward Carol, whose difficult battle with her patriarchal husband Harge (Kyle Chandler) over the custody of their daughter Rinny threatens to destroy the women's relationship and casts Carol in an increasingly vulnerable role. We follow the subtle but unmistakable signs of desire shaping their meeting—the chance encounter at a department store toy counter at Christmas, their exchanged glances signaling both attraction and uncertainty, Carol asking Therese for advice on what to buy her young daughter for Christmas, leaving her leather gloves on the counter "by accident"—and then follow the blossoming of their relationship, however furtive and hidden, until its near destruction, thanks to the efforts of Carol's jealous and wounded husband. If this had been a more traditional or conventional "melodrama of the unknown woman," as those Cavell studies, the story would likely have followed Carol's trajectory, her failed attempts to find happiness in some alternative kind of life, having sacrificed her daughter and, most likely, her hopes of happiness for a tragically "impossible" love.

As a lesbian love story, however, *Carol* combines these elements with romance, the experience of love with its anxieties, ecstasies, and obsessions, exploring how romantic love between two women might be possible within an intolerant, prejudicial world.[39] As remarked, Therese is an ingénue, still unformed, finding her way in life, attracted to, but not quite comprehending, the magnetic allure of the more experienced, worldly Carol. Both women undergo a shared experience of love that is profound and transformative, and both come to understand themselves and the possibility of a shared life together that will require invention and independence. The fact that this is a lesbian love affair, one that challenges many 1950s boundaries of moral prejudice and social convention—not only concerning heterosexuality but boundaries of age, class, parenthood, and social experience—makes the romance between Therese and Carol both transformative and tragic, passionate and political. The film also combines elements of the "remarriage" motif with the melodrama, with the younger woman having to decide whether to see Carol again after the seeming demise of their relationship, whether to recommit to their love and live together as a couple, the film ending with a moment of possible reconciliation and fragile sense of shared futurity.

I have chosen to focus on *Carol* because it raises an important issue that has dogged Cavell's accounts of the more "traditional" (heterosexual) melodramas and remarriage comedies: the asymmetry between the woman's moral perfectionist quest or transformative ethical trajectory and the man's relatively static, unchanging status and experience, as though she has to learn the nature of her desire in order to become who she is, whereas the male characters, by and large, do not.[40] As a lesbian romance, there are elements of the melodrama of the unknown woman in both protagonists: not only Therese but Carol too is presented as, and to an extent remains, an unknown woman but one who clearly also undergoes a profound shift or transformation of perspective, thanks to her relationship with Therese. Both women are caught between worlds: Therese between the worlds of photography, journalism, the student bohemian set and Carol's world of social privilege and bourgeois propriety; and Carol between the worlds of motherhood, married respectability, and the possibility of an alternative world that neither she nor Therese can yet name or describe. Therese's world offers the possibility of a career in photography, being part of the (male) world of journalism, but also relationships with women that may have to remain clandestine and fleeting (the young woman who appears interested in her at a friend's party toward the end of the film). Carol renounces the lie of claiming that her homosexual affair was a psychological aberration due to mental distress brought about by her husband's harsh conduct, claiming in a moving speech before the divorce lawyers that she freely chose this affair and that she would rather give up custody of her daughter Rinny (while insisting on visiting rights) than continue to live a lie that "goes against my grain."

There are no clear alternatives, however, available for either woman to find genuine acknowledgment, their shared love having to remain concealed and ambiguous, furtive and discreet, while also claiming subtle forms of social visibility and moral acknowledgment.[41] At the same time, Therese and Carol have the possibility of inventing a new path, the open possibility of finding a way of life that would allow them to live their love and transform each other within a world that remains marked by ideological, moral, and social constraints. Their relationship nonetheless offers a more mutual exchange than many of the more traditional melodramas Cavell reflects upon, a genuinely transformative relationship in a reciprocal sense, educating both women in different ways so as to enable them to become who they are, despite the prejudices they face and the uncertain acknowledgment they seek. As remarked, their relationship also has elements of the "remarriage" theme: Therese must choose again, in her own way, whether to recommit to her relationship with Carol, this time more autonomously, with the benefit of experience. She knows that it may mean abandoning her place within her current social milieu and embarking on an uncertain life together, the two women having to find or invent ways to live and express their love in a world that will continue to stymie or thwart it.

The film's rich visual style is beautifully attuned to these psychological tensions, emotional demands, and moral ambiguities. Cinematographer Ed Lachman shot the film on retro Super 16mm film stock in order to capture the grainier and muted style of 1940s and early 50s street and documentary photography (by Saul Leiter, Ruth Orkin, Helen Lovitt, Esther Bubley, and Vivian Maier) that served as visual models for the world of the film.[42] The careful attention to color, muted and harmonious—greens, browns, and pinks, with occasional splashes of red—set against an urban milieu that is elegant and restrained but also gritty and subdued, serves as an expressive medium directing the viewer visually as well as emotionally. So too with the music, composed by Carter Burwell, which combines period melancholy love songs with beautifully scored, mood-setting sequences. Both characters use music to express mood and feeling in ways they could not otherwise verbally articulate (the importance of the record player, the record store, and the radio playing in key scenes are cases in point). The film itself does the same with the musical score, however, creating moods that both reveal the subjectivity of the characters and attune us to the social world of early 1950s New York. Costuming is another key element complementing both the individual expression of character—Therese's woolen pom-pom beret, her fashion transition from student ingénue to independent young urban photographer; Carol's opulent furs, elegant frocks, stunning hair, and striking jewelry, revealing aspects of her surface persona and of her hidden depths—and the expressive composition of an ambiguous social milieu.

The film's expressive visual style has often been noted and praised.[43] There are numerous shots incorporating various forms of framing and reflection (using car windows, mirrors, glass doors, window frames, interior/exterior thresholds). There are shots using abstraction as well as partial obscuring of vision (close shots within a car on a rainy night, of hands, faces, and arresting objects within a carefully controlled frame) and shots that foreclose background in favor of focused intimacy (the withholding of establishing shots or wider framings and the use of shallow focus in order to emphasize textures, fabrics, jewelry, clothing, and make-up, not to mention Blanchett's and Mara's facial expressiveness). All of these stylistic choices contribute to showing the inner emotional states of the characters as well as the interplay between image and world, interior and exterior, social self-presentation and sensuous inner feeling. The expressive and intimate visual style of the film helps convey the ambiguous imbrication of image and desire, complicating the characters' maneuvering of the dialectic between "illicit" forms of desire and deadening social convention.

Dialogue in the film is muted, understated, punctuated by pauses and silences, but also complemented by subtle facial expressions, significant gestures, and telling glances. When Carol and Therese sit down for cocktails and lunch in a discreetly lit restaurant booth, ostensibly to thank Therese for returning Carol's leather gloves, the scene focuses closely on their face-to-face encounter in the expressively lit, evocative restaurant setting. The dialogue is both formal and intimate; each phrase Carol utters having to be at once conventional and suggestive. As their meals arrive, Carol asks what Therese does on Sundays, to which she replies, "nothing," asking Carol the same question in turn, to which Carol gives the same reply, with a certain emphatic note inflecting her otherwise languid, sophisticated diction.

After a pause, Carol invites Therese to visit her on Sunday, barely able to glance at Therese directly, combining a casual politeness with anxious poignancy. The shift in tone from Carol's haughty elegance, now more intimate and vulnerable, and from Therese's doe-eyed innocence to her subtle frankness in accepting Carol's offer without hesitation, while also hinting that she understands what it really means, is all conveyed through tone and gesture, glances and intonation. Carol glances briefly up at Therese, who is now smiling openly, Carol adopting her feline suggestive smile in return, gazing briefly in admiration and perplexity at Therese. "What a strange girl you are." "Why?" Therese asks innocently, "Flung out of space," Carol remarks, almost whispering to herself.

This kind of subtle but suggestive exchange, communicating at the level of interpersonal expression and shared affect rather than explicit dialogue or action, is emblematic of their relationship. The careful framing, attention to visual detail, and aesthetic mood evoking longing as well as fascination, anxiety as well as desire, is a remarkable achievement of the film. Style and substance perfectly complement one another, combining artfully to express the "moral perfectionist" desire to transform oneself in partnership with an other, where this transformative ethic of open-ended becoming becomes complicated, thanks to both the ambiguity of romantic love and the social constraints of the characters' world.

Like so many melodramas, visual style and aesthetic "excess" stand in for, or supplement and intensify, what cannot be openly communicated or explicitly articulated. Drawing on masters such as Douglas Sirk but adding the restraint of tragic romance (as in David Lean's *Brief Encounter*, an explicit reference point for Haynes[44]), *Carol* shows how the moral perfectionist quest, within the context of a lesbian romance, necessarily encounters the prejudices and prohibitions of a straight world that cannot openly acknowledge alternative forms of love and desire.

Carol shows us both the possibilities and limits of the melodrama of the unknown woman, multiplying the ethical dimensions of the romantic relationship. By following the mutual transformation of two women in love, rather than the asymmetrical trajectory of the woman and relative stasis of the man in traditional melodramas, *Carol* highlights the struggle for acknowledgment that the couple will experience together within a socially imperfect world. The ethics of moral perfectionism, at one level, defines the lovers' quest, their shared experiment to find out who they are, and what they might become together, while also stressing the failure of this path to allow these women to pursue their love without fear of exposure, censure, or sacrifice. To its credit, *Carol* eschews the conventional path of ultimately "punishing" its queer characters for their transgressive desire, opting for a more affirmative yet ambiguous denouement that suggests how the transformative experience of romantic love between women may yet make possible the invention of new ways of living. It does so, moreover, while acknowledging the uncertainty and difficulty of achieving this within a world that continues to constrain or limit the possibilities of moral perfectionism for individuals who do not conform to social and cultural norms of identity, sexuality, or desire.

Recalling Cavell's "classic" melodramas of the unknown woman, *Carol* both explores and extends the dialectic between acknowledgment and rejection, individual self-realization and the satisfaction of desire, the quest to become who one is in a world bent on denying that quest. Carol and Therese embark on a reciprocal form of self-transformation, a moral perfectionist rejection of the world of marriage and men, struggling to invent a new mode of existence and form of community for themselves, while contending with the unavoidable prejudice they will face in living a queer life together. We might describe *Carol,* in short, as a *self-critical* melodrama of the unknown woman, one that, by transposing Cavell's model to a same-sex romance, reveals both the possibilities and the constraints, the promises and disappointments, of moral perfectionism in an imperfect world.

Notes

1 Stanley Cavell, *Contesting Tears: The Hollywood Melodrama of the Unknown Woman* (Chicago: The University of Chicago Press, 1996), xii.

2 D. N. Rodowick, "Ethics in Film Philosophy (Cavell, Deleuze, Levinas)" (n.d), unpublished manuscript (rejected entry for *The Routledge Encyclopedia of Film and Philosophy*), 1–2: https://www.academia.edu/36412056/Ethics_in_film_philosophy_Cavell_Deleuze_Levinas_

3 Rodowick, "Ethics in Film Philosophy (Cavell, Deleuze, Levinas)," 1–2. See also Robert Sinnerbrink, *Cinematic Ethics: Exploring Ethical Experience through Film* (London and New York: Routledge, 2016).

4   Stanley Cavell, *The World Viewed: Reflections on the Ontology of Film*, Enlarged Edition (Cambridge: Harvard University Press, 1979). The first edition of *The World Viewed* was published in 1971.
5   See Martin Heidegger, "The Age of the World-Picture," in *The Question Concerning Technology*, trans. W. Lovitt (New York: Harper and Row, 1977), 115–54.
6   Heidegger and Wittgenstein have featured prominently in the "film as philosophy" literature in recent decades, not least thanks to Cavell's influence.
7   Cavell, *The World Viewed*, 16.
8   Ibid., 20.
9   Ibid., 23.
10 Ibid., 188.
11 See Stanley Cavell, *Cities of Words: Pedagogical Letters on a Register of Moral Life* (Cambridge: Belknap Press of Harvard University Press, 2004); Stanley Cavell, *Pursuits of Happiness: The Hollywood Comedy of Remarriage* (Cambridge: Harvard University Press, 1981); and Cavell, *Contesting Tears*.
12 Cavell, *Cities of Words*, 12–13.
13 Ibid., 13; Pierre Hadot, "There Are Nowadays Professors of Philosophy but no Philosophers," trans. J. Aaron Simmons, *Journal of Speculative Realism* 19, no. 3 (2005): 229–37; Pierre Hadot, *Philosophy as a Way of Life: Spiritual Exercises from Socrates to Foucault*, trans. Michael Chase, ed. Arnold Davidson (Oxford: Basil Blackwell, 1995).
14 Martha C. Nussbaum, *Love's Knowledge: Essays on Philosophy and Literature* (Oxford: Oxford University Press, 1992).
15 See also Simon Critchley, *Very Little . . . Almost Nothing: Death, Philosophy, Literature*, Revised Edition (London: Routledge, 1997).
16 Robert B. Pippin, *Modernism as a Philosophical Problem: On the Dissatisfactions of European Higher Culture*, 2nd edn. (Oxford: Basil Blackwell, 1999); Charles Taylor, *Sources of the Self: The Making of Modern Identity* (Cambridge: Cambridge University Press, 1989).
17 Cavell, *Cities of Words*, 2.
18 Ibid.
19 Ibid., 13.
20 Ibid., 11.
21 Ibid.
22 Ibid., 90–91, 218–26. See Paul Patton, "Cavell and Rawls on the Conversation of Justice: Moral versus Political Perfectionism," *Conversations: The Journal of Cavellian Studies* 2 (2014): 54–74. Patton defends Rawls and Nietzsche on perfectionism but does not address Cavell's central focus, which is how a moral perfectionism of the everyday is elaborated in a range of melodramas and romantic comedies expressed in a cinematic manner.
23 Cavell, *Cities of Words*, 49.

24 Ibid., 27–34.
25 Stanley Cavell, "A Capra Moment," *Cavell on Film*, ed. William Rothman (Albany: State University of New York Press, 2005), 136.
26 Cavell, *Cities of Words*, 4.
27 Cavell, "A Capra Moment," 137.
28 Cavell, *Cities of Words*, 6.
29 Ibid.
30 Cavell, *Contesting Tears*, 9.
31 Ibid.
32 Ibid., 10.
33 See Sinnerbrink, *Cinematic Ethics*, 123–25; Cynthia Willett, *Irony in the Age of Empire: Comic Perspectives on Democracy and Freedom* (Bloomington: Indiana University Press, 2008); Linda Williams, "'Something Else Besides a Mother': *Stella Dallas* and the Maternal Melodrama," *Cinema Journal* 24, no. 1 (1984): 2–27.
34 Thomas Elsaesser, "Tales of Sound and Fury: Observations on the Family Melodrama," in *Home Is Where the Heart Is: Studies in Melodrama and the Woman's Film*, ed. Christine Gledhill (London: British Film Institute, 1987), 65.
35 Williams, "Something Else Besides a Mother," 4.
36 Cavell, *Cities of Words*, 6.
37 See Alison L. McKee, "*The Price of Salt, Carol*, and Queer Narrative Desire(s)," in *Patricia Highsmith on Screen*, ed. Wieland Schwanebeck and Douglas McFarland (New York: Springer/Palgrave Macmillan, 2018), 139–58; Jenny M. James, "Maternal Failure, Queer Futures: Reading *The Price of Salt* (1952) and *Carol* (2015) against Their Grain," *GLQ* 24, no. 2–3 (2018): 291–314; Victoria L. Smith, "The Heterotopias of Todd Haynes: Creating Space for Same Sex Desire in *Carol*," *Film Criticism* 42, no. 1 (2018): 1–15; Patricia White, "Sketchy Lesbians: *Carol* as History and Fantasy," *Film Quarterly* 62, no. 2 (2015): 8–18.
38 Richard Rushton, "Cavell and the Politics of Cinema: On *Marie Antoinette*," *Film-Philosophy* 18 (2014): 8–18; Richard Rushton, "Acknowledgment and Unknown Women: The Films of Catherine Breillat," *Journal for Cultural Research* 14, no. 1 (2010): 85–101; Wim Staat, "Christian Petzold's Melodramas: From Unknown Woman to Reciprocal Unknownness in *Phoenix*, *Wolfsburg*, and *Barbara*," *Studies in European Cinema* 13, no. 3 (2016): 185–99.
39 Haynes asked Blanchett and Mara to read Roland Barthes' *A Lover's Discourse* in order to prepare for their roles as Carol and Therese. See White, "Sketchy Lesbians: *Carol* as History and Fantasy." White discusses the significance of Barthes' text for the ways in which the love relationship is explored in the film.
40 See Sinnerbrink, *Cinematic Ethics*, 123–25.

41 Therese's own ambivalence about how her relationship with Carol may or may not fit within the subcultural New York lesbian community is signaled in the record store scene where two older lesbians, in mannish dress, stare pointedly at Therese, who also seems unsure how to respond to their gaze. That she and Carol do not fit into this subcultural world, let alone the "straight" world, only adds to the tragic pressure to which their perfectionist romance is submitted.

42 See the illuminating interview with Haynes about the making of the film by Nick Davis, "The Object of Desire," *Film Comment* 51, no. 6 (2015): 31–35.

43 Walter Metz, "Far From Toy Trains," *Film Criticism* 40, no. 3 (2016): 1–4.

44 The film's circular structure—commencing with a restaurant scene in which their relationship hangs in the balance, recounting the story of their relationship and how they reached that point, and reprising the same scene having traversed the story and realized the pathos and gravity of their exchange—recalls *Brief Encounter* in structure, mood, and style. *Carol*, however, also departs from the earlier film in leaving open the possibility of Carol and Therese renewing their romance on a more equal and hopeful basis.

8

Overcoming Skepticism in *Casablanca*

Thomas E. Wartenberg

THE PHILOSOPHER WHO HAS WRITTEN MOST EXTENSIVELY and with the greatest insight about film and romantic love is, of course, Stanley Cavell.[1] Identifying two genres of traditional Hollywood film—the comedy of remarriage and the melodrama of the unknown woman—Cavell argues that film can be a source of important philosophical insight.[2] With nuanced and penetrating interpretations of such films as *It Happened One Night* and *Stella Dallas*, Cavell argues that films in these two genres offer profound examinations of what he calls the problem of skepticism and the possibility of overcoming it. Although in his later work,[3] Cavell prefers to talk about moral perfectionism, in this chapter I shall retain his earlier emphasis on skepticism.

By skepticism, Cavell refers to what analytic philosophers call "the problem of other minds," the question of whether—and, if so, how we can know—other people have minds, that is, an interior life with thoughts and emotions much like our own. This is a problem for those post-Cartesian philosophers who have retained Descartes' assumption that we have "privileged access" to the contents of our own minds, something lacking in regard to those of other people.[4] The only access we have to others' minds, these philosophers maintain, is through their behavior, which yields less certainty than what is attained through introspection. Indeed, the standard argument from analogy's attempt to bridge the gap between our own minds and those of others has repeatedly come in for devastating critique.[5] Hence, the skeptical possibility of doubting that we can ever know with certainty what others think or feel.

Philosophers from Spinoza and Leibniz to Heidegger and Wittgenstein and beyond have attempted to resolve this problem or, as some would have it, dis-solve it. Cavell's own innovative solution denies that it can be resolved theoretically, as many philosophers had attempted. Rather, other minds skepticism, according to Cavell, requires an ethical or practical solution. He calls this solution "acknowledgment," by which he means that one has to open oneself to the other in all the uncertainty and with all the vicissitudes this entails. This "solution" does not attempt to point out an error at the base of other minds' skepticism but treats it as an ongoing threat facing us as we live our lives, one that needs to be repeatedly confronted and accepted.

Cavell discusses the issue of acknowledgment in various different contexts, finding it present in literary and dramatic texts as well as philosophical ones. He claims that the comedies and melodramas he discusses do more to examine the problems that skepticism poses for us and what the possibilities for overcoming it are than most of the works of post-Cartesian Western philosophy. Through their narratives, we are presented with individuals succumbing to the ever-present temptation of skepticism yet finding a way to accept the other in all their messy finitude.

In interpreting these films and their presentation of skepticism, Cavell focuses on their central female characters. He claims that these women need to be "saved" from the perils of skepticism by the men they are involved with. In the comedies, they are faced with a choice between a man who offers comfort and conformity, and one who offers an adventurous if less traditional life. In choosing the latter, the heroines of these films are portrayed as learning to live with the dangers of skepticism in order to embrace a more fulfilling life than available with a more conventional partner.

Cavell has been criticized for the sexism inherent in his view by many people including both feminists and myself. My own criticism is that Cavell misinterprets the films he discusses by overemphasizing the women characters' need to be saved by the male counterparts, and failing to see that these men are in as much need of assistance in confronting their own skeptical doubts as the women they supposedly are engaged in saving.[6] To cite just one example, the Clark Gable character in *It Happened One Night* is equally in need of shedding his elitism and solipsism as the Claudette Colbert character is of embracing a more egalitarian vision of humanity. By failing to acknowledge that the films' male characters are equally prey to the threat of skepticism as the female ones, Cavell gives a one-sided interpretation of the films he discusses.

Nonetheless, Cavell's emphasis on skepticism illuminates the philosophical interest of many films, including, as I shall argue in this chapter, *Casablanca* (1942, dir. Michael Curtiz). I see *Casablanca* as focusing on a male character who has succumbed to the threat of skepticism from which he needs to be saved, and will be through the agency of a woman. So, on this view,

Casablanca is a film depicting the threat skepticism poses even as it provides an important corrective to Cavell's one-sided emphasis.

Rick's Isolationist Individualism

Early on, *Casablanca* presents Rick Blaine (Humphrey Bogart) as a mysterious, isolated figure at the center of the vibrant café he owns, *Rick's Café Américain*. Even the Nazi officer, Major Strasser (Conrad Veidt), who has come to Casablanca to investigate the deaths of two couriers and to retrieve the letters of transit stolen from them, tells the corrupt but charming local police officer, Captain Louis Renault (Claude Rains), that he has heard of the place.

Our first glimpse of Rick emphasizes the mystery surrounding him. After we enter the main room of the café, seeing its elegant tables with white tablecloths while hearing Sam (Dooley Wilson) and his ensemble entertaining the customers with a jazz tune, we move into the back room where illegal gambling takes place. When one of the female customers asks if Rick will join her party for a drink, she is informed that "Rick never drinks with customers," establishing his isolation.[7] When her companion tries to use his status as the manager of the second largest bank in Amsterdam to get Rick to join them, he is told that Rick won't be impressed by his boast since the pastry chef was that city's leading banker. (Throughout this scene, the film plays on the fact that many of its secondary characters are played by refugee actors who fled to the United States to escape Hitler and who had been major European film stars.) We then see a gambling chit placed on a table with a white tablecloth and a man's hand picking it up to study it. The signature he places on it—"OK, Rick"—identifies the man for us as having the authority to approve a check and the camera then pans up to reveal Rick. He sits alone despite there being a crowd in the club, playing chess by himself. He then looks at the door to the back room where various people are trying to gain entrance. After nodding to allow an exotically attired couple to enter, Rick shakes his head, denying entrance to a German banker, who is enraged. As he tries to force his way in, Rick tells him that his money is good at the bar.

What these encounters signal to us is that Rick fulfills the stereotype of many Hollywood male characters, the rugged individualist who needs no one else, the "strong, silent type." In the context of this film and its use of its narrative as a metaphor for politics, we could say that Rick is an isolationist, someone who, as he will later say more than once, sticks his neck out for no one.

In these opening shots, the film conveys Rick's isolation and eschewal of intimate relationships including romantic ones. He drinks alone, is his own chess opponent, and shows no affection for the attractive young woman,

Yvonne (Madeleine Lebeau), he had been sleeping with. At this point, the only person for whom Rick shows any signs of affection is Sam (Dooley Wilson), his black piano player, who he has refused to sell to Signor Ferrari (Sydney Greenstreet), the owner of a competing establishment, the Blue Parrot, saying he doesn't "buy or sell human beings," thereby distinguishing his Americanness from European urbanity. Aside from Sam and the various employees in the café, Rick's only other contact is with Renault, and their relationship is governed by their mutually benefiting from each other, with Renault turning a blind eye to the illegal gambling taking place in the back room in exchange for being paid off.

The incident that cements our sense of Rick as a cynical isolationist shows him failing to help Ugarte (Peter Lorre), a small-time black marketeer. Ugarte enters *Rick's* and quickly tries to ingratiate himself with Rick. Although Rick refuses to drink with him in accordance with his isolationist policy, he and Ugarte share an easy camaraderie. This results in Ugarte asking Rick to do him a favor: to keep the two letters of transit that are now in Ugarte's possession. Rick accepts the letters under the provision that he not have to keep them overnight and hides them in Sam's piano. Ugarte is the thief Renault plans to arrest in a dramatic fashion to impress Strasser.

That evening, as Ugarte is gambling in the back room, he is apprehended. As he attempts to flee, he encounters Rick. "Rick, Rick, help me," he cries. Rick responds, "Don't be a fool. You can't get away," making not even the slightest attempt to help Ugarte, despite the latter's repeated pleas for help. Ugarte is captured and, we later learn, killed. (Renault later remarks that he can't decide whether Ugarte died trying to escape or committed suicide in his cell, emphasizing his corrupt morals.) When a bystander says that he hopes Rick will do more to help him "when they come to get" him, Rick repeats the ethical stance he had earlier articulated in response to Renault's worry that he would help Laszlo leave Casablanca: "I stick my neck out for nobody."

This incident does two things. First, it anchors our sense of Rick as an isolationist individualist. Rick is completely unmoved by Ugarte's request for help, for he is impervious to the ethical claims others have on him. He is the only person whose welfare he is concerned with, with the exception of Sam, and Sam is a black man who is dependent on Rick, his "boss."[8] Rick's relationship with Sam is important, despite its echo of a master-slave relationship.

Second, Rick winds up with the letters of transit as a result of Ugarte's apprehension. Narratively, this is what allows Rick to become the obstacle to—and later the vehicle for—Ilsa (Ingrid Bergman) and Laszlo's escape from Casablanca.

The initial sense we get of Rick, then, is that he is a strong individualist who thinks of himself as needing no one. The character played by Bogart is one that fulfills a basic stereotype employed for leading men in classical Hollywood cinema. Although the political agenda of the film overlays Rick's individualism with a disregard for politics, the film has not strayed far from standard representations of Hollywood's leading men.

The Origins of Rick's Skepticism

Rick's attitude of isolationism or noninvolvement with others parallels the political stance of many anti-interventionists who had opposed the United States' entry into the Second World War, the time when *Casablanca* was filmed. However, the film moves beyond a typical portrayal of the male rugged individualist by showing how Rick came to have this attitude. Rather than treating Rick's individualism as fundamental, the film suggests that this attitude is a reaction engendered by the wound caused by betrayal. According to the film, Rick's more fundamental character is that of a caring and committed person who fights for freedom even at great personal cost. His belief that his lover betrayed him makes Rick cynical about love and results in his adopting an isolationist attitude that embodies his distrust of others. What I am going to suggest is that this cynical attitude is best understood as a form of skepticism.

The revelation of how Rick evolved into the isolationist he now appears to be—we should note that even during the opening sequence there are some "cracks" in his refusal to get involved, as he demonstrates by his antipathy to the Nazis in the café—takes place at night in the café the evening after Ilsa's appearance there. Rick had been taken aback by Ilsa's sudden entrance into the café. He only becomes aware of Isla's presence when he hears Sam playing "their song," "As Time Goes By," despite his ban on it. Rick's subsequent transgressive sharing a drink with Ilsa and Laszlo underscores the significance Ilsa has for him, a fact remarked upon by Renault, an acute observer of Rick's behavior.

Later that night, Rick is sitting alone with a bottle of bourbon when Sam enters.

Continuing in his role as Rick's protector, Sam urges Rick to leave with him and go fishing, echoing, as many have noted, Huck and Jim's adventures on the raft. Rick demurs, and soon mutters one of the film's classic lines: "Of all the gin joints in all the towns in all the world she walks into mine—!" Clearly, Ilsa's appearance has overturned the calm, controlled exterior that we have so far seen Rick exhibit. Sam's attempt to divert Rick fails, as Rick reflects on his relationship with Ilsa.

Rick and Ilsa had a torrid affair in Paris on the eve of the Nazi invasion, something the film reveals through a flashback whose contents we see depicted on the screen. One interesting feature of the flashback is that, even though it supposedly presents us with the contents of Rick's memories, it allows us to see aspects of what transpired during that period of which Rick himself is unaware. The film's creation of a gap between Rick's understanding of these events and ours is significant, as we shall see.

In Paris, Rick was involved in anti-Nazi activities, a part of his past that had already been hinted at by Strasser and Renault in an earlier scene at the café, but that Rick refused to attribute to any motive other than the pay he received for running guns. Although Ilsa was married to Laszlo, she believed he had been killed, so her affair with Rick does not tarnish her ethics in the way that a knowingly adulterous affair would have.

What we learn about their affair from the flashback is that it was brief and very intense. In its first shot, we see them driving in a convertible sports car with the Parisian countryside in the background. Rick, in particular, looks less severe, more relaxed, and infinitely happier than he does in Casablanca. We then see them boating on the Seine, drinking champagne, and dancing, activities indicative of the intensity of their romantic relationship. Their reverie is interrupted by the imminent invasion of Paris by the Nazis, conveyed through another newsreel-like montage that abruptly changes the romantic mood.

The longest scene in the flashback takes place at *La Belle Aurore*, the establishment Rick owned in Paris. We see Rick and Ilsa sipping champagne together with Sam who plays "As Time Goes By." Rick toasts Ilsa with a line that became Bogart's signature, "Here's looking at you, kid." But Ilsa seems troubled. When the film moves from a three-shot to a close-up of Ilsa, she is shown looking down apprehensively. Although we may take this to be due to the danger he faces from the imminent Nazi takeover of Paris, it's actually something else much more threatening to their future, though we don't learn what until later in the film. Rick, however, caught up in their romance, fails to even notice the divergence between Ilsa's mood and his, as he proposes a toast repeating his famous line, "Here's looking at you, kid."

The presence of a Gestapo soundtruck loudly announcing the immanence of the German invasion of Paris, brings them up short. It's clear that Rick is in danger because of his anti-Nazi activities, so they have to make plans to escape.

Rick suggests that they take the Marseilles train together in the morning and proposes picking Ilsa up at her hotel, but she demurs. As he proposes to her, she cries, saying that she hates the war and loves him so much. She tries to tell Rick that something is amiss but can't bring herself to—she worries that he might not leave Paris if he knows she won't—and asks him to kiss her "as if it were the last time," presaging their impending separation.

Throughout this scene, the film clues us into a disparity between Rick's complete involvement in their relationship and Ilsa's hesitation. For example, when Rick suggests picking her up at her hotel, her expression clearly indicates a problem, as she looks down as if she is seeing some danger or concern. But Rick has averted his gaze and notices nothing. While the film depicts Ilsa's hesitation to commit to Rick's plan, it also shows us that Rick does not pick up on this, thereby establishing an epistemological gap between our knowledge and his, as well as between Ilsa's and his feelings.

The next day, as Rick stands waiting in the pouring rain, Ilsa does not show up as she had promised. In her stead is a brief letter she gave to Sam that Rick reads in the pouring rain, blurring the ink. Although in the letter Ilsa assures Rick that she loves him, she doesn't explain why she won't be going with him, only telling him that she can't. Sam manages to get the devastated Rick onto the Marseilles-bound train and out of harm's way.

This brief flashback sequence supplies important information about Rick and Ilsa that explains Rick's attitude toward her. It hints that the film may be a remarriage film, though perhaps not a comedy in any standard sense, for we can anticipate Rick and Ilsa acknowledging their love for one another in Casablanca and resuming their romance. The problem standing in their way—or, at least, the one internal to their relationship—is Rick's attitude toward Ilsa.

As the flashback ends, Ilsa enters the closed café. During her interaction with Rick, his bitterness over her failure to meet him at the station emerges. This scene is shot with Ilsa, clad in a white coat, dramatically lit with the rest of the café, Rick included, in shadow, as light from a searchlight periodically sweeps the room. This lighting allows Ilsa's beauty to be emphasized, but it also gives us clear access to her reactions to what Rick says, reactions that indicate she is not the heartless betrayer Rick takes her to be. Wallowing in self-pity, Rick does not notice that Ilsa still loves him, as indicated when she tells him that she can understand how he feels, a revelation he simply dismisses by brutally asking her "How long was it we had, honey?" As in the flashback scene, we are privy to Ilsa's feelings in a way that Rick is not.

Rick then tells Ilsa how he felt when she didn't show up at the Paris train station, saying that he remembers every day of their relationship, especially the last one: "A wow finish. A guy standing on a station platform in the rain with a comical look on his face because his insides had been kicked out."

Ilsa tries to explain to Rick why she couldn't join him on the train to Marseilles by telling him "the story" of her relationship with Laszlo, but Rick puts her off telling her that he hears stories all the time, so that hers is nothing special. Rick's anger emerges even more strongly when he asks her if she left him for Laszlo and casts aspersions on her character: "Was it Laszlo [that she left him for]—or were there others in between—or aren't you the kind that tells?"

The Rick we see in this scene is a bitter, vulnerable man, who has suffered inordinately from the perceived betrayal of his lover. And this aggrieved lover is also different from the happy, loving person we saw during most of the Paris flashback. Clearly, there are depths to Rick's character that seeing him as an isolationist with no need for or interest in others simply fails to take account of.

This portrayal of his vulnerability complicates our initial sense of Rick's character. In addition to seeing how different Rick was when he was in Paris with Ilsa—both she and Sam call him Richard there, as if to register that he was a different person then, a committed partisan and caring lover—we also see the pain that Rick conceals in Casablanca by adopting the "tough guy" cover. The strong, silent figure we see at the film's outset is revealed to be a pose, an appearance, protective of a more vulnerable self.

We can best understand the nature of Rick's isolationist attitude by characterizing it as a form of skepticism. To see this, consider the following sentence from the first of Descartes' *Meditations on First Philosophy*, which brings the ancient skeptical tradition to the heart of modern European philosophy. Descartes introduces the theme of deception with this thought: "But occasionally I have found that [the senses] have deceived me, and it is unwise to trust completely those who [*qui*] have deceived us even once."[9] Descartes' worry is that he will never be able to attain certainty—his epistemic goal—if he trusts a source of beliefs that has deceived him even once. For this reason, he resorts to skepticism, the universal doubting of all sense perception, as a way to avoid error and attain certainty. But such certainty is based on a very exacting standard for knowledge—that one never be misled—that has come in for a great deal of criticism from subsequent philosophers.

Rick's cynical, skeptical attitude about love and other human beings is the result of his applying a similar overly exacting standard to his relationship with others. He has been so deeply hurt by Ilsa's failure to leave Paris with him that he attempts to protect himself from being hurt again by not trusting anyone, a move akin to Descartes' skeptical rejection of beliefs grounded upon the senses because they had deceived him. As in the case of Descartes, Rick's self-protective stance is faulty for its radical rejection of trust simply because it brings with it the possibility of deception and error.

Trust plays a constitutive role in our relationships with others. In order to have a romantic relationship with someone, we need to trust them to be telling the truth, so that we can take our understanding of what they are feeling to be an accurate guide to how they actually do feel. During our initial views of Rick and Ilsa during the Paris flashback, they shared such a trusting relationship, something the film indicated in many of its shots of the two of them, by the lighting, and the expressions of the two actors. But we already noticed that, toward the end of that sequence, there was a disjunction between what Ilsa was feeling and what Rick took her to be feeling, something the film was able to indicate to us by allowing us to see her expression in a way that emphasized how Ilsa did not share Rick's fantasies about their future.

One element needs to be added in order to fill out our understanding of the Cartesian skepticism I have attributed to Rick, namely, how it allows one to avoid the vulnerability to another human being that romantic love brings in its wake. To love someone is to allow one's own happiness to be dependent on them and how they relate to you. Anyone who has experienced romantic rejection is aware of this dependency. In Rick's case, the fact that Ilsa's perceived rejection of him comes when he believes she is truly in love with him makes the pain of his dependency all the greater.

The skeptic, the person who distrusts other human beings and suspects their motives, is able to protect himself from being deceived, but only at the price of rejecting all intimate human relationships. The film asks us to understand isolationism such as Rick's as just such a skeptical reaction to the experience of loss.

So, *Casablanca* demonstrates that there are reasons why people find romantic love along with its concomitant acknowledgment of another threatening: in a love relationship, one makes oneself vulnerable to the other. Should they betray your trust—as Rick believes Ilsa did—your entire sense of self can be undermined. Such betrayal is a violation of trust, and once one loses one's trust, which after all has to do both with one's relationship to others and also to one's own experience, it is difficult to develop an appropriate relationship to the world and others in it.

Casablanca thus rejects the notion that skepticism is a basic stance toward experience reflective of a person's innate character. Instead, it presents it as reactive. The film thereby criticizes how many films present the rugged male individual, a staple of Hollywood film— think, for example, of the character Charles Bronson played in the various *Death Wish* films. Rather than accepting the portrayal of such "he men" as embodying a fundamental form of masculinity, through its portrayal of Rick, *Casablanca* suggests that this character type is developed to protect a man's natural vulnerability.

This understanding of the film's take on skepticism and masculinity is supported by the fact that Bogart's screen persona is in transition in this film. Earlier, in films like *King of the Underworld* (1939, dir. Lewis Seiler), Bogart played gangsters, characters who fit the "strong, silent type" mold. But with *Casablanca*, Bogart was being transitioned into the romantic hero of films like *The Big Sleep* (1946, dir. Howard Hawks). In *Casablanca*, Bogart is being used "off-cast," that is, in a manner that contradicts the type of character he had previously been cast as, allowing the film to critically depict that very type.[10]

Restoring Trust, Overcoming Skepticism

I have suggested that *Casablanca* prepares us for Rick and Ilsa's "remarriage." However, the film does not fulfill its suggestion that Rick and Ilsa will remarry, in part because the complexities of the sociopolitical context make such a reunion impossible. But, before their remarriage is even possible,

Rick will have to shed his skepticism, something he does in a scene that takes place with Ilsa in his office once again.

Ilsa has returned to Rick's office with the intention of getting the letters of transit from him so that she can leave Casablanca with Laszlo. She does so despite Rick's hostility toward her and his repeated brusque refusal to give the two of them the letters, even when Laszlo offers to pay handsomely for them.

Ilsa appeals to Rick by asking him to put aside his animosity toward her, hoping to reach the person she knew him to be in Paris, calling him "Richard" in an attempt to reach the deeper self underneath his cynical, skeptical shell. She tells him that giving her the letters will serve "something more important" than his own hurt feelings, hoping that Laszlo's role in the fight against fascism will move Rick, since he previously had worked for that cause. But emphasizing Laszlo's importance only exacerbates Rick's animosity. "I'm not fighting for anything anymore—except myself," he responds. "I'm the only cause I'm interested in," reiterating the cynicism of his skeptical, isolationist stance. That skeptical stance has become deeply ingrained in Rick, although not without certain "leakage," as when he helps a young Bulgarian woman get the visa she needs, an incident we'll explore more fully in a moment.

When Ilsa tells him if he "only knew the truth" he'd act differently, Rick dismisses her in a manner that emphasizes his skeptical distrust. "I wouldn't believe you, no matter what you told me." Rick thinks that Ilsa will use any means at her disposal to get what she wants, so that his distrust of her utterances is warranted.

Ilsa responds by calling him a coward for responding to her supposed betrayal by adopting a universally skeptical stance. Abruptly shifting her emotions, she plaintively tells Rick that he is "their last hope." To Ilsa's plea that unless he gives her the letters, Laszlo will die in Casablanca, Rick blithely responds, "What of it? I'm going to die in Casablanca. It's a good spot for it." Horrified by his response, Ilsa pulls out a gun, much to Rick's surprise as he turns and sees her. She hopes that the threat of violence will get Rick to yield: "I tried to reason with you. I tried everything. Now I want the letters." What she hadn't counted on was how deeply her perceived treachery had wounded Rick. He refuses to hand over the letters and tells her as he moves closer to her, "All right, I'll make it easier for you, go ahead, shoot. You'll be doing me a favor."

Ironically, Ilsa can't follow the advice she just gave Rick and put aside her own feelings in service of something more important. Faced with shooting the man she truly loves, she finds her resolve falter. "Richard," she says, "I tried to stay away. I thought I would never see you again." As she turns away from Rick in despair, to the sound of deeply romantic music, Rick's face registers the feelings he has been denying. His skeptical distrust has been overcome by her confession of love.

Rick then goes to her and the two of them embrace to the strains of romantic violins. With their faces in shadow, Ilsa confesses, "If you knew how much I loved you, how much I still love you," and the two of them share a deep kiss. No longer the skeptic, Rick is able to acknowledge his love for Ilsa despite the vulnerability that accompanies it.

What is it that allows Rick to alter his skeptical distrust of Ilsa and acknowledge her suffering and her love for him? As Cavell has emphasized, skepticism cannot be overcome by a proof, a demonstration that such an attitude is ill-founded, because skepticism is founded on an important truth about human relationships. The only successful way to "overcome" skepticism is for the skeptic to change his or her attitude toward the other, his or her lover. Ilsa's inability to follow through on her threat to shoot Rick and her subsequent breakdown are what prompt Rick's abandonment of his skepticism in regard to her, what get him to see her differently. The film depicts this through a series of close-ups of their two faces, with each of their faces illuminated with a bright light from behind that casts strong shadows on the side of their faces facing us. As Rick takes in the emotion that overwhelms Ilsa, she sheds a tear before she turns away from him and walks to the window. As we see his face registering genuine concern for her, he moves toward her and embraces her as she explains why she was not able to meet him. Having shed his skeptical shell, Rick now allows himself to acknowledge the love he had been repressing.

During the Paris flashback, Rick and Ilsa's feelings were out of sync; now, the two are completely in harmony. The face-to-face encounter that was precipitated by Ilsa's threat and Rick's response has ironically resulted in their reunification rather than in Rick's death at Ilsa's hands. The film seems poised to provide the two lovers with the remarriage we had ardently been hoping for, though this will not come to pass.

Central to *Casablanca*'s philosophical achievement is its rejection of the standard Hollywood depiction of heroic masculinity through its presentation of Rick's cynical skepticism not as a basic attitude but as one formed in reaction to a lover's betrayal. *Casablanca* depicts its male hero's independence as a symptom of his skeptical withdrawal, and the latter as a result of his wounded narcissism. It was this narcissism that was responsible for the epistemic gap between him and his beloved, a gap that contributed to his being blindsided by her failure to join him at the station.

In all of this, *Casablanca* involves a significant departure from the narrative central to Cavell's account of both comedies and melodramas, where the character needing saving is a woman. Here, Rick is clearly the character who needs to undergo a change in order for the couple to be able to remarry, the standard outcome of the comedies Cavell is concerned with. Although Rick and Ilsa's remarriage is only brief, lasting but a single night, it is made possible by Rick's shedding his skepticism. This happens because

Ilsa's refusal to harm him and her subsequent acknowledgment of her love for him pierce the cynical shell with which he has armed himself.

Rick's transformation or, perhaps, recovery opens up the possibility of their "remarriage." After two dissolves indicative of the passage of time—perhaps they made love—Ilsa completes her explanation of her failure to meet him at the station. Rick responds by saying "It's still a story without an ending," prompting Ilsa to say that she only knows that she'll "never have the strength to leave him again." When Rick asks her about Laszlo, she asks him to help Laszlo escape, since then he'll have his work. After Rick points out that Laszlo won't have her, she collapses into his arms, saying, "I don't know what's right any longer. You'll have to think for both of us. For all of us." Her realization of the personal cost of putting the political before the personal makes her unable to follow through on her plan to be, as Rick later puts it, "noble." Unable to follow through on the course of action she has chosen, Ilsa turns to Rick, asking him to provide a means of rationally deciding what the right, that is, moral, thing to do is.

Conveniently, Rick exhibits no ambivalence about being asked to determine how they should act and accepts Ilsa's proposition: "All right. I will." And he then reprises once again the great line uttered twice during the Paris flashback that here signifies the resurgence of his love for Ilsa and his jettisoning of his skepticism: "Here's looking at you, kid."

At this point, it seems that Rick and Ilsa's story has an ending. The two of them, having rediscovered their love for one another, will be remarried and Laszlo will go to the United States to continue his anti-fascist agitation. Nonetheless, the film can't actually end with such a remarriage.

Two things stand in the way. First, Laszlo's fate is a factor that Rick and Ilsa's remarriage won't solve. Unlike the alternative male figure in some of the remarriage comedies—King Westley (Jameson Thomas) in *It Happened One Night*, for example—Laszlo is not someone for whom we have no sympathy, even if he appears stilted and unattractive in comparison with Rick. His anti-fascist efforts make him admirable, so remarrying the couple at the cost of his unhappiness would not provide a morally satisfactory ending for the film.

Second, there is an important factor external to the narrative of the film that won't allow for a successful remarriage of Rick and Ilsa. Given the role that the Motion Picture Production Code still played in Hollywood, presenting an adulterous relationship positively would likely have gotten the film banned even though the film would have still supported resistance to the Nazis, though not in as strong terms as it actually did. The problem facing the filmmakers is to provide a morally satisfying and emotionally compelling resolution to this "three-body problem."

Before turning to that, I want to emphasize the gendered nature of the remarriage. Ilsa, the woman, is overcome with emotion and tells Rick, the man, that he has to do the thinking for her. Presumably, she thinks he'll be able to distance himself sufficiently from his emotions—despite not having been able to since leaving Paris—to make the correct ethical decision about what to do.

The film here uses a standard sexist trope: "Man is to woman as reason is to emotion." This disempowers Ilsa, who otherwise has been shown to be a strong, capable woman. In the following scene, matters get even worse, as all the thinking is done by Rick and Ilsa is completely passive in the final resolution of their situation. So, despite its critical examination of one form of masculinity, the film eventually embodies a stereotypical conception of gender.

A Different Lesson in Love

The lesson about love that *Casablanca* offers seems to be that, despite the danger involved in making one's happiness depend upon another, it is a mistake to skeptically deny its importance. However, the film's ending highlights a different claim about love, namely, that love requires the lover to give priority to the well-being of the person they love, even if doing so is not in the lover's own self-interest. It is this recognition that motivates Rick to make the noble sacrifice in the film's well-known final scene.

The ending of *Casablanca* is one of the great twists in Hollywood cinema. Everyone, both the members of the audience and all the characters assembled at the Casablanca airport, expects Rick to send Laszlo off to Portugal while he and Ilsa remain in Casablanca. This is, after all, what he and Ilsa had agreed to. But Rick turns the tables in a hugely romantic, emotional scene, sending Ilsa off with Laszlo and remaining behind himself.

What explains Rick's decision, and how does it reflect his doing the thinking for all of them, the task Ilsa had bequeathed to him? Basically, Rick comes to believe that love requires prioritizing the well-being of one's lover. He learns this, most pointedly, through his earlier interaction with a minor character in the film, Annina Brandel (Joy Paige).

She, like most of the film's characters, needs an exit visa. It turns out that Captain Renault controls their distribution. Renault has one major vice—young women—and he uses his control of the visas to extract sex from them in exchange for the visas. It is this situation that the film uses to present Annina's ethical dilemma in a manner that presages Rick's own.

Annina is a young and very beautiful Bulgarian woman. From the first time *Casablanca* presents her to us, she is portrayed as a character with whose plight we have sympathy. She is filmed in a manner emphasizing her attractiveness and thus activating our empathy for her situation. Paige's acting also foregrounds her innocence and sincerity. Annina has fled her homeland with her husband Jan (Helmut Dantine) in the hope of getting to America and having a better life not just for themselves but for their future children. The difficulty they face is obtaining exit visas. They are poor and can't afford the black-market price for a visa, so Jan decides to gamble at Rick's in the hope of winning sufficient funds to buy the visas from Renault. It appears, however, that Jan will lose all of their money—the roulette wheel is fixed—so that the only way for them to obtain the visas is for Annina to sleep with Renault.

Annina clearly is faced with an ethical dilemma. On the one hand, she has the ability to obtain the exit visas she and her husband need. On the other, the cost of doing so is serious, for Renault would be coercing her into having sex with him even though doing so would involve violating her marriage vow to "forsake all others." Having grappled with this issue previously, she has decided to go ahead and sleep with Renault but only if she can resolve two worries. She turns to Rick for help in resolving them.

First, she needs to be assured that Renault won't back out of the deal once she has slept with him. After Rick assures her that Renault has always proven trustworthy, thereby resolving that qualm, Annina brings up the second one. In a scene shot in increasingly tight shot-reverse shots of Annina and Rick, with Annina's face illuminated with an eye-light that creates a glimmer in her eyes—something that establishes a connection between her and Ilsa not just for us but in Rick's mind as well, for Ilsa's face is illuminated identically in a number of scenes to emphasize her beauty and attractiveness—Annina asks Rick, "M'Sieur, you are a man. If someone loved you . . . very much, so that your happiness was the only thing in the world that she wanted and . . . she did a bad thing to make certain of it, could you forgive her?" These lines emphasize both Annina's naïveté and her sincerity. Turning to a stranger, indeed, a cynic who doesn't want to become involved with others' difficulties, shows her innocent and trusting nature, features of her character that make her attractive to the film's audience.

Rick's response shows that he has been moved, but also that he won't get involved. "Nobody ever loved me that much," he responds in a line brimming with self-pity. Refusing to be discouraged, Annina continues: "But, M'seur, if he never knew . . . if the girl kept this bad thing locked in her heart . . . that would be all right, wouldn't it?"

Initially, Rick seems to abide by his skeptical moral stance when he tells Annina that his advice to her is to "go back to Bulgaria" and eventually dismisses her by telling her that "Everyone in Casablanca has problems." However, because he has been moved by her plight, he extricates Annina from her difficulty. He has his croupier (Marcel Dalio) let Jan win enough money to purchase the exit visas, thus revealing his "sentimental" (Renault's term) side in action, that is, his empathy with the young lovers.

The reason that Rick is so affected by Annina is that she claims that her love for Jan is the most important thing in her life. This means that Jan's happiness matters so much to her that she is willing to sacrifice her own to help him attain satisfaction. What Rick learns from her is that love means caring so deeply about fostering the happiness and well-being of one's lover that one is willing to sacrifice oneself to achieve it.

This view of love as requiring the normative prioritization of the beloved's welfare is further emphasized in a short interchange Rick has with Laszlo, shortly before the film's final scene. Laszlo, who is almost always taken to be a one-sided character defined by his loyalty to "the cause," exhibits an adherence to Annina's understanding of love. After commenting on Rick's running from something, Victor tells Rick that he knows they both love Ilsa, and then makes an unexpected request.

> LASZLO: I ask you as a favor to use the letters to take her [Ilsa] away from Casablanca.
> RICK: You love her that much?
> LASZLO: Apparently you think of me only as the leader of a cause. Well, I am also a human being. . . . Yes, I love her that much.

Here, the earnest Victor is motivated by something other than his political commitment. In fact, by asking Rick to use the letters to take Ilsa away from Casablanca, Laszlo seems willing to forsake "the cause," since he will likely be imprisoned by the Nazis if he remains in Casablanca and that would keep him from his anti-fascist work.

The twist in *Casablanca*'s final scene is the result of Rick's decision to act on the basis of this conception of love. Keeping his intentions quiet, Rick masterfully arranges for things to transpire according to his plan in a manner that surprises both the characters and the film's audience.

Ilsa is, of course, shocked when she hears Rick tell Renault to put her and Laszlo's names on the letters of transit, for she had expected to remain with Rick. Ironically, when Rick explains his reasoning to her, he doesn't expressly point out its basis on his new understanding of the requirements of romantic love. Instead, he tries to get Ilsa to see the rationality of his decision.

Rick's justification begins with two attempts to show Ilsa that she will be better off with Laszlo. First, he explains that staying in Casablanca is not the attractive alternative it appears to be. Rick points out that a dreadful fate likely awaits them there, even estimating its likelihood: "Nine chances out of ten we'd both land in a concentration camp." This clearly makes her staying in Casablanca a lot less attractive, for this outcome will almost certainly put her in a dreadful situation. It also explains *to the film audience* why he has chosen to let her go with Laszlo, for staying with him will only endanger her.

Rick's second attempt points out the value she attributes to her role in supporting Laszlo's anti-fascist work. Rick argues that not assisting Laszlo is something that "you'll regret. . . . Maybe not today, maybe not tomorrow, but soon, and for the rest of your life." This suggests that Ilsa has not adequately taken into account the long-term consequences of her actions, weighing only its short-term benefits. Here, she is vulnerable to a particular cognitive bias that many of us are also prone to, "hyperbolic discounting."[11] Rick supplies an important corrective to a faulty assessment of the relative merits of different courses of action. Effects lying in the distant future are no less significant than those occurring nearly immediately. Ilsa has been, he thinks, guilty of ignoring the long-term consequences of staying with him. Rick presents his thinking as doing a better job of accurately assessing the alternatives available to her.

Rick's final rationale places his and Ilsa's dilemma in the broader context of the threat to humanity posed by the Nazis: "It doesn't take much to see that the problems of three little people don't amount to a hill of beans in this crazy world. Someday you'll understand that. . . . Here's looking at you, kid." Rick's point is that the welfare of the three of them is simply not that significant ethically. What matters is the pressing need to support the anti-fascist movement.

Even if it were true that Rick and Ilsa would enjoy their lives together—something that he has already argued would not be the case—Rick now asserts that their happiness is inconsequential in comparison with the need to protect the millions of people who stand to benefit from Laszlo's presence in America that would enable him to continue his anti-fascist activities.

It's significant that, as part of his reasoning at this point, Rick tells Ilsa that, no matter what happens, "we'll always have Paris." That is, Ilsa has given *him* back Paris by confessing her love. It's that which allows him to reexperience their love as a positive feature of his life, rather than as the prelude to a painful rejection. And that fuels his ability to do what is best for *her*, even though this will entail their parting. And so, *Casablanca* ends with Rick making the noble gesture he claims not to be good at.

One aspect of Rick's decision-making raises doubts about its legitimacy, namely, his disempowerment of Ilsa. (Although Laszlo is also disempowered, that matters less for us than what happens to Ilsa.) As he explains *his* decision to her, she wants to respond. But each attempt she makes to express her dissent is interrupted by Rick with another argument supporting his decision. He even tells her, without waiting for her assent, that she had misjudged her own feelings and instructs her on the right way to feel. If, following Cavell, we think that there has to be a mutuality to a love relationship, since each must acknowledge the other, Ilsa's inability to speak indicates that things have gone awry.[12]

So, even though we may not be either surprised or offended by how Rick does "the thinking for all of them," the film does show the underside of Rick's doing so: it leaves no room for Ilsa's dissent to be taken into account, let alone expressed. Her final line in the film, "God bless you," does little to restore her agency as she goes off with Laszlo not into the sunset but into the fog.

Casablanca's ending involves a surprising twist not only because it fails to support the remarriage of its two protagonists as we might expect, but also because it involves a significant departure from the understanding of love that had come to the fore in Rick's story. The film's first ending, so to speak, occurred when Rick was able to acknowledge Ilsa's love for him and reject the skeptical position he had arrived at because of her apparent betrayal of him, thereby choosing to love despite the risk posed to his own happiness. But now, as Rick gives up the woman he loves so dearly, he has thought through the consequences of that love. Because he loves Ilsa, he must act to protect her from harm. But this entails a willingness to make a noble sacrifice in the name of the very love he chooses to forgo—and thus preserve.

Notes

1 This chapter originated in a talk prepared for the Princeton University Symposium on "Love and Friendship in the Movies." It has benefited from comments from the participants in that event, as well as suggestions from Cynthia Freeland and, especially, Paul Schofield. Nina Kleinberg saved me from a number of mistakes about the structure of the film. Additional references consulted while composing the chapter include the stage play, upon which *Casablanca* is based, by Murray Burnett and Joan Alison, *Everybody Comes to Rick's* (New York: Wharton & Gabel, 1940). http://vincasa.com/Screenplay- Everybody_Comes_to_Rick's.pdf; Laura T. Di Summa-Knoop, "The Philosophical and Cognitive Achievement of Cult and Ethical Puzzle of *Casablanca*," *Film and Philosophy* 19 (2015): 115–26; Noah Isenberg, *We'll Always Have Casablanca: The Life, Legend, and Afterlife of Hollywood's Most Beloved Movie* (New York: W.W. Norton, 2017); and my own *Thinking on Screen: Film as Philosophy* (New York: Routledge, 2007).

2 Stanley Cavell, *Pursuits of Happiness: The Hollywood Comedy of Remarriage* (Cambridge: Harvard University Press, 1981) and *Contesting Tears: The Hollywood Melodrama of the Unknown Woman* (Chicago: The University of Chicago Press, 1997).

3 Stanley Cavell, *Cities of Words: Pedagogical Letters on a Register of the Moral Life* (Cambridge: Belknap Press, Harvard University Press, 2004).

4 René Descartes, *Meditations on First Philosophy* (1641), accessed on May 15, 2018, at http://earlymoderntexts.com/assets/pdfs/descartes1641.pdf.

5 The inadequacies of the argument from analogy as the basis for believing in the existence of others' minds have been discussed by philosophers for many decades. For a good summary of this and other issues related to this question, see Alec Hyslop, "Other Minds," *Stanford Encyclopedia of Philosophy*, 2014; http://plato.stanford.edu/archives/spr2019/entries/other-minds/.

6 Thomas E. Wartenberg, *Unlikely Couples: Movie Romance as Social Criticism* (Boulder: Westview Press, 1999).
7 There are many discrepancies between the film's dialogue and its published script: Julius J. Epstein, Philip G. Epstein, and Howard Koch, *Casablanca* (1942), accessed on March 14, 2017 at http://mckeestory.com/wp-content/uploads/Digital-Casablanca.pdf. All quotations from the film are from my transcription of the soundtrack done in conjunction with the published script.
8 The issue of the film's representation of a black man has been the focus on some controversy. Although Sam is not portrayed in any of the stereotypical ways then dominant in Hollywood cinema, neither is he presented as a full-fledged human being with desires and interests of his own. He is primarily Rick's "guardian angel." See Robert Gooding-Williams, "Black Cupids, White Desires: Reading the Representation of Racial Difference in *Casablanca* and *Ghost*," in *Film and Philosophy*, ed. Cynthia Freeland and Thomas E. Wartenberg (New York: Routledge, 1995).
9 Descartes, *Meditations on First Philosophy*.
10 I owe this point to Murray Smith.
11 See, for example, S. Frederick, G. Loewenstein, and T. O'Donoghue, "Time Discounting and Time Preference: A Critical Review," *Journal of Economic Literature* 40, no. 2 (2002): 351–401.
12 I owe this point to Paul Taylor.

9

A Skeptic's Reprieve: Cavell on Comedy in Shakespeare and the Movies

LAWRENCE F. RHU

STANLEY CAVELL WROTE A BOOK ABOUT SHAKESPEARE and several books about film, and his thinking about these two topics overlaps and intertwines in provocative and fruitful ways. Most notably, in *Pursuits of Happiness: The Hollywood Comedy of Remarriage*, Cavell relies on ideas of genre brought to bear on Shakespearean comedy by Northrop Frye. In employing such an approach Cavell's primary aim is "not to establish a classification of objects"—films, in this case, with the right features to qualify for admission to the generic category of remarriage comedy. Rather, he seeks "to articulate the arguments among them."[1] In other words, he identifies recurrent features and their analogues to promote mainly thematic analysis of a group of films whose shared qualities suggest that they are in conversation with one another already.

Cavell is not offering us a catalogue or an itemized list of requirements that secure these films an inarguable place in the canon of such movies. Rather, he offers us topics of discussion already in play among them and invites us into ongoing conversations he overhears on screen between particular films and others of their kind.

Such topics include marriage, a couple's shared past, the role of the woman's father, and the Green World—the last two of which are explicit borrowings from Frye. To demonstrate how these concerns are usefully taken up in Cavell's consideration of remarriage comedy, we could pick any of the seven films he chooses to discuss at length under that rubric. Say, *The Awful Truth*, for example.

In discussing marriage, Cavell memorably remarks that ever since Henry VIII got divorced and Martin Luther married, neither the state nor the church has maintained its former authority to legitimize marriage. Of course, Luther was a priest who ultimately married a nun, and he persuasively argued for the removal of marriage from the church's consideration as a sacrament. Henry was a king whom the Church of Rome dubbed Defender of the Faith for his response to such Lutheran heresy. Little more than a decade later, however, the Pope's refusal to grant Henry a divorce prompted schism, such as Luther had inspired in German principalities.

So, Henry nationalized the Church of England in order to secure a divorce of his own granting. These shaken foundations of Christian authority constitute Cavell's historical allegory of the uncertain idea of marriage we inherit ever after in the West.

Since modern marriage is always subject to the possibility of divorce, Cavell appeals to another historical marker for an apposite sense of what marriage has come to mean in our time: John Milton's *Doctrine and Discipline of Divorce*. In 1643 Milton petitioned Parliament to expand the grounds for divorce beyond carnal infidelity to include "household unhappiness." That sad state of affairs sounds something like "emotional incompatibility," a modern predicate for divorce proceedings. As an alternative, Milton summoned the phrase "meet and happy conversation" to describe the essence of a good marriage, and Cavell considers it an effective expression of the happiness marriage nowadays legitimately hopes to achieve. But he also emphasizes the law's lack of any force in determining a couple's success in attaining such a relationship. We can better come to understand what constitutes such happiness at the movies.

Milton redefined marriage in asking for a divorce (which he received, along with bitter notoriety as a "divorcer"), and that paradox sheds considerable light on films that Cavell identifies as comedies of remarriage. They are not, like Shakespeare's romantic comedies, accounts of a struggle against external obstacles like a father's refusal of his permission for a daughter to marry and the patriarchal laws that reinforce it. Hollywood replaces those shades of the *senex iratus*, or angry old man, of Roman comedy with fathers who often discern their daughters' true desires better than they do themselves. Such fathers actively facilitate their daughters' efforts to achieve those desires.

Under the threat of divorce, however, modern romance dramatizes not marriage but remarriage—not getting together, but getting *back* together, or getting together *again*. When breaking up is a legal option, staying together is freely chosen, and a crisis may inspire the reaffirmation of such a choice. Remarriage comedies dramatize the experience of couples who undergo such crises. In the process they rediscover the rightness of their original choice of each other and make the further choice of staying together.

During the first decades of Hollywood talkies, movie studios engaged in a robust love affair with witty dialogue. With Milton's support, Cavell understands such conversation as the sign of mutual intelligibility or marriage. In *The Awful Truth* (1937, dir. Leo McCarey), the couple actually takes their marriage to court, and the movie runs the length of fictional time that the law requires for their divorce to almost become final. Meanwhile Lucy Warriner (Irene Dunne) reminisces about her life with her soon-to-be ex-husband Jerry (Cary Grant). "We've had some grand laughs together," she remarks to her Aunt Patsy (Cecil Cunningham); and we can fairly construe this comment as an acknowledgment of her "meet and happy conversation" with Jerry. Thus, we begin to notice that the new guy in Lucy's life, Dan Leeson (Ralph Bellamy), doesn't get her jokes. To put it metaphorically (and metaphysically), he and Lucy are not in conversation with one another, though they may often be found together talking, apparently, to one another.

On the other hand, Jerry repeatedly elicits Lucy's laughter, or her anger, whether it's with a pencil in the ribs from behind the door while she listens to the cringe-worthy sappiness of Dan's corny love poem or with the clumsiness of Jerry's jealous interruption of Lucy's performance at a musicale. She is a trained singer, but her voice is basically inaudible to Dan, who cannot bear up under Lucy's harmonizing with his rendition of "Home on the Range," Dan's signature tune. "I've never had a lesson in my life," Dan informs Lucy with evident pride in gifts he seems to suppose Nature has lavished upon him. Though he manages with some apparent effort to identify the aptly named nightclub singer Dixie Belle's accent as southern, Lucy's cultivated voice is beyond his appreciation. In 1937 Irene Dunne arrived at this film with an established reputation as a trained singer due especially to her performance in *Show Boat* (1936) the year before. Three years later Ralph Bellamy cashed in on his reputation for cluelessness, again opposite Cary Grant, in *His Girl Friday* (1940, dir. Howard Hawks), where he passionately protests, "I'm innocent," as if we didn't know. But in *The Awful Truth* we have already seen Cary Grant playing the piano deftly enough to sync the beat with the barking of Mr. Smith, the couple's dog, whose custody the judge obliged them to share during the trial period of their separation. This hilarious musical gag so infuriates Lucy that her anger seems, all the more, a telling index of the grand laughs they have shared before their marriage began to deteriorate.

Such moments project vivid images of a lively relationship that has gone stale, and these sophisticates readily acknowledge, or display, their boredom in each other's company, which reveals the impasse that their marriage has reached. Yet, they make their lucky way back into conversation with one another, and their progress in that direction culminates in a genuinely philosophical dialogue—about continuity and change, and identity and difference—that reminds Cavell of Plato's *Parmenides*. Such a text hardly seems a typical resource for makers of Hollywood movies, or an analogue for the usual ambitions of popular culture. Nonetheless, Cavell recognizes the inherent demand of remarriage comedy, as a genre, for philosophical speculation. Besides, who cannot imagine, or easily remember, in his or her own experience, a moment when it was natural, even necessary, to ask a friend, or a companion, or an exciting new acquaintance, "Do you ever think about getting married?" From such a question about thinking, many sorts of conversation might ensue, but it would be rash to rule out the philosophical.

Couples in remarriage comedy typically share a past. They've grown up together, or they've known one another all their lives. If that's not the case, at least they feel that way about each other, which is more to the point. During the marital crisis in *The Awful Truth*, such feelings seem faintly pathological; at least in the movie's terms, they border on incest. Of course, sentiments of that kind can go a long way toward explaining the staleness or boredom that is shutting down freshness and spontaneity of emotional connection between Jerry and Lucy. He accidentally casts her as his own sister when Lucy visits his apartment and inadvertently answers a call from Jerry's fiancé, Barbara Vance (Molly Lamont). When he tells her that lie in an effort to cover up the fact of his soon-to-be ex's presence in his new place, Barbara naturally expresses a wish to meet her future sister-in-law, a.k.a. Lola, a nightclub singer (mainly in Europe). This quickly conceived fantasy leads to Lucy/Lola's bawdy rendition of Dixie Belle's theme song, "Gone with the Wind," in the otherwise staid atmosphere of a family gathering in the Vances' living room. In Lucy's surprising improvisation, her cultivated voice revels in a funkier register than we've heard from her before, which, together with a few new moves, clearly begins to recapture Jerry's interest in her. When she urges the assembled Vances to use their imaginations about her impromptu performance off-stage, Lucy's suggestion thematizes one of the defects at the root of the Warriners' lost interest in one another: their lack of imagination or, at least, their failure to exercise that faculty empathetically in their understanding of one another. Lucy's disruptive sister act gives them a fresh chance to reconceive of their relationship together.

The absence of Lucy's father in this film may seem to eliminate the opportunity for such a figure to obstruct or facilitate her heart's desire, but Aunt Patsy rather competently fills this merely apparent void in the remarriage structure. Indeed, the strange journey the couple takes to her cabin in Connecticut includes a brief encounter with someone Lucy calls "Dad" when they learn of Aunt Patsy's absence upon their arrival. Moreover, she accurately describes Lucy's sudden interest in Dan as a mere "rebound" from her breakup with Jerry, and, in this exchange, she identifies the central problem Lucy faces, both in and out of her marriage: boredom and complacency.

> PATSY: But what a girl really wants is dependability and security.
> LUCY: Yes, I suppose so.
> PATSY: Then she ought to buy an annuity.

The last line above sounds like a prophecy of Ralph Bellamy's reappearance as an unworldly insurance salesman in *His Girl Friday*. By then, as a rancher from Tulsa in *The Awful Truth*, he has already shown off his chops as the safe option, an automatic default for wives on the rebound.

In five of the seven remarriage comedies examined in *Pursuits of Happiness*, the Green World is called Connecticut. In one of those five, *The Lady Eve* (1941, dir. Preston Sturges), the title character gets into such a cockeyed conversation about how she got to Connecticut from wherever she comes from—and she hits the silent "c" of that word's second syllable so hard with her fake British accent—that it seems there must be something special, if not vaguely transcendental, about such a place. Like Emerson's "new yet unapproachable America," it's unapproachable because you are already there, yet you must change to experience its presence—and, vice versa, your own presence, being there. As though the Centaurs *needed* to be invited to this remarriage, the trip Lucy and Jerry take to that destination ultimately requires what Cavell calls "mythological motorcycles." It is a comic sort of transport, or slapstick rapture, which delivers Lucy and Jerry into a mood of playful abandon. From such a place in the heart they begin to drop their guard and see each other with a fresh sense of possibility.

The Green World is the main idea Cavell derives from Frye about Shakespearean comedy, where it is routinely a place of retreat from the court or the city. For example, in *A Midsummer Night's Dream*, "a wood near Athens" becomes such a place for the beleaguered couples. Athenian law requires young women either to obey their father's will and marry whom he chooses or to suffer the consequences: death or "the livery of a nun, / For aye to be in shady cloister mewed, / To live a barren sister all your life, / Chanting faint hymns to the cold and fruitless moon."[2] Needless to say, there allegedly is an upside to that second alternative, beyond just staying alive a little longer. It's what Duke Theseus calls "[dying] in single blessedness," but there are no Athenian takers for that option. Instead, the young lovers flee and camp out overnight in the woods. There they participate unintentionally in a farcical comedy of errors. With some help from Puck's magic love potion, each discovers the route to his or her true desires, though one of the guys must remain on medication.

Of course, this structural feature of Shakespearean comedy recurs in other such plays. It is called Belmont in *The Merchant of Venice* and the Forest of Arden in *As You Like It*, and it helps qualify them as members of that genre. But it is harder to locate in certain instances of this kind of play. For example, in *Much Ado about Nothing* the action all occurs in the Sicilian town of Messina, where the governor, Leonato, hosts Don Pedro, the Prince of Aragon, and leaders of his army. The men are returning victorious from the suppression of a rebellion against Don Pedro's rule by the Prince's illegitimate brother, Don John. The masked ball in celebration of their success provides an occasion where identities become confused enough to unsettle some established views and perspectives, but the next day's staged performances by their friends trick the allegedly hardened resistance to marriage of both Beatrice and Benedick into allegedly reluctant submission. Their Green World is the fictional realm of lovesickness and rejection concocted and elaborated within their hearing by friends who see through the guise of their "merry war." When such merely theatrical revelations ring true in the overhearing of their target audience, Beatrice and Benedick each become more willing to finally acknowledge love for the other. But the traumatic event of Claudio's denunciation of Hero at the altar, which both Beatrice and Benedick witness, is the proximate cause of the confession of love that each makes to the other.

Similarly, in *The Philadelphia Story* (1940, dir. George Cukor), after a preliminary vignette in the offices of *Spy* magazine, virtually all of the action of the movie transpires on the Lords' estate and the suburban village nearby. The night before the wedding, however, includes a harsh exchange between bride-to-be Tracy Lord (Katharine Hepburn) and her father. His wounding words and Tracy's hard partying immediately thereafter bring about her altered consciousness under the influence of champagne, which leads to an eye-opening transformation in her views about what really matters and what she really wants. It turns out to be remarriage to her ex, C. K. Dexter Haven (Cary Grant), not her current fiancé, George Kittredge (John Howard) and her imminent second marriage, whose celebration has already begun.

In a comparative essay such as this, the name Kittredge itself requires an intervention that more fully shows how Shakespearean details permeate this film and Cavell's commentary on it. George Lyman Kittredge was a famous Shakespeare scholar at Harvard, where Philip Barry (1896–1949), who wrote *The Philadelphia Story*, attended George Pierce Baker's renowned playwriting course, "47 Workshop." (Alumni of Baker's course, in addition to Barry, include Eugene O'Neill and Thomas Wolfe.) Kittredge may seem an odd source for Barry's character of that name, but, like the film itself, Cavell's chapter on *The Philadelphia Story* directly addresses challenges of privilege and snobbery that American democracy has faced in a variety of elite institutions ever since its inception in Constitution Hall in Philadelphia, which serves as a backdrop for the credits that scroll down the screen as this movie begins.

Distinctions between popular and elite culture constitute such a challenge for American critics and artists, and this film dramatizes tensions between the privileges of wealth and the exigencies of wage-earning in Tracy's exchanges with both Dexter and Mike (James Stewart). Mike is the reporter from *Spy* who is covering the wedding, but he also writes high-quality fiction for a very small market. Indeed, we learn that Dexter already has some acquaintance with Mike's stories, and we see how pertinently one of them moves Tracy when she exclaims, "They're almost poetry!" Further, when she singles out "With the Rich and Mighty" as her favorite, Mike explains that its title comes from a Spanish peasant proverb, "With the rich and mighty always a little patience," an adage altogether suitable to the drama unfolding on screen.

In its own way *A Midsummer Night's Dream* engages early modern English versions of such tensions in its play-within-the-play, which is produced for an audience at Theseus' court by the "rude mechanicals," who are skilled laborers or craftsmen—like Bottom, the weaver, whose name refers to the core on which a skein of yarn is wound, among other things, like the status of such workers vis-à-vis aristocratic courtiers or Bottom's anatomical "bottom." When the Duke welcomes these blue-collar troupers who have won the prize of his patronage, moralism muffles the condescension in his initial greeting, "For never anything can be amiss / When simpleness and duty tender it."[3] As Peter Quince and his players proceed, however, their hilarious sequence of malapropisms and maladroit acting elicits sarcastic asides from members of the aristocratic audience, and the Duke fully participates in the snide critical roasting of their performance of "Pyramus and Thisbe."

Shakespeare references are scattered throughout *The Philadelphia Story*. Kittredge may count as one of those, and so may "Uncle Willie" (Roland Young), who briefly trades places with his brother-in-law Seth Lord (John Halliday) in an effort to deceive *Spy* magazine into thinking that Tracy's father will be attending her wedding. With Uncle Willie we begin to discern suggestions of Bottom in *A Midsummer Night's Dream*. "Uncle Willie is a pincher," as Tracy knows from experience, and Bottom is transformed ("translated") into an ass, which, in another sense of the word, is what Uncle Willie pinches on two occasions—first Tracy's and then Liz Imbrie's (Ruth Hussey). When he rides to the wedding in Dinah's (Virginia Weidler) strange donkey-driven cart, Uncle Willie says his head falls off. He is referring to his hangover from drinking too much at the party he hosted the previous night, but his remark is reminiscent of his reputation as a pincher and rhymes with the ass' head, with its long ears, which are usually the prominent features of Bottom's transformation onstage. Also, Dinah's "dream" echoes "Bottom's dream" in Shakespeare's play.[4] Though Bottom becomes the bedmate of Titania, Queen of the Fairies, Dinah merely suspects Tracy of a similar lapse with Mike because she caught a suggestive glimpse of their late-night return from the pool.

Moreover, when the hungover Tracy appears in the morning, she begins to assert her grounded common sense by saying she is "standing on her own two hands," which sounds like the sort of synesthetic confusion that Bottom visits upon St. Paul by echoing 1 Corinthians 2.9ff.[5] In sorting out dream from reality Dinah asserts that she actually did see Mike and Tracy coming "out of the woods," suggesting a wood near Athens, or, in Northrop Frye's terms, the Green World of *A Midsummer Night's Dream*. The Lords' estate is expansive, no doubt, but Tracy and Mike are coming out of the back yard, where the pool is located. Still, our mythical imaginations are receiving considerable encouragement. Given all the emphasis on opening Tracy's eyes, a repeated phrase in the next-to-last scene of the movie, we are obviously being directed to the ultimate Green World in the Judeo-Christian tradition, the Garden of Eden. There, of course, Adam and Eve fell—fortunately, in some readings. *The Philadelphia Story* follows that tradition. Tracy's fall humanizes her in the sense that her now-evident fallibility inspires her newfound understanding and acceptance of the faults of others.

The change Tracy undergoes exemplifies another feature that Cavell singles out as characteristic of the Hollywood comedy of remarriage. He calls it the creation of the woman, as though, in the process of rejecting the marriage she has been readying herself for with George, Tracy becomes a new person in order to remarry Dexter. The same could be said of Lucy Warriner in *The Awful Truth*: she distinguishes herself from her previous self via her sister act under the new name of Lola. This performance serves as a prelude to Lucy's dialogue with Jerry, in the Green World of Connecticut, about similarities and differences, an exchange that leads them to their decision *not* to get a divorce. Now that they both have disentangled themselves from impending second marriages, they decide to get back together. Moreover, under the rubric of the creation of the woman, Cavell's indebtedness to Shakespeare as a resource for thinking about Hollywood movie genres, and vice versa—Hollywood movies as a resource for thinking about Shakespeare—stands out in bolder relief. In Shakespeare, however, the creation of the woman, when it occurs, requires change in the man, whose skepticism has mistaken his wife, or bride, for the creature of his darkest doubts.

Although Cavell's first Shakespeare essay, "The Avoidance of Love: A Reading of *King Lear*," made a memorable impact among literary scholars who specialize in the English Renaissance and in Shakespeare in particular, it was still an outlier. Harry Berger, Jr., aptly dubs it "an essay from outer space," though he promptly acknowledges his gratitude and esteem for Cavell's readings of Shakespeare and the skeptical crises he describes as disowning knowledge.[6] But Cavell's discernment, in *Othello*, of an existential agon masquerading as an intellectual crisis more precisely elaborates the kinship between ordeals of skepticism and those of sexual jealousy than we could fairly expect in his reading of *King Lear*. After all, *Othello* is Shakespeare's most domestic of tragedies. When Othello and Desdemona die, along with Iago and Emilia too, Venice remains pretty well unshaken, though minus a few of its citizens. Even on the outskirts of empire in Cyprus, the very opposite of a Green World, only a few wounds need dressing for things to go back to normal, as far as the state is concerned. Othello's apocalyptic proclamation that "chaos will come again" warrants only a local application, which, given the absence of "an huge eclipse," evaporates into the pathetic and continuing self-deception of "one who loved not wisely but too well." On the other hand, Kent's vision of "the promised end" in *King Lear* describes a comprehensive condition of the realm Edgar embarks upon ruling after the deaths of all the direct heirs to the throne and their British husbands.

Cavell also notes that *Othello*'s structure shares fundamental elements of traditional comedy: an older husband and a younger wife, as well as a potential rival, Cassio, who is nearer the wife in age. Iago ably develops that potential by exploiting Cassio's weaknesses—a low tolerance of alcohol and a high degree of self-love—while he works on the self-confessed insecurities that Othello specifies, via soliloquy, right in the middle of the play's lengthy temptation scene: his color, his age, and his inexperience in courtly conversation.[7]

Among these possible vulnerabilities in Othello's own sense of himself, Cavell shows a striking concern for Othello's color and a memorable appreciation of Desdemona's implicit consideration of it in her account of her love for Othello. In response to her father's midnight denunciation of Othello before the Venetian Senate, Desdemona replies, at the Duke's prompting, "I saw Othello's visage in his mind."[8] Cavell reads this statement as Desdemona's way of saying that she sees Othello as he sees himself, which requires no color-blind metaphysics. She is making a full-throated claim of their mutual intelligibility, which, in Cavell's discussion of remarriage comedy, signifies that a couple is married. Such clarity in understanding another serves as the equivalent of "meet and happy conversation," regardless of whatever weight the law and its legitimating documents may carry in the eyes of others and the state. In fact, Cavell describes *Othello* as a failed comedy of remarriage precisely because the central couple's like-mindedness is lost beyond recovery.[9] Yet why is that? What causes such an irremediable failure? The terrible speed of this tragedy—one night in Venice and another day and a half in Cyprus—rhymes nicely with the typical precipitousness of the skeptical crisis that overtakes Othello. The play almost seems over when it has just begun. Had they Green World enough and time, perhaps their tragic fate could have been avoided.

Cavell's intervention on behalf of Othello's intelligence is even more striking and memorable, especially because he considers skepticism prone to tragic misuse of epistemological arguments.[10] Doubt masquerades as earnest inquiry in regions where scientific criteria of knowledge need not apply.

Such criteria distort human predicaments into problems to solve rather than circumstances we need to inhabit and abide, or resist. We thus make something false and unreal of situations that require patience, intuition, and attunement, or courage and determination—not evidence, arguments, and proofs. But Cavell's marvelous outburst, that Othello is not a lunkhead, seeks to reclaim him from an influential line of modern criticism that condescends to this character and treats him as though he were simply confused on a variety of scores.

> I mean merely to ask that we not, conventionally but insufferably, assume that we know this woman better than this man knows her—making Othello some kind of exotic, gorgeous, superstitious lunkhead; which is about what Iago thinks. However much Othello deserves each of these titles, however far he believes Iago's tidings, he cannot just believe them; somewhere he *knows* them to be false.[11]

With his caricature of Othello's final monologue in self-explanation as *bovarysme* and merely an effort to cheer himself up, T. S. Eliot had a significant hand in establishing this view, and F. R. Leavis compounded this sort of dismissal by describing Othello as self-deluded from the beginning.[12] Laurence Olivier as Othello on screen in 1965 was the most unforgettable incarnation of this sort of attitude in his blackface performance of Othello as an eminently dupable sensualist, poised for a fall. But Cavell's treatment of this figure, as well as his approach to Hollywood movie genres via Shakespearean analogues, invite us to consider Othello in a more capacious context where film and Shakespeare's dramatic art may shed clarifying light on one another in various ways.

Over a period of a dozen years and in three different genres, Shakespeare wrote a trio of plays centrally about the same subject: *Much Ado about Nothing* (1598), *Othello* (1604), and *The Winter's Tale* (1610). All of these plays feature ordeals of jealousy and crises of doubt as central agons of their generically different plot structures, which are, respectively, comedy, tragedy, and tragicomedy or what we now call romance. For example, in the earliest of these three plays, *Much Ado about Nothing*, the climactic scene at the altar rehearses an earlier Shakespearean version of Desdemona's fate in *Othello*. Thus, it is pertinent to remember the reaction that it elicits from interested parties on stage who witness those events as they unfold. They can serve as a stand-in for the audience who behold such an action, as we do when we see a production of *Othello*.

Hero, the daughter of the governor of Messina, is engaged to marry Claudio, a young Florentine who has distinguished himself in battle. In the immediate aftermath of his military success and on the brink of his marriage to Hero, Claudio has been deceived into thinking that his fiancée has betrayed him. Therefore, he intends to shame Hero publicly during the wedding ceremony by denouncing her for infidelity, and he carries out this plan in collaboration with his leader, Don Pedro, Prince of Aragon. Claudio's denunciation of Hero at the altar emphasizes his skeptical crisis as he decries the disjunction between what Hero seems and what she is. In the process he extrapolates from the unreadability of her character to the indecipherability of women in general; and, in Shakespearean crises of this kind, that is a fact of life that makes being a man traumatic and being a woman potentially fatal.

Or, rather, it is such a fact if it is perceived in a certain mood, and otherwise it is no fact at all. In the dawning of such a perception, we hear Othello threaten and command Iago, "Be sure you prove my love a whore." Othello's insistence upon certainty betrays his readiness for that mistaken conviction and for a proof that will be no proof at all. Its achievement is merely an exercise in reaching a foregone conclusion, and it is a cover story for darker reaches of his soul that he would rather not reveal, even to himself. In Claudio we have a callow youth who pales by comparison with so accomplished and seasoned a military hero as Othello; but his anxieties and suspicions nonetheless smack of similar shortcomings, as do those of Leontes in *The Winter's Tale*, who notably requires no villain like Iago in *Othello* or Don John in *Much Ado* to set him upon his course of destructive jealousy. In the evolving crises of all these plays there are discerning characters who find such claims incredible: Camillo and Paulina in *The Winter's Tale*, Emilia in *Othello*, and Beatrice in *Much Ado*. All three of them express a shock of disbelief when they hear the charges leveled at the women accused, even though in all of these plays there also circulates a predisposition to believe that the infidelity of wives and the cuckoldry of husbands is simply the way of the world.

When the drama of fiercely aggressive confrontation unfolds at the altar in *Much Ado*, we can behold auguries of *Othello* not only in Claudio's cruel retaliation but also in the patriarch Leonato's vindictive death wish for his daughter, Hero, an impulse akin to Brabantio's outbreak at the loss of Desdemona to the Moor. Moreover, we can also behold the heartfelt impression that the attack upon Hero makes upon two of its witnesses in particular, Beatrice and Benedick, who watch this violent expression of misguided passion, in Hamlet's phrase, "like guilty creatures at a play." Since they *are* characters in a play who have just witnessed the very incident of violent denunciation that we have watched in the audience, their reaction can influence ours as a model response that exemplifies and confirms what the play expects of us. It seems like an extended version of the sort of guidance a reaction shot in a film offers to an alert audience in validation of the emotions each may passively undergo at witnessing the sequence of events projected on the screen. Indeed, Kenneth Branagh's film version of this play uses the camera to just this effect in showing how Beatrice and Benedick are affected by what they have seen. Although stage actors have to project such feelings out to the audience somehow, film actors are subjects of the camera's power to project from close-up the passions they undergo in such a critical moment. Those intimate takes tell of feelings strong enough to threaten a tragic action of revenge, as Benedick agrees to Beatrice's passionate command, "Kill Claudio."

Avowals of a love long disguised as hostility in their contest of wits now are promptly forthcoming, as though the shock of Claudio's fierce attack made the truth of this pair's deepest feelings undeniable and urgently in need of expression. Beatrice's call for fatal revenge seems equally primal, as though masks were suddenly dropped and everyday dodges no longer possible. Even when we hear the play's recurrent puns on "nothing" recycled in this fraught exchange, the words hardly sound self-conscious, and the camera's intimacy with these actors' faces puts us in proximity to emotions unmediated by second thoughts. When Benedick agrees to Beatrice's chilling proposal, he makes a decisive break from the bonds of male camaraderie and joins with her in a new alliance that makes him the man to perform the duty of clearing her kinswoman Hero's honor.

Fortunately, Beatrice and Benedick are characters in a comedy. Their entanglement in this moment brings *Much Ado* nearer the brink of tragedy than any other Shakespeare comedy, but it will happily unravel and set them free, along with Hero and Claudio, to marry and dance in celebration of their personal reconciliation and the restoration of social harmony overall. Or, rather, to dance and then marry, as Shakespeare reverses the usual comedic sequence in a parting twist of generic expectations that distinguishes *Much Ado* from other Shakespearean examples of this kind of play. *Much Ado*'s nearly tragic moment, as mentioned, anticipates *Othello* in its skeptical crisis and in the violent response of its protagonist to suspicions of a young woman's infidelity, but *Othello* also mingles elements of its opposite genre. While not exactly a May-and-January marriage of the Chaucerian kind in "The Merchant's Tale," the mismatch in the ages of its newlyweds reprises a customary imbalance in comedies of cuckoldry where benighted older husbands are gulled by the ingenuity of youth, which emerges as virtually a force of nature; and other elements of this tragedy's plot and characters further align it with comic convention.

The spirit of comedy spares us from tragedy in *Much Ado*, where defensive raillery about female infidelity generally releases male anxieties and preempts the tragic violence that such fears can otherwise produce. Claudio alone takes irreversibly to heart the possibility of this painful sort of betrayal in his intimate life; but, in the nick of time, good luck befalls both Claudio and the entire community in Messina, and it dispels the mortal danger of murderous revenge. Othello has no such good fortune. He displays a fatalism that promptly accepts the worst as a necessity of life—the inevitable cuckoldry of husbands and the vulnerability of both the older lover and the outsider.

> Haply for I am black,
> And have not those soft parts of conversation
> That chamberers have; or for I am declined
> Into the vale of years—yet that's not much—
> She's gone. I am abused, and my relief
> Must be to loathe her. O curse of marriage,
> That we can call these delicate creatures ours
> And not their appetites! I had rather be a toad
> And live upon the vapor of a dungeon
> Than keep a corner in the thing I love
> For others' uses. Yet 'tis the plague of great ones;
> Prerogatived are they less than the base.
> 'Tis destiny unshunnable, like death.
> Even then this forkèd plague is fated to us
> When we do quicken.[13]

For Othello resignation in this regard is no such joking matter as it becomes for Benedick and his cohort. It inspires grandiose delusions in which Othello casts himself as an agent of justice saving other men from the serial adultery that Desdemona will surely commit unless he kills her sacrificially in a good cause.

In his alleged quest for truth Othello travels between the extremes of perfection and disgust intimately audible in his own avowal that, "Her name, that was as fresh/As Dian's visage, is now begrimed and black/As mine own face."[14] The mythical ideal of such a vision of freshness, like a platonic form, is meant to sponsor an ascent; but it becomes the foil for a descent into a drastic extreme made visible by what passes for honesty, the comradely confidences of Iago. In the process, that extremism not only undoes the divine Desdemona and the noble Moor but also Roderigo and Emilia, who, in a show of courageous defiance, brings down her husband Iago's murderous wrath upon herself. Moreover, it nearly puts an end to Desdemona's friend and encomiast, Cassio, who, as Iago spitefully confesses, has "a daily beauty in his life that makes [him] ugly."

The fixated idealism of Othello's view of Desdemona becomes painfully audible in the moments before he murders her, as he contemplates her sleeping body and fastens his gaze upon "that whiter skin of hers than snow/And smooth as monumental alabaster." Even *post mortem*, Othello retains such an ideal of the world he has just lost in the person of Desdemona when he imagines "such another [world] . . . of one entire chrysolite."[15] Chrysolite is a precious gem sometimes identified as topaz, and this second comparison with stone again suggests precisely the reverse of the transformation whose recounting in Ovid's *Metamorphoses* serves as the primary source of Hermione's fate in *The Winter's Tale*: Pygmalion's creation of the marble statue of a woman, whom that sculptor's prayers move Venus to bring to life as the flesh-and-blood Galatea. Similarly, Hero's swoon under attack from Claudio and the subsequent pretense of her death suggest this sort of mortifying astonishment or petrification in *Much Ado*, where Hero's blush gives onlookers a last vivid chance at charitable interpretation of her conduct before the fiction of her death is circulated in the ultimately disappointed hope that the "idea of her life" will become recoverable through Claudio's grief over the loss of her. The fixed ideas that provoke action in both these plays are causes of destruction, not progress, until grace somehow intervenes to turn events into happier outcomes than tragedy customarily produces.

In *Much Ado* the specifically Pauline Christian terms of that event are audibly glossed by this summary line: "What your wisdoms could not discover, these shallow fools have brought to light."[16] This echo of such sentiments as we hear, for example, in First Corinthians, where worldly wisdom is mocked as divine folly, can remind us of a pattern that *Much Ado* follows but that *Othello* precisely fails to fit, although up to the very last moments of its brief course in time there is a chance that things could go otherwise. In the comedy the stupidest character of all, Dogberry, helps decisively to bring the truth to light before irreversible tragedy can occur; in the tragedy, the character who best fits that description, Roderigo, helps in this way only after nearly all of the deaths have occurred, including his own, when explanatory evidence is discovered in his clothing. In *The Winter's Tale*, Paulina performs a kindred function as an agent of grace, and, of course, her name reveals this Christian aspect of her role in the proceedings. However, she has become the king's chief adviser in the course of the play, and this part aligns her with Iago's role as the general's confidante and ultimately most trusted adviser despite his initial griping about losing the lieutenantship to Cassio. The contrast between how Paulina and Iago fill their comparable roles tells us a great deal, not only about them as characters, but also about the sorts of response these various plays seek to elicit and the purpose of playing in the different genres that they represent.

In Europe during the age of Shakespeare and for centuries thereafter, no book more influentially defined the role of those who serve as advisers to powerful leaders than *The Book of the Courtier* by Baldassare Castiglione, and this book memorably epitomizes the job of such counselors in terms that we most readily may recognize from the Disney version of P. L. Travers' classic chapter book, *Mary Poppins*. In Italy, where all three of the Shakespeare plays under discussion are set and whose writers supply Shakespeare with primary sources for all three of these plays, Renaissance humanists pioneered the recovery of classical texts such as Lucretius' long philosophical poem *On the Nature of Things*, which gives word to the most widely circulated Latin expression of those sentiments that Mary Poppins so memorably threatens to preempt. It describes poetry as a means of delivering sound doctrine by a comparison of the philosopher with the wise physician who smears with honey the rim of a cup full of bitter medicine to trick sick children into recovering good health. The half-dozen lines of this simile appear repeatedly in canonical works of Shakespeare's culture, and they also become a way of demonstrating the moral value of poetry to suspicious critics who claim it promotes idleness and vice. When Paulina brings Leontes' dead wife Hermione back to life, she requires him to awake his faith in order to experience the benefit of this miracle. Her insistence upon the necessity of faith reveals the Pauline theology that she encourages in her exchanges with Leontes as she leads him to the climactic moment of the play's final scene, and his willingness to follow expresses the mixture of sweet and bitter sensations that he has become ready to experience in this process:

> PAULINA: I am sorry, sir, I have thus far stirred you, but
> I could afflict you farther.
> LEONTES: Do, Paulina,
> For this affliction has a taste as sweet
> As any cordial comfort. Still, methinks
> There is an air comes from her. What fine chisel
> Could ever yet cut breath? Let no man mock me,
> For I will kiss her.[17]

The work of art that all are focused upon is a statue of Hermione, and the sculptor has rendered her likeness with such success that she seems alive (which she will turn out to be). The sweetness of this experience specifically outstrips the pain associated with all that has gone before in this regard, and the art of its achievement wins the ultimate tribute of perfect verisimilitude, imitation that seems uncannily real.

The final scene of *Othello* has elicited sentiments quite the opposite. Within the scene itself Ludovico describes the tragic loading of the bed as a poisoning sight and in need of immediate covering; and within the reception history of this play, Samuel Johnson expresses a significant tradition in finding this scene unendurable. Of course, such reactions attest to the tragic nature of the experiences that the final scene represents, and, as such, they register the trials that tragedy forces an audience to undergo. Indeed, there is a widely circulated anecdote about *Othello* that tells of a spectator who is so convinced of the reality of what he is witnessing that he rushes onto the stage to rescue Desdemona from the murderous violence of Othello.

Cavell uses it to illustrate a basic failure in understanding what tragedy expects of us and what it teaches us: clear-eyed patience in the face of suffering, an opening of the heart to ordeals that are woven into the texture of human experience, an alertness to how things can go tragically wrong despite every reason to hope otherwise.[18] This anecdote has also been used to read the play as a cautionary tale specifically against miscegenation, and perhaps unsurprisingly, such readings have been associated with audiences in the American South where the legacies of slavery and segregation are constantly subject to review and reconsideration.[19]

In this regard the figure of Paul Robeson looms especially large, and his performance as Othello in 1943–44 is a landmark event in stage history. The New York production with Robeson in the title role set a record for the length of a run of a Shakespeare play on Broadway and was duly celebrated as an extraordinary accomplishment. The first 340 years of this play's performance history almost exclusively featured white actors in and out of blackface as Othello. The African-American Robeson was said not only to have played Othello but to have become him, an achievement of verisimilitude that makes that term itself sound woefully inadequate to the tribute it seeks to confer upon an artistic feat and a historical event of the greatest significance. Still, little more than two decades thereafter, the appearance of a film version of *Othello* starring Lawrence Olivier, the preeminent British Shakespearean actor of his day, stirred a controversy that epitomizes questions now being asked about *Othello* more vocally or, perhaps, more audibly, than before. Simply put as a single question they amount to this challenge: who would ever want to become Othello? A dominant line of interpretation during the twentieth century emphasized Othello's gullibility as the fall guy of a clever con man. He swallowed malicious lies, as we say, hook, line, and sinker; and he became no longer the noble Moor of the play's opening scenes but the dull Moor of Emilia's harsh condemnation, as ignorant as dirt. T. S. Eliot and F. R. Leavis exemplify this trend; and, in his influential reading of skepticism at the core of this tragedy, we can hear Cavell defending himself against such views of Othello when he specifically denies that Othello is stupid or, as he puts it, a lunkhead. Similarly, in *A Season of Migration to the North*, the Sudanese novelist Tayeb Salih constructs an *Othello*-like story whose protagonist emphatically disavows any likeness between himself and Shakespeare's protagonist. In brief, from Robeson, via Eliot and Leavis, to Olivier, Cavell and Salih, we see a reversal of the force of this Shakespearean character and a diminishment of Shakespeare in general as a source of ratification for an artistic achievement.

An effort to recuperate Othello from such developments becomes visible on screen in Lawrence Fishburne's performance under the direction of Oliver Parker. One of Othello's final moments responds in a particular way to the script's explicit question: How does Othello get the weapon he will use to kill himself? The whole of this complex scene, of course, warrants extended discussion. For now, however, let me call your attention to a few of its features. We can initially note a striking contrast between Cassio and Othello, on one hand, and Lodovico on the other. With his wavy hair and silk hose, Lodovico represents those contemptuously dismissed in Act I as Othello's rivals for Desdemona's hand—"the wealthy curly-headed darlings of our nation." More importantly, it is key to note that Cassio hands, or should we say, slips, Othello the dagger with which he will take his own life.

Their exchange of looks in this process is also a crucial index of possible reconciliation and mutual understanding, and it is a way of recognizing more fully Othello's conscious resolve to take his own life. Also, in this presentation, Cassio's lines about having thought Othello unarmed are baldly transformed into a lie that further indicates his collusion in Othello's recovery of agency in his final action. While suicide itself is not esteemed an honorable option in the religious culture of Christianity that Othello has embraced and pictures himself as defending in his final long speech, Stoicism views it otherwise, as we know from Horatio in *Hamlet* and from several leading figures in Shakespeare's Roman plays, like Brutus and Cleopatra. The dignity of such a death is thus not entirely a fantasy, such as T. S. Eliot famously makes it sound when he derides Othello for "cheering himself up" in this speech. Once again the terrible solemnity of Othello's tragic fate becomes momentarily more available in this film's way of presenting it, and the demonic intelligence of Iago loses some of the appeal it may have achieved in other renderings, which would thereby limit Othello's powerful claim upon our pity and fear.

Notes

1 Stanley Cavell, "Psychoanalysis and Cinema: The Melodrama of the Unknown Woman," in *The Cavell Reader*, ed. Stephen Mulhall (New York: Blackwell, 1996), 222–52, 230.

2 1.1.70-73. All quotations are taken from *The Norton Shakespeare*, 2nd ed. (New York: Norton, 2008).

3 Shakespeare, *A Midsummer Night's Dream*, 5.1.82-3.

4 Shakespeare, *A Midsummer Night's Dream*, 4.1.200ff.

5 "I have had a most rare vision. I have had a dream, past the wit of man to say what dream it was: man is but an ass, if he go about to expound this dream. Methought I was—there is no man can tell what. Methought I was—and methought I had—but man is but a patched fool, if he will offer to say what methought I had. The eye of man hath not heard, the ear of man hath not seen, man's hand is not able to taste, his tongue to conceive, nor his heart to report, what my dream was" (4.1.199-207).

1 Cor 2:9-10 (RSV): "But, as it is written, 'What no eye has seen, nor ear heard, / nor the heart of man conceived, / what God has prepared for those who love him,' God has revealed to us through the Spirit."

6 Harry Berger, Jr., *Making Trifles of Terrors: Redistributing Complicities in Shakespeare* (Stanford: Stanford University Press, 1997), xii.

7 Shakespeare, *Othello*, 3.3.262-81.

8 Shakespeare, *Othello*, 1.3.251.

9 *Pursuits of Happiness: The Hollywood Comedy of Remarriage* (Cambridge: Harvard University Press, 1981), 142.

10 Or, as Jerry Warriner puts it, "The Road to Reno is paved with suspicion." For he is as benighted as Othello in this regard.
11 Stanley Cavell, *Disowning Knowledge in Seven Plays of Shakespeare*, updated edition (New York: Cambridge University Press, 2003), 133.
12 William Shakespeare, *Othello*, 2nd ed., ed. Edward Pechter (New York: W. W. Norton and Company, 2017), 209, 270–71.
13 Shakespeare, *Othello*, 3.3.262-76.
14 Shakespeare, *Othello*, 3.3.391-3.
15 Shakespeare, *Othello*, 5.2.4-5, 151-2.
16 Shakespeare, *Much Ado about Nothing*, 5.1.217-8.
17 Shakespeare, *The Winter's Tale*, 5.3.73-9.
18 Cavell, *Disowning Knowledge*, 98.
19 Michael Bristol, *Big-Time Shakespeare* (New York: Routledge, 1996), 198–99.

PART IV

Film, As If Made for Philosophy

10

Film Exists in a State of Philosophy: Two Contemporary Cavellian Views

Shawn Loht

THE QUESTION OF WHETHER PHILOSOPHY can occur *through* film (sometimes called in the shorthand "film-as-philosophy") has been especially lively during the last twenty years of scholarship in the philosophy of film. Specifically, the question has concerned whether films can "philosophize" in a primarily cinematic fashion, and if so, how do they do this? Prominent figures in Anglo-American philosophy of film including Noël Carroll, Paisley Livingston, and Murray Smith have all leveraged strong arguments *against* this capacity in films.[1] These counter-arguments frequently hold that a film's purported philosophizing is really expressive of and parasitic upon one's philosophical reading of it; that films can only philosophize on the shoulders of previously formulated philosophical theses in texts; or that films cannot present theses or claims with any kind of precision in their own right; and so forth. In contrast, some philosophers of a more continental persuasion have suggested that much of the affirmative side of the debate hinges not on fixed aesthetic possibilities of films as much as it depends on the philosophical power individual films reveal in and of themselves. From this latter perspective, whether a given film philosophizes is a function of the film's very viewing, or ultimately, what the film gives the viewer to replay and contemplate critically and thoughtfully.

Stanley Cavell was one of the first philosophers to suggest that there are ontological grounds for how films can be said to exist in an inherent condition of philosophy. And much of the contemporary debate concerning the possibility of philosophy's occurrence "in" film has its roots in Cavell's legacy. Stephen Mulhall and Robert Sinnerbrink are two contemporary Cavellian philosophers of film who regard film in the mold of this legacy. Mulhall and Sinnerbrink have both produced bodies of work that suggest expansive ways of appreciating the philosophical capacity of films and of assessing film's philosophical relevance for the twenty-first-century world. In this chapter I wish to compare the approaches of these two contemporary philosophers, and to highlight and dissect some of the Cavellian foundations that support their views. The larger underlying question I wish to address concerns the grounds upon which one can defend the very notions of film's claim to philosophy, and of philosophy's possibility to occur through film.

Stephen Mulhall on Philosophy in the *Alien* Films

Stephen Mulhall's work, principally his influential book *On Film* (currently in its third edition) has been a watershed text, albeit controversially so, in the post-Cavellian conversation about film's philosophical capacity. Decisive about Mulhall's approach, vis-à-vis its Cavellian roots, is his unabashed defense of the view that films can function not merely as inspiration for philosophical thought or as handy illustrations of philosophical ideas, but rather, that they can provide bona fide contributions to philosophical debate. In other words, Mulhall eschews holding simply that films sometimes offer material to viewers that can be parsed into the traditional language of philosophers, as if a film's purported philosophizing can only be parasitic on philosophical conversations and analyses external to it. Mulhall claims that films can be on par with actual philosophers in providing new insights about perennial philosophical questions.[2] Films can comprise, in a memorable locution he employs in this light, "philosophy in action," and for this reason certain films convey something like a reflective thought process, an exercise in the study of ideas. Mulhall does not advocate a global thesis regarding necessary or sufficient conditions underwriting a given film's operation in the condition of philosophy. He also emphasizes the fruitlessness of attempting to nail down exactly what it would mean for films to philosophize purely cinematically, outside of a few very general parameters.[3] Indeed, Mulhall holds that the best illustration of the medium's philosophical capacity is an ostensive (and experiential) one, only possible through examination of particular films.[4] Let us then consider what he says about some of the specific films that have seized his attention.

Given that Mulhall's readings of the *Alien* films (to date, six films in number) have arguably been the most influential and widely read in his body of work, I will restrict the present discussion to his interpretations of these cinematic works, although it is worth noting that he reads these films with frequent reference to some of their cousins in the science fiction genre, among which Mulhall holds that there is a steady cross-flow of films mutually informing one another (for example, the *Terminator* series, *Blade Runner*, *The Abyss*).

A synopsis of the *Alien* series is as follows. The premise is a science fiction scenario initiated in the first film, *Alien* (1979, dir. Ridley Scott). In this film, a mining crew traveling through distant space aboard the ship *Nostromo* encounters a terrifying and violent alien species on an unoccupied planet. While exploring the planet—on which they had landed by pure happenstance, responding to an anomalous radio signal—the crew unwittingly unearths one of the creatures, waking it from a dormant, incubational state. The octopus-like creature is immediately aggressive, attacking by leaping up and attaching itself to the face of one of the astronauts, Kane (John Hurt). Shortly thereafter, it is discovered that Kane has become impregnated with an alien fetus. When a live creature bursts from Kane's stomach and effectively takes over the ship, it becomes evident that these alien creatures require a human host to propagate. The aliens emerge as nonrational, yet highly proficient killing machines that strongly outmatch humans in speed, strength, and resiliency. And although the human characters quickly find themselves faced with an existential threat, their encounter with the aliens takes on a counterpoint dimension of amorality, as the alien species is, in fact, just another life-form striving to persist and now given an opportunity to do so. Unfortunately for Kane and company, it so happens that the humans fit the bill for a viable carrier. The ensuing films in the series each continue this narrative, revealing new and surprising ways in which the human and alien transform one another.

The various hermeneutic, historic, and biological relations borne out between the two species becomes a recurring, almost symphonic theme. For instance, the narrative of the first and second films explores the aliens as an object of study for the advancement of scientific knowledge and human utility. In the third film, *Alien*^{3} (1992, dir. David Fincher), the main character and star of the series, Ellen Ripley (Sigourney Weaver), has become impregnated with an alien fetus. At the film's end she destroys herself by blowing up her space station in order to prevent any more carnage the aliens might cause. And the fourth film in the series, *Alien: Resurrection* (1997, dir. Jean-Pierre Jeunet), portrays Ripley as a reborn alien-human hybrid. She has been cloned from the DNA of the original Ellen Ripley and cross-bred with the alien creatures, who by this point have finally been subjugated by the human race in efforts to engineer them for military-industrial use. In contrast, the fifth film in the series, *Prometheus* (2012, dir. Ridley Scott), a prequel to the series' first film, suggests that this deadly alien species was, in fact, created by a long-dead, proto-human species called the Engineers. The characters in *Prometheus* hypothesize that the alien creatures are the product of an experiment in military technology conducted by the Engineers that went horribly wrong.

In general, as the series has played out over the last three-plus decades, the overarching narrative exceeds the tropes of the horror-science fiction film genre, exploring more deeply mythological themes related to the nature of life, self-awareness, and historical destiny.

Additionally, a theme that ostensibly has become more pronounced in the last two installations of the series, *Prometheus* and its sequel *Alien: Covenant* (2017, dir. Ridley Scott), is the anthropomorphic, existential disposition of the android beings that figure into the storyline—an aspect that inspires Mulhall's interest in *Blade Runner* and the *Terminator* movies. A central character of these latter two *Alien* films is David (Michael Fassbender), an android built to be immortal and perfectly rational, yet who lacks certain human features he finds himself wanting, particularly autonomy and the ability to procreate. The storyline of *Alien: Covenant* provides a number of clues to suggest that David aims both to conquer his human creators and to populate the universe with a breed of alien-human hybrids cultivated through his own creation.

On the surface, it is easy to justify Mulhall's inclination to analyze the *Alien* films through a philosophical lens. For these films certainly thematize in various degrees a number of ready-made philosophical issues. Particularly decisive in Mulhall's view is the sustained meditation the *Alien* films show in their portrayals of biological life, humanness, and the moral teleologies bound up in the interaction of the two. Mulhall also draws attention to these films' ways of subverting traditional Western philosophical paradigms of gender, sexuality, embodiment, birth, and death. For instance, human men are "impregnated" (indeed, more provocatively, raped) by an invasive species; human life as we know it is pitched as the child of an ancestor species of a higher order of intelligence; living creatures are portrayed as products of engineering; machine-based beings take on God-like status; and so forth. Mulhall highlights the questioning, reflective character of these films' explorations of many of our "inter-related anxieties about human identity" with questions such as:

> What exactly is my place in nature? How far does the (natural) human ability to develop technology alienate us from the natural world? Am I (or am I in) my body? How sharply does my gender define me? How vulnerable does my body make me? Is sexual reproduction a threat to my integrity, and if so, does the reality and nature of that threat depend on whether I am a man or a woman?[5]

More controversially, however, Mulhall proposes that these films actually comprise original philosophical thinking on these topics in their own right; in particular, he sees the *Alien* films as worthy participants in the perennial

Cartesian question of whether one's being relates to one's body. In one of his most striking series of claims, he writes:

> The sophistication and self-awareness with which these films deploy and develop [the relation of human identity to embodiment] ... suggest to me that they should be taken as making real contributions to these intellectual debates. ... I see them rather as themselves reflecting on and evaluating such views and arguments, as thinking seriously and systematically about them in just the way philosophers do. ... They are philosophical exercises, philosophy in action—film as philosophizing.[6]

Mulhall's core claim appears to center on the fact that the *Alien* films equally concern issues that, in and of themselves, are of fundamental philosophical significance, *and at the same time* that the films foster a kind of philosophical contemplation precisely by putting into focus human scenarios in which the aforementioned metaphysical and moral issues take on a natural philosophical weight. A special qualification Mulhall highlights on this last score is the rather minimalist science fiction setting of the films, which allows for a stripped-down aesthetic in which the philosophical themes can emerge front and center.[7] A further premise in his reasoning is that the appearance of multiple sequels in the *Alien* series, each by a different, influential director, renders the subsequent films a series of reflections on the first (and prior) film's premises.[8] In this light, he comments that the series progresses philosophically by "reflecting upon the conditions of its own possibility," a feature that lends these films "as good a characterization as could be desired of the way in which any truly rigorous philosophy must proceed."[9] Mulhall implies that the philosophical significance of the films' sequeldom lay in the way each installation responds to a logical challenge for how the storyline might continue while maintaining a conceptual continuity in its philosophically laden premises. For one of the films to demonstrate reflection on its conditions would thus entail creative thinking on the filmmaker's part, to take logical conditions that have been provided in the previous films and expand their implications while remaining true to what was initially given (not unlike proofs performed in an undergraduate symbolic logic course). The "questioning" or "reflective" character posed by these films thus gains its *philosophical* character just insofar as the films persistently *engage, problematize, and analyze the facts* of what it means to be human—including the conditions of the claims already made about that status.[10] A line of logical continuity persists throughout the films according to which new paradigms appear for understanding the logical and metaphysical possibilities underlying humanness, for example, being existentially threatened by a superior species, being a carrier vessel for that species' progeny, bearing a hybrid offspring of multiple species, etc. So Mulhall's (to some) controversial claim about these films comprising "philosophy in action" is strongly redeemed in the power these films show for adducing new truth-values for humanness and its philosophical concomitants. Described differently, these films can be considered as participants in philosophical debate on mind, body, and identity just insofar as they instantiate new ways for us to understand ourselves and our relation to other life forms.

Mulhall's approach has been criticized for stretching the conventional boundaries of how philosophy is typically conceived. Mulhall's critics, do, in fact, have reasonable grounds for holding that it is generally unclear how precisely we might assess the philosophical accomplishments the *Alien* films provide.[11] Do the films defend a philosophical thesis? If so, what is it? How has that thesis been defended? Has a definitive philosophical insight been achieved? What have we actually learned? In brief, films are not exempt from the claims of reason.[12] Moreover, Mulhall makes broad conclusions about film as such, on the basis of his own interpretations of this limited set of *Alien* films—what they are about and what he sees of philosophical importance in them. (It would appear you are out of luck if you disagree with the details of his readings.)[13] In any event, supposing even that the reading of Mulhall (or anyone else) were correct or at least compelling, it seems difficult to deny that it is the film *interpreter*—that is, the philosopher, not the film, who is doing the philosophy. All of the philosophical themes highlighted in the paragraphs above require a human critic to express them in words.

Contra Mulhall, it would seem that a film's "philosophy in action" is actually realized in and through the viewer. With these objections in mind, I turn to Robert Sinnerbrink, who defends and expands Mulhall's position while also offering views that significantly widen the implications of the debate about film's philosophical credentials.

Robert Sinnerbrink on Philosophical Film Criticism

In his book *New Philosophies of Film*, Sinnerbrink takes up a number of the principal criticisms in the philosophical literature regarding philosophy's occurrence through film. As a counter-thesis to Mulhall's opponents, Sinnerbrink defends the suggestion that the possibility for film to operate in the condition of philosophy is predicated not on what a given film accomplishes per se, but, instead, on the discursive, aesthetic, and critical insights the film affords the viewer.

Sinnerbrink emphasizes that such criteria need not be limited to epistemic knowledge-building dimensions of film-viewing; this is so because the multivalent material of films often communicates views and ideas that exceed the carrying capacity of logical propositions.[14] Films do not merely tell, they *show*.[15] Furthermore, Sinnerbrink's emphasis on the primacy of viewership is attractive because it avoids the quagmire of trying to describe film-as-philosophy as if films have some kind of independent agency. Instead, the philosophical capacity or achievement of a film is a function of the insights we as viewers are able to articulate and defend upon viewing the film. In this light, a film's purported philosophical achievement is ultimately seated in the critical receptivity of its viewer, and in the viewer's subsequent ability to give a persuasive account of what the film achieves. Overall, the conditions of thoughtful, defensible film interpretation are fundamentally rooted in the philosophical, aesthetic, or discursive ways we might engage with a film.[16] Sinnerbrink drives the point home when he describes the phenomenon this way: "We can only 'demonstrate' whether a film makes a philosophical contribution by offering aesthetically receptive, hermeneutically defensible and philosophically original interpretations of the films in question."[17] A film's operation in the condition of philosophy can only be made evident through one's own defensible interpretation of the film. Such an interpretation must be minded toward what the film shows and how it shows it.

Like Mulhall, Sinnerbrink envisions film in the condition of philosophy in local, particular terms rather than in a one-size-fits-all conceptual formulation, given that to hold otherwise would deny film's capacity as an art medium to accomplish the new and unexpected.[18] Indeed, a single-size view of film-as-philosophy risks begging the question regarding both what film is and what its aesthetic teleology allows. Sinnerbrink provides some vindication to Mulhall's approach by emphasizing why interpretive viewer experience is so crucial. The viewer's interpretive experience is decisive because it is the locus of *film's* capacity to occasion new pathways of thinking, new perspectives and questions—and this is so precisely by virtue of the particularity a film can present *to* the viewer. Sinnerbrink suggests that some films— Terrence Malick's *The New World* (2005), Lars von Trier's *Antichrist* (2009), and Ingmar Bergman's *Persona* (1966) and *Scenes from a Marriage* (1973)—simply are natural candidates for the film-as-philosophy designation because they are inherently interpretive, proffering new modes of cinematic experience. The works of these filmmakers often expand the reach of cinema to reveal combinations of image, montage, sound, and narrative the likes of which have not been seen before. Consequently, such films stand to foster philosophical insights not realized hitherto.

Terrence Malick's trademark technique of employing voice-over narration that is in tension with the visual depiction of the film's on-screen characters, as seen, for instance, in *The Thin Red Line*, prompts a unique cinematic insight into the dichotomy of people's interior and exterior lives.[19] Similarly, we could cite the philosophical power of new thought patterns occasioned by the striking visual composition in the films of diverse masters such as

Andrei Tarkovsky, Yasujiro Ozu, and Wes Anderson. The unconventional and challenging cinematic achievements of such films often do not simply call upon preexisting philosophical discourses in order to realize their philosophical import. Rather, such films often invite the viewer to entertain new filmic ways of thinking and sense-making.[20] As Sinnerbrink writes, to defend film's operation in the condition of philosophy, "we will have to engage with aesthetic, hermeneutic and other relevant criteria that fall outside the domain of philosophical argumentation, narrowly construed. In sum, we can only defend the film-as-philosophy thesis by interdisciplinary means."[21]

To step away from Sinnerbrink for a moment and focus on just one such interdisciplinary means, consider the instructive, aesthetic power of images in art. Photographs, portraits, and paintings oftentimes allow us to see something we have never noticed before in their subject. We are even tempted to say, on occasion, that they even reveal their subject "more truthfully" than the subject's in-the-flesh appearance.[22] Philosophers have long recognized the instructive power of images and, especially, the use of images in the human thought process. Both Aristotle and Kant, for instance, remark that there is either no thought without images, or else very little thought without them. Many of the most powerful arguments of Plato and Descartes employ cinema-esque thought experiments (e.g., Plato's cave allegory; Descartes' evil genius dilemma). Also apposite here in contemporary philosophy is Gilles Deleuze's account of cinema, where he holds that cinematic shots comprise units of thinking duration, the universe revealing itself cinematically as it were.[23]

To illustrate Sinnerbrink's position on the measure of art's instructiveness for philosophy, then, I turn to an occasion when Sinnerbrink reads one such work: Pedro Almodovar's *Talk to Her* (2002). In the film, two men become close friends by happenstance. Marco (Dario Grandinetti) is a travel writer whose romantic partner, Lydia (Rosario Flores), has been seriously injured in a bull-fighting match. He meets Benigno (Javier Cámara), a nurse, in the hospital where Lydia lay in a coma. Although Benigno is a competent, gentle nurse, he is something of a stunted, social misfit. He is in love with Alicia (Leonor Watling), another comatose patient he cares for. As the film's narrative unfolds, it is revealed that Benigno was infatuated with Alicia previous to her coma-inducing accident and, in fact, sought out situations in which he could bump into her. A climactic point in the film occurs when, in a series of events communicated only elliptically on screen, Benigno rapes comatose Alicia, causing her to become pregnant. When the hospital discovers the crime, Benigno is quickly turned over to the authorities and jailed. He later commits suicide in prison once he realizes he can no longer be with Alicia.

Cinematically speaking, what offers some redemption to this admittedly horrifying storyline is the juxtaposition of Benigno's love for Alicia with

Marco's love for Lydia. Whereas (aside from the troubling fact of rape) Benigno demonstrates a loving, respectful appreciation of Alicia even in her clearly compromised state, Lydia's injury and hospitalization cause Marco to become distant and uninvolved. This contrast is revealed in some dialogue spoken by Benigno in which he praises the virtue of talking to a woman as a loving means of understanding her. Benigno spends much of his time with Alicia talking to her, whereas Marco can only stare at Lydia in silence. Benigno wholeheartedly believes that his "talk" to Alicia is genuine; he does not look at her as if she were an empty vessel, even with the assumption she will never wake from the coma. Nonetheless, after Benigno's suicide, it is revealed in a voice-over by Marco addressed to Benigno that Alicia did, in fact, wake up. Marco suggests that it was Benigno who "woke" her. In the end, Benigno earns some indirect (albeit post-mortem) redemption, through the implication that his attentive care for Alicia—his talking to her—led to her miraculous recovery, whereas Lydia dies in the hospital as a comment on Marco's lack of care for her (expressed by his lack of "conversation" with her).

Sinnerbrink highlights *Talk to Her* for its contribution to film-as-philosophy in the various ways it portrays a morally challenging situation *without* foisting a particular stance onto the viewer; the film is not moralistic. Instead, the film comprises what Sinnerbrink labels a "moral melodrama," which he characterizes as a film genre "particularly apt at evoking complex forms of ethically ambivalent experience, eliciting simultaneously sympathetic and antipathetic responses, thereby generating a dynamic dialectic of emotional engagement and critical reflection."[24] As such, Sinnerbrink holds that moral melodramas often exemplify "cinematic ethics" or ethical philosophy through film. *Talk to Her* does not accomplish these effects through a (merely) unconventional storyline; rather, it *shows* its characters in ambiguous situations, at the same time moving the viewer in competing empathic and critical directions. Also employed are a number of other nondiscursive, aesthetic features that contribute to the film's philosophical outlook, including an allegorical dance sequence, abundant use of music, and a film-within-the-film that metaphorizes Benigno's rape of Alicia.[25] Sinnerbrink concludes that *Talk to Her* elicits a unique ethical experience in its viewer, upon whom it is incumbent to accept a persistent tension between condemnation of Benigno's criminal actions *and* sympathetic comportment toward him, given his gentle nature and stunted maturity. Sinnerbrink puts it this way:

> The film deliberately thus positions the viewer—much like the majority of the characters—in a morally ambiguous, compromising space. . . . *Talk to Her* evokes a profoundly unsettling, ambivalent form of ethical experience—an ethical estrangement rather than engagement—that demands a considered, thoughtful response; an experience of ethical

cognitive dissonance or moral self-questioning that lasts well after the movie has ended.[26]

And what is the thoughtful response *Talk to Her* engenders? Presumably one could formulate many defensible conclusions for which the film provides some hermeneutical support. In Sinnerbrink's reading, the film affords "the disturbing ethical experience that there are moral situations in which conflicting impulses toward sympathy and condemnation, empathy and criticism, remain irreducibly at odds."[27] In general, this film and Sinnerbrink's interpretation of it serve to illustrate the phenomenological character embedded in his thesis regarding film-as-philosophy as a defensible, aesthetically receptive criticism. While Almodovar's film offers very little in terms of direct philosophical discourse, it does nonetheless position the viewer to formulate a unique, aesthetically multilayered philosophical view.

As a rejoinder to critics of Mulhall's and Sinnerbrink's approaches to film, namely, to those who view film's operation in the condition of philosophy in the narrow, restrictive terms of traditional philosophical discourse, one can say it is unproblematic that a film requires the interpretive articulation of its *viewer* in order for its philosophical achievement *qua* thoughtful, defensible criticism to be realized. For, if I am afforded a unique philosophical insight *by* a film, then I am going to have the task of translating that insight in order to make it communicable and justifiable to others. Nonetheless, my interpretive criticism is the basis for any kind of demonstration of the film's philosophical accomplishment. Moreover, the new insight I am afforded in cinematic terms may be predicated upon modes of discourse entirely other than traditional philosophical propositions.

While Mulhall and Sinnerbrink are concerned with articulating the same phenomenon, Sinnerbrink's position completes much of the unstated philosophical groundwork that Mulhall's approach requires in order to succeed. Mulhall's account remains insufficient in unravelling the hermeneutic, phenomenological dimensions of what it means to claim that films can operate in the condition of philosophy; in particular, Mulhall seems to overlook what makes viewers' philosophical experience of film so decisive. Sinnerbrink's account helps, however, to explicate the phenomenological, hermeneutic underpinning of the experience that lies at the heart of any defensible account of film-as-philosophy.

Cavellian Origins of Contemporary Film-Philosophies

Stanley Cavell's philosophy of film is at work in both Mulhall's and Sinnerbrink's philosophical projects, and in this concluding section I wish to highlight some areas in which Cavell's formulations are decisive for resolving ambiguities in Mulhall's and Sinnerbrink's work addressed thus far. One important issue I have not attended to fully concerns how philosophy is to be defined in the scope of the present discussion, so I aim to clarify the notion of philosophy as it occurs "through" film and how it lends itself to appropriation *by* film. What is philosophy, we could ask, such that film can exist in a state of philosophy? In what follows I hope to adjudicate a reply by discussing a selection of passages in Cavell's work that speak to this question. As a complement to this task, I invoke some work by Martin Heidegger, a philosopher with whom Cavell often engages and whose thought seems to underpin Cavell's own intuitions regarding philosophy's occurrence though film.

Cavell describes at length how films naturally present their subjects as material for reflection and study. Film images possess a character of enlarging and emphasizing what they show. In the essay "The Thought of Movies," Cavell describes this phenomenon as that of the insignificant moments of life becoming significant on film: "It is part of the grain of film to magnify the feeling and meaning of a moment."[28] Likewise, this phenomenon can occur in inverse fashion; significant moments can be deliberately passed over in the film image, making their very neglect decisive. In general, these observations are of a piece with Cavell's often-cited passage in *The World Viewed*, that films afford us the ability to see the world while unseen, "displaced from our natural habitation in it."[29] Seeing from this aesthetic, removed distance allows us to behold things themselves,[30] often for the first time, or in a totally original light.[31] In *Contesting Tears* and other writings, Cavell describes this phenomenon equally in terms of film's "transfiguration" (borrowing a locution from Arthur Danto) of the human. Films project, screen, and amplify human beings into types. This transfiguration causes the human types to come to life on screen, to achieve a self-commanding, luminescent presence, and to contribute to the creation of genres.[32] In this guise, the human cinematic image functions something like an animated philosophical concept, exerting its own visual, metaphysical weight. A passage of Cavell's that illustrates this aspect of film appears in a remark on *The Awful Truth* (1937, dir. Leo McCarey) in the essay "The Thought of Movies":

> I find in *The Awful Truth* that when the camera moves away from an immanent embrace between Cary Grant and Irene Dunne to discover a pair of human figurines marking the passage of time by skipping together into a clock that has the form of a house, that in the image something is being said about what marriage is, that it is a new way of inhabiting time.[33]

These observations foreground Cavell's view that films incline toward a philosophical disposition, or perhaps stated better, that the film viewer is naturally privileged with a philosophical vantage point. But what is meant by "philosophy" here? Cavell's perhaps most explicit statement in the film writings regarding the nature of philosophy appears in the following remark: "I understand philosophy . . . as a willingness to think undistractedly about things that ordinary human beings cannot help thinking about."[34] Cavell makes this statement principally in the context of discussing the compatibility of film and philosophy and the prima facie reasons for why these should not be considered at odds with one another. If films foster undistracted thinking about issues embedded in ordinary life, then the ultimate court of appeals for the film medium's claim to philosophy is simply the experience one has in viewing such films.[35]

Although he does not mention it in these contexts, Cavell's conception of a film viewer's experience seems strongly grounded in Heidegger's conception of *Dasein*. In Heidegger's *Being and Time*, a text of lasting interest for Cavell, *Dasein* is defined as the being whose own being is an issue and matter of reflexive concern for it.[36] Insofar as you and I are *Dasein*, our being is such that we take an interest in it. Cavell often portrays philosophy's occurrence in film in precisely this way: it is derivative of the fact that we take an interest in our own experience.[37] Philosophy, Cavell says, exists "in its very discovery."[38] It is "responsive" to the situations and contexts to which one is exposed.[39] For Heidegger, because our existence as *Dasein* includes a cognition (and subsequent recognition) of our own finitude, an awareness of our ungrounded thrownness, we possess an inherent questioning—or philosophical—disposition. And we possess a corresponding capacity to recognize a state of our being as questionable and worthy of contemplation.[40] For these reasons, according to Heidegger, the realization of finitude is the ultimate cause for individual moments of our lives to have authentic, self-possessed meaning. The crux of Heidegger's central claim in *Being and Time* lies in his claim that temporal finitude is the horizon out of which everyday experience gains meaning.[41] When Cavell characterizes films as possessing the power to "transfigure" their subjects and command a necessary philosophical outlook for the viewer, I suggest that this feature of films—and their constituent, constituting images—*activates* in us this existential feature of questioning self-concern. In other words, we might say that *Dasein* is conditioned (or constituted) to recognize moments when films magnify and transfigure their subjects, prompting our questioning, philosophical reflection.

Mulhall's thesis regarding the philosophy embedded in the *Alien* series appears to channel Heidegger by way of Cavell. Mulhall observes an inherent philosophical weight in the portrayals of humans and aliens in the series, such that the films' imagistic explorations of how the two species encounter and appropriate one another render the camera's subjects into, as it were, embodied, expressive philosophical arguments.[42] When Mulhall characterizes these films as "philosophy in action," he seems to mean that the film images and corresponding narrative operate akin to a kind of philosophical thinking, a process in which the concepts of human and alien morph into one another in different shapes, where a viewing *Dasein* cannot help but take reflective interest in these movements of self and other. Mulhall also refers to something like the "thrown," existential dimension of the viewer's innate philosophical capacity as a *Dasein* when he writes that the *Alien* films reflect on "inter-related anxieties" laden in the human condition, such as our preoccupations with gender, sexuality, finitude, embodiment, and personal identity.[43]

Another important feature of Cavell's conception of philosophy lay in his assertion that philosophy is not limited to any subject matter. As he describes in *The World Viewed*, given that film comprises a popular art form, film's philosophical potential is equally open for all.[44] Film operates in the condition of democratic poetry,[45] such that one does not need special training in order to comprehend or appreciate a film's philosophical accomplishment. Film takes the unseen, philosophically weighted aspects of everyday life and makes them available for anyone who is paying attention.[46] Here the philosophical stakes of film's power are joined to its sociopolitical significance; the everydayness of film is part of its potency for activating and cultivating thought. In Mulhall's account the democratic feature of film viewership entails that there is no philosophical privilege, either in the kinds of films that can function as vehicles for philosophy, or in the precise manner that these films convey their philosophical material. On this score, it is decisive that big-budget action movies, animated films, and superhero serials can operate in the condition of philosophy; these works show, time and again, that film-as-philosophy need not be limited to the self-conscious art-house film, the structural film, the existential film, etc.[47] Sinnerbrink reaches a similar conclusion and emphasizes that film-as-philosophy is made manifest in philosophical criticism of films. From Sinnerbrink's perspective, the films in question (including their specific content, themes, style, etc.) are, in fact, less decisive than the *disclosures* (another word with Heideggerian resonances) they give the viewer to articulate. As an attentive, thoughtful viewer, I am not at liberty to hold that a film presents anything and everything that I please, though I am privileged to describe the philosophical import in what I perceive so long as I can persuasively communicate it. Philosophy exists in the state of film and film exists in the state of the everyday, so by transposition, the philosophical weight of films—even those with unremarkable themes—can be shown to be significant.

Mulhall makes a Cavellian observation that in certain film genres, the achievement of a new perspective on existence occurs in tandem with a new place, typically removed from the familiar setting of one's life. Cavell observes that in Shakespeare this is the Green World, a place in nature or wilderness outside or apart from the bustle of everyday life and commerce, such as the Forest of Arden in *As You Like It* or Prospero's island in *The*

Tempest.[48] Decisive, transformational experiences of life so often take place in foreign, unfamiliar spaces, or turned another way, we could say that such spaces reveal themselves as conducive to such transformations. Mulhall invokes a similar trope with the overtly metaphysical character of the science fiction setting that stages the *Alien* films. In his view, part of the reason these films can operate in the condition of philosophy is that the topology of the "Green World"—in this case, the "Black World" of the outer expanses of the universe—places key subject matter in more direct focus, distanced as it is from the familiar terrain of ordinary routine. We are poised to see the problem at hand more clearly because the *Alien* films offer a more stripped-down, minimalistic view of their subjects and situations. Indeed, although Mulhall downplays his account's reliance on a science fiction scenario (given the cliché that science fiction films are often philosophical by default[49]), I believe the point about science fiction's special capacity for achieving this focus (by showing us "outer" spaces set against our familiar and inner ones) is especially convincing vis-à-vis Cavell's observation of the philosophical power of place as well as his conception of genre in the film medium.[50]

Science fiction films are (especially) conducive to philosophy because they place the human subject into foreign, "experimental" worlds where themes of humanness, mind, embodiment, free will, and destiny occupy our central focus. The minimal Black World of deep space is a place in which only one's *humanness* stands out for change because it is, in some sense, all that is meaningfully present. Consider other examples in this regard: *2001: A Space Odyssey* (1968, dir. Stanley Kubrick), *Solaris* (1972, dir. Andrei Tarkovsky), *Moon* (2009, dir. Duncan Jones), and *Gravity* (2013, dir. Alfonso Cuarón). For Cavell, films fall into genres by reflecting on their shared conditions of possibility, and genres thereafter mutually inform one another.[51] Genres treat similar thematic questions regarding the possibility of their subject matter in different ways, and in treating such questions differently they complement and respond to other films that do the same.[52] If we follow Mulhall's overall reading, the *Alien* series and its cousins (noted above) comprise a Cavellian genre—"outer-space science fiction," we might say—by virtue of mutually negotiating the skepticism and existential uncertainty bound up with familiar but ungrounded aspects of the human condition. Indeed, this unique characteristic of science fiction films in particular seems just as decisive in the present zeitgeist, given that this genre's philosophical preoccupations continue to figure prominently in the "common cultural inheritance" of the human condition in the twenty-first century.[53]

In this dialogue between Mulhall, Sinnerbrink, and Cavell, we should take note of the Cavellian notion of film interpretation as performance. As summarized above, Sinnerbrink defends film's claim to philosophy via the practice of justifiable, philosophical film criticism. Sinnerbrink's thesis is attractive, in part because it dispenses with awkward claims regarding a film's "agency" and the thorny issue of how films philosophize "cinematically."

Sinnerbrink's account illuminates the aspect in which film-as-philosophy is achieved and realized through the viewer's experience of what the film affords in various modes of aesthetic, hermeneutic, and emotive experience. Nonetheless, a potential weak-spot in Sinnerbrink's thesis emerges when we regard *philosophical* film criticism as amounting to nothing more than a high-flown kind of film reading or interpretation. Noël Carroll, for instance, argues that most purported instances of film-as-philosophy simply *are* philosophically minded film criticism—no different from what a movie reviewer might publish in a newspaper. And as such, according to Carroll, there is no special status to assign to the *film* in its own right.[54]

There are some passages in Cavell's work that, I believe, contra Carroll, lend credence to Sinnerbrink's position. In *Pursuits of Happiness*, Cavell remarks that, among the ways he might describe his method of film analysis, one preferable characterization is to call it "performance." The preference for this term stems from the dialectical quagmire involved in trying to determine the boundary between the primary text—in this case, the film—and one's reading or interpretation of the film. Cavell's implication is that any claim about what the primary film text actually is versus what one interprets in the film risks begging the question. Cavell suggests that calling film interpretation a "performance" helps to convey that one's interpretation stems from an analysis borne in *viewing* the film. This critic-centric account is analogous, Cavell says, to the way a musician first analyzes a piece of music in its written text, and subsequently manifests his or her way of hearing it in the notes he or she performs.[55] The thrust of the analogy is that the music "text" *receives interpretation* through the musician's performance; interpretation and performance are inseparable. So too, then, one ought to understand a film's accounting—its meaning, say—to rely on its interpretation or "performance" by a critic. Sinnerbrink's notion of philosophically minded film criticism attentive to the various criteria proffered in a film benefits from this idea of performance. For criticism of film, books, or other art media is a form of discourse, of gathering and articulating for others the disclosures one experiences in the work. As such, criticism is performative; it involves a kind of rehearsing or replaying of what has been given in the work. And to the extent that films often "do" their philosophical, discursive work in mediated, unspoken fashion, it is ultimately the thoughtful viewer's justifiable criticism that connects the dots a film initially sketches.

There is also a relevant Heideggerian undercurrent at work in Cavell's notion of performance, which we find in *Being and Time*'s conception of discourse (*Rede*) as a specific existential mode in which *Dasein* experiences disclosures of meaning. Discourse for Heidegger is the fundamental, irreducible mode in which we experience things in terms of language, codes, and signs.[56] On one hand, discourse refers to the ontological condition through which human beings have or possess the phenomena of spoken and written language; we seem wired to communicate using language and would certainly be hard-pressed to make ourselves mutually understood without it. Yet, on the other hand, discourse is also a pre-linguistic mode in which our understanding of reality operates. This is to say, we do not construct our comprehension of the world from bare sense-data, as if our role as rational beings involves building from scratch interpretations of every sense-experience. Heidegger cites as examples the sounds of a bustling street, of a motorcycle engine, or even of people talking in a foreign language (that we hear as a vocalized language, not as nondescript noise). Each of these examples is a holistic disclosure—we might say, performance—whose discursive meaning comes across ready-made. We do not need to invent such meaning because it is already given in the performative disclosure. We know the sound without being told what it is or what it means. I suggest that a phenomenological conception of film interpretation as performance finds vindication in this kind of "disclosive" character in Heidegger's notion of discourse. To call a film reading a "performance" is a fitting label because *Dasein*'s existential mode of discourse fosters performance as both a dative mode of disclosure from film to viewer, and an outward-looking, critical mode of film viewership. In other words, one's performative interpretation of a film is borne out of the *film's* performative disclosure. I am suggesting that the performance provided by what Cavell calls the "text" of a film is therefore reflected in and by the discourse it gives the viewer to perform.

Such a notion of performance (and criticism as performance) seems at the heart of Cavell's observation that "[a] reading of a film sets up a continuous appeal to the experience of the film."[57] To be sure, this reading does not entail that a film interpreter and "performer" can easily repeat or replay a film's performance or translate it painlessly, much less fully, into words. Cavell writes on this score: "This is an epitome of the nature of conversation about film generally, that those who are experiencing again, and expressing, moments of a film are at times apt to become incomprehensible . . . to those who are not experiencing them."[58] Recounting the experience of a film is often fuzzy and predicated on memory, but this is further complicated when the recounting is met by other people who have not seen the film at all.

Without a shared experience of the film, communication is strained; but then, when we both have seen a film, our *interpretations* of the film are not saved by a magical ability to confer our meanings. These limitations (for the unseen and the seen) are general features of ordinary intentional, minded experience, which is nearly always a mixture of clarity and obscurity, intelligibility and hiddenness, presence and absence.[59] Films exemplify this muddled phenomenon as much as anything else for they so often reflect our complexity as muddled beings; one's (performative) interpretation of a film cannot always be perfectly lucid because filmic disclosures are often obscure. As Cavell puts it, "it is as if an inherent concealment of significance, as much as its revelation, were part of the governing force of what we mean by film."[60] Cavell's sentiment about film's double character as disclosive and hidden echoes Sinnerbrink's view that purported instances of film-as-philosophy do not lie in purely epistemic affordances of films, but, instead, require our consciousness of other, concealed, unspoken, and unseen criteria.

Notes

1. See for instance their respective contributions to *Thinking through Cinema: Film as Philosophy*, ed. Thomas E. Wartenberg and Murray Smith (Malden: Blackwell, 2006).
2. Stephen Mulhall, *On Film*, 3rd edn. (London: Routledge, 2016), 3.
3. Ibid., 99–102.
4. Ibid., 3–6.
5. Ibid., 3.
6. Ibid., 3–4.
7. Ibid., 3.
8. Ibid., 4.
9. Ibid., 5.
10. "This cosmic backdrop makes it all but impossible to avoid grasping the narrative and thematic structure of the films in metaphysical or existential terms—as if the alien universe could not but concern itself with the human condition as such." *Ibid.*, 7.
11. Julian Baggini, "Alien Ways of Thinking: Mulhall's *On Film*," *Film-Philosophy* 7 (2003).
12. Mulhall, *On Film*, 89.
13. Todd DuFresne, "*On Film*, Theory, & 'Film as Philosophy': Or, Philosophy Goes Pop," *Film and Philosophy* 15 (2011): 150.
14. Robert Sinnerbrink, *New Philosophies of Film* (London: Continuum, 2011), 132–33.
15. Ibid., 132–33.
16. Ibid., 134–35.
17. Ibid., 134.
18. Ibid., 135.
19. Robert Pippin, "Vernacular Metaphysics: On Terrence Malick's *The Thin Red Line*," *Critical Inquiry* 39, no. 2 (2013): 252–53. See also *The Philosophy of War Films*, ed. David LaRocca (Lexington: The University Press of Kentucky, 2014), 385–412.
20. Sinnerbrink, *New Philosophies of Film*, 137–39.
21. Ibid., 134–35.
22. Robert Sokolowski, *Phenomenology of the Human Person* (Cambridge: Cambridge University Press, 2006), 138ff. Robert Sokolowsi, "Visual Intelligence in Painting," *Review of Metaphysics* 59, no. 2 (2005): 333.

23 Gilles Deleuze, *Cinema I: The Movement-Image*, trans. Hugh Tomlinson (Minneapolis: University of Minnesota Press, 1991) esp. Chapter 2, Section 2.
24 Robert Sinnerbrink, *Cinematic Ethics* (Abingdon: Routledge, 2016), 126.
25 Ibid., 128.
26 Ibid., 133–34.
27 Ibid., 134.
28 Stanley Cavell, "The Thought of Movies" in *Themes Out of School: Effects and Causes* (San Francisco: North Point Press, 1984), 11.
29 Stanley Cavell, *The World Viewed: Reflections on the Ontology of Film*, Expanded Edition (Cambridge: Harvard University Press, 1979), 40–41.
30 Daniel Shaw, "Stanley Cavell on the Magic of the Movies," *Film-Philosophy* 21 (2017): 118–19.
31 Stanley Cavell, *Pursuits of Happiness: The Hollywood Comedy of Remarriage* (Cambridge: Harvard University Press, 1981), 10–12.
32 Stanley Cavell, *Contesting Tears: The Hollywood Melodrama of the Unknown Woman* (Chicago: The University of Chicago Press, 1996), 7; Cavell, "The Thought of Movies," 7.
33 Cavell, "The Thought of Movies," 7.
34 Ibid., 9.
35 Ibid.
36 Martin Heidegger, *Being and Time*, trans. Joan Stambaugh, rev. Dennis J. Schmidt (Albany: SUNY Press, 2010), Section 4.
37 Cavell, *Pursuits of Happiness*, 12.
38 Stanley Cavell, *Cities of Words: Pedagogical Letters on a Register of the Moral Life* (Cambridge: Harvard University Press; Belknap Press, 2004), 7.
39 Stanley Cavell and Andrew Klevan, "Stanley Cavell in Conversation with Andrew Klevan," in *Film as Philosophy: Essays on Cinema after Wittgenstein and Cavell*, ed. Rupert Read and Jerry Goodenough (Bastingstoke: Palgrave Macmillan, 2005), 186.
40 Heidegger, *Being and Time*, Section 2.
41 Ibid., Section 5.
42 Mulhall, *On Film*, 3.
43 Ibid., 3–4.
44 Cavell, *The World Viewed*, 14.
45 Cavell, "The Thought of Movies," 14.
46 Ibid., 14–17.
47 Mulhall, *On Film*, 6–7.
48 Cavell, "The Thought of Movies," 13.
49 Mulhall, *On Film*, 98.

50 This is a noteworthy quirk in Mulhall's body of work, given that nearly all of the films he takes up are in fact science fiction or otherwise operate in the realm of the supernatural and fantastic.
51 Cavell, *Pursuits of Happiness*, 28–30.
52 Shaw, "Cavell on the Magic of the Movies," 116.
53 Cavell, *Pursuits of Happiness*, 9.
54 Noël Carroll, "Philosophizing Through the Moving Image: The Case of *Serene Velocity*," in *Philosophy Through Film*, ed. Thomas E. Wartenburg and Murray Smith (Malden: Blackwell, 2006), 182–83.
55 Cavell, *Pursuits of Happiness*, 37–38.
56 Heidegger, *Being and Time*, Section 35.
57 Cavell, *Pursuits of Happiness*, 11.
58 Ibid.
59 Edmund Husserl, *Logical Investigations*, vol. II (Atlantic Highlands: Humanities Books, 2000), 711.
60 Cavell, "The Thought of Movies," 11.

11

The Conception of Film for the Subject of Television: Moral Education of the Public and a Return to an Aesthetics of the Ordinary

SANDRA LAUGIER

STANLEY CAVELL WAS NO DOUBT THE FIRST to account for the transformation of theory and criticism brought about by reflection on popular culture—such as so-called mainstream cinema. However, Cavell is less concerned with reversing artistic hierarchies or inverting the relation between theory and practice than with the self-transformation required by our encounters with new experiences. Robert Warshow, Cavell's inspiration on these matters and the author of remarkable analyses of popular culture, put it thus:

> We are all "self-made men" culturally, establishing ourselves in terms of the particular choices we make from among the confusing multitude of stimuli that present themselves to us. Something more than the pleasures of personal cultivation is at stake when one chooses to respond to Proust rather than to Mickey Spillane, to Laurence Olivier in *Oedipus Rex* rather than Sterling Hayden in *The Asphalt Jungle*. And when one has made the "right" choice, Mickey Spillane and Sterling Hayden do not disappear; perhaps no one gets quite out of sight of them. There is great need, I think, for a criticism of "popular culture" which can

acknowledge its pervasive and disturbing power without ceasing to be aware of the superior claims of the higher arts, and yet without a bad conscience.¹

Is there still any sense in talking about "popular culture?" Or has this sense been transformed to the extent that we now use the expression without really knowing what we are saying—or, to take the title of one of Cavell's essays, without *meaning* what we say?² In *The Claim of Reason*, Cavell defined philosophy as the "education of grownups," parallel to his goal in his major works on cinema—*The World Viewed*, *Pursuits of Happiness* (on remarriage comedies), *Contesting Tears* (on melodrama), and *Cities of Words* (which covers the entirety of his teaching at Harvard, alternating between lessons in philosophy and studies of films)—to give popular culture (Hollywood movies in particular are his main interest) the power to change us.³ According to Cavell, the value of a culture lies not in its "great art" but in its transformative capacity, the same capacity found in the "moral perfectionism" of Emerson and Thoreau. Philosophy consists in "bring[ing] my own language and life into imagination," in "a convening of my culture's criteria, in order to confront them with my words and life . . . and at the same time to confront my words and life as I pursue them with the life my culture's words may imagine for me: to confront the culture with itself, along the lines in which it meets in me."⁴

How can we imagine continuing to grow after the end of childhood? Cavell's philosophy defines growth—once childhood and physical growth are over—as the capacity to change. This capacity is at work in Cavell's favored object of study, the apparently minor genre of remarriage comedies, which stage characters' mutual education and their transformation through separation and reunion: "In this light, philosophy becomes the education of grownups. . . . The anxiety in teaching, in serious communication, is that I myself require education. And for grownups," he writes, "this is not natural growth, but *change*."⁵

Cavell also gives this philosophical enterprise the outdated name "moral education," or "pedagogy," as in the subtitle to *Cities of Words*. For Cavell, whose childhood and youth were haunted by Hollywood movies, the culture in question is popular cinema, whose productions reached the greatest number at the time. The educational value of popular culture is not anecdotal. Indeed, it seems to me to define what must be understood both by "popular" and by "culture" (in the sense of *Bildung*) in the expression "popular culture." Within such a perspective, the vocation of popular culture is the philosophical education of a *public* rather than the institution and valorization of a socially targeted corpus. The way in which Cavell has claimed the philosophical value of Hollywood cinema—placing it on the level of the greatest works of thought without, however, thinking of cinema as great art—may have seemed too easy, demagogic, or populist, as if such a claim could not be real. What Cavell claimed for mainstream Hollywood cinema in the 1970s has been transferred to other practices and bodies of work, such as television series, which have taken over for cinema, if not replaced it, in the task of educating adolescents and adults.

Philosophy has not yet adequately observed or analyzed the democratization of art in the digital age, nor has it addressed the blurring of the distinction between amateur and professional in certain artistic settings and practices. This is because philosophy has lacked the necessary analyses and theoretical tools and has not clearly grasped the pragmatic shift of culture toward the public space. Thus, it is essential to use and invent new tools to examine the democratization of art and, conversely, the emergence of artistic practices as resources for renewing democratic claims and forms.

In 1939, Walter Benjamin reflected on the consequences of new techniques of mechanically reproducing visual and musical works of art. Erwin Panofsky stressed that "film was first and foremost a medium of popular entertainment, devoid of aesthetic pretention, which reestablished the 'dynamic contact between art production and art consumption'" that is "sorely attenuated, if not entirely interrupted, in many other fields of artistic endeavor."

A profound change is underway in the field of culture and its hierarchies, and it is marked by the change in attitude toward television series,[6] which are now seen as spaces where artistic and hermeneutic authority can be reappropriated and where viewers can be reempowered by constituting their own unique experiences. This is what the critic, Robert Warshow had in mind when he wrote in *The Immediate Experience* (1962) that "culturally, we are all 'self-made men': we constitute ourselves in the particular choices we make within the dizzying array of stimuli that offer themselves to us."

The democratization of artistic production promised by romanticism would thus be realized in the new artistic forms and modes of participation and interaction that digital technology allows, opening the way for new forms of subjective authority. The question of democracy is thus also a question of our capacity for individual expression and unique aesthetic actions and choices. Art and film have gone from being elitist to being essential drivers of social intervention and innovation. In this, they have become creators of true democracy—if by democracy we mean not an institution but, rather, the demand for equality and participation in public life.

What is meant by popular culture today is no longer exactly popular in the social or political sense in which certain arts—for example, songs or folklore—were popular, even if it draws on the resources of these arts. When it comes to defining our shared, accessible heritage, we must think, instead, of the material of ordinary conversation. At a certain time—and still today in certain milieus—this could have been a recent film or a controversial book.

Today, among the young and a good number of adults, it is just as often a television series. Popular culture turns out to be a site for "the education of grownups," who, through this intermediary, return to a form of education and cultivation of the self: subjective improvement (*perfectionism* = *meliorism*); more exactly, a subjectivation that takes place through sharing and commenting on public and ordinary material that is integrated into ordinary life. It is in this sense that "we are all self-made men" and that cinema, for Warshow and Cavell, is at the heart of "popular culture" and the stakes of its criticism, as Warshow notes: "Such a criticism finds its best opportunity in the movies, which are the most highly developed and most engrossing of the popular arts, and which seem to have an almost unlimited power to absorb and transform the discordant elements of our fragmented culture."[7] There is here a new assessment of importance, which Wittgenstein called for when he asserted the importance of ordinary language philosophy and attention to real life:

> Where does our investigation get its importance from, since it seems only to destroy everything interesting, that is, all that is great and important? (As it were all the buildings, leaving behind only bits of stone and rubble.) What we are destroying is nothing but houses of cards and we are clearing up the ground of language on which they stand.[8]

In *Cities of Words*, Cavell writes:

> "Importance" is an important word for Tracy's former (and future) husband C. K. Dexter Haven, who applies it, to Tracy's chagrin, to the night she got drunk and danced naked on the roof of the house—it is her saying impatiently to him that he attached too much importance to that silly escapade that prompts him to say to her, "it was immensely important."[9]

And said earlier, in *The Claim of Reason*:

> What feels like destruction, what expresses itself here in the idea of destruction, is really a shift in what we are asked to let interest us, in the tumbling of our ideas of the great and the important.[10]

Cavell's main point is a reassessment of importance, which implies the collapse or *relocation* (just as radical) of hierarchies between great art and ordinary cultural practices. He remarks parenthetically: "(This relocation of importance and interest is what in *The Claim of Reason*, following my reading of Wittgenstein's *Investigations*, I call the recounting of importance, and assign as a guiding task of philosophy)."[11]

The Democracy of Cinema

In *The World Viewed*, Cavell's starting point was the popular nature of cinema, which he connected to a certain relation to ordinary life: an intimacy with the ordinary. A first aspect of this intimacy lies in cinema's integration in the ordinary lives of movie enthusiasts. In an excellent essay on the ontology of cinema in Cavell, Emmanuel Bourdieu defined cinema's realism by its entanglement with our ordinary life: "Cinema is common, ordinary, shared aesthetic experience, implicated in and bound up with everyday life (a movie before or after dinner and before returning home; a night perhaps spent dreaming of it; breakfast, etc.)."[12]

One of Cavell's goals, and one of his greatest successes, is to make apparent the intelligence (understanding) that a film has already brought to bear in its own making, which also amounts to "letting a work of art *have its own voice* in what philosophy will say about it." This is not only a methodological point, for it supposes that cinema is equal to philosophy as a mode of approach to the world. Consequently, cinema interests us as *experience* and not as *object*, and this is the basis of an ordinary criticism and theory of cinema.[13]

Understanding cinema's relation to philosophy thus implies two tasks:

1. Learning what it means to "check one's experience," to use an expression from *Pursuits of Happiness*, that is, to examine one's experience and "to let the object or the work of your interest teach you how to consider it."[14] This means that it is necessary to educate one's experience in such a way that one can be educated by it. There is an inevitable circularity here, which Emerson pointed out: *having* an experience requires having confidence in one's experience.

2. Finding the words to express one's experience. This theme is central in Cavell's work: the will to find one's voice in one's story, against the temptation of inexpressiveness.[15] The possibility of *having* an experience is inseparable from the question of expression and the possibilities, which cinema explores, for human beings' natural expressivity. This discovery, rooted in a reading of Wittgenstein, is Cavell's mode of approach to cinema and it serves as his entry into its different genres: the conversations in remarriage comedies do not duplicate ordinary conversations, but *express* a relation to ordinary words. "A mastery of film writing and film making accordingly requires a mastery of this mimesis of ordinary words."[16]

The fact that this conversation is not "only" discourse, and implies what Cavell calls photogenesis—the projection of living characters onto the screen to speak these words—shows that this conversation can only exist in cinema, that it even constitutes the experience of cinema, and that it inscribes the ordinariness of language in cinema: (talking) films put us in the presence of a body and a voice, of ordinary language. Thus, to find the ordinary would be to find an adequacy between our words and our world; it would be to come closer to our experience. This is the claim of popular and democratic culture, already expressed by Emerson: "I ask not for the great, the remote, the romantic; what is doing in Italy or Arabia; Greek art or Provencal minstrelsy; I embrace the common, I explore and sit at the feet of the familiar, the low."[17]

For this, it is not a matter of the critic interpreting, but, rather, letting the film say what it has to show and hearing what it says: its voice. This means letting oneself be educated by the experience of the film and finding passivity in the experience and its repetition. For Cavell, cinema is a response to skepticism, to the loss of an experience that escapes me, but it is not a way of recovering an inaccessible experience, of regaining the world in the projection of the world: it is, instead, a mode of recognizing the loss. The paradox of the idea of a *return* to the ordinary is that one returns to something one never had, where we have never been.

The genre of remarriage comedies expresses this aspiration to return to the ordinary—acceptance of repetition, and of the everyday—which in these films is only possible through death (the loss of the other and of the world), and then rebirth. The genre marks a unique proximity between the experience of cinema and what constitutes our experience as ordinary. The experience of these films makes it possible to "be interested in one's own experience." People bear these films "in their experience as memorable public events, segments of the experiences, the memories, of a common life. So that the difficulty of assessing them is the same as the difficulty of assessing everyday experience, the difficulty of expressing oneself satisfactorily, of making oneself find the words for what one is specifically interested to say."[18]

Cinema, answering the Emersonian call for democratic and ordinary art, is able to describe everyday reality. Our experience as spectators comes out of an ordinary, shared culture—access to the "physiognomy" of the ordinary: to quote Emerson's "The American Scholar" again, "the literature of the poor, the feelings of the child, the philosophy of the street, the meaning of household life."[19] The idea that the highest culture is shared culture is one of the fundamental values Cavell defends in "Film in the University," the afterword to *Pursuits of Happiness*. Cavell teaches us that an ordinary aesthetics of cinema must defend not the specificity of the individuals who created a work, nor the singularity of a work, but, rather, our common aesthetic experience—for example, the experience of a movie viewer who goes to see a movie less for its director than for the actors in it, whom he or she liked in earlier films and now wants to see again in new incarnations ("the same, but different," as Cary Grant says in *The Awful Truth* [1937, dir. Leo McCarey]).

The experience of cinema is at once mysterious and ordinary. Here, we touch on the very finitude of the experience of film, which is always repeatable but also always circumscribed. In spite of new viewing conditions that have been established over the last several decades (with videos, DVDs, etc.), the temporality of film is always the temporality of finitude. There is always a moment when it stops, and this feeling is part of the experience of a film, making it a type of the ordinary experience of life.

This proximity between the experience of cinema and what makes our experience ordinary—its evanescence and endurance—constitutes the pedagogic and democratic aspect of the cinematographic experience, which comes out of shared *care*. As Cavell writes in *The World Viewed*: "Rich and poor, those who care about no (other) art and those who live on the promise of art, those whose pride is education and those whose pride is power or practicality—all care about movies, await them, respond to them, remember them, talk about them, hate some of them, are grateful for some of them."[20]

Another democratic characteristic of the experience of cinema is that in cinema we like the exceptional as much as the common: the movie enthusiast is by definition eclectic (in a way the art or literature enthusiast is not always). As Marc Cerisuelo reminds us, Panofsky had already noticed this element: if cinema is important for us, it is because it has not lost contact with a wide audience, unlike the traditional great arts. Panofsky was the first to insist "on the fact that film was first and foremost created as popular entertainment without aesthetic pretension, and revitalized the connections between artistic production and consumption, which are more than tenuous—if not broken—in many artistic disciplines."[21] This is the basis of the relation of cinema to its genres. "In the case of films," Cavell writes "it is generally true that you do not really like the highest instances unless you also like typical ones. You don't even know what the highest are instances of unless you know the typical as well."[22]

The Importance of Film

Cavell's goal is to propose a change of perspective—which he sometimes calls a *revolution*—on cinema and popular culture in general. In order to do this, it is necessary to truly take cinema seriously, to see its importance—to accept, for example, as Cavell indicates in his essay "The Thought of Movies,"[23] that Hollywood movies have as much to tell us about certain questions (such as the possibility of establishing contact with the world) as philosophy as we know it does; that reflection on skepticism in Capra is as radical as it is in Hume or Kant. We must take Cavell seriously when, in *Pursuits of Happiness*, he associates the argument of *It Happened One Night* (1934, dir. Frank Capra) with that of *The Critique of Pure Reason*.

Obviously, there is something shocking in this, and this very scandal is what interests Cavell. It is not the association of cinema and philosophy that is scandalous (it has become all too common), but, rather, making them equal in their competence and capacity to educate and shape. The philosophical relevance of a film lies in what it itself says and shows, not in what criticism discovers in it or develops in relation to it. The "nightmare of criticism" is to be unable to see "the intelligence that a film has *already* brought to bear in its making." The perspective on popular film introduced by Cavell now applies to television series and to everything that comes out of the exploration and mixing of "genres": art forms that not only maintain contact with the public, but also educate it, possibly through the creation of a specific universe based on its own culture, which it produces (the cult series *Buffy the Vampire Slayer* is an example of this).

Cinema is not (or for Cavell, not foremost) a matter of art: it has to do, rather, with shared experience. In this respect, cinema heralds the reign of television series. Cavell does not speak of seeing a film but of "moviegoing." It is less a matter of aesthetics than of *practice*, a practice that connects and reconciles public and private, subjective expectation and sharing in something common. Cinema's relation to popular culture shifts as a result. From the outset, Cavell nullifies a response that would claim that every art, in its youth, goes through a "popular" phase. He sees two biases in such a response: first, in the possibility of measuring the lifespan of an art and seeing it as a living being with a youth and adulthood, and second, in the hierarchy between or evolution from popular to great art. Panofsky wanted to show that cinema took up the popular genres of tragedy, romance, crime, adventure, and comedy "as soon as it was realized that they could be transfigured . . . by the exploitation of the unique and specific possibilities of the new *medium*."[24] The word "transfigure" can here be understood as the creation of another figure, another representation or expression ("dynamization of space" or "spatialization of time," the ability to show several events unfolding at the same time, "possibilities of the cinematographic *medium*.") The theme of cinema as the exploration of new aesthetic possibilities is fairly central to the philosophy of film, but does not interest Cavell. For him, cinema is important because of its place in our lives and its exploration of genres, and because of its capacity to absorb and produce fragments of our experience—an essential aspect of popular culture and which ordinary criticism must account for.

Emmanuel Bourdieu, in the essay cited above, explains that one of the characteristics of cinema is its internal reference to genres, as a specific modality of its examination of its own expressive potentials. Of course, other arts also appeal to the notion of genre, but retrospectively, in order to classify the productions of the past or to distinguish themselves within a genre. For Cavell, on the other hand, cinema only exists in its genres, and this defines its popular nature: there is no essence of cinema or authorial mystique. In contrast to aristocratic distinction, popular culture opposes the model of the self-made spectator who creates his or her taste through his or her favorite genres: action, romantic comedies, Westerns, science fiction, vulgar-comedies-for-teens, vampire movies, etc.

For Cavell, the constitution of these genres, and their pregnancy, rests on a specific property of film creation: its collective nature. The production of a cinematographic work is a collective enterprise that mobilizes not only the film's team, led by its director, but also, indirectly, the entire community of other filmmakers and all their works, since team members are always likely to participate or to have participated in the making of other films produced by the community in question. Henceforth, the system of reference relative to which the work of art was understood—that is, the author and his unique inspiration—dissolves. To understand a cinematographic work, it is necessary to find a system of reference that transcends individual wills and inspirations. This system of reference is the collectively constituted genre.[25]

Stephen Mulhall has convincingly described what sets Cavell's approach apart from those of other philosophers of cinema.[26] The dominant approach consists in describing essential properties of the medium in order to prescribe its possibilities and possible genres. Cavell, on the other hand, advocates describing certain artistic successes or certain genres in order to describe the possibilities of the medium—just as for Wittgenstein there is no "essence of language" that would prescribe its norms and usages, and no definition of our concepts that would determine their possible future application. We may here turn to Victor Perkins' analysis:

> I do not believe that the film (or any other medium) has an essence which we can usefully invoke to justify our criteria. We do not deduce the standards relevant to Rembrandt from the essence of paint; nor does the nature of words impose a method of judging ballads and novels. Standards of judgement cannot be appropriate to a medium as such but only to particular ways of exploiting its opportunities. That is why the concept of the cinematic, presented in terms of demands, has stunted the useful growth of film theory.[27]

Cavellian genres are defined in relation to a certain body of actual works—for example, a group of comedies produced within a given period, the 1930s and 1940s, within a certain structure of production, the large Hollywood studios of the time. As Bourdieu notes: "The expressive possibilities of cinema as an aesthetic medium are created by their realization. Thus, for Cavell, the potentialities of the medium—in particular its technical potentialities—are not even possibilities as such as long as they haven't been given meaning within a particular work."[28]

A genre of cinema or television is thus not an a posteriori principle of classification, or a normative system, but, rather, a creative force. The genre strives "toward a state of absolute explicitness, of expressive saturation. At that point the genre would have nothing further to generate."[29] Thus, none of the traits that enter into the definition of a genre is a necessary and sufficient condition for belonging to this genre—the list of characteristic traits is "radically open-ended." And the absence of a trait characteristic of a given genre (for example, the absence of a heroine's mother in remarriage comedies) can always be made up for by a "compensating circumstance." However, belonging to the remarriage comedy genre does seem to suppose that the heroine be a woman on a quest for perfection and that the starting point of the film be a divorce, or something of that order, and its endpoint be (something like) her remarriage. But this structure does not constitute a set of properties necessary and sufficient for a given work to belong to a genre; the list of properties that defines a genre is never closed.

It is a genre's openness and creativity that allows for its productivity, including in the derivation of new genres: for example, the perfectionist quest in the genre of melodrama; remarriage or the equivalent (reconciliation/conversation) in romantic comedies or comedies for teens such as *Knocked Up* (2007, dir. Judd Apatow) and *Superbad* (2007, dir. Greg Mottola).

Not to mention the productivity of genres in television series, which have clearly inherited the conversational capacities of couples in Hollywood comedies, which provide them with the grammar of their expressions, interactions, and emotions.

There is thus, in genre, an aspect of empowerment for later generations of characters. In an apparently banal comedy, *The Holiday* (2007, dir. Nancy Meyers), genre has a determining role, allowing the heroine of one of the storylines (Kate Winslet, whose character discovers an entire series of remarriage comedy films during a trip to California, where she meets an old screenwriter and a young composer) to find the strength to reject her former, toxic lover and to express new confidence in herself. *The Holiday* is sprinkled with micro-extracts of films (including *The Lady Eve* and *His Girl Friday*), which underscores this heritage and the expressive fecundity of the genre.

A genre provides an expressive grammar, including for the spectator, who—like the heroine of *The Holiday*—finds within it resources for his or her own sentiments and situations. This ordinary pedagogical aspect has been radicalized in television series, which are explicitly sites of ordinary expression. They are themselves fed by moments of conversation in recent or classic comedies, which make up their referential and moral universe (think, for example, of the constant allusions to television or movie characters in *Buffy*, *Lost*, or *How I Met Your Mother*, or the more recent *Love*). The spectator's ordinary expertise turns out to be a capacity for expression that comes from knowledge, even mastery, of a genre. Once again, a genre is not an essence—its worth lies in the expressive possibilities it opens up for actors and spectators. Thus, the remarriage comedy genre proposes a grammar of moral education, which Cavell elaborated in *Cities of Words*. The democratic nature of cinema and television series is also found in this capacity for education. This is because, as Cavell notes, cinema shows the important moments of life, when life changes imperceptibly—moments which, in real life, are fleeting and indeterminate, or whose importance it takes years or an entire life to understand. In order to rethink the concept of popular culture, it is necessary to understand that cinema is not a specialized art and that it can transform our existences by educating our ordinary experience.

The Public

No reflection on popular culture can ignore the question confronted by Cavell, who rejects both the critic's contempt for forms seen as degraded and the condescension of the intellectual who claims interest in television series or popular movies while remaining certain of a position of superiority over the material. Cavell bases his hermeneutic work on "the intelligence that a film has *already* brought to bear in its making." The perspective Cavell introduces on popular cinema and the demand it places on criticism is now, in my opinion, valid for television series and for everything that emerges out of the exploration and mixture of "genres" of culture. The education provided by these series comes from the fact that they are polyphonic, contain a plurality of singular expressions, stage arguments and debates, and are permeated by a moral atmosphere.

There is an education provided by the very form in which television series are presented, and the radical turn that took place with series produced beginning in the 1990s (e.g., *ER, Friends, The West Wing*): the integration of characters into viewers' ordinary and familiar lives; viewers' initiation into new forms of life and new, initially opaque vocabularies that are not made explicit, without any heavy-handed guidance or explanation, as there was in earlier productions.[30] This methodology and the narrativity of series are what make for their moral relevance and power. But this leads to revising the status of morality—to seeing it not in rules and principles of decision-making, but, rather, in attention to ordinary behavior, to everyday micro-choices, to individuals' styles of expressing themselves and making claims. Some philosophers, weary of an overly abstract meta-ethics, have already called for such transformations. The material of television series allows for even greater contextualization, historicity (regularity, duration), familiarization, and education of perception (attention to the expressions and gestures of characters the viewer learns to know; attachment to recurring figures integrated into everyday life; the presence of faces on the "small screen").

This answers the question raised by Cavell concerning the moral function of "public" works and the form of education they generate in the public *and* the private they create. This intertwining of the private and the public is also an intertwining of modes of constituting a public. The address to the public/audience also becomes the constitution of a public discourse and its norms. Morality is constituted by the claims of individuals, and by the recognition of others' claims; the recognition of a plurality of moral positions and voices within the same world. Hence the polyphonic nature of television series, the plurality of singular expressions, the staging of arguments and debates, and the moral atmosphere that emanates from them.

Television series rearticulate the private and public differently—they create their audience by slipping into private life.[31] In order to understand this, it is necessary to take seriously the moral intentions of the producers and scriptwriters of television series and movies, as well as the constraints imposed on these fictions—here again in line with Cavell's reading. Breaking with traditional criticism, which made the intelligence and meaning of films a by-product of critical interpretation, Cavell affirmed the importance of the collective writing of films, and of the function of screenwriters, directors, and also actors in creating films' meaning and educational value. It is therefore necessary to show, within the moral expression constituted by television series, the moral choices—both individual and collective—negotiations, conflicts, and agreements that are at the basis of morality: the choices and itineraries of fictional characters, plot twists, conflicts, reconciliations, slips of the tongue, and repressions. To see this, we need only think of the importance, within adolescent culture, of *Buffy the Vampire Slayer*, conceived by its creator, Joss Whedon, as a feminist work intended to morally transform a co-ed adolescent audience by showing an apparently ordinary girl who could also fight; or, of the show *How I Met Your Mother*, which makes it possible to take different perfectionist trajectories across various ordinary life situations of young adults and the variety of regimes of expression that constitute their grammar.

The perspective on ordinary culture inaugurated by Cavell and Warshow makes it possible to perceive the moral importance of television series, which now generate immense interest in the intellectual world, but for which a critical discourse befitting the richness of the material and the creativity of the discipline has not yet been found. This is undoubtedly due to the fact that those interested in these series lack the resources for reconciling the moral education they gain from frequenting these series and their characters with their status as enthusiastic fans and with the conceptual overstimulation generated by the material's richness and diversity, typical of popular culture.

If we also recall that in *The Public and its Problems*, John Dewey defines the public on the basis of a confrontation with a problematic situation where people experience a particular difficulty which they initially perceive as coming from private life and where the answer, never given in advance, emerges out of the play of interactions of those who decide in turn to give it public expression, we realize that television, understood in this way, inherits the moral education at stake in popular cinema. The characters in television fiction can be "let go" and opened up to the imagination and usage of all; "entrusted" to us, as if it were up to all of us to take care of them by taking care of ourselves; this is particularly clear at the conclusion of a show. Indeed, characters show trajectories of personal transformation and exigency and testify to a hope for the educability of the spectator, who is obliged to pay attention, familiarize him- or herself, and little-by-little shape him- or herself, like the child Wittgenstein (citing Augustine) describes at the beginning of the *Philosophical Investigations*, who is integrated into a form of life, and has to let go, or, as in *The Americans*, to accept to be left, abandoned.

When seen in this light, popular television is not a primal state or inferior version of culture but a democratic culture that creates shared values and acts as a resource for education of the self—becoming a subject by virtue of discussing public material that is integrated into everyday life. The digital revolution has allowed for new forms, agents, and models of artistic action that contest both elitist conceptions of "great art" and "populist" conceptions of popular art. Television shows, and the serial format, are, however, special. Television series are spaces where ethical and hermeneutic authority can be reappropriated and where viewers can be empowered by constituting, sharing, and discussing their own unique experiences; as democratic spaces for developing the capacity for individual expression, tastes, and choices.

For Cavell, films are fully constitutive of spectators' experiences; memories of moments in film are memories. But television inherits this power: television series accompany us over the years as the plot unfolds and evolves, as we unfold and evolve. The importance of television series is further reinforced by audiences' attachment to characters: viewers truly *care* about/for television series' protagonists. Television series also take care of their audience.[32] They provide communities with words for conversations and a common language to approach the world, empower individuals with moral judgment, and present varieties and differences in moral points of view. The realism of television series, the "pressure of reality" on them, is also connected to the practices of world viewing.[33] Television series belong to both private life and to the public realm: they occupy the most public spaces (for example, some people will watch an episode on their phone on public transportation) and the most private (people watch television series at home, even in bed). That which Cavell claimed in the twentieth century for popular movies has, in part, been transferred to television series, which have taken over for, if not replaced, movies in the task of providing an education to the public. By virtue of their aesthetic format, television series entail viewers' initiation into forms of life that are not made explicit, and are initially opaque and sometimes disturbing. The "pilot" episode (rightly named) of each series of the corpus guides and leads us into a specific universe, with its codes, and vocabularies, and rules (the introduction of a seemingly naïve character in the DGSE quarters in the wonderful French show *The Bureau*).

Television series are the site of an "education for grownups" through the transmission and discussion of material that is widely available and shareable. To put this into view requires taking seriously the intentions of those who create, write, and make television series and again to pursue Cavell's conception of film for the subject of television. Serious study of television undermines a critical tradition that held that the intelligence of a show is a by-product of the critical reading of it, and demonstrates, instead, the intelligence a show brings to its own production—the importance of the function of the screenwriter, the work of actors, the choices made by editors. This also, as television series do in general, transforms the conception of single authorship. Actors' modes of expression and embodiment of characters and moral positions (moral texture, gait, style of speaking and behaving) in television series are central to the moral education made possible by such dramas, through collective and individual moral choices, negotiations, conflicts, and agreements that are at the basis of this education; trajectories of characters or ensembles; narrative turns and arcs; plot twists, and so on.

We can thus account for the powers of influence of television series, along with their potential for the transmission and sharing of meanings and values. This means taking into account and demonstrating their degree of reflexivity: introducing agency into the concept of "reception" by studying some underestimated phenomena (attachment to shows and characters; re-appropriation of scenes and episodes online; online amateur critiques; the influence of series on personal ethical choices or career choices, etc.). Television series and the conversations they initiate are a unique way of depicting the competing moral positions of protagonists as they are lived every day, and help viewers understand another's point of view through the representation of radically different ethical and political positions. For instance, the Israeli television series *Fauda*, which depicts the hard reality of situations of tension in the Palestinian occupied territories, is appreciated both by Israeli *and* Palestinian viewers.

The movie or television actor or actress has the mysterious ability of what Cavell defined as "photogenesis": the capacity to make him- or herself perceptible to spectators, and thereby to constitute the spectator's experience. In popular cinema as in television series, we can see the emergence of a specific entity that once again subverts the mystique of authors or works: the moral type constituted (on the model of family resemblance) by an actor's or actress' different roles or phases. Television series and the place that they, and their universes, have taken in the existences of spectators have only confirmed this incorporation to experience. The educative force of television series, indeed, lies in their integration into everyday life, in ordinary and repeated contact with characters who become intimates—no longer on the overused model of identification and recognition, but, rather, the model of frequenting, familiarization, and attachment: processes that leave open the possibility of the other's independence and unknowability. In this way, television series continue the quest for the popular cinema's pedagogical task of creating an inseparably subjective and public education. This intertwining of the private and of modes of constituting a public translates into new modes of subjectivation by the public. This brings us back to the question of *what counts* for a given individual. Cavell noted with respect to Warshow that once criticism begins to focus on these public objects, it requires both a specific attention and "personal writing," which can be defined by care for the self.

> While the likes of T.S. Eliot and Henry James . . . are great artists, unlike those who create the comic strip *Krazy Kat* and write Broadway plays and make Hollywood movies, the latter say things he (also) wants to hear, or rather things he (also) can and must understand his relation to; this relation manifests the way he lives, his actual life of culture. He concludes that to say what he finds in these more everyday concerns he needs to write personally, but it seems clear that the reverse is equally true, that he wants to attend to them because that attention demands of him writing that is personal, and inspires him to it.[34]

This does not imply a false revolutionary inversion of aesthetic values, but, rather, a new assessment of importance, which Wittgenstein called for when he asserted the importance of the ordinary.

To overcome skepticism and this vulnerability is to overcome our inability or refusal to *see what matters*, as Cavell wrote: "To fail to guess the unseen from the seen, to fail to trace the implications of things—that is to fail the perception that that there *is* something to be guessed and traced, right or wrong." This is at the core of the redefinition of ethics, and of the pursuit of happiness, through the search for importance.

> Any of the arts will be drawn to this knowledge, this perception of the poetry of the ordinary, but film democratizes the knowledge, hence at once blesses and curses us with it. It says that the perception of poetry is open to all, regardless as it were of birth or talent, as the ability is to hold a camera on a subject, so that a failure so to perceive, to persist in missing the subject, which may amount to missing the evanescence of the subject, is ascribable only to ourselves, to failures of our character; as if to fail to guess the unseen from the seen, to fail to trace the implications of things—that is to fail the perception that that there is something to be guessed and traced, right or wrong—requires that we persistently coarsen and stupefy ourselves.[35]

This revelation of one's own pertinence, of the possibility and above all the necessity of making use of who one is, is something that all Cavell's readers and students owe him. This redefinition of the task of philosophy, the pursuit of happiness, through the search for importance (what is important to me, what is important to us) and the recognition of our failures to acknowledge importance, to "guess the unseen from the seen," may be his main teaching. As he writes in *The World Viewed*: "We involve the movies in us. They become further fragments of what happens to me, further cards in the shuffle of my memory, with no telling what place in the future. Like childhood memories whose treasure no one else appreciates, whose content is nothing compared to their unspeakable importance for me."[36]

The injunction to appropriate and re-collect one's experience and *what counts* within it, to take yourself seriously, defines the new demand of the *culture of the ordinary*. As Cavell puts it in his assessment of *The Immediate Experience*: Warshow "expresses his sense of the necessarily personal in various ways in his opening essay ('The Legacy of the 30s')—namely, a sense of the writer's having to invent his own audience, of the writer's having to invent all the meanings of experience, of the modern intellectual's 'facing the necessity of describing and clarifying an experience which has itself deprived him of the vocabulary he requires to deal with it.'"[37] Here again we discover perfectionism in the aesthetic demand to find and invent an audience, as a "personal" search for words to describe an experience that *has precisely deprived you of the vocabulary necessary to deal with it*. This is both a definition of popular culture and the expression of a new requirement for criticism and for ordinary ethics and politics. Popular culture is, indeed, the place for "the education of grownups" who, through it, can arrive at a kind of self-education or self-cultivation, a perfecting of the self: the process of becoming a subject by becoming part of, discussing, and sharing in, material that is both public and private, ordinary, woven into everyday life. It is in this sense that, as Warshow said, "we are all self-made (wo)men."

Notes

1 Robert Warshow, *The Immediate Experience*, Expanded Edition (Cambridge: Harvard University Press, 2001), xxxvii. Acknowledgments: this chapter is a follow-up to an earlier article on film genres and popular culture: Sandra Laugier and Daniela Ginsburg, "Popular Cultures, Ordinary Criticism: A Philosophy of Minor Genres," *MLN*, vol. 127, no. 5 (2012), 997–1012. I would like to thank Daniela Ginsburg, as well as Paola Marrati, for sharing these interests for more than a decade now, and David LaRocca for his encouragement and advice regarding the extension to television series.

2   Stanley Cavell, "Must We Mean What We Say?" in *Must We Mean What We Say* (Cambridge: Cambridge University Press, 1969, reissued 2002).

3   Stanley Cavell, *The World Viewed: Reflections on the Ontology of Film*, Enlarged Edition (Cambridge: Harvard University Press, 1979); *Pursuits of Happiness: The Hollywood Comedy of Remarriage* (Cambridge: Harvard University Press, 1981); *Contesting Tears: The Hollywood Melodrama of the Unknown Woman* (Chicago: The University of Chicago Press, 1997); *Cities of Words: Pedagogical Letters on a Register of Moral Life* (Cambridge: Belknap, Harvard University Press, 2004). Warshow, *The Immediate Experience*, xxxvii.

4   Stanley Cavell, *The Claim of Reason: Wittgenstein, Skepticism, Morality, and Tragedy* (New York: Oxford University Press, 1979), 125.

5   Ibid.

6   Martin Shuster, *New Television: The Aesthetics and Politics of a Genre*, (Chicago: University of Chicao Press, 2017).

7   Warshow, *The Immediate Experience*, xxxviii.

8   Ludwig Wittgenstein, *Philosophical Investigations*, 2nd ed., trans. G. E. M. Anscombe (Oxford: Basil Blackwell, 1958). See Sandra Laugier, *Why We Need Ordinary Language Philosophy* (Chicago: The University of Chicago Press, 2013).

9   Cavell, *Cities of Words*, 40.

10 Cavell, *The Claim of Reason*, xxi.

11 Ibid., 262.

12 Emmanuel Bourdieu, "Stanley Cavell—*pour une esthétique d'un art impur*," in *Stanley Cavell, Cinéma et philosophie*, ed. Marc Cerisuelo and Sandra Laugier (Paris: Presses de la Sorbonne Nouvelle, 2000), 57.

13 See Laugier, "Popular Cultures, Ordinary Criticism."

14 Cavell, *Pursuits of Happiness*, 10.

15 Sandra Laugier, *Le mythe de l'inexpressivité* (Paris: Vrin, 2010); Andrew Norris, *Becoming Who We Are: Politics and Practical Philosophy in the Work of Stanley Cavell* (Oxford: Oxford University Press, 2017).

16 Cavell, *Pursuits of Happiness*, 12.

17 Ralph Waldo Emerson, "The American Scholar," in *The Essential Writings of Ralph Waldo Emerson* (New York: Modern Library Classics, 2000), 57. Cited in Ibid., 14.

18 Cavell, *Pursuits of Happiness*, 41.

19 Emerson, "The American Scholar," 57.

20 Cavell, *The World Viewed*, 4–5.

21 See Marc Cerisuelo "The Importance of Cinema" ("*L'importance du cinéma*"), in *Stanley Cavell, Cinéma et philosophie*, 19.

22 Cavell, *The World Viewed*, 6.

23 Stanley Cavell, "The Thought of Movies" (1983), in *Cavell on Film*, ed. William Rothman (Albany: State University of New York Press, 2005).

24 Erwin Panofsky, "Style and Medium in the Moving Pictures," in *Film*, ed. Daniel Talbot (New York: Simon and Schuster, 1959), 18. Cited in Cavell, *The World Viewed*, 30.
25 Bourdieu, "Stanley Cavell—*pour une esthétique d'un art impur*," 44.
26 See Stephen Mulhall, *On Film*, 3rd ed. (New York: Routledge, 2016).
27 V. F. Perkins, *Film as Film* (London: Penguin Books, 1972), 59.
28 Bourdieu, "Stanley Cavell—*pour une esthétique d'un art impur*," 47.
29 Cavell, *Pursuits of Happiness*, 30.
30 Sabine Chalvon-Demersay, "*La confusion des conditions: une enquête sur la série télévisée* Urgences," *Reseaux* 95 (1999): 235–83.
31 See Sandra Laugier, "*Les séries télévisées: éthique du care et adresse au public*," *Raison publique*, no. 11 (2009), and Norris, *Becoming Who We Are*.
32 See Sandra Laugier, *Nos vies en séries* (Paris: Flammarion, 2019).
33 Cavell, *The World Viewed*, 165.
34 Stanley Cavell, "After Half a Century," in *The Immediate Experience*, Expanded Edition (Cambridge: Harvard University Press, 2001), 292.
35 Stanley Cavell, "The Thought of Movies," *Themes Out of School: Effects and Causes* (San Francisco: North Point Press, 1984), 14.
36 Cavell, *The World Viewed*, 154.
37 Cavell, *The Immediate Experience*, 292.

12

On Film in Reality: Cavellian Reflections on Skepticism, Belief, and Documentary

Mathew Abbott

I don't try to make you believe *something you* don't *believe, but to do something you won't do.*
—LUDWIG WITTGENSTEIN[1]

PEOPLE ARE MILLING ABOUT AT A TRAIN STATION. *A train arrives and they move up and down the platform, some bustling past the camera. The train stops. Passengers exit and others board.* That is a brief description of the content of a famous Lumière brothers film depicting the arrival of a train at a station. Though it was not one of the shorts they showed in their inaugural 1895 screenings, the work has become "an icon of the medium's origins," playing a distinctive role in "constructing the founding myth of cinema's birth."[2] As he traces its reception, Martin Loiperdinger shows that the film's history is rather more complex than commonly acknowledged, with commentators repeating ideas about it that are not borne out by the evidence. Most notoriously, they have claimed that screenings of the film caused panics in audiences. This from a 1994 issue of *Der Spiegel* is exemplary: "One short film had a particularly lasting impact; yes, it caused fear, terror, even panic. . . . [As] the cinematographic train was dashing toward the crowded audience . . . the spectators felt physically threatened."[3]

Journalists are not the only ones who have repeated the story: it turns up in different guises in classics of film history and theory. But there are no contemporaneous reports of audiences panicking at the sight of a locomotive (apparently) bearing down on them, nor is anything of the sort mentioned in the published letters of the Lumière brothers. In fact, the notion doesn't start appearing in print until about half a century after the first screenings.[4] And there are other reasons to be dubious: advertising material produced for the screenings do not depict them with the sensationalism one might expect had they regularly produced panics in audiences; the venue in which the screenings took place—the basement of the Grand Café in central Paris—was so cramped and crowded that panics would have almost certainly resulted in injuries, if not deaths, yet there are no press or police reports of that; and conditions were not amenable to creating effective illusions, as the film was silent, the images were black and white, and the two-bladed shutter on the rattling Cinématographe Lumière would have produced a distracting flicker.[5]

Something stranger and more telling is going on here than a rumor taking on a life of its own. Loiperdinger is right to call the story of panicking audiences mythic,[6] and not just because it is probably false. We repeat stories of this kind because we like them; whether they are true is less important than that they seem to clarify something. This particular myth provides a neat way of explaining cinema's power over spectators: the answer it appears to offer is that films are affecting because they can convince us of the truth of illusions. As well as being neat the explanation is gratifying because it allows us to indulge ideas about naïve film audiences, giving an image of credulous spectators from which we can distinguish ourselves as sophisticated viewers, theorists, and scholars.

Apocryphal stories about early cinema are not the only place we find the notion that film produces an illusion of reality. We find inklings of it in a range of everyday beliefs, practices, and expressions regarding cinema and its affective powers, for example in phrases like "the magic of the movies." It has been important to a great deal of film theory, from accounts of the apparatus to the gaze, from psychoanalytic theories of identification to materialist, structuralist, and Marxist theories that critique narrative cinema for its ideological effects. The notion has also been the subject of some ridicule in contemporary philosophy of film, with cognitivists such as Noël Carroll, William Seely, Gregory Currie, and Berys Gaut attacking "cognitive illusionism"[7]: the idea that successful films somehow get audiences to believe in the reality of what is depicted on screen.

A problem with cognitive illusionism is that—no matter how absorbed in a film they might become—audiences do not typically behave as though they believe in the reality of what happens on screen. When a disaster film depicts imminent doom via asteroid, audiences do not switch on their phones to text final words to loved ones. If a monster film shows a gigantic reptile ripping up their city, they do not flee the cinema to find safety elsewhere. Audiences may be shocked, terrified, or even traumatized by gruesome murders in horror films, but they do not leave the cinema calling for those who played the villains to be prosecuted for their heinous crimes. If cognitive illusionism were true, film audiences would regularly acquire false beliefs from watching films; they do not typically appear to acquire such beliefs, so the theory is false.

This argument against cognitive illusionism is so obviously convincing that it should give us pause. Surely those sympathetic to the idea that films create illusions of reality know that movie audiences do not usually act as though they believe in those illusions. Isn't part of the attraction of this myth that it seems to be an exception proving the rule? It involves a naïve audience first encountering cinema, not an audience prepared with the knowledge, codes, and conventions surrounding film and its fictions that coalesced over time as the art and technology of cinema developed. Film audiences do not respond now in this way, but if they did when cinema arrived on the scene (the thought seems to be) it might tell us something about audiences now. Here is Christian Metz:

> Any spectator will tell you that he "doesn't believe it," but everything happens as if there were nonetheless someone to be deceived, someone who really would "believe in it." . . . This credulous person is, of course, another part of ourselves, he is still seated *beneath* the incredulous one, or in his heart, it is he who continues to believe, who disavows what he knows (he for whom all human beings are still endowed with a penis). But by a symmetrical and simultaneous movement, the incredulous person disavows the credulous one. . . . That is why the instance of credulousness is often projected into the outer world and constituted as a separate person, a person completely abused by the diegesis.[8]

Metz wants a more sophisticated account of the role of illusion and credulity in cinema. Naturally, spectators do not believe in the reality of what they see on screen in the way they believe in the reality of what they see off screen. In an important sense, they know what they see isn't real, and that is why they do not act on the false beliefs they would acquire if they mistook illusion for reality. But the conscious spectator is not the only one. Another spectator, disavowed by and in the conscious one, *does* mistake illusion for reality. We let ourselves be swept away—if not completely away—and we are inclined to deny the indulgence involved in maintaining that credulity. As the conscious spectator disavows the unconscious one, so the unconscious one disavows the conscious one; hence, apparently, the capacity for viewers to entertain contradictory beliefs at the same time ("a train is hurtling toward me" *and* "I am watching a film depicting a train hurtling toward me"). Metz goes on:

> This instance which believes and also its personified projection have fairly precise equivalents in the cinema: for example, the credulous spectators at

the 'Grand Café' in 1895 [or thereabouts], frequently and complacently evoked by the incredulous spectators who have come *later* (and are no longer children), those spectators . . . who fled their seats in terror when the train entered La Ciotat station (in Lumière's famous film), because they were afraid it would run them down.[9]

The point about complacency is worth registering. It captures something of the gratification to which I referred above: that when repeating the myth about what happened in the Grand Café, journalists, historians, and theorists have enjoyed distancing themselves from naïve audiences.[10] It is unclear if he endorses the truth of it, but the story clearly resonates for Metz, who understands such complacency as a denial of the fact that deep down we are all the dupes of cinema.

But there is something going unstated here, which is important not only to Metz but also to the cognitivists. In this passage from his essay on *King Lear*, Stanley Cavell is describing the arrival of skepticism on the philosophical scene in early modernity:

> At some early point in epistemological investigations, the world normally present to us (the world in whose existence, as it is typically put, we "believe") is brought into question and vanishes, whereupon all connection with the world is found to hang upon what can be said to be "present to the senses"; and that turns out, shockingly, not to be the world. It is at this point that the doubter finds himself cast into skepticism, turning the existence of the external world into a problem.[11]

Cavell's scare quotes around "believe" show what is distinctive about his contribution to the problem of philosophical skepticism. Rather than beginning where the skeptic usually does—by raising questions about whether we can justify our belief that the world exists outside our minds, or that others are minded in the way we are—Cavell *begins from belief* because it has logical priority in the skeptic's account. The skeptic's problem is not quite what he takes it to be, and there is a sense in which it runs deeper than he thinks it does, because the skeptical outlook first gets a hold on him—on us—not with the thought that there is no rational justification for our belief in reality, but with the thought that we believe in reality—for that is what leads to the thought that our belief stands in need of rational justification. In another essay, Cavell writes the following about a remark of Wittgenstein's: "The *Investigations* has this: 'I am not of the *opinion* that he has a soul.' Nor am I of the opinion that there is a world."[12] As Wittgenstein states that he is not of the opinion that the other is ensouled (or minded), Cavell states that he is not of the opinion that the world exists. But neither philosopher is raising doubts about these apparent "facts" (a term that, like "believe" in the passage from the *King Lear* essay, also belongs in scare quotes here).

The point is that these "facts" are not of the same order as the fact that it is cloudy today, or the fact as to whether audiences panicked at the sight of cinematographic trains in the basement of the Grand Café near the end of the nineteenth century.

Consider the point in contention between a theorist like Metz and contemporary cognitivists. Metz thinks that cinema's power over us must be explained by its capacity to make us believe in the reality of what we see on screen. On his account, the fear we might feel as an on-screen train hurtles toward us is no different in kind from the fear we would feel were an off-screen train coming our way. But the fear we feel while watching the train on screen is checked by our conscious minds, which cling to the knowledge that what we see is not actually real, or—it amounts to the same thing—disavow that we do take it to be real.

Cognitivists reply that the fear must be different in kind. Too empirically minded to take seriously the notion of the unconscious that Metz relies upon, cognitivists think we need another way of accounting for how the content of films is entertained in the minds of spectators, and how it ends up affecting them. Currie offers an exemplary alternative theory when he argues that fictions engage our minds in "off-line" mode, "severing the connections between our mental states and their perceptual causes and behavioral effects."[13] "With fictions," he writes, "what we acquire instead of beliefs [are] *imaginings* which simulate belief."[14] These imaginings can simulate "sometimes pleasant and sometimes unpleasant bodily states" in us, states we "associate with being emotionally moved by events."[15] Whatever we feel when responding to fictional events on screen is different in kind from the emotions we feel when responding to off-screen events because the feelings are not based on belief but upon "imaginings": the feelings may be powerful in their own way, but they do not come out of our belief and so we will not act on them. Indeed (and this should strike us as peculiar), Currie seems to be implying here that we are not really moved by fictional events on screen: instead, bodily states are stimulated, states we merely "associate" with the states stimulated when we are emotionally moved by events.[16]

What is not in contention between Metz and the cognitivists is that the standard case, against which the case of film has to be distinguished, must involve belief in reality. Now if I panic because a train is hurtling toward me in reality, there is nothing necessarily wrong with saying "I believe" a train is hurtling toward me. But we should note that in everyday life it would be unusual to put things like this. After all, "I believe a train is hurtling toward me" is the kind of thought I might have in a situation of unusual epistemic unclarity, say if I have woken from a daze to find myself blindfolded and tied to (what feel like) train tracks, which have just begun to vibrate: "believe" marks that I am doing my best in extraordinary circumstances. This gives us an inkling of what is peculiar about the skeptic's argument.

Of course, the skeptic's argument is not directed against the rational justification of any particular bit of knowledge. He often makes his argument on the basis of (what looks like) a particular claim to knowledge, as Descartes does with his fire and his bit of wax. But it is important that it does not matter what example he chooses, that any object will serve as well as any other. As Cavell argues, "it cannot be the investigation of a concrete claim if its conclusion is to be general."[17] And the skeptic's conclusion needs to be general if it is to implicate our knowing in general. Cavell does not want simply to deny that conclusion but to draw our attention to what makes it seem inevitable: the thought that we believe in reality. But what is the alternative to thinking that? Here is the beginning of Cavell's response: "What skepticism suggests is that since we cannot know the world exists, its presentness to us cannot be a function of knowing. The world is to be accepted; as the presentness of others is not to be known, but acknowledged."[18]

It is useful to refer to the example of pain in this context (Cavell—like Wittgenstein—often does just this). Imagine you are playing a game: your opponent hides a ten-dollar bill in one of her fists, then puts both forward saying, "I have ten dollars in my left hand." You need to consider her facial expression, body language, tone of voice and so on, and say "I believe you" or "I don't believe you" (get it right and you get the money). The game may be an odd one, but there is nothing odd about how language is being used here: a proposition is forwarded, you weigh up the evidence in favor of its truth and state a conclusion. Consider now the statement "I have a terrible pain in my left hand." The grammar of this sentence looks similar to the grammar of the one above: they both seem to forward propositions regarding the state of the speaker's hand. But reflect on the oddness of a similar reply. To say "I believe you" when someone says "I have a terrible pain in my left hand" is likely to seem like an insulting change of subject, as though the relevant issue is the honesty of the speaker and not her pain. The statement "I am in terrible pain" is not (usually) put forward for its truth value to be weighed up: it is (typically) put forward to elicit sympathy, or perhaps as a plea for help. As Wittgenstein says, "one can resolve to say 'I believe he is in pain' . . ." but this is really to exchange "one way of talking for another which, while we are doing philosophy, seems to us the more apt."[19]

Philosophers have a tendency to want to reduce everything to belief and knowledge, treating all statements as though they have the same logical form ("there exists a hand such that it is my left one and it has terrible pain in it"). Yet statements that appear to philosophers to have the same form can call out for different kinds of response, revealing different forms in themselves. Hence Cavell: "Your suffering makes a claim upon me. It is not enough that I know (am certain) that you suffer—I must do or reveal something (whatever can be done). In a word, I must acknowledge it."[20] It is not that "I have a terrible pain in my left hand" expresses no proposition about the world, nor that there is no circumstance in which saying "I believe you" might be an appropriate response (think of a doctor treating someone with a history of opioid addiction, who has made false reports of terrible pain before—in that case, "I believe you" could be the beginning of an offer of help). It is that, when we are doing philosophy, we start to lose our grip on distinctions we have no problem making—and demands to which we have no problem responding—in ordinary life.

Cavell is not putting forward some moral prescription that we *should* acknowledge others, nor is he telling us to accept the world. For without invoking platitudes, try to imagine what a prescription to accept the world in general or acknowledge others in general could actually ask of us. It is not the whole world that we have to accept, or all others that we have to acknowledge: it is the world I am *in* that I am to accept (or which I might deny), and the various claims made on me by others in that world that call for my acknowledgment (and which I might reject). The skeptical method can look like a kind of defense against this.[21] Skeptical questioning is also a means of isolating ourselves, of setting ourselves against a world that makes no specific claims on us. We "achieve" this by giving priority to belief and knowledge, treating response and action as though they play supporting roles. If I can accept the world it is because the problem it presents to me just is the problem of my life: that I have to live and act in this world as I find it. That means giving up on my pretensions to being something other than a finite being, answerable to reality. Cavell takes the fact that we seem to have no way of satisfactorily denying skeptical conclusions to indicate something of our finitude. Philosophical skeptics locate that finitude in our knowledge, but Cavell wants us to see that it runs deeper than that. He holds that skepticism has its source in the philosopher's tendency to prioritize belief by taking for granted that our relation to the world and to others can be cashed out in terms of it. But he finds a rather ordinary human need or wish driving that philosophical tendency: a fantasy of denying the answerability to reality in which our finitude consists.

If Cavell's fundamental thought about skepticism is that it emerges out of a denial of our finitude, then his fundamental thought about film is that it seems to offer us the opportunity to indulge that fantasy of denial. He writes that film is a "moving image of skepticism"[22]; that it "screens me from the world it holds—that is, makes me invisible"[23]; that movies reproduce the world "not by literally presenting us with the world, but by permitting us to view it unseen"[24]; that cinema "present[s] the world by absenting us from it."[25] Film makes the world present to us. But the world it presents is one to which *we* are *not* present, to which we need not respond. Film seems to offer us the world by severing our connection with it, allowing us to view a world to which we are not answerable. This is what Cavell means when he says that film does not "have to establish presentness to and of the world."[26]

Rather, film achieves the latter at the expense of the former. And as film expends the former, it can achieve the latter naturally, automatically (it may be as easy as pointing a cinematograph at an oncoming train and turning the crank). Which gives us another way of understanding what has been so attractive about the story of panicked audiences in the Grand Café at the *fin de siècle*. We like and repeat the story because we are gratified less by the thought that *film is like reality* than by the thought that *reality is like a film*. And we are gratified by *that* thought because it indulges our fantasy that we are just spectators, that we can take reality as philosophical skeptics do (or say they do).

Film's status as a moving image of skepticism gives it a particular philosophical propensity to raise and then exacerbate problems of knowledge.[27] *The Arrival of a Train at La Ciotat* (*L'arrivée du train à La Ciotat*) is a case in point. The film raises problems (which we may not have known we had) about reality and pretense, about what it means to view people going about their daily lives, people who are nevertheless acting in awareness of the camera. For it contains elements that appear to have been staged. The porter moves his baggage cart to reveal a view of the station platform "just in the moment when, in the back right, the locomotive of the arriving train becomes discernible."[28] The movements of the stationmaster and the ladies walking with their children also appear to be choreographed. It turns out that many of the people on the platform were members of the Lumière family, including the wife of Louis Lumière, as well as his "sister-in-law, his mother, three little children, and two nannies."[29] Perhaps most pointedly, "[n]obody looks directly into the camera!"[30] In view of the novelty of the cinematograph used to capture the images, this has to be explained by direction from a filmmaker (indeed, this feature of the film is not shared by a number of other Lumière shorts, where subjects are often seen staring, waving, or doffing their hats at the camera).

Consider again the brief description of what happens in the film I provided at the start of this chapter. The recognition that some or even all of the people on film were acting under direction will not challenge anything in it. But it can appear to put pressure on the idea that the film is true *actualité*: a nonnarrative film depicting real events. Hence Loiperdinger argues that we should, instead, regard *The Arrival of a Train at La Ciotat* as an amateur film.[31] Yet, his claim will only challenge the idea that the film is an *actualité* if we take "real events" to mean something like "unstaged events," where "unstaged" means "taking place without regard for the camera." And look how quickly these thoughts get tangled. For the most significant tell that we are watching staged events here is that the people depicted in the film do *not* look at the camera. The fact that they act without regard for the camera, in other words, is evidence they are taking it into account. The thought seemed to be that the filmmaker cannot capture reality as it is (in itself) unless he sneaks up on it unawares, filming it without affecting it—but the outcome of that thought in practice is that the filmmaker must ensure that everything is prearranged, that his presence on the scene is regarded. Note how Loiperdinger asserts that the sense of reality the film imparts depends upon the elision of "anything that points to the presence of a recording apparatus, such as people looking into the camera during shooting."[32] But his argument is also that the staging of aspects of the pro-filmic scene undermines this film's claim to reality. Would the events have seemed more "authentic"[33] if the people on the platform were not acting under direction, if they gathered and gawked at the cameraman and his novel, rattling device? What if a handful had stopped to stare, while others continued the charade (if that is what we should call it)? We are told that the film fails to document real events because the events it records were staged. But we are also told that if the events weren't staged then the people on the platform would have acknowledged the cinematograph and spoiled the film's claim to reality. This tangle of thoughts implies that reality can be achieved only if it is undermined.

On Noël Carroll's influential account, documentaries are films intended to make claims—or "presumptive assertions"[34]—about how things stand in the real world, claims audiences are asked to believe. Fictional films, by contrast, put forward what Carroll calls "suppositions": claims about fictional worlds, which audiences are asked not to believe but to entertain in their imaginations. Partly because the theory of presumptive assertion does not rely on any version of the contentious notion of indexicality,[35] it is a powerful account of documentary. But it is weakened by its inattention to the status of the documentary *as film*. Medium does no real work in the theory: we could substitute "written texts" for "films" in "films intended to persuade audiences to believe claims about how things stand in the real world" and end up with a structurally identical theory of what distinguishes fictional writing from (say) journalism, biography, or other forms of non-fiction writing. Carroll is right that documentaries make claims about the real world, but the theory is not attentive to what is distinctive about cinematic images, and the kinds of claims they can make.[36]

As Carl Plantinga argues, the problem with Carroll's theory comes out particularly clearly if we try to apply it to observational documentaries, such as the works of Frederick Wiseman or the Maysles brothers, and of which the films of the Lumière brothers are prototypical.[37] Unlike expository documentaries, which tend to feature voice-overs, forms of narration, or interview questions, the makers of these documentaries are typically happy to present images of the world, the significance of which is not determined to the same extent.[38] One problem raised for Carroll by such works is that it is usually unobvious what filmmakers want to say with or in their films—indeed, that they like to treat their material with an ethos of experimentation and open-endedness, rejecting the very idea that a documentary should be used as a vehicle for convincing audiences of the views of its maker. On Plantinga's account, the issue is that filmmakers "cannot have in mind, when making the film, all the propositions that might plausibly be gleaned from the film's images." And that is because "the moving photograph and the sound recording are to some degree belief-independent."[39]

We can bring out Plantinga's point by comparing films with paintings. With both films and paintings it is natural to ask *why* some element was included in an image. In the case of paintings, that means asking about the intentions of the painter: asking why some element was included just is to ask why the painter painted it (or painted it that way), hence what she meant by it or intended with it. With films the issue is more complicated. Some elements may have been selected (or, indeed, "staged") by a filmmaker, but others may have just happened to be included in a scene—not because the filmmaker wanted them there (meaning something by them, intending something with them), but because they simply *were* there and the camera (automatically) recorded them.[40] Michael Fried illustrates this in discussing three remarkable paintings by Jean-Baptiste-Siméon Chardin: "In the *Soap Bubble* our attention is caught by the tear in the young man's jacket; in the *Game of Knuckle Bones* by the upper corner of the young woman's apron that has become unpinned; and in the *Card Castle*, in the immediate foreground, by the negligently half-opened drawer containing a pair of playing cards."[41] Fried claims that in each of these cases Chardin is "singling out . . . at least one salient detail that functions as a sign of the figure's obliviousness to everything but the operation he or she is intent on performing."[42] According to Fried, in other words, these elements tell us something important about what Chardin was trying to achieve in his works, and so about their meaning. But what of the subjects in *The Arrival of a Train at La Ciotat*? Loiperdinger remarks at one point that some of the men appear to "have their hats pulled down strikingly low over their foreheads."[43] Was this meant to dissuade them from looking at the cinematograph, or to obscure any furtive glances they might have taken of it? Were they instructed, in other words, to pull their hats down? Or did they just happen to be wearing their hats in this way? That we do not know tells us something important about cinematic images, and how different their content can be from the content of paintings. For these low hats are not like the torn jacket or unpinned apron in the Chardins. Fried might be wrong about the meaning of those representations, but he is clearly talking about *Chardin's* meaning. With the hats on film the question is not just what they mean but whether they were meant.

As this indicates, another feature of observational documentaries that troubles Carroll's proposal is the complicated, in fact sometimes intractable nature of the relationships at work in them between filmmakers and subjects, and the interpretative problems this dynamic introduces. Consider again that porter. Was he directed to move in the way he did, so as to increase the visual drama of the train's arrival by revealing the platform for a moment beforehand? Or was he just doing his job, so absorbed in his task of preparing for the arrival of a new set of passengers that he was oblivious to the cinematograph and the aesthetic effect he happened to be creating for it? We can speculate about whether his movements were intended by the filmmakers, of course, and there may be a good case for saying they were. But there is a mystery here, and we are likely to find similar problems if we go asking after the meaning of the behaviors of any subject in the film: *Just what are the filmmakers trying to persuade us of?* Pursued too relentlessly, that question will obscure more than it clarifies. That is because film (like reality) can make claims on which believing has awkward purchase. Unlike the reality to which we are answerable, however, the claims films make do not call for our acknowledgment. That follows from Cavell's point that film does not make us present to the world it presents. But Cavell's point must hold differently of documentaries, for the world they make present is our world. And *The Arrival of a Train at La Ciotat* shows the weakness of belief's grip on some of the claims to reality a documentary can make.

Late in his paper Loiperdinger identifies a partial exception to his earlier claim that nobody in the film looks directly into the camera: using a frame enlargement, he shows that a little girl does, indeed, take a glance at the cinematograph about halfway through the film.[44] Her look is not an especially curious one. For she is Marlene Koehler, a niece of Louis Lumière, and she has "been in front of the camera many times and knows both the apparatus and the man who is turning the crank."[45] In the way a child of her age might, she appears momentarily to have forgotten (or decided to disregard) the direction not to look. James Conant's description of what he calls "the problematic of movie acting" can help us understand why this is significant:

> An aspiring movie actor is repeatedly enjoined (in terms roughly opposite of those screamed out by the parent filming his children in a home movie): "Don't look at the camera!" He must never look directly into the lens of the camera. . . . But if we say to an aspiring actor: "Forget about the camera! Act as if the camera did not exist!" he must know how to understand our injunction. . . . The test of whether he has fully achieved this mode of awareness consists in its being the case that nothing he ever does, not even a glance or a facial expression, offer any indication of his controlling awareness of the presence of the camera whose absence his every glance and gesture serves to declare.[46]

Conant is referring here to conventions crucial to what he calls "the movie": a fictional, narrative film with a basis in a photographic medium. His claim is that having people on screen avoid looking into the camera is one of the "constitutive principles"[47] of the movie. He supports the claim with reference to the idiosyncratic *Lady in the Lake*, which constantly violates this principle and so does not "succeed in being a movie."[48] He also supports it with reference to painting, and specifically to Fried's influential interpretation of the works of Chardin and other painters from the French pre-modernist period. Conant cites a remark from Fried about the need painters like Chardin felt to create "the illusion that the audience did not exist, that it was not really there or at the very least had not been taken into account."[49] This had a distinctive outcome for the practice of painting. Chardin and others tried to create works with convincing depictions of oblivious human subjects, subjects so absorbed in their activities—blowing a soap bubble, playing knucklebones, constructing a card castle—that they seemed unaware of being looked at. This is the source of Fried's reading of the unpinned apron and the torn jacket: he thinks Chardin's representations are meant to show the unaffectedness of the subjects, so absorbed in their activities they have let things slip. For what Chardin and the painters who followed his lead were after was something like authenticity. And what was in question was not just the potential for affectation in the depicted subjects, but that potential in the painters: what worried the painters was that *they* would appear to be trying to produce effects on audiences. Yet, paintings *are* meant to produce effects on audiences. The paradox is that to produce the right effect, artists had to paint as though they were not trying to produce an effect (note that while these painters were aiming to convince audiences, there is little temptation to say they were aiming to get them to believe in the reality of the depicted scenes: conviction means something different here, something more like what we mean when we call a poem or piece of music convincing.) Conant argues there are intriguing similarities between the constitutive principle of movies he identifies and the injunctions under which Fried claims these painters worked:

> No amount of realism lavished on the sets or invested in the quality of the cinematography or achieved in the performance of the actors in a film can restore the illusion of worldhood that is shattered through a systematic failure to respect a supreme underlying fiction that is a constitutive condition of the possibility of the presentation of a movie-world: namely, that the camera—and its viewpoint onto the world of the movie—does not exist.[50]

In both cases, artists are seeking to avoid the aesthetic disturbance that would be caused by an acknowledgment of audience. But there is a difference between the problems facing Chardin and his contemporaries and the problems facing the makers of fictional films. In the context of French pre-modernism, any acknowledgment of the beholder was felt to undermine authentic painting. In movies, a look at the camera will not undermine authenticity—it is important that it is hard to say what that would mean in this context—but threaten the very integrity of the narrative world itself, such that the characters "all come down out of the world of the movie.... The narrative world of the movie is emptied out; it collapses into our world."[51] Now Conant never quite says that this emptying out effects a break in the audience's *belief* in the movie world (he speaks, instead, of the audience's absorption in it).[52] Rather, what is broken is the audience's sense, crucial to the establishment of a movie world, of that world's separateness from their own. Were the makers of *The Arrival of a Train at La Ciotat* caught up in a thought like this when staging elements of the scene on the platform? If they were, it must have been a nascent (hence perhaps inchoate) version of it, for there was no such thing as a movie when they produced the film. But it is fascinating that even here, in the creation of one of the first works of cinema, there was an awareness of the complications filming can introduce into reality, and what appear to be attempts at controlling them.

And there is a difference between the problems facing the makers of movies and the makers of documentaries, especially observational works and *actualités*. For the world of a documentary is not a fictional world but the real one, so there are no characters to come down out of it.[53] The thought that someone's glance at a camera will upset an *actualité's* claim to reality is itself a skeptical one, turning on a fantasy of a world without the spectator in it. If something like that fantasy is constitutive of movie worlds, then letting it take hold in relation to the real one is to deny some of the difficulties that are part of it. It is hard to know what to believe about the images in *The Arrival of a Train at La Ciotat*—how to tell the intentions, aims, and attitudes of the filmmakers apart from other aspects of the scene they were filming, or what is pretend and what is not in a context where stealing a glance at a camera and acting without regard for it are both ways of acknowledging it—but this does not simply spoil their claims to reality.

Pretense here does not mean what it does in a movie world, in which actors play characters (note that we often call good performances "believable," but that does not imply we are somehow duped by them). And it is different from the kinds of pretense that the French pre-modernists sought to neutralize, for there is nothing necessarily inauthentic about it (Loiperdinger acknowledges this when he says that the scene does not "come across as contrived"[54]).[55] *The Arrival of a Train at La Ciotat* gives us a glimpse into our world—but it is not the pristine, untouched world we might have expected or (thought we) wanted. It shows our world when cinema was arriving in it, with all the problems it brought on board. The people on the platform were discovering a new capacity for pretense, which is both displayed and elided in the film. That capacity was part of who they were, part of their real lives. Though there is a sense in which they were acting, they were not playing characters. It would be better to say they were playing themselves, that they were doing so in reality, and that they were among the first on our planet to do this on film.

Notes

1. Wittgenstein's remark to a student; italics in original. Quoted in *Discussions of Wittgenstein*, ed. Rush Rhees (London: Routledge and Kegan Paul, 1970), 43.
2. Martin Loiperdinger, "Lumière's Arrival of the Train: Cinema's Founding Myth," trans. Bernd Elzer, *The Moving Image* 4, no. 1 (2004): 90.
3. Quoted in Loiperdinger, "Lumière's Arrival of the Train," 90.
4. There are further complexities. One pertains to the date of the screening itself: the film is often taken to have been screened in the first suite of films the brothers showed in 1895, but it was not until early in the following year that the Lumières publicly screened a film depicting the arrival of a train at a station. Another is that the brothers produced at least three films depicting trains arriving at stations. That makes it difficult to know which film is being referred to in contemporaneous reports, and in some of the scholarly literature. When I turn in depth to the film later in this chapter, I will follow Loiperdinger's lead and focus on film #653 from the Lumière catalogue, *L'arrivée du train à La Ciotat*.
5. See Loiperdinger, "Lumière's Arrival of the Train," 94–97.
6. Tom Gunning also describes the story as "mythical." See "An Aesthetic of Astonishment: Early Film and the (In)credulous Spectator," in *Viewing Positions: Ways of Seeing Film*, ed. Linda Williams (New Brunswick: Rutgers University Press, 1995), 115.
7. See Gregory Currie, *Image and Mind: Film, Philosophy, and Cognitive Science* (Cambridge: Cambridge University Press, 1995), 19–47. See also Noël Carroll and William Seely, "Cognitivism, Psychology and Neuroscience: Movies as Attentional Engines," in *Psychocinematics: The Aesthetic Science of Movies*, ed. Arthur Shimamura (New York: Oxford University Press, 2013), 53–75; and Berys Gaut, *A Philosophy of Cinematic Art* (Cambridge: Cambridge University Press, 2010), 62–65.
8. Christian Metz, *The Imaginary Signifier: Psychoanalysis and the Cinema*, trans. Celia Britton (Bloomington: Indiana University Press, 1982), 72.
9. Metz, *The Imaginary Signifier*, 73. Note that Metz's account elides an important distinction between cognitive illusionism and what Currie calls "perceptual illusionism": the thesis that the cinema creates illusions of perception, for example the illusion that the images on screen are moving (or the illusion that there is a train coming toward the viewer). Currie is right to argue against the "tendency to assume that the (alleged) truth of Perceptual Illusionism somehow supports the claim of Cognitive Illusionism" (*Image and Mind*, 30). But the fact that so many theorists have been inclined to run them together supports the idea that there is something tellingly strange about film theoretic accounts of belief in cinema.
10. See Gunning's account in "An Aesthetic of Astonishment," 115–16.
11. Stanley Cavell, "The Avoidance of Love," in *Must We Mean What We Say?* (Cambridge: Cambridge University Press, 1976), 323.

12 Stanley Cavell, "Knowing and Acknowledging," in *Must We Mean What We Say?* (Cambridge: Cambridge University Press, 1976), 240.
13 Currie, *Image and Mind*, 149.
14 Ibid., 148.
15 Ibid., 156.
16 In this sense Currie's account is reminiscent of Kendall Walton's "make-believe theory," which requires him to posit the existence of "quasi-emotions." Walton writes of Anna Karenina: "It is fictional that we are aware of her suffering, and we experience quasi pity as a result." *Mimesis as Make-Believe: On the Foundations of the Representational Arts* (Cambridge: Harvard University Press, 1990), 251.
17 Stanley Cavell, *The Claim of Reason* (Oxford: Oxford University Press, 1979/1999), 220.
18 Cavell, "The Avoidance of Love," 324.
19 Ludwig Wittgenstein, *Philosophical Investigations*, trans. Anscombe, Hacker and Schulte, 4th edn (Chichester and Malden: Wiley Blackwell, 2009), §303.
20 Cavell, "Knowing and Acknowledging," 263.
21 As David Macarthur writes: "Vitally important aspects of our lives are covered up, lost to us, by treating them in epistemological terms as items of objective knowledge, justification, belief and doubt." "Cavell on Skepticism and the Importance of Not-Knowing," *Conversations: The Journal of Cavellian Studies* 2 (2014): 22. My argument here is that this "cover-up" is not just the idle outcome of a peculiar mode of thinking (which nevertheless seems natural to philosophers). It also seems to offer us a means of denying our answerability to reality. See Cora Diamond's "The Difficulty of Reality and the Difficulty of Philosophy," in *Philosophy and Animal Life* (New York: Columbia University Press, 2008), especially her claim that philosophy "does not know how to treat a wounded body as anything but a fact" (59).
22 Stanley Cavell, *The World Viewed: Reflections on the Ontology of Film* (Cambridge: Harvard University Press, 1979), 188.
23 Ibid., 24.
24 Ibid., 40.
25 Ibid., 226.
26 Ibid., 118.
27 I give an account of why in *Abbas Kiarostami and Film-Philosophy* (Edinburgh: Edinburgh University Press, 2016), 1–31.
28 Loiperdinger, "Lumière's Arrival of the Train," 108.
29 Ibid., 111.
30 Ibid., 108.
31 See Ibid., 110. For more on home movies, see the next chapter in this volume, by David LaRocca.
32 Loiperdinger, "Lumière's Arrival of the Train," 108.

33 Ibid., 110.
34 Noël Carroll, "Fiction, Nonfiction, and the Film of Presumptive Assertion: Conceptual Analyses," in *Engaging the Moving Image* (New Haven, CT: Yale University Press, 2003), 207–12.
35 In this sense Carroll's account is opposed to the theory of documentary Currie outlines in "Visible Traces: Documentary and the Contents of Photographs," *Journal of Aesthetics and Art Criticism* 57, no. 3 (1999): 285–97. See also Carroll and Currie's contributions to *The Philosophy of Documentary Film: Image, Sound, Fiction, Truth*, ed. David LaRocca (Lanham: Lexington Books of Rowman and Littlefield, 2017), 75–94 and 95–112.
36 Carroll may be happy to accept my criticism, as he is a well-known critic of the notion of medium specificity. See Carroll, "The Specificity of Media in the Arts," *The Journal of Aesthetic Education* 19, no. 4 (1985): 5–20. In *Abbas Kiarostami and Film-Philosophy*, I critique the more general idea that being moved by film (whether fictional or documentary) must entail entertaining propositional content (see in particular 129–46).
37 It is therefore a bit surprising to find Carroll claiming that the works of the Lumière brothers are "paradigmatic documentaries." See Carroll, "Photographic Traces and Documentary Films: Comments for Gregory Currie," in *Engaging the Moving Image* (New Haven, CT: Yale University Press, 2003), 231.
38 Plantinga is drawing on the influential specification of documentary subgenres given by Bill Nichols in *Introduction to Documentary*, 2nd edn. (Bloomington: Indiana University Press, 2010).
39 Carl Plantinga, "What a Documentary Is, After All," *The Journal of Aesthetics and Art Criticism* 1, no. 2 (2005): 110.
40 Of course a painter may include an element just because it happened to be present on the scene she was painting—for example, part of a model's clothing or a feature of the furniture on which she posed. But the painter has nevertheless *decided* to include everything she includes in a painting, while a camera will include the elements that are present regardless of the intent of the filmmaker. And a painter has a much deeper kind control over *how* to depict the elements she includes. Fried's account of Thomas Demand's photography is useful in this context because Demand's work is an exception that clarifies the rule: by producing photographs of scenes whose elements have all been constructed by the artist, Demand seeks to regain the loss of intentional control his medium introduces. See Michael Fried, *Why Photography Matters as Art as Never Before* (New Haven: Yale University Press, 2008), 261–76. See also Fried's account of a film by Demand in "Thomas Demand's *Pacific Sun*" in *Another Light: Jacques-Louis David to Thomas Demand* (New Haven: Yale University Press, 2014), 251–69.
41 Michael Fried, *Absorption and Theatricality: Painting and Beholder in the Age of Diderot* (Berkeley: University of California Press, 1980), 25–26.
42 Ibid., 25.
43 Loiperdinger, "Lumière's Arrival of the Train," 122.

44 See Ibid., 109–10.
45 Loiperdinger, "Lumière's Arrival of the Train," 124.
46 James Conant, "The World of a Movie," in *Making a Difference: Rethinking Humanism and the Humanities*, ed. Niklas Forsberg and Susanne Jansson (Riga: Thales, 2009), 322.
47 Ibid., 320.
48 Ibid., 298.
49 Quoted in Ibid., 320.
50 Conant, "The World of a Movie," 320.
51 Ibid., 319.
52 Note also the claim from Fried's "Art and Objecthood" that movies offer "absorption not conviction." Michael Fried, *Art and Objecthood: Essays and Reviews* (Chicago: The University of Chicago Press, 1998), 164.
53 There are interesting exceptions to this. A full account of the ontological differences between documentaries and fictional films is beyond the scope of this chapter, but it would have to attend to the complexities introduced by generic hybrids, like some of the works of Sacha Baron Cohen. See, for example, Part V of *The Philosophy of Documentary Film*, ed. LaRocca, for engagement on these issues.
54 Loiperdinger, "Lumière's Arrival of the Train," 110.
55 In "An Aesthetic of Astonishment," Gunning writes: "For Fried, the painting of Greuze and others created a new relation to the viewer through a self-contained hermetic world which makes no acknowledgment of the beholder's presence. Early cinema totally ignores this construction of the beholder. These early films explicitly acknowledge their spectator, seeming to reach outwards and confront," 123. My account in this chapter may explain why early cinema could ignore this construction of the beholder without reintroducing the problems of inauthenticity that French pre-modernists sought to neutralize: because the medium of film is reality, films irreparably complicate the issue of artistic intention. It also troubles Gunning's claims about spectators of *The Arrival of a Train at La Ciotat*, which ignores the measures the makers of this film took to prevent acknowledgment of the camera.

13

On the Aesthetics of Amateur Filmmaking in Narrative Cinema: Negotiating Home Movies after *Adam's Rib*

DAVID LAROCCA

TOWARD THE BEGINNING of George Cukor's *Adam's Rib* (1949), there is a scene of friends gathering in the city to watch a home movie featuring their hosts in the country. By this point, Adam (Spencer Tracy) and Amanda (Katharine Hepburn)—their almost-anagram names announcing their entwined lives, and perhaps their incapacity to be separated—are in a fight, and watch the home movie that, to their shared chagrin, pronounces their shared joy; in the company of their friends, they watch themselves, he especially, with stubborn dismissal and annoyance, she with empathy and bewilderment. Here is an older couple standing in judgment of its early incarnation: "Who are those people?" "Are we to think 'We are them,' or 'We are no longer them. We have changed'?" Watching a couple on film watching a couple on film thus begs at once an assessment of the media's ontology *and* something of the emotive and moral import of our findings about that media. That said, the encounter with the home movie in *Adam's Rib* wouldn't be nearly as interesting as it is—some seventy years on—if it weren't for Stanley Cavell's incisive study of the film, that is, the film-within-the-film, *The Mortgage the Merrier*, in his chapter "The Importance of Importance" in *Pursuits of Happiness: The Hollywood Comedy of Remarriage*.

In returning to Cavell's prismatic reading of this metacinematic moment (one among many in the comedies of remarriage), I wish to get Cavell's claims clearly before us so that we can use them to think further about the many instances—since *Adam's Rib*—when home-movie-like objects find their way into Hollywood feature films, and, indeed, into other modes of narrative and nonnarrative production (including non-Hollywood domestic and "foreign" films, documentary, experimental, and avant-garde works—while also making room for their appearance in contemporary streaming serials *and* considering how self-made moving images posted to or streamed on social media platforms present an evolution of the subject). Given the proliferation of these instances and types, we find ourselves (as the subtitle suggests) negotiating what it is we can say about the nature of the home movie as such, and by extension, the home movie "in" narrative cinema, or narrative-cinema-as-home movie, and related filmic expressions; if we find ontological significance in the question "what is a home movie?" we also find it in the question "when is a home movie?"

On this occasion, I aim to explore how the aesthetics of amateur filmmaking (that is, since the home movies in these films are made by professionals) are used in specific ways to signal ontological spaces and times that are distinct from those featured in the main narrative fiction (for example, the past of the home movie set against the present of its screening in the film). I wish to see how the "nested" film—the imposition of this cinematic object or, perhaps better, *reality*, and the moment of its revelation through projection, often to members of the diegetic world—can lead to two transformations: one in the lives of the characters (who watch their past selves or other depicted histories) and another in our thinking about the film we are watching, that is, the film that seems to encompass and contain this miniature work of art. In short, two scenes or scenarios of movie watching occur simultaneously, and yet on different temporal and ontological registers (that is, two films yield three temporal layers or levels).[1] Cavell's articulation of the role of *The Mortgage the Merrier* not only provided a crucial intervention into our understanding of *Adam's Rib*, it also continues to be generative for our contemporary approach to a wider range of home-movie-type representations; in particular, Cavell's account offers an essential and much-needed heuristic for reading *other films* that use amateur film—and the aesthetics of amateurism more generally—to substantiate primary filmic narratives and temporal modes by means of subordinated works of cinematic art.

One of the guiding questions before us, then, is *how* the presence of these films—little artworks, fabrications, moments of metacinema, often films-unto-themselves (with their own styles and sensibilities), somehow showing up in the course of a narrative—shape our understanding of the fiction, figuration, characters, time, place, etc., in the rest of the film. Or, put another way: the long title of this chapter might be paraphrased—and abbreviated—to say we are "Watching Home Movies with Stanley Cavell," for that is the spirit of what I am doing.[2] Or better, "Home Movies" in quotation marks, since our interest in these pages is in the *aesthetics* of home movies as they appear in narrative cinema—the way narrative films (but especially Hollywood movies) recurrently deploy the look (and we want to add "the feel") of the low-tech to tell its (often high-tech) stories.[3] If we will study *how* a home-movie aesthetic is featured (how that "look" and "feel" is achieved), our central question is further clarified: Why is it featured—to what end?

In an earlier work on the nature of documentary film, I explored how prominent, big-budget, feature films often use documentary or news-style footage (real or fabricated to look real) to bolster what might be called the reality credentials of the fictional world.[4] In another piece, I attended to the way home movies can suddenly shift into documentary films, or become footage of historical significance (for example, ethically and politically).[5] The present study is kindred to those projects, since here I am asking how the home-movie aesthetic functions as a mechanism of storytelling, and also what it betokens about the metaphysics of film worlds—in particular, the way a fictional world is made to feel as if it "contains" a real world (with more on containment below).

The home movies we will be watching in what follows will *not* be homemade—that is to say, casual audiovisual captures by (genuine) amateur movie-makers—rather they are created by cinematic professionals who draw upon the aesthetics of amateur filmmaking. These home movies are, then, works of art. But as home movies, they are also fakes, frauds, and aimed at achieving a kind of audiovisual hypnosis: to make you think you have seen things that are impossible, with characters who somehow, in the midst of their stories, appear to have gone on holiday. Or for some reason carried a camera with them, or, for that matter, managed to be in the frame while some unacknowledged other acted as resident filmmaker. In these moments, we not only visit "other places"—places that are not the primary scenes of the story's action, even as we are said to be "in" the mainstream flow of narrative events—but also other *times*. We "go back," sometimes with them in our company (as in *Adam's Rib*), sometimes without them (as in Martin Scorsese's *Raging Bull* [1980]), and catch a glimpse of an alternate reality. But where is this place and how does its ontology on film affect our understanding of the fictional worlds we are summoned to inhabit?

What such an "alternate reality" consists in—how it is produced or what it provides—will be the preoccupation of the following remarks, motivated as they are by questions about the presence of (fabricated) home movies in the midst of (mostly) mainstream (American) cinema. What are, in short, such films doing there? What does this nesting—of films within films—mean to signal? Beyond these foundational ontological questions lie the ethical and emotive effects of that home-movie presence, which might be translated as asking: first, how does the home movie provide access to "a more real" reality (even if feigned in the context of the film's fabrication), which, in turn, sheds light on the present-day circumstances of characters? How does the home movie offer a space in which to address and explore existing, persisting ethical conundrums as we find them in the film—for example, as experienced or treated by its characters (who are often *also* an audience)? And secondly, how does the home movie function as an agent of melodramatic force? If "ethics and aesthetics are one," as Wittgenstein attested, then our look into the ontological features of the home-movie aesthetic will naturally shed light on the ethical nature of the diegetical world, and we can only hope, on our own.[6]

To begin at the beginning, a naive encounter with a home movie conjures its most elemental emotive force: it is a moving picture (in the early days, often without sound, now more commonly with sound) of a world that we take to be our own. In this way, it harbors a core attribute of the "documentary film" as we have come to call and know it. The home movie is or compels us to *think* it is, in a word, authentic. Early in our personal lives, we are typically the subject of such domestically made documentaries—first steps, birthday parties, picnics and camping, family outings and travel, perhaps even a bit of stagecraft in the form of class performances or plays on the home front. As we age, and as moviemaking technology has become more portable and compact, less expensive, and with higher sound and image fidelities, we may become the unwitting creators of such documentaries of one another, and perhaps, of the lives of children. These are sound and image files that are all too easily "lost" on tapes or hard-drives, but when they are recovered, or even stumbled upon while searching for something else, they often contain a rare "glimpse" of some past reality, some time or place that has since then existed mainly as a private memory, if that. Indeed, even a few seconds of the sight and sound of a past event—watching someone walk, hearing someone's voice—can stimulate and expand one's recollections, and in time, may even come to displace whatever it was one did, in fact, remember. In this way, the home movie simply becomes one's memory of one's past.[7] Moreover, when we watch these clips and files, we do not doubt that these are images of us (or familiar others), sounds we made, and the like; we "travel back" to those earlier moments as if in a bit of time travel. Not harboring any skepticism about the veracity of these files, we treat such moving pictures and audio expressions as natively created—as genuine, as real—and often for that very reason, we are moved by them.

The postulations of the previous paragraph may contain all the evidence we need to wonder why dramatic or melodramatic films—regularly in their mainstream narrative forms—might want to trade on the familiarity of home movies and the feelings they conjure: since home movies are easily forged, the results can be just as easily taken to be, treated as, real documents of real lives and by extension contain the conditions for genuine emotional impact—which, in turn, often catalyzes profound existential and ethical effects. If these generalities are recognizable by readers (that is, fellow home movie makers and watchers), then it must be in the close reading of specific films—along with criticism of home movies as a category of art *and* as a presence in mainstream film fictions—that we will advance our thinking on the matter. It is at this juncture that we seek the counsel of Stanley Cavell.

* * *

At an early point in *The World Viewed: Reflections on the Ontology of Film*, Cavell asks of film, and of us: "Why, for example, didn't the medium begin and remain in the condition of home movies, one shot just physically tacked on to another, cut and edited according to subject? (Newsreels essentially did, and they are nevertheless valuable, enough so to have justified the invention of moving pictures.)"[8] Cavell's fascinating question captures the very spirit of Erwin Panofsky, who wondered after "the unique and specific possibilities of the medium."[9] What, in effect, can film be for? Cavell sustains Panofsky's provocation with an explanation: "The answer seems obvious: narrative movies emerged because someone 'saw the possibilities' of the medium."[10] Yet, Cavell is quick to notice that "cutting and editing and taking shots at different distances from the subject" are "mere actualities of film mechanics" and as such "every home movie and newsreel contains them," so how do we account for the transformative leap to a cinema of narrative?[11] Cavell offers a reply: to "make them 'possibilities of the medium'"—that is, to make the mechanics of film do something other than provide us with home movies and newsreels—"is to realize what will give them *significance*—for example, the narrative and physical rhythms of melodrama, farce, American comedy of the 1930s."[12] For our purposes here, I wish to suggest that part of the invention of significance in narrative cinema beyond home movies and newsreels, nevertheless, traded on attributes of those earlier forms. Home movies and newsreels, in short, become a genre, or if you prefer, an idiom by which we call upon certain features of significance in the context of other genres and styles of filmmaking.[13] Let us make this more concrete with a canonical example from Cavell's peerless oeuvre of closely read films.

I will not rehearse here the entire plot of *Adam's Rib*, a task Cavell himself has completed with aplomb in the opening notes (of twenty small segments) to his chapter on the film in *Cities of Words*, but I will say we are watching a movie about a married couple, both lawyers, who find themselves on opposite sides of a legal case in which a wife is tried for shooting her husband, who survives the attack.[14] In the early part of the contest that gives narrative shape to the film, and we are meant to consider is one of a series of such contests a couple such as Amanda and Adam Bonner take as familiar to their marriage, we find them at home, in the company of guests gathered to celebrate the paying off of the mortgage on their country house in Connecticut (the Shakespearean "green world" that lies beyond the congested, concrete streets of Manhattan, as in other films such as *Bringing*

Up Baby [1938, dir. Howard Hawks] and *Mr. Blandings Builds His Dream House* [1948, dir. H. C. Potter]—both films sharing Cary Grant as part of the cast, and the former also starring Katharine Hepburn).[15] As Cavell glosses the scene: "Amanda tells one of the judges, in Adam's hearing, that she has taken the Doris Attinger (Judy Holliday) case. After dinner a home movie is shown of Adam and Amanda's country house. . . . Adam, seething from Amanda's news, has further to contain himself throughout the enforced silence of the screening, the seething and the silence heightened by [neighbor and sometime interloper] Kip's parodic, grating narrative of the film."[16]

Only thirty-four years removed from D. W. Griffith's *The Birth of a Nation* (1915), which itself innovates from the home movie and the newsreel (including remarkable fantasy sequences, such as the invocation of Abraham Lincoln, as if his presidency was contemporaneous with the art of moviemaking), Cukor's *Adam's Rib* treats its audience to a startling innovation of metacinema: for as we are watching *Adam's Rib*, we are *also* watching a home movie—entitled *The Mortgage the Merrier*—with its characters (as it were "inside" the diegesis of the film). In this doubling of movies, much is created and much is revealed. Let us call this invocation of home movies within the cinematic space of popular narrative cinema—both in its comedy and (if Cavell would allow) in its melodrama—the realization of one (or more) of the "possibilities of the medium," possibilities that, as I will explore further below, have hardly run their courses, but are continually renewed over the seventy years that separate us from Cukor's exemplary instance of the practice.

While many viewers of *Adam's Rib*, then and now, might barely register the presence of *The Mortgage the Merrier* in the stream of the story— especially because the emotion of the scene is so fraught, charged as it is with a bona fide fight between the principal leads of the story—it is a metacinematic intervention worth dwelling upon. For one thing, while we are rightly distracted by the marital conflict—which is itself compounded by the further self-referential fact that Katharine Hepburn and Spencer Tracy were nearly a decade into a relationship when they made *Adam's Rib*, we may well miss—as we so often do in our habitual encounter with such recursive elements—how the interpolated home movie is providing us with a rich semantic field.[17] By extension, we are prompted to think not just about the independent qualities of the two films (their participation in genres, for example, or their *allusion* to genres), but also how they are interacting and what that conjugation of genres (real and invoked) might mean. Indeed, a fascinating way in which medium specificity (say, the way this home movie is without sound and so resembles a silent movie) is mobilized by Cukor and company to play out a specific kind of commentary—what Cavell is noticing or anointing as melodrama.

Hepburn and Tracy were both staying at George Cukor's house, off and on, while Tracy avoided his wife. The mores and sexual politics of such an affair, in the context of Golden Age Hollywood and the prevailing Hays Code, are familiar territory for film and cultural historians. I merely wish to underscore how the Hepburn-Tracy domestic intimacy off-camera might be pertinent to what we have come to find in *Adam's Rib*, in short, a home-movie-like testament to their rare rapport: "Tracy and Hepburn were never more relaxed with the audience or each other," writes Patrick McGilligan in his biography of Cukor, and focusing on the production of *Adam's Rib*: "It was as if the camera was peeking through a keyhole in their hideaway on Cukor's grounds. Cukor did not force the point: He let them be themselves. Their scenes together are marvelously supple."[18]

The home movie entitled *The Mortgage the Merrier* begins about twenty-seven minutes into the film and is announced by a seemingly hand-etched title card. What stands out on repeated viewing is the unexpected manner in which the title card overlays (by superimposition) the scene of the party underway—*not* the home movie it purports to announce. We are, as it were, given a second title (a subtitle?) to the film already in progress that, moreover, contains its own subtitle. The nesting of these commentaries and metacommentaries is deep, indeed, and we are invited (a fitting gesture for such a party) to consider, as noted just above, that *Adam's Rib* is itself a home movie of sorts, or, indeed, operates at several levels of depiction at once (for example, as feature film, as documentary-of-its-own-making, as home movie, etc.).

Bonner Epics

present

"THE MORTGAGE THE MERRIER"

A Too Real Epic

Married screenwriters Ruth Gordon and Garson Kanin, I wish to believe, surely relished the francophilic double entendre loaded in the chosen surname, Bonner (and thus made yet another registration of metacommentary), namely, that the Bonners—Amanda and Adam—possess a name defined by *happiness (bonheur)*. Moreover, the title of their home movie about their marriage playfully calls forth the mood of the *merrier* in conjunction with the figure of the *marrier* (that is, the one who marries and may be merry when being wed). Fans of Kanin's prodigious screenwriting, including his steady collaborations with Cukor (and, of course, Gordon), will also delight in the punned and repurposed film title, *The More the Merrier* (1942, dir. George Stevens).[19] In the context of Cavell's book—with *its* main title alerting us to pursuits of happiness—we seem to have found our ur-couple, a veritable Adam and (not Eve—despite the *rib* on offer) but *Amanda*, that is, one who is deserving of love, or worthy of being loved. And her worthiness as an object of love is caught up in the question of Amanda's relation to knowing what *a man* is or does or is worth (a man understood as a human and so a woman *too*—but also in the "little difference" that distinguished man *from* woman). Amanda's name is a (subtle?) way of calling her "a man"—as if she were wearing a badge or label at odds with her personage, and thus not one who would be taken or mistaken for a man (though we admit another internal reference to a time, fourteen years earlier, when she was just that—in Cukor's *Sylvia Scarlett* [1935]).[20] Meanwhile, less subtle, often playful, commentary—for example, when Adam's mock rival, Kip Lurie (David Wayne) is around—tests what makes a man and who would or would not want to be one; at one point, Kip takes offense at the name. As Mrs. Bonner rebuffs his peculiar advances to "trade kisses," Amanda says: "Now, you look here, Kip, . . . it's clear you're behaving, I hate to put it this way, . . . but like a *man*." Kip replies: "You watch your language."[21]

While "epic" may likely intone more than a touch of sarcasm (since grandiosity about one's home movies can be playfully undermined this way), the gloss of a "too real epic" (the word epic repeated to assure us that the Bonners are aware it would only be these two, this couple, who would treat the foregoing glimpses *as* epic) also reminds us of the sorts of claims a veritable home movie might want to make at this point in a fabricated story: namely, that it is *real* (and of significance). Since we are in the hands of witty screenwriters, though, who enjoy the levels of meaning they are creating, we are called to remember that home movies of the time (and for some time to come) would have been shot on "reels," and so a "too real epic" is also a "two reel epic."[22]

Anyone who has "held" a mortgage (a locution that reflects the felt weight one carries) might have also looked up its etymology, and sure enough it is kin with mortality (*mortuus*, Lat., dead) and promise-making or pledge-taking (*gage*, Fr., pledge). Thus while the having or "holding" of a mortgage is a burden laden with the double-stroke of death and commitments (many last thirty years, which is perhaps longer than most marriages), the discharging of a mortgage should certainly be a source of cheer (hence, the merriment of the home movie's title). The Thoreauvian word is intentional for it reminds us that the solitary woodsman of Walden Pond worried that it was not we who own our homes but the homes that own us—"our houses are such unwieldy property that we are often imprisoned rather than housed in them."[23] And yet the Bonners, who should be happy in this moment when their faraway Green World is, at last, theirs—when the deathly insinuations of the mortgage are traded for the life-affirming pleasure of ownership—are, instead, angry and resentful about the more pressing pressures of their city life.

It is a testament to the artful editing and thus sinuous integration of *The Mortgage the Merrier* that the full scene that includes the home movie is a mere four minutes in total.[24] Despite the economy of screen time, these handful of minutes provide a rich site of significance for what Cavell has called *Adam's Rib*'s "allegory of the nature of viewing film."[25] In this allegory, the film is—or the filmmakers are—keenly aware of the "stages" on offer: from the *Punch and Judy* motif to the courtroom to the bedroom, and, of primary concern here, the home movie (which is, indeed, depicting the couple "at home"—or complicates where home is: in the country and not in the city?). Cavell notes that *Adam's Rib* is, "with one minor exception, the only member of our genre in which we see the pair in their own home at all"—and, as just noted, we are meant to think they have two such places.[26] And so we might emphasize that though we see them in two homes—in town and in the country—we are left to wonder where they are "at home" (in one, the other, both, neither?). Part of the intrigue of *The Mortgage the Merrier*, though, is that while it is screened "at home" (in town), it purports to show its audience of friends and colleagues—and perhaps even more so, us, as the gathered audience for the screen (hence the deepening allegory Cavell calls to our attention)—that Amanda and Adam are "even more at home" in the country. The home movie is not just a mock-up ploy, but, to use the language and logic of the diegesis, it is *making a case*, in particular, that Amanda and Adam are fit for one another: they know how to speak, how to love, how to negotiate the "courting of marriage," as Cavell puts it in his usefully double entendre-laden chapter title, "The Courting of Marriage." Despite all the tears and shouting, the harsh words and proffered weapons, we are meant to think that Amanda and Adam are capable of *bonheur*, that is, the seeking for and the finding of their happiness.

In this sense, the home movie is "more real" or "too real," since it reminds us what we are failing at, or have lost or are at risk of losing, in the present moment. Adam and Amanda do love one another; they are fit for marriage; and the home movie shows them (and us) why. Indeed, they argue immediately after seeing *The Mortgage the Merrier* precisely because they are reminded how far they are from their idyll. What they see on film is a love to save and, as often happens, to fight for. Adam's "rib" of Amanda, and likewise her "rib" of him, therefore, involves love and anger, flirt and taunt, jest and confession.

Among Cavell's salient points, if also remarks that stand in need of further elaboration, context, and commentary, we are told that "both films are equally real, equally films; they have, so to speak, the same dimensionality."[27] On this front, we could remember that *The Mortgage the Merrier* does not exist as an "independent film," but, as noted, has achieved a kind of integration into the film on the marquee. And yet, within the reality (or "dimensionality") of *Adam's Rib*, *The Mortgage the Merrier* makes more than a passing appearance. It is announced! It has titles and credits! It is bona fide. Despite its standing—that it stands out (in ways many home movies, in other films, do not)—Cavell regards the relationship between the two works (or is it one work of two types?) as revealing further nuances, and thus, as calling for further reflection:

> The containing-contained relation makes the containing film essentially more complex than the film it contains (since it contains something the

other cannot contain), but we do not know what significance attaches to this complexity. It may go with this to say that the home movie is meant for a private audience and the commercial movie for a public, but then to consider this relation is something we know to be a goal of the more complex movie as a whole.[28]

Adam's Rib is ipso facto more "complex" than *The Mortgage the Merrier* because the former "contains" the latter, yet it does more than *include* a short home movie: it also encloses a genre or a style or an idiom, something that makes the home movie stand apart from the movie that incorporates it. In what follows, I hope to add a few notes to offset the sense that "we do not know what significance attaches to this complexity." For one thing, we can consider the relationship between private and public in *Adam's Rib* as a dispatch from an earlier era. We know, for example, in contemporary instances, that there are home movies (something shot initially for personal purposes, "meant for a private audience") that in time, or in turn, are "made public." In these cases, ordinary life becomes newsworthy—as in *5 Broken Cameras* (2011, dir., Emad Burnat and Guy Davidi), when Burnat takes up the camera to film his son's birthday and ends up becoming a war cinematographer (since the border between home front and the war front collapsed, or never was). And when Diamond Reynolds live-streams the death of Philando Castile, a further complication in the evolution of the private/public divide is presented to us; the expanding instinct for filming—surveilling—our own lives because news-may-be-happening in it or to it, suggests that the home movie is now, perhaps permanently, liberated from the domestic (as it was, partially, by the mobility of cameras that could accompany a family while traveling).[29] Where Reynolds anticipated an escalation of violence, Abraham Zapruder was merely rolling his camera—yet in that moment announced the shift from private home movie to public surveillance, now a permanent and familiar part of our image/sound-capturing environment. As we have become increasingly aggressive documenters of our experiences using mobile devices—ones that put the movie camera in a permanent state of readiness (from Instagram clips to Facebook videos to terabytes of content uploaded to YouTube—at present, three hundred hours per minute)—the private realm not only has more coverage, but also significantly more distribution. The home is where the camera is.[30] The home movie has gone global.

Typically, that is, as a measure of cliché, home movies are boring; that is, or has been, one of their claims to fame. A home movie's meaning, then, seems caught up with private interpretation (that the importance of its importance is perpetually private). When we become aware of our interest in the significance of home movies in feature films, as in *Adam's Rib*, we can ask how they became of interest to a viewing *public*. What in Adam and Amanda's life on the Connecticut farm seems to escape their privacy and the intimacy of their domestic life? One answer is that we are interested in their experience of watching their own home movie—or, as depicted by Cukor, not watching it but watching each other (that is, the two people who should be most interested in *The Mortgage the Merrier* seem the most distracted from its claims for interest.) What a trick: Cukor has managed to create a home movie that captivates the *public* but not those featured in it. He has, along with Gordon and Kanin's savvy screenwriting, and at least two indelible actors, inverted the customary patterns of valuing and evaluating home movies.

As part of his noticing and note-taking on the "two films" (indeed, are they one or are they two?), Cavell emphasizes two further differences: "*Adam's Rib* has better production values than *The Mortgage the Merrier*" and "*Adam's Rib* is a talkie whereas *The Mortgage the Merrier* is not."[31] Combining these points of difference we might describe *The Mortgage the Merrier* as a silent home movie. No doubt, early cinema is replete with silent films, some of them with high production values (for the time), yet there is something seemingly essential to the common definition—or sensibility—of "home movie" that its production values remain "lesser" than any film that might aspire to (or achieve) the label "feature film." This point has been complicated in recent years by the appearance of high-resolution, high frame-rate smartphones—such as the iPhone—that are not only readily available for increasing the production values of one's home movies (as, say, compared with celluloid 8mm and 16mm, not to mention the video-based Betamax, VHS, Hi-8, and mini-DV formats of yore), but are also co-opted by professional filmmakers to create feature works that stand as reasonable contributions from a productions-level assessment.[32] Sean Baker's *Tangerine* (2015; shot entirely on three iPhone 5Ss) and Steven Soderbergh's *Unsane* (2018; using the slightly upgraded iPhone 7Plus) are feature films shown in competition, while Michel Gondry used an iPhone 7 to make the short, *Detour* (which includes techniques such as stop-motion and time-lapse). Such references would not, *could not*, be part of the landscape of possibilities Cavell was contending with in the seventies and early eighties when he was writing *The World Viewed* and *Pursuits of Happiness*, even as his principle areas of focus were films from the late 1930s and 1940s.

Reviewing Cavell's two points of difference just noted—namely, production values that avail themselves to differentiation (for example, gradations of higher and lower) and silence in one film and not in the other—provides an indication of how a home-movie aesthetic was achieved in the black-and-white feature cinematography of the Hollywood studio system of the 1940s. The availability of silent 8mm film cameras would have allowed amateur cinéastes to create home movies that "looked like" *The Mortgage the Merrier* (though likely without such capable intertitles and deprived of such compelling feature players). Cukor, and his creative team would—then as now—have to be in touch with what the presiding low-end, mass-market technology was and what it could afford creatively. With these machines and materials in mind, a director, cinematographer, production designer, editor, and others, could reverse-engineer "the look" of the home movie circa-whenever—and Cukor and others do just this with the introduction of skipping frames, sped-up frames, upside-down frames, titles, dialogue cards ("Censored!" reads one), as well as operating without diegetic sound or a soundtrack (for example, while screening *The Mortgage the Merrier*, the steady, loud purring of the running projector can be heard).[33] (Whether Cukor and company, in fact, *shoot* the home movie with an 8mm or 16mm film camera is a further question—as is what format Adam and Amanda *would* shoot in.[34]) We even get a shout-out that calls the status of the director (of both films?) into question: "Who took these pictures? Your cow?"[35] The traits of the quintessential home movie (and isn't it interesting that we all, somehow, have a sense of what that "looks like," perhaps regardless of technological traits?) help identify *The Mortgage the Merrier* as a home movie, but these very characteristics also bring the medium of film to mind, which in this case, makes it appear as if we are watching *two* films seemingly at once.

Following after this logic and the points made in the previous paragraphs, a director making a film today would have to be familiar with the kinds of technologies that are available and in use for the mainstream of home-movie makers. For example, are most of them using smartphones for movie cameras? What software are they editing with? What traits—such as coloration or typeface—have become regularized? Discerning the prevailing home-movie aesthetic—what it is, or what is possible from a given technology at a given time—is crucial to the creative implementation of a (staged or faked) home movie in the context of a larger narrative fiction. One can imagine a failure to do so: it might result in an implanted home movie that, as it were, "looks too good," or for that matter, "doesn't look good enough." In another instance, a viewer may find that the production values of the home movie are simply "too close" to those of the main feature underway, and so there is not properly a home movie "contained in" the film so much as a gesture to the visual, sonic, and kinetic sensibility of amateur filmmaking. *The Theory of Everything* (2014, dir. James Marsh), which I discuss briefly below, employs this approach.

Even more conspicuously, the cinematography of *First Man* (2018, dir. Damien Chazelle) aims for the veritable *digestion* of the home-movie aesthetic; for an instance of *ingestion*, one might look to *The Man in the High Castle* (2015–19), in which 8mm footage—and its projection within the *mise-en-scène*—plays a significant role in plotting. *First Man* was shot in the familiar home-movie technology of its 1960s era—16mm—that is, until Armstrong & Co. land on the moon, whereupon we are given the world, this new world, in a wider frame and in the hyper-real high-definition of the IMAX format. Chazelle explains a technological choice and its intended effect on the *mise-en-scène*: "The thinking was, what if this was actual authentic documentary footage and we could use that style to maybe de-glamorize, de-mythologize this part of history."[36] Cinematographer Linus Sandgren adds: "We felt that by committing to that kind of language, shooting handheld with a zoom [in 16mm], was the most immersive way of telling the home-life story because it would signal that you are there for real, like in a documentary." Indeed, when Sandgren saw the results of shooting with contemporary, high-quality film, he diagnosed the problem: "It looked too much like a movie"—and continues—"It didn't feel as authentic and real as the inspiration, which was [NASA's] actual footage that we'd screened. To be authentic 60s, to be emotionally connected as well, the grain and 16mm softness is something we felt was more human and connected with them, while the moon was so far away." Sandgren's language, especially, admits and encodes what might be deemed a popular or naive sense of the powers of documentary cinema; the use of words such as "real," "authentic," "more human," call out to *associations* we have with documentary films more than any actual truth content they may contain. (Each year during the Academy Awards, I marvel at the way presenters frame the practice of documentary film in Sandgren's terms. Proximity to the production of film does not necessarily bequeath a sophisticated understanding of what it is or does or achieves). Yet, it is precisely this power—this cult of vivid, indelible associations with documentary film—that Chazelle and Sandgren so smartly capitalize on in *First Man*.

Instead of recuperating an older incarnation of the film medium, as Chazelle and Sandgren do in their use of an antiquated technology, or adapting traditional home movie projection as Steven Spielberg does in *Minority Report* (2002), Denis Villeneuve exploits present-day, leading-edge technologies to map out a future in *Blade Runner 2049* (2017).[37] In particular, it is the (digital) projection of a character, Joi (Ana de Armas), that draws our interest, since K's (Ryan Gosling) holographic/AI girlfriend presents—in her very presence on screen—a new expression of the home movie.[38] In her changing of outfits for K upon his return home, for example, she seems to be rehearsing what kind of home movie she is—what genre their domestic life will inhabit or enact. As AR and VR need to be further theorized for their relation to home movies, Joi offers an indication of how an *interactive* home movie might one day be a familiar part of daily life.

Turning back now to Cukor's cinematic coupling, Cavell is also keen to point out *similarities* between the two films, the containing and contained—indeed, to describe *Adam's Rib* as "acknowledging the autonomy of the film it incorporates, declaring it to be a complete (primitive) film on its own."[39] Perhaps it would be wise to describe that as the *effect Adam's Rib* has on the viewer of *The Mortgage the Merrier*, since we know that that short film, that home movie, is intercut within or overlaid upon the proceedings known as *Adam's Rib*, and moreover, that there are remarkably clever editorial apparatuses at work to get us to "blend"—one is tempted in this context to say *marry*—the two films (for example, as the title card of *The Mortgage the Merrier* does not overlay the country house [and scene or setting of the home movie], but, instead, the cocktail party in the city where the home movie is screened). Sure, we are meant to *notice* that a home movie of some sort is being projected in Amanda and Adam's living room, but not so much that we leave the diegesis of *Adam's Rib*. Cukor and his cinematographers and editors are sure to cut back and forth between the cocktail party and the projected home movie *and* to make plain that a viewer ought not to get caught up in some separate, second film named *The Mortgage the Merrier*, but, instead, remain persistently aware of its status as a projection for the gathered company, including Adam and Amanda (the stars of, as it were, both films). As Cavell notes, the home movie is a projection in their midst, something they can see as a projection since it often does not fill the frame:

> The sequence of the film-within-the-film in *Adam's Rib* is organized by alternating shots of showing the home movie screen with shots showing the home movie audience, never mixing these subjects. The first two times the home screen is shown its screen is distinctly smaller than ours; while our shot contains no other equally distinct subjects, the top border can be seen to be occupied by a stretch of ceiling and the top segment of a column which are part of the room in which the screening is taking place, visible beyond the depicted screen. In subsequent shots of this screen we have moved closer, nothing whatever is visible beyond the depicted screen, but yet the frame of that movie is not allowed quite to coincide with ours. So it is not quite accurate to say about the film-within-the-film of *Adam's Rib* . . . that we are given a shift from the depicting of a film to the projecting of that very film by identifying ours with it. Rather, in *Adam's Rib*, we shift from a clear case of depiction to a position in which it is ambiguous whether we are meant to understand the film as depicting or as projecting the film it contains.[40]

The lengthy extract here of Cavell's careful description and account is meant to get just right the stakes of our presumed concern with what we might call the ontological status of *The Mortgage the Merrier*, in effect to ask: What kind of film is it? Given that, as Cavell notes, the "latent content" of the film-within-a-film is not readily forthcoming, we might have to satisfy ourselves with a series of conjectures and considerations. Sometimes film criticism does not come down to proving something one way or another—even with the evidence apparently right before us, willingly subjecting itself to repeated inspection—so much as making sense of things at a given time, perhaps in the grip of a certain mood or set of preoccupations. How else can it be that our opinions of films can change so radically from screening to screening, and over years of repeat viewings?

Let us say that Cukor and his team have—for the sake of early techniques of continuity editing—marshaled their skills to preclude our total immersion in *The Mortgage the Merrier* by making sure to show us those bits of ceiling and column, by maintaining Kip Lurie's running (Cavell calls it "grating") narration as well as the aforementioned cutting back to the gathered crowd-as-audience for the film.[41] In this sense, it is not that ambiguous to claim that the film *is* projected and the creators of *Adam's Rib* want it to be seen that way. Like Kip's commentary, a voice-over that occupies the diegesis of *Adam's Rib* but not the home movie screened in it, and which Cavell finds reason to liken to the role of a film critic (since Kip's remarks appear to "[affirm] that what he is criticizing is a film"), we, the audience (of *Adam's Rib*) and they, the audience (of *The Mortgage the Merrier*) may "share" the home movie, but we are, importantly, never without the cocktail crowd and Kip's persistent annotation, as Cavell describes it, "of pedant, or village explainer."[42] Indeed, as Kip prepares the scene, welcoming a next round of guests to the soirée—"Are you the judges? Somebody said judges were coming," we the audience are invited in as well.[43] And aren't we judges too?

Amanda and Adam will show us a home movie testifying to their marriage—put it on trial for us—and we are to sit back and make our judgments, and as Kip and the crowd do, find language for pronouncing them. No wonder Amanda, like anyone about to screen a home movie for casual acquaintances, if not proper family, would ask nervously: "Are you all sure that you *want* to see this?" Keeping to character, Kip replies in deadpan: "I don't."[44] Just a moment before, as the opening title card is put up, Kip anticipates the genre: "The trouble with this picture? It drags."[45] To which Amanda replies: "Shut up, Kip." With another comment worth appending to the vast majority of home movies, Kip declares: "I would say this movie has a rather limited appeal."[46] The metacinematic frisson of this moment, of course, is that we can take him to (also) mean *Adam's Rib*, which is funny because it is untrue. In his penultimate dig, Kip keeps the presumed boredom of such films, that is home movies, ready at hand: "Seems much slower than the other eight times I've seen it."[47] And makes his final derisive note on the genre—and this particular instance of it: "We say goodbye to Bonner Hill and the sickening home movie."[48] (We might reserve such an epithet for arguably the most indelible film of the twentieth century—*also* a home movie—that was captured by Abraham Zapruder on November 22, 1963, in Dallas, Texas.)

Do we wish to revisit our assurance that *The Mortgage the Merrier* is, in fact, an "autonomous" film within *Adam's Rib*, and that this is something the latter film "acknowledges" (a consequential Cavellian master-term, to be sure).[49] To do so, we can benefit from Cavell's perceptive observation that "in thus identifying its own enterprise with that of *The Mortgage the Merrier*, *Adam's Rib* is claiming the continuity of Hollywood sound comedy with two primary sources of the art of film: with the fact and the tradition of documentary film (of which home movies form a massive if peculiar species, and for which the home movie we are shown here suggests, in turn, a fictional basis), and with the fact and the tradition of silent film, especially melodrama."[50] Even before we would make any attempt at a continuity of subject matter (between the Hollywood sound comedy and its two predecessors, or is it three?—namely, documentary, home movie, and silent), perhaps we can simply dwell on the obvious formal continuity: these are all types of film, that is, all entertainments caught on celluloid and projected onto screens (or for us we might say, *originally* caught on celluloid but now largely held in digital form, "streamed" to various platforms, and the like). Such a basic notation of a shared medium goes a long way to establishing something like the common ontological condition of any cinematic works (for example, shot on film, in these cases, and so prompting the need for further investigation in the digital age and its attendant "film" creations; how, for example, might the ontology of a feature film or a home movie, for that matter, be ontologically affected by a shift at this granular—or better, pixelated—level of medium specificity?[51]).

As part of an effort to understand Cavell's appeal to documentary, including the "massive if peculiar species" of home movie, consider how Cavell refers to both films—*The Mortgage the Merrier* and *Adam's Rib*—as *documents*: a "document of marriage" in the first case, and a "document of remarriage" in the second.[52] Since we can safely assume that Cavell understands both films as fictions, the use of the term "document" may stand out, perhaps even seem out of place. Documents, we are often told, are objects attesting to facts and realities: forensic images of a crime scene are documents; replies to an official exam form a document; an internal memo from the clandestine services is a document, and so on. In Cavell's nomenclature, however, a document can be or may contain a fiction. We may simply call documents of this sort art. (Is this a modernist impulse on Cavell's part? Say, the way a document can be treated or taken as art, much as a found object [for example, a urinal, a Brillo box, etc.] was and is?).

Yet, these are two films (if we can say they are two) that form a special kind of art object, ones that are artfully staging an awareness of themselves as art (for example, as stylized creations, as acted performances, as self-referential texts, as metacinematic documents, etc.). At a literal level, echoing a sentiment familiar enough to be ascribed to a number of apocryphal sources (but usually attributed to Jean-Luc Godard and Jacques Rivette), we can say that any fiction film is always already a *document* of the making of the film.[53] (Again, whether this statement holds up or requires refinement when the moving pictures derive from computer-generated imagery remains a further question.) With Godard and Rivette offering an insight-as-evidence, allow me to say provocatively but genuinely that all films are, *in this sense*, home movies; indeed, a trio of films—allegedly shot without screenplays—by former Cavell student Terrence Malick (*To the Wonder*, *Knight of Cups*, and *Song to Song*) would seem to petition for this kind of recognition, where, despite abundant voice-over, plot and character development have been suppressed in favor of the ellipsis and evocation customary of vignettes—and home movies.⁵⁴ Or, if stated with a lot more qualification, we seem poised to say that the films under our consideration here—*Adam's Rib* and *The Mortgage the Merrier*—are at once documents and art objects. If they are, in fact, two films, they *also* possess the qualities of two kinds of things.

And so we go back to Cavell's note above—namely, "the tradition of documentary film (of which home movies form a massive if peculiar species, and for which the home movie we are shown here suggests in turn a fictional basis)"—and find ourselves faced with the ways home movies (presented as "documents" of a given life or lives) are glimpses of life *performed* (as we say "for the camera").⁵⁵ The "tradition" Cavell alludes to is replete with exemplars of the form—Robert Flaherty and John Grierson come to mind— since they not only made documentary films but made them early enough in the tradition that they were forced to contend directly with the application of the word "documentary" to the kind of films they were making. Flaherty remarked that "one often has to distort a thing to catch its true spirit," while Grierson defined documentary as the "creative treatment of actuality."⁵⁶ Grierson's marvelous phrase can be further enriched by the way we come to speak of "actuality" in the context of (explicitly) fictitious works such as *Adam's Rib*. There is a sense in which Katharine Hepburn and Spencer Tracy are in "actuality," or in today's casual parlance, "actually," acting—in this studio, at this time, in Los Angeles, and so on⁵⁷—but, soon enough, when the print is locked (marveling for a moment that the professional name for such a thing is a "married print") and the editing is complete, we have *Adam's Rib*, and clearly Hepburn and Tracy have moved on (since we see them in other films). And now, of course, they are dead. The fact that we can still hear their voices and admire their gaits and gestures on screen must remain an astonishment, even to those of us who are supposed to be inured to the miraculous conjuring that takes place every time a film is presented. The definition "creative treatment of actuality," then, is one we should want to reserve *also* for the kind of film that *Adam's Rib* is, for that seems to be precisely what George Cukor, along with his screenwriters, technicians, and actors, achieved.

Importantly, then, the "fictional basis" Cavell ascribes to *The Mortgage the Merrier* is not a one-off or accident of *Adam's Rib*'s production but, should be treated, instead, as an acknowledgment (playfully made by *Adam's Rib* or otherwise provocatively suggested by the present author) that home movies *are* fictions. That is, they are simultaneously documents *and* works of art. "Of course we acted all this out afterwards. It isn't actual." says the judge who was invited over for the evening—meaning what?⁵⁸ That *The Mortgage the Merrier* is not a documentary film, since what we see on screen (for example, the judge, Amanda, Adam) is *not*, in fact, a scene of the mortgage being paid off, as we have been led to believe it is. That "act" will happen, the judge tells us, "afterwards"—off-camera and thus off-screen. And even then, in another playful double entendre, the true paying off of the mortgage is *also* "acted out." The judge's account of the home movie (in the position of audience member and film critic) makes us also wonder, beyond the frame of *The Mortgage the Merrier*, whether Amanda and Adam "keep on acting" after Kip switches off the projector—which, of course, they do *for us* as stars in *Adam's Rib*, but in the diegesis, it would be a surprise to think that they continue to *act*. So the home movie is an act? And the diegetic world of the film is also an act? Indeed, someone in the gathered crowd shouts out in praise of the judge's performance in *The Mortgage the Merrier*: "You oughta be on the stage, judge," to which Kip quickly quips: "Anywhere but in this picture."[59] We, then, return to earlier remarks on the various stages *Adam's Rib* puts before us (courtroom, law office, bedroom, the varied domestic spaces of the home movie [city apartment, country house], . . . *Punch and Judy* show) and ask anew what it means to *act* upon them.

Perhaps there was a time, a long time, in fact, when the home movie was the best picture we had of "real life"—life unadorned, the everyday and ordinary, the unstaged, or if staged then within the private theatrical space of the domestic sphere, and so on—but now we have alternatives. For example, perhaps we are now inclined to think that "raw" surveillance footage is a better picture of "real life," since in these moving images we are not acting, though perhaps (only) because we have forgotten (or didn't know or suspect) we were "on camera." The surveillance clips repurposed by Xu Bing in *Dragonfly Eyes* (2017) indicate a certain (and increasing) cultural obliviousness to the ubiquity of cameras; they see us but we do not see them. We can turn to Garrett Stewart's *Closed Circuits: Screening Narrative Surveillance* to join us on this path, in part, to help us take a measure of the way the medium has evolved to include what we might call "foreign parts." For example, consider the practice of inset imaging that we find in Michael Haneke's *Caché* (*Hidden*, 2005) so that, as Stewart notes: "the ultimately unsourced amateur VHS 'home movies' (again, a second movie or the same?) would stand out more dramatically as deviant and invasive" when placed "within" the high-definition frame.[60] Moreover, we are left to consider that "the whole panoply of inset surveillance screens in thrillers and science-fiction is an often real-time mutation of the home movie," for example, in the remarkable panning across surveillance screens found in the BBC limited-series, *Bodyguard* (2018, dir. Thomas Vincent and John Strickland). In most of these cases, the invasive motion picture is used principally as a homing device (the pun duly noted) rather than as a chronicle.

The ever-expanding uses of surveillance footage in feature films may remind us that rather than watching, it is we who are, in fact, being watched. There are now some places (and more and more places as time passes), such as marquee national monuments and prominent public forums, where we should assume that we are almost always being captured by some kind of surveillance apparatus. A reader can ask herself: when I am in such a place—airport security, a high-profile public event, etc.—do I change my behavior or simply become more self-conscious because I think or know I am being recorded? The Benthamites and Foucauldians alike will presumably assure us that the panopticon has, in fact, despite its technological efflorescence, gone fully internal. We are policing ourselves. But to the point at hand: Does that self-consciousness and self-monitoring mean we are always "acting" and never "actual"? The very notion of "acting naturally" becomes oxymoronic. If the home movie is not the repository of "real life" that we have been told and trained to believe it is; if, in fact, it is thoroughly underwritten by a "fictional basis" (as much, say, as *The Mortgage the Merrier*), then we could ask first, what the contained film's fictionality means for its role in *Adam's Rib*, and more broadly, what the role of the home movie is (or has been) in fiction features more generally and up to the present day (more on this below).

    I want to return to these two crucial queries in a moment, but first touch on Cavell's other point of reference in relation to *The Mortgage the Merrier*, namely, the silent film. Cavell is intent on placing *The Mortgage the Merrier* in a sequence that finds it as an *expression* of silent film, since this home movie-of-a-sort replicates certain "terms of plot, character, and setting" befitting the melodramatic mode.[61] From our distance in time—2019 to 1949—some seventy years, one feature of the two films may strike us as overtly, undeniably matched, namely, that both are shot in black and white. Though color film reaches back to the nineteen teens, with hand-tinting arriving even earlier, many use *The Wizard of Oz* (1939, dir. Victor Fleming—with our George Cukor an uncredited director!) as a touchstone for the emergence of color as a prominent feature of mainstream cinema (quickly pointing out that the Kansas scenes are shot in a sepia black and white . . . and directed by still another, King Vigor). Even in the late 1940s and into the early 1950s, comedies and melodramas were customarily shot in black and white. This point about the characteristics of medium specificity in *Adam's Rib* and *The Mortgage the Merrier* finds a fitting gloss in *The World Viewed*, where Cavell speaks about the difference color made to filmed works of art:

> The inherent drama of black and white film further clarifies what it is about film that invited the outline clarity of types and justified those decades of melodramas, comedies. . . . In accepting these works are movies we accepted what they depicted as reality. Of course it *was* reality, but reality—whether of land or city—dramatized. I do not say that our acceptance of film created the acceptance of this reality. On the contrary, I suppose that the ease with which we accepted film reality came from our

having already taken reality dramatically. The movie merely confirmed what the nineteenth century completed.⁶²

Thus, in Cavell's chapter on color, we, the viewers of *Adam's Rib* and *The Mortgage the Merrier*, are not just reminded that these are black and white films—and given a reason to consider the pertinence of that fact—but also bidden to assess the claim of the "inherent drama of black and white film" (is this so? is it a controversial notion?). Perhaps as fitting to our present inquiry is the proposition that film's capacity for showing us "reality dramatized" is predicated on the prevailing fact that we already took "reality dramatically."—Or, as Cavell puts it in a different part of *The World Viewed*—on automatism: "Movies convince us of the world's reality in the only way we have to be convinced . . .: by taking views of it."⁶³ "Movies seem more natural than reality" because "they are reliefs from private fantasies"—call these the fictions we make up for ourselves and that, so often, trouble us. The relief of movies, then, is a liberation to see the world "unseen."⁶⁴ At this point, in the light of our position vis-à-vis the movie and its screening, one might say that the "inherency" of drama is not *just* a function of black and white film (that is, since we do not live in such a world without color, black and white film must strike us as strangely, uncannily enhanced—as in "Bergman's harsh black and white mysteries"⁶⁵), but also a matter of the (mere?) *projection* of drama in the goings-on presented by filmed entertainments. The human experience of the film screened, we could say, after Cavell, fulfills the human "wish for the condition of viewing as such."⁶⁶

To give Cavell's claim more due, should we allow that—from a certain vantage, say, the moviegoer of the 1930s and 40s, such as Cavell was—black and white film was inherently dramatic because black and white (as such) *abstracts* our (otherwise) "colorized" reality—one that we are, for its ubiquity and everydayness, inured to? Few of us notice that we see in color (however many variations may obtain in the specific realities of the perceived colors). At such moments, we are reminded that we are invoking an experience of the sighted, and at that, of those who perceive the color spectrum. What might be said for the "inherent drama" of other, non-optical, non-chromatic modes of perception? As a companion to a query about sight in cinema, the experience of *sound* in cinema might be a fecund place to turn.⁶⁷

Whether we are confident that drama is inherent to black and white film-as-such, or more so to black and white film than color, are questions that need not hold up this deliberation. Rather, we may simply wonder how or why it is that *The Mortgage the Merrier* stages drama (or melodrama or comedy) differently than *Adam's Rib*, the film it appears "in" (or "with"?). Perhaps that difference can be marked by the nature of black and white film, but, as I wish to emphasize, a further, enriching clue may reside in the particular (and peculiar) functionality of the home-movie aesthetic within a familiar narrative progression (say, of the films Cavell anointed "comedies of remarriage"). A first indication that this may be the case rests in the way Cavell marks the silent film *The Mortgage the Merrier not* as a comedy, but as a melodrama. Since they are both black and white films, we can say, along with Cavell, that they are both full of "inherent drama," but for differences in sound (one is silent, one is not) as well as shooting style, editing, etc., they are operating in different genres. *The Mortgage the Merrier* is a melodrama *and* a home movie.

At this point, we may want to ask if all home movies are inherently melodramatic. What would make them so? For Cavell, there appear to be two salient qualities that must reveal themselves to the viewer—"first whether there is a narrative here at all, second, if there is, whether it contains a villain, a despoiler of virtue."[68] After having called *The Mortgage the Merrier* a melodrama, Cavell has his doubts, which he then dispenses with in short order; so, for him, *this* home movie qualifies. If Cavell's criteria hold for what counts as a melodramatic home movie, perhaps it is analytic that home movies as such, as the broad, ranging genre it is, are not inherently melodramatic. But the question is generative for, among other reasons, pressing us to consider whether we think of our lives as inherently melodramatic (echoing Cavell's thought that we were primed to take film dramatically because, as noted just above, we already took "reality dramatically"). For example, the cliché—and cliché because it is true—that strangers (and even some family and dear friends) find the sharing of home movies rather insufferable suggests that home movies *are* inherently melodramatic for the *subjects* of such films. Perhaps this is why Kip's animated, gossipy snide, "grating" voice-over narration of Amanda and Adam's home movie, is so peculiar: How has he arrogated the right to voice this track? To make this consecutive commentary on the lives of others? Then again, perhaps Kip's intimate outsider narration is just what the gathered audience needs in order to overcome their customary boredom with such domestic depictions on film. Far from being an interloper who ruins the melodrama, Kip supplies it—makes it available to friend and stranger alike, even to the two stars of the film who sit within earshot, one pouting in the corner, the other solicitous and confused.

* * *

As we continue to hold and fold these various attributes (formal as well as in matters of content), for example, black and white, sound, silent, containing, contained, etc., we might say, that in 1949, Cukor had little or no choice—as a matter of the prevailing style of such films, or for budgetary reasons from the studio office—but to make a black and white film, and moreover, if it should "contain" another film that would have to be black and white, too.

When the movies went color, by and large, so did the home movies. Yet, from our vantage, more than a half-century on, we might consider anew, and with so many instances to choose from, how home movies have, in some sense, kept pace with their more expensive and elaborate counterparts (that is, the films that "contain" them)—such as we see in the recent pop Marvel offering, *Logan* (2017, dir. James Mangold), in which the titular hero (Hugh Jackman) watches movies of Gabriela (Elizabeth Rodriquez) on her phone. In addition to the issue of color, we should also emphasize that from *Adam's Rib* to the present, home movies function as an efficient device for exposition.[69] Like a dream or flashback, a well-crafted, artfully edited amateur film can propel a plot forward (as in *Raging Bull*), fill in backstory (as in *Paris, Texas*), and in some cases, indeed most cases, enrich our capacity to connect with the diegetic world through the introduction of details that deliver clarity, as well as the nuance and ambiguity so necessary for art.[70] Yet, the home movie is not just a metaphysical curiosity in the space of a given film, but in some cases (for example, *Adam's Rib*, *Paris, Texas*, and others), it is also a sentimental object *for the characters*. Footage of an earlier time adds genuine pathos—a sense of an unrecoverable past coupled with a hope for a recovery, reclamation, or restoration of some sort. So though flashbacks, for example in the Bourne series, provide *the viewer* with a certain kind of access to past events—including a glimpse into Jason Bourne's own mind and memory—they are not themselves artifacts.[71] Jason cannot "play" his memory for Marie (Franka Potente) or Nicky (Julia Stiles), as *The Mortgage the Merrier* can be projected for the principal pair as well as their friends and acquaintances (who appear "in" the film we call *Adam's Rib*) and also, for strangers (that is, we, the viewers).

As a unique case, with a rare orientation to color and plotting, consider Martin Scorsese's Oscar-winning black and white boxing epic, *Raging Bull* (1980), which includes home movies—in color. We can look to Patricia Erens' foundational work on this topic, for example, in "Home Movies in Commercial Narrative Film" (1986)—in an issue of the *Journal of Film and Video* devoted to "Home Movies and Amateur Filmmaking"—where she notes:

> Occurring half-way through the feature, the home footage serves to chronicle the courtship, marriage, and growing family of Jake [Robert De Niro] and Vickie [Cathy Moriarty], creating a montage sequence accompanied by a lyric musical passage. The home movies cover a period of four years, which are indicated with titles, giving dates of various fights, setting up further contrast between Jake's professional career and his private life.[72]

If Scorsese's celebrated "grimy black and white" cinematography in *Raging Bull* projects that "inherent melodrama" of the pre-color era, what kind of drama/melodrama can be claimed for the color footage marked out as taken on the home front instead of inside the ring?[73] Noticing that broad span of time covered in the color footage—four years—how could we not say that such a period (defined, in this case, by courtship, marriage, children, etc.) is inherently melodramatic? I don't mean to answer a question with a rhetorical question, but, instead, ask after the particular logic of the home movie's role in *Raging Bull*, seen as it is on this occasion, in correspondence with the home movie's position in *Adam's Rib*. For one thing, it may be the case that Scorsese's use of black and white for the containing film and color for the contained film creates a confrontation between genres. But what to call them, one and the other? When Cavell suggests that *The Mortgage the Merrier* is a melodrama tucked into *Adam's Rib*'s comedy, he sees a parallel with Amanda's own decision to "take her happy marriage to court."[74] In this way, the courtroom is another stage for the projection of a particular way of life. Yet, it is a perilous gambit, since Amanda may not just be trying Doris Attinger's case against her husband, but Amanda's own—"risking the turning of her romance into melodrama."[75] Here again, the *doubleness* that attends the containing and contained films (namely, that there are two of them) finds another variant in the paralleling of marriages (that is, Doris' and Amanda's)—their types, tempers, and trials.

But these "conversations" between framing/enframed films (again, the feature and the home movie) along with the storylines of two marriages that come into communion, for a time, find further permutations in *Raging Bull*. As Erens adduces, in *Raging Bull*, we find a public life (in black and white) contrasted with a private life (in color) and in *Adam's Rib* we inhabit the public courtroom and the private apartment (notably the kitchen, but also, more boldly for 1949, the bedroom—and with our principal pair in bed, under the covers, if fully clothed). In both films, the private life is *extended*, we could say, by the home-movie footage—in *Adam's Rib* it arrives as a pre-edited short complete with titles, intertitles, and a live commentary covering a moment in the past; in *Raging Bull*, however, while the color footage continues the audience's access to a couple's history it does so, for us, by propelling the story *forward*, into the future (that is, instead of "taking us back," as is a customary purpose for expounding "backstory"). Moreover, Scorsese's color footage is *not* presented as a narrative featurette (like *The Mortgage the Merrier*) but as a montage, a mode or method of exhibition that is much more in keeping with the way we, as an audience to home movies, would encounter them: from one reel to the next, unedited. Or if edited, then unprofessionally.

As Erens notes, the home-movie aesthetic is in full effect in the middle of *Raging Bull*, Scorsese clearly attuned—as we would expect, say, Steven Spielberg to be—to the particularities of the medium used for domestic filmmaking:[76] "The pseudo-home footage utilizes almost all of the 'mistakes' . . . , including: jump cuts, light flashes, tilt shots, over-exposed lighting, and shaky camera movements. Likewise, the content replicates the content of thousands of home movies—wedding ceremonies, playing at the local swimming pool, mugging for the camera.... Scorsese even includes a continuity mistake"—a "mistake" made, presumably by some unknown, unnamed editor of this footage. It may be the case that Vickie (Cathy Moriarty) has simply changed her clothes—swapped her black suit for a white one (she has already opened a box containing a white hat that she is still wearing when she appears a few frames later in a white outfit[77]), but the so-called continuity error is perhaps better treated as a reminder of the compression of a few of life's moments into a relative handful of images we make of them (though this is beginning to change, as noted, because of digital surveillance and obsessive self-recording). Indeed, some four years are covered in a mere two-and-a-half minutes (of a home-movie montage in color that is interspliced with black and white images)—which should make this cinematic phrasing a textbook example of radically concentrated filmic exposition. Yet, for all it achieves—by showing—its brevity leaves much to wonder about, and for this latter reason, the homemade footage in *Raging Bull* has about it the character of a memory or a dream: it is not so much a record, after all, as a faint indication, a sketch, a gesture toward remembering. Though the home movie, in this case, moves us into the future, it compels us to look back.

In watching this segment—placed about a third of the way into the film[78]—we are not, for example, to think that Jake (Robert De Niro) has fired up the projector for his friends, and neither for us, the audience. Rather, the color footage—silent, without voice-over narration—arrives as if from a deus ex machina (call him Scorsese), who has come upon a box of old 8mm reels and wants to study them and share them with us. Scorsese motivates the show-and-tell with a neorealist meditation on a wrecked hand submerged in a bucket of ice: with music beginning to swell, a slow-zoom pulls us into thought, and leaves us open to what might be on Jake's mind, or Scorsese's. Jake and Vickie are not aware of the screening of their private lives (in color) and therefore cannot be harmed or benefited by their exposure (the way that Amanda and Adam may be by theirs), still less are they crafting the sumptuous black and white stills and slow-mos, and the intertitles that provide names, dates, and locations of various boxing matches. Though Jake and Vickie remain alienated from the colorful illumination of their private histories, we may be prompted anew to ask if montage itself—perhaps especially as it is used in home movies, and in the manufactured but unnamed micro-dramas we are discussing here—is narrative in nature (and for that reason also dramatic, even [inherently?] melodramatic).

The foregoing notes may prompt an interest in, if not a settled explanation of, a lexicographical distinction Cavell makes in *The World Viewed* between a fictive world "projection" (where there is no unconstructed off-screen space) and a "recording" of elapsed events (such as those in an actual past life, where images of *the* world, not just a world, are on offer). Cavell puts it tersely and emphatically: "First of all, movies are not recordings."[79] We may have perceived some slippage in these two conceptually distinct terms, in part, because of the way surveillance footage has been (increasingly) integrated into movies, for example, in the black and white home-movies-as-registry-of-trauma taken by a coercive psychologist father in the expressively colorful world of *Peeping Tom* (1960, dir. Michael Powell); in the convulsive, multimodal experiment of war cinema, *Redacted* (2007, dir. Brian De Palma)[80]; in the dreary metacinema of *The Final Cut* (2004, dir. Omar Naim), in which an organic camera-implant records every moment of life in POV for replaying widescreen at a "rememory" service, and later, when the camera-implant notion was picked up effectively if unnervingly in the *Black Mirror* installment, "The Entire History of You" (s1:e3, 2011, dir. Brian Welsh); and where the emotional core of memory and its "moving" images found captivating expression, in Charlie Kaufman's *Eternal Sunshine of the Spotless Mind* (2004, dir. Michel Gondry).[81] In short, the ongoing and expanding use of filmed "recordings" has encouraged us to forget that these examples are not recordings in the way Cavell means the term in *The World Viewed*.

Given that the home movie in feature film is, let us say, always part of the fiction (despite the illusion of authenticity it creates), we should return again to the queries above: (1) what the contained film's fictionality means for its role in *Adam's Rib*, and more broadly, (2) what the role of the home movie in fiction features is (or has been), more generally. On that first front, we might note the ways in which the home movie in feature fiction occupies a role akin to documentary (or better, pseudo-documentary), namely, as a resource for establishing the reality and authenticity of people, places, and temporal locations. Pseudo-television coverage—what we could designate as subspecies of a documentary aesthetic—is also a prevalent device, for example, in such major motion pictures as *World War Z* (2013, dir. Marc Forster) and *Mission Impossible—Fallout* (2018, dir. Christopher McQuarrie), both of which use variations of news coverage to situate their opening scenes—in the first case, crosscutting animal documentary footage with newscasts, and in the latter case, enlisting Wolf Blitzer to creative effect.[82] These contemporary instances of CGI-rich, mega-budget productions belie the longevity of this particular documentary instinct: consider the opening of *The Magnificent Ambersons* (1942, dir. Orson Welles), in which the narrator (Welles) provides voice-over for a sequence of shots that one is tempted to re-describe as "movies of a home." At the beginning of the film, we are not yet *in* the story, but told about it—what it promises to contain, as the narrator says: "against so home-spun a background."[83] Evoking a Griffith's-like fantasia *avant la lettre*—that cameras were around in 1873— we watch a heavily vignetted square-frame with a slight flicker that seems to provide a "glimpse" of a world *before* the movie camera.

Yet another significant point of reference, in the flow of such meditations, is the subgenre of found footage films or (after David Bordwell) "discovered" footage films—especially as they are imbricated or embodied in horror movies.[84] As a maneuver in some contemporary and conspicuous horror movies—gathering momentum with *Cannibal Holocaust* (1980, dir. Ruggero Deodato) and continuing in a lineage up through *The Blair Witch Project*, *Paranormal Activity*, *[REC]*, and *Cloverfield*)—footage, often made on consumer-grade equipment (or made to look that way), is attributed to people who are now lost or dead or otherwise absent. A parallel practice is discernable in works of science fiction, such as *Chronicle* and *Europa Report*. Whether in horror or science fiction, the film itself becomes an unintended testament and an inadvertent bit of forensic evidence—but for what specifically we often remain unsure. The proximity of home movie and snuff film, however, provides much of the thrill or chill, depending on one's taste.

All of this artful repurposing and fabrication of film—for instance, making fake footage resemble genuine content—isolates the crucial role that the (attempted) *suppression* of fictionality takes on at the precise moment such work is deployed. We could turn this point inside out by saying that *The Mortgage the Merrier*'s fictionality-as-film is not its purpose; it is, instead, meant to exist in communion with a realm (our realm as viewers and makers of home movies?) whose credentials for authenticity are not in question. One may, rightly I think, treat *The Mortgage the Merrier*'s presence and role as a case of cinematic legerdemain, for what else are directors, cinematographers, editors, actors, and screenwriters doing but using filmic sleight of hand to insist on the emotional and ethical tonality of amateur film capture? By "imbedding" *The Mortgage the Merrier* in *Adam's Rib*, the creators know that—by contrast—the contained film will come across as truer, more real, and the like.

Strangely, though, the very invocation of home movies in this narrative context makes us forgetful of how much fiction is contained in them—or better, how they simply *are* fictions. For example, we could consider how selective home movies are in terms of the time and space they capture, as well as the framing of that space, the editing of content, the particular distortions of color, the presence or absence of diegetic sound, the use of music, the fact that people may (instinctively, self-consciously) *act* in a home movie—which is to say, these are *all* qualities familiar to the creation of fiction films.

* * *

Shifting to the second question—namely, what the role of the home movie in fiction features is (or has been), more generally and up to the present day—it may prove illuminating to account for some other uses of the home-movie aesthetic, this time in additional contemporary films, with an eye toward how the foregoing remarks on Cavell—and *Adam's Rib* and *The Mortgage the Merrier*—might enrich our current relationship with the ongoing use of, and thus the presence of, "home movies" in feature films.

Some of these feature films are treated as documentaries, that is, the films were produced and then *promoted* as documentaries—and only later revealed to be otherwise. Salient examples include *F For Fake* (1975, dir. Orson Welles) and, more recently, *I'm Still Here* (2010, dir. Casey Affleck), *Stories We Tell* (2012, dir. Sarah Polley).[85] Flipped the other way, there are features we want to treat as documentaries: given the intermittent temporal progress of Richard Linklater's *Boyhood* (2014), we are compelled to say that the footage holds up as a documentary of the lead actor (Ellar Coltrane), even as the characters are fictionalized and the narrative is scripted. Meanwhile, we encounter an enthralling case of role reversal in *The Act of Killing* (2012, dir., Joshua Oppenheimer), a documentary that "contains" feature films (or at least scenes of reenactment in varied cinematic styles); here, fictionalized performances of genocidal acts yield unexpectedly genuine and appropriate emotive effects, as when Anwar Congo heaves.[86] Oppenheimer solicits confession indirectly, not by police-style interrogation but by casting a Hollywood spell: make them stars and they will tell you everything.

We might say that documentary itself *began* in a state of fakery—as accounts of Robert Flaherty's production of *Nanook of the North* (1922) attest to the fabrication at the heart of the "documentary" project.[87] Documentary-as-fabrication—or, in John Grierson's apt phrase noted above, "the creative treatment of actuality"[88]—is an old idea that was overlooked for a long time and in the new century has been recovered. Indeed, the necessary state of *fiction* that documentary seems to contain as an attribute of its medium specificity, has, especially in recent years and experiments, become a more prominent part of the very modus operandi of some works. *I'm Still Here* is an example of a feature documentary that gets "outed" as a feature fiction; the film was intended as an artistic stunt—a provocation—but it became a controversy, and one that left many feeling alienated and cheated. Similar to *Stories We Tell*, *I'm Still Here* "contains" digital video that invokes and evokes its authenticity—handheld, camera-in-mirror, direct address, grainy VHS footage, and so on—yet, upon the film's release in theaters it was accused of being a hoax. Seemingly by accident, *I'm Still Here* provides an instance of a new subgenre: hoax *vérité*.[89] Caught up in the controversy within and unleashed by what Joaquin Phoenix and Casey Affleck called an "art experiment," we might lean back a moment to notice that *I'm Still Here* is *one long home movie*—including footage from childhood (later revealed to be erzatz), with most of the coverage attributed to the star's brother-in-law. When taken as *genuine*, the film can seem like an affirmative answer to the question: "If celebrities make home movies do we simply treat those creations as feature films?" While in the domestic melodramas of our own creation *we* are the "stars," legitimate celebrities come differently equipped to make the casual shots from a nearby camera into an indelible performance—as when the professional musician picks up the child's instrument and makes a sound that awes us.

In Sarah Polley's metacinematic cultivation in *Stories We Tell*, she pursues hoax-like methods of *mise-en-abîme*, and yet—for all her fabulism and dissimulation—she resolves the controversy within the film's running time (as Welles did earlier in *F for Fake*). That is, we learn that the entire film is a kind (or, better, *more than one* kind of) home movie; for this reason, the purported authenticity of what appear to be home movies is a ruse: the interior ("contained") home movies are fictions, while the containing film—absent the customary grain, scratch, and jitter of 8mm film, and featuring the director herself—is the *truer* portrait of a family (however ambiguously, however suggestively, the film itself may conclude).[90] Meanwhile, in Oppenheimer's inventive, genre-aggregating *The Act of Killing*, which becomes the first part of a tandem pair, later joined by *The Look of Silence* (2014), he enlists historical perpetrators in the telling or "acting out" of their personal histories. (To be sure, there is plenty of "acting out" in *Stories We Tell*—since Polley and her relations are all, for the most part, actors). The performances in *The Act of Killing*, though, are drawn from private memories and then "translated," as it were, through a series of cinematic genres (and their familiar tropes), such as the gangster film. While the assailants "act" (in what appear to be scenes-from-a-poorly-produced-movie), Oppenheimer films the occasion, thereby generating a documentary of a fiction that is based on historical events—mass human atrocities and genocide—and the first-hand testimony of those who perpetrated these events, those who "acted" to carry them out.[91]

Such explicitly hybrid (film) forms provide a heuristic for any approach to the use of the aesthetics of amateur filmmaking (and the inclusion of "home movies"—or, for that matter, documentaries and pseudo-documentaries) in contemporary feature films, since we are primed to ask anew about the very state of fictionality that obtains in one designation or another. Habit and culture have trained us, effectively, to treat documentaries as true, or more true, than fiction films (and to *believe* in this truth status). Noël Carroll's notion of "films of presumptive assertion" and Gregory Currie's description of the "trace," help to negotiate this varied, unruly terrain.[92] If, after Carroll, we think about the ways documentary films "make assertions," which we as an audience are meant to *presume* are veritable (and likewise for Currie's "trace"), let us ask, in the present context, what sort of assertions fiction films are making when they imbed or otherwise adopt amateur aesthetics, such as the home movie or the pseudo-documentary? Asking this question may highlight the unarticulated purposes of this overt (yet relatively undertheorized) operation. As a partial remedy, I will conduct a quick tour of some salient examples, disobeying chronology (for the most part) in favor of logical and thematic progression.

When was a home movie first used in a feature film? I wouldn't be surprised to learn it was among the first gimmicks to be explored, since, like mirrors and lenses, the pleasure of nesting seems a particular trait of meta-art from antiquity to the present (as suggested by scale modeling, *trompe l'oeil*, metafiction, and metatheater, among other cases). William Rothman directed my attention to Yasujiro Ozu's *An Adult's Picture Book View—I Was Born, But* . . . , a 1932 black and white silent film (later adapted in *Good Morning* [1959]), in which sons inadvertently see a home movie of their otherwise stern father behaving like a fool in front of his employer. Moreover, Rothman transforms our relation to Billy Wilder's *Sunset Boulevard* (1950), released the year after *Adam's Rib*, by alluding to the way Norma Desmond (Gloria Swanson) screens her Hollywood films for herself, in the privacy of her home, thus making the "home theatre" a space of transmutation—since, for Swanson, the films her fans know as fictional entertainments are to her documentaries of her youthful exploits as an actor.[93] What Swanson does as a character, however, feels very much in keeping with what *we* can do with our own relationship to films (that are not home movies). In this context, re-read the opening line of Cavell's Preface to *The World Viewed*: "Memories of movies are strand over strand with memories of my life."[94] For Cavell to remember *The Philadelphia Story*, for instance, is simply to remember his life of screenings of that film, and his thoughts and memories about it. In this way, Cavell suggests that the public can, in fact, be made private, both intellectually and emotionally. *The Philadelphia Story* is (somehow, yet clearly true) a special series of facts from his personal history.

While Michael Powell's use of home movies in *Peeping Tom* (1960), mentioned above, is another conspicuous precedent for the implementation of home movies in narrative cinema, let us turn to Alain Resnais' third feature, *Muriel* (1963), which only momentarily varies its visual resolution (for example, changing film stock once, at midway), but ranges over multiple, indiscernible time signatures and realities (for example, dreams, memories, etc.)—indeed, the full title of the film is *Muriel, or the Time of Return (ou le temps d'un retour)*; as viewers, we are in the present, and then, also compelled to consider what a remembered or imagined past might look like on film, as well as how it might find integration with the proceedings of the present.[95] In addition to the familiar purpose of the home-movie object to conjure and represent the past (for example, personal memory, younger selves, lost time, etc.), this film shares the rhythm of the jump cut (defining for its immediate Nouvelle Vague forebear, *Breathless* [1960, *À bout de souffle*]); like Godard's work, Resnais' construction often reveals a kinship in framing, point of view, and the kinetics of a handheld camera. At one point, Marie-Do (Martine Vatel) asks: "Is this a documentary?" And Bernard (Jean-Baptiste Thiérrée) replies: "Even worse." She pauses: "You scare me."[96] Shortly thereafter, the man (shown) with the movie camera becomes the voice-over narrator to films projected to full frame that we may presume he shot (he has returned from the Algerian war, which had recently ended), intoning enigmatic things that do not seem to map onto the motion pictures of soldiers at work: "Nobody knew this woman. . . . They said her name was Muriel. It probably wasn't her real name."[97] The sound of the projector is discernible. And then, suddenly, we see Bernard again: discovering at once that the narrator is not "in the movie" (as a voice-track) but in a room, speaking the voice-over live, beside another man; they have been watching these homemade movies together. As in *Adam's Rib*, we are an audience to an audience for a home movie. And the gestalt repeats itself on many other occasions, for example, in *Paris, Texas* (1984, dir. Wim Wenders), when Travis and Jane Henderson (Harry Dean Stanton and Nastassja Kinski) watch home movies together, in the company of others, while we watch all of them watching.[98] Or in *Home for the Holidays* (1995, dir. Holly Hunter), when we come upon Henry Larson (Charles Durning) watching family home movies alone in the basement—and at the very end of the film discover that one of his *memories* ("Great moment in my life. Great. ... Ten seconds, tops. I wish I had it all on tape.") was, somehow, "recorded" on the family movie camera, and now, at last, is screened for us (in our living rooms, as we watch the Larson home movies innumerable times).

In *The Way We Were* (1973, dir. Sydney Pollack), the visual signature of the home movie is also given explicit reference, here keeping close company with strategies and effects in *Adam's Rib*, and other films just noted, where the practice of amateur film capture and display is an intimate part of the diegetic realm. In correspondence about this aspect of Pollack's film, starring Barbra Streisand, Garrett Stewart has pointed out to me the scene of Katie Morosky's (Streisand) college-era, anti-Franco speech, which is "rendered twice-over." As Stewart says: "The scene is given once in real narrative time, later replayed in a Hollywood producer's screening room in the form of 8mm home movie meant to recapitulate the good old days: that latter film footage becoming, in effect, the story's metacinematic title scene. Such is the pervasive malady of regret, when viewed in company by her gradually estranged husband, whose evidence is preserved here on celluloid in the full nostalgic equivalent of a flashback made over to diegetic technology instead."[99] Like Adam in *Adam's Rib*, it is Hubbell's (Robert Redford) revisitation of the past, by way of film, that strikes a note of significant parallel. The screening of documentary footage (the "8mm home movie" Stewart references) provides an arresting example of the way amateur aesthetics can mobilize commentary (and by structural necessity, metacommentary), since, in this case, the producer's vantage is like our own: we are both watching Katie. But the interstitial position of the producer—he is somehow, we want to say, "between" us and Katie—provides a natural moment in which to account for the latent misogyny and anti-semitism Katie encounters on campus *and* in the screening room.

Other examples that are worth further study might include *Down and Out in Beverly Hills* (1986, dir. Paul Mazursky)—in which Max (Evan Richards) gives his father, Dave (Richard Dreyfuss) a VHS copy of an experimental compilation film as a form of son-to-father or child-to-parent communication. Such home-movie mediated missives find similar expression a few years later, in *Cousins* (1989, dir. Joel Schumacher), where son Mitch (Keith Coogan) plays his own experimental compilation film (also on the era-appropriate VHS format) as a mode of public address to his family—and includes what amounts to surveillance footage that reveals his stepmother's affair. As Mitch's father, Larry (Ted Danson), watches, he manages a genuine smile of pride at his son's bold expression while also taking stock of the stunt's dire, private implications. Both fathers, thus, acknowledge their sons' creative efforts—Dave says, half-proud, half-dejected, "My son, the filmmaker"—but, like us, are forced to interpret these works of art that have arrived in the midst of a Hollywood feature fiction. The doubling of film-types or genres enables us to smoothly change subject positions: to empathize with the sons who need experimental home movies to "talk" with their fathers (and families)—Mazursky, for example, gives over his frame to Max, so we see Dave shouting at his son, and since he breaks the fourth wall, shouting *at us*; and then, later, when Dave watches the film in which he appears, we share the father's untutored efforts at film analysis and self-introspection.

The home movie as memory device, indeed, as a kind of emotional recall system—for on-screen characters as well as serving an expository role for the audience—can be seen in *My Life* (1993, dir. Bruce Joel Rubin), in which Bob (Michael Keaton), recently diagnosed with terminal cancer, takes up a camera for parental-pedagogical purposes, to record himself "teaching" his first child, still *in utero*.[100] More recently, *After Life* (2019, dir. Ricky Gervais) is structurally—and emotionally—built around Tony (Gervais) watching homemade videos of his now-dead wife. The archival valences of the home movie are prominent in these works, as they are in a range of films that treat the presence of amateur film as an inheritance for posterity: as if the films amounted to the deceased or soon-to-be-deceased's memory or experience on file (a sort of metaphysical proxy for embodied life). Yet, sometimes the film does not merely preserve a life, but also a love, as in *Cinema Paradiso* (1989, dir. Giuseppe Tornatore), in which Salvatore Di Vita is played by three actors, the oldest incarnation of which (Jacques Perrin) watches movies of a young Elena (Agnesse Nano) that he made during their earlier, life-defining romance. His archival shot of her fills our frame, then we see him watching the same footage projected, then we are given a reverse shot of him watching the moving pictures. "Our" footage of them as youthful lovers (what we just think of as the film) is displaced by "his" home-movie footage of Elena; as it is screened for us, his home movie becomes, as it were, ours—and so, depending on temporal and phenomenological descriptions, the feature and the home movie present as adjacent or overlapping, and perhaps both. Having become a film director, Salvatore is moved, no doubt, by this reencounter with a formative love made possible by a filmic representation of her and also, at the same time, by cinema's power—in the form of a home movie—to return him to his memories: the Italian *ricorda*, "remember," that he speaks to an older Elena, resonates in English, where the nature of moviemaking (recording) and memory-making (*ricorda*) is especially poignant for private films such as these.[101] By contrast, in *Falling Down* (1993, dir. Joel Schumacher, again), when William Foster (Michael Douglas) plays home movies for himself, the realization seems to be (only) ours to have—as we are given evidence to believe that he wasn't the father he imagines himself to have been; in this case, the home movies are used not as a confirmation but as a counterfactual for the benefit of the audience's (truer, more direct) knowledge of this character's past.[102]

The very notion of "a legacy" (in the bourgeois sense) is remade in the light of these remnants of privately fabricated audiovisual culture. As shown in *My Life*, a central motif of such films is a parent's love for children—even those unborn (again, *My Life*), or not yet conceived, as in *127 Hours* (2010, dir. Danny Boyle), based on a true story, in which Aron Ralston (James Franco) uses a small DV-camera to record himself while trapped by a boulder and facing near-certain death. A remarkable cycle of documentary films exist along this plane as well, most of them focused on fathers and sons, among them: *Capturing the Friedmans* (2003, dir. Andrew Jarecki); *Dear Zachary: A Letter to a Son About his Father* (2008, dir., Kurt Kuenne), a sort of substitute home movie made by a friend of the son's deceased father; *My Architect* (2003, dir., Nathanial Kahn); *The Wolfpack* (2015, dir. Crystal Moselle), with a unique take on the role of metacinema; and *Three Identical Strangers* (2018, dir. Tim Wardle), which contains home movies, studio interviews, reenactments, and what might be called "clinical home movies" (those shot by psychologists). In all of these cases of mainstream narrative cinema and documentary films, we may glean some of the *philosophical* presumptions the creators reveal (intentionally or not) about the power of home movies (whether as fabrications or as legitimate historical artifacts), since we can recognize that in addition to being efficacious for their expository efficiency and emotional agitation, home movies (genuine and imagined) draw us further into our own deeply held convictions about the ontology of such objects. We are left asking not just what is real, but also *when* is real. And what such (filmed) realities could mean for me as time passes—and *after* my time is up.

While an extensive taxonomy of instances of other contemporary films that stage an amateur/homemade movie aesthetic could be adduced, allow a handful of suggestive representatives to suffice here: *American Beauty* (1999, dir. Sam Mendes)—with a floating bag on mini-DV tape that is declared by Ricky (Wes Bentley) to be the "most beautiful thing I've ever filmed"; *The Family Man* (2000, dir. Brent Ratner), in which Jack (Nicolas Cage) sings to his wife; *The Life Aquatic with Steve Zissou* (2004, dir. Wes Anderson), where the eponymous Steve (Bill Murray) is the captain of a ship *and* a documentary filmmaker (with his ship's crew doubling as a film crew); *The Adderall Diaries* (2015, dir. Pamela Romanowsky) that integrates faux home movies; *Vice* (2018, dir. Adam McKay); and *Vox Lux* (2018, dir. Brady Corbet).[103] In *Vice*, McKay uses home-movie-style footage, going so far as to include sprocket holes; the overtness of the display of an outmoded technology (one likely unfamiliar to the memory of much of the audience) announces the fabrication, or better, the faux-fabrication of this material: we are at once shown a home movie and told (by emphasis) that it is fake. In this way, McKay may be going further into the *mise-en-abîme*, as he was in *The Big Short* (2015), into what might be named meta-metacinema; he seems to be saying: "this is how films, for one example *this film*, claiming to participate in the genre of biopics, might try to fool you—these films might use ersatz home-movie footage and time and again you fall for it, but not us, we the filmmakers: we make sure you know *we* are aware that this is fake, and also that we believe that *you*, the audience, should know that *we* know (and that we know *you* know)." As for *Vox Lux*, Manohla Dargis susses out its reason for employing the technique: "First heard over images resembling home movies of Celeste [Natalie Portman] and her family, the voice-over—which introduces Celeste by placing her on the 'losing side of Reaganomics' and refers to her 'predetermined destination'—also tips that she isn't the only creator of her story."[104] Metacinema is, in these cases, distinctly complicating auteur theory, a crucial development that calls for separate investigation.

Two final, recent instances as indications of the many permutations of—indeed, evolutionary adaptations of—amateur filmmaking, each reveal how home-movie techniques can be inventively cast within the context of a narrative feature. Consider, first, the novel use of the home-movie aesthetic in the opening credit sequence of *The Theory of Everything* (2014, dir. James Marsh), in which we are shown warm-toned, blurry glimpses of figures—one in a wheelchair—roving about in large, high-ceiled, ornamental halls. The time register shifts suddenly, the color goes pale and blue—we are sent to 1963—assuming what? That we have traveled back in time. Such an assumption is verified with only ten minutes of screen time remaining, that is, when the soft sepia tones of the title sequence *return*, and we find Stephen Hawking (Eddie Redmayne) and his loving family at Buckingham Palace, having been invited to visit the Queen. The blur comes into focus and we realize that the home-movie aesthetic (for example, by way of subtle shifts in grading and grain, color and frame rate, as well as a visual allusion to a certain buttery film stock) provided cues to frame the story and to signal that whatever we were seeing at the outset was from a different time, in this case, a later time.[105] While the first point is worth noting (that is to say, since framing by aesthetic contrast is familiar—taking us all the way back to *The Cabinet of Dr. Caligari* [1920, dir. Robert Wiene]), the second point is worth underscoring—namely, that here we have, as it were, a home movie *from the future*. Where in *Adam's Rib* and so many other indelible instances, home movies send us back in time, to the past, or in the case of *Raging Bull*, propel us onward through the present (speeding up exposition through a form of miniaturist compression), *The Theory of Everything* begins with a rethinking of our experience of temporality. How fitting for a film about time-theorist Stephen Hawking.

Lastly, we move from the rarefied groves of academe and the Queen's palace to the truly terrifying halls of middle school in *Eighth Grade* (2018), Bo Burnham's devastating glimpse of life for those who came to consciousness with the iPhone. Given all that has changed since we—and then our *children*—began carrying these devices, these miniature film studios, we should not be surprised that we see a still further evolution of the home movie. Even as the film uses the making of inspirational YouTube talks by Kayla (Elsie Fisher) to punctuate the contrast between lived life and life on screen, it is the creation of a home movie of herself, stored on a flash drive that I wish to emphasize. When Kayla plugs in the SpongeBob thumb drive (itself meant as a cultural time-marker), she watches and listens to a dispatch from her younger self. It's too much to bear. Horrified by what she sees and hears, she burns the drive—a kind of self-immolation by proxy. The violence against the media itself (figured here as an effigy) calls to mind not just the intensity of adolescent feelings (for example, where one is decidedly *not* caught up in some "archive fever," despite various fevers of sentiment), but, instead, caught off-guard by the embarrassment associated with the undeniable evidence that one exists.

* * *

If we have nodded to a few salient instances (among the many mainstream candidates in contemporary film that use the home-movie aesthetic as part of their storytelling device), there is, and remains—with Cavell still in mind—a need to explore those cases in which avant-garde and experimental cinema, ostensibly in a home-movie mode, in part, aspires not only to something like the conditions and criteria that constitute a feature film, but, in some cases, to the creation of or contribution to a film ontology of its own.[106] In this respect, the title of this chapter's parameter-setting notion of "in narrative cinema," at last, in these closing remarks, should be expanded to include its presumed opposites, namely, nonnarrative, experimental, and avant-garde film. The stakes for narrative cinema are still very much at hand, since any insight into the way(s) home movies—and/or the aesthetics of amateurism—are deployed in nonnarrative film enriches the present study (and the thoughts it might yield or inspire).

In a letter, Chris Marker, one of the foremost cinematic experimentalists of the twentieth century, said of his now canonical *Sans Soleil* (1983): "On a more matter-of-fact level, I could tell you that the film intended to be, and is nothing more than a home movie. I really think that my main talent has been to find people to pay for my home movies. Were I born rich, I guess I would have made more or less the same films, at least the traveling kind, but nobody would have heard of them except my friends and visitors."[107]

Turning to another innovator of experimental cinema, Jonas Mekas, we might describe his *Walden: Diaries, Notes, and Sketches* (1969) as a 180-minute home movie in the form of a feature film. Indeed, at one point in *Walden*, Mekas, speaking as himself in a bit of voice-over made with a Cartesian inflection: "I make home movies, therefore I live. I live, therefore I make home movies."[108] Moreover, trading on Thoreau—another decisive point of reference for Cavell—we see how Mekas' film "journal" (with footage captured over the course of five years) transforms fragments of film and the glimpses they offer (or obscure) into a sustained, hypnotic, revelatory epic. Indeed, the magnitude of a work such as *Walden* can make us rethink the very entrenched notions we customarily have about the criteria for "what counts" as a movie—feature fiction and otherwise—and everything else that (somehow) doesn't. Why, for example, should *The Mortgage the Merrier* enjoy its status as a home-movie/movie "inside" a bona fide Hollywood film and not, say, someone's private recordings (namely, those made at home)? What else, after all, were Marker and Mekas up to, if not that? Marker again: "I was naturally alone from beginning to end [of production], but with some exceptions that's my usual way to work."[109] Mekas' artistic transformation of his created footage—culminating in *Walden*—entreats us to consider the legitimacy of the home movie *as movie*. In an important way, Hollywood has long conferred this respect (if unintentionally) by employing its lower-tech aesthetic in the midst of its higher-tech, often stratospherically higher-budget, mainstream entertainments. Yet, despite the prevalent use of such home-spun techniques in the midst of big-budget fare, the art form familiar to amateurs and experimentalists is itself seldom spoken of with the explicit respect and reverence we regularly bestow on lesser creations of the studio system and its heirs. The containing/contained film relationship that has us looking for metacinematic traits and the fecund, if occasionally befuddling, contours of *mise-en-abîme*, are transformed in Mekas yet again, so that our thinking of what is possible "as home movie" and "as narrative cinema" (however avant-garde it may be!) is altered in the process of our encounter with these works of art.

As an indication of my concluding thesis—that the work of experimentalists, such as Marker and Mekas, illuminates new things about mainstream narrative cinema—we are shown by *Sans Soleil* and *Walden*, among other avant-garde forays, that "home movies" are not just about narcissistic self-regard, or private family archiving, but more so and more generally, about our fascination with the everyday: for example, those people and places and objects that contribute to our sense of reality at any given time, thus a house, its décor, the light and shadows, movements, speech inside and landscapes beyond the window, children, pets, etc. Cavell is sensible to this observation, and endorses it as standing in kinship with the motivations of Austin and Wittgenstein's ordinary language philosophy, and, more proximately to Mekas, the underwriting of the ordinary by Thoreau and Emerson before him.[110] As in the writing of fiction, so we are told that in the making of movies, it is the specificity of detail—not clichés and generic tropes, but the highly nuanced immediacy of objects, and the histories and memories people share—that makes us lean toward the screen. Likewise with home movies: their power is in their particularity. Tolstoy wrote that "all happy families are alike; each unhappy family is unhappy in its own way," but the reason a home movie *can* be interesting to everyone is the same reason a novel can be interesting to everyone: its radical specificity. And happiness or unhappiness is part of the moral and emotional gradation we come to know by watching home movies, by reading novels. Such is a lesson of the interaction between *Adam's Rib* and *The Mortgage the Merrier*: the unhappiness is very specific, but, to be sure, it is also comprehensible by us, the viewers—and across more than seventy years.

"One of the ways Godard defines the difference between fiction and documentary—as obsessive an issue for him as prostitution—is that documentary cannot contain the entirety of its subject; fiction is by definition self-contained,"[111] writes Amy Taubin in the critical notes for the Criterion DVD of *2 or 3 Things I Know About Her* (1967, *2 ou 3 choses que je sais d'elle*). When home movies "become" fiction (as they must in the hands of artificers and fabulizers), then they also become "self-contained." In this sense, we cannot ask for more footage from *The Mortgage the Merrier*, whereas we can for Mekas' *Walden*. Using a master-term from Cavell's discussion, we might repurpose things to say that home movies are always "uncontained"—and it is this emotional and ethical expansiveness that, we might at last conclude, is part of why an amateur home-movie aesthetic is desirable for feature fiction films. The impression of a world "uncontained"— of an existence beyond the confines of the story, of the narrative fiction, indeed, *beyond the frame*—is just too tempting not to exploit.[112] Since 1949, we have had our fixed sense of the fiction of *Adam's Rib*, while we are encouraged to fantasize beyond the boundaries of *The Mortgage the Merrier* to imagine Amanda and Adam's life in the Connecticut countryside. Thinking of Godard's distinction between fiction and nonfiction, then, we gain some orientation to the presence of the home movie in narrative cinema generally. While following Godard we could say that the fictional narrative is whole and self-contained, yet for the presence of this so-called home movie we are compelled to imagine its expansiveness—to imagine that it is part of the world that is in effect *not captured* on film, that exceeds the nature of narrative and thus of art. Again, Cavell's distinction between "projection" and "recording," invoked earlier, may be profitably recalled for giving conceptual expression to these vexing, increasingly blurred scenarios of cinematic (and post-filmic) experience.

One of the things home movies—and the aesthetic of amateur filmmaking—do, not just in their mainstream classic and contemporary variations, or even in their avant-garde and experimental instances, is remind us of something Garrett Stewart noted at the outset of the volume, namely that "since Cavell wrote, and long since the films that counted for him, the fact that cinema is not a recording but a projection may seem all the clearer when it is no longer film at all."[113] I ask rhetorically: What else is a metacinematic scene in which characters watch home movies (and we, of course, watch them watching) but a picture of this account of film's (or cinema's) ontology? The home movie "in" a movie (while also *being* a movie) announces how cinema's world is a projected one. For this reason, we return to Stewart's observations at the beginning of these proceedings on Cavell's understanding of film ontology that there is "something centrally underspecified in Cavell's definition of film as a 'succession of automatic world projections'—rather than just world *pictures*."[114] In the subtitle to Cavell's first book on film (referenced in the present book's subtitle), we have again, on this occasion, and seemingly ever anew, to contend with the rich, ineluctable doubleness of our senses of *reflection*.

With *Adam's Rib*—and its little gem, *The Mortgage the Merrier*, made to look like a home movie—and in company with Stanley Cavell's astute, enduring criticism of both, we are better positioned to think about the broad expanse of uses home movies are put to, and not just in mainstream narrative cinema, but also in the capacious collection of works that can and should draw our critical interest: from installation art to independent films, from avant-garde and experimental pieces to mainstream confections, from private archives to public performance art, from smartphone footage to high-end Hollywood productions. The seemingly modest little genre, plotting technique, and exposition device often hides in plain sight, and for its tenacious hold on our imaginations, it continues to proliferate in inventive instances worthy of our sustained and savvy deliberation. The humility of the home movie belies the deep and dynamic moral and emotional registers it can achieve as well as the transformative effects it can reveal for our thinking about cinematic ontology more generally. And so, for all of these reasons, when the home movie starts playing, we do not—as conventional wisdom would have it—turn away. As a medium and as a genre, as an approach to storytelling, or better, story *creation*, the melodrama of the home movie feels inherent, something we recognize, no doubt, because it is just the kind of film we might find ourselves in. A persistent fascination with the ontology of the film (perhaps for most a largely unconscious or unarticulated allure), coupled with a more readily discernable and abiding interest in ourselves and each other (especially as we appear on screen), confirms our historical and ongoing obsession with the aesthetics of amateur filmmaking. We are as we were, as if stars made for one another.[115]

Notes

1   The two films under consideration are *Adam's Rib* and *The Mortgage the Merrier* and the three temporal levels include the time of the home movie (at the country house in Connecticut), the time of the soirée in the city (the diegetic space of *Adam's Rib*), and whenever we screen *Adam's Rib* in our present. (Whether *Adam's Rib* and *The Mortgage the Merrier* are, in fact, two films will be discussed below).

2   "Watching Home Movies with Stanley Cavell" is the title of the remarks I offered at "Le Pensée du cinéma: en hommage à Stanley Cavell," Université Paris 1 Panthéon Sorbonne, Paris, June 2019, organized by Sandra Laugier and Elise Domenach.

3   For a set of crucial touchstones on related points, including home movies *without* quotation marks, see Patricia R. Zimmermann, *Reel Families: A Social History of Amateur Film* (Bloomington: Indiana University Press, 1995); Michelle Citron, *Home Movies and Other Necessary Fictions* (Minneapolis: University of Minnesota Press, 1998); James M. Moran, *There's No Place Like Home Video* (Minneapolis: University of Minnesota Press, 2002); *Mining the Home Movie: Excavations in Histories and Memories*, ed. Karen L. Ishizuka and Patricia R. Zimmermann (Berkeley: University of California Press, 2008); and *Amateur Filmmaking: The Home Movie, the Archive, the Web*, ed. Laura Rascaroli, Gwenda Young, and Barry Monahan (New York: Bloomsbury, 2014). Also, at the outset, I wish to express special and emphatic thanks to dearly appreciated collaborators: to Garrett Stewart and William Day who, along with other and anonymous readers, have provided crucial feedback and incisive commentary on earlier versions of this chapter; and to Paul Cronin, who was an indispensable ally in this venture—so full of pertinent resources, along with wit and care, and generosity with all of them.

4   David LaRocca, "Introduction: Representative Qualities and Questions of Documentary Film," *The Philosophy of Documentary Film: Image, Sound, Fiction, Truth*, ed. David LaRocca (Lanham: Lexington Books of Rowman & Littlefield, 2017a), 9.

5   See David LaRocca, "Shooting for the Truth: Amateur Documentary Filmmaking, Affective Optics, and the Ethical Impulse," *Post Script: Essays in Film and the Humanities* 26, no. 2 and 3 (Winter/Spring/Summer 2017b), Dan Geva and Yvonne Kozlovsky-Golan, guest editors.

6   Ludwig Wittgenstein, *Tractatus Logico-Philosophicus* (London: Kegan Paul, 1922), 88, § 6.421, where he writes "Ethik und Asthetik sind Eins."

7   I have speculated, on another occasion, that a civilian's "memories of war" may simply (and solely) be those images of war films watched—and sounds

heard—over the course of a lifetime. See David LaRocca, "Introduction: War Films and the Ineffability of War," in *The Philosophy of War Films*, ed. David LaRocca (Lexington: The University Press of Kentucky, 2014), 41. For a related sense of the integration of cinematic experience into personal memory, see *The World Viewed*, where Cavell puts it this way: "We involve the movies in us. They become further fragments of what happens to me, further cards in the shuffle of my memory." 154.

8   Stanley Cavell, *The World Viewed: Reflections on the Ontology of Film*, Expanded Edition (Cambridge: Harvard University Press, 1971/1979), 31.

9   Erwin Panofsky, "Style and Medium in the Moving Pictures," in *Film*, ed. Daniel Talbot (New York: Simon and Schuster, 1959), 18; cited in Cavell, *The World Viewed*, 30.

10 Cavell, *The World Viewed*, 31.

11 Ibid., 31. On the question of the "mere actualities of film mechanics," we can see resemblances and hear resonances of the tradition of *actualités*, which has been given account by Tom Gunning in "The Cinema of Attraction[s]: Early Film, Its Spectatorship, and the Avant-Garde," in *The Cinema of Attractions Reloaded*, ed. Wanda Strauven (Amsterdam: University of Amsterdam Press, 2006), 381–88; and "Before Documentary: Early Nonfiction Films and the 'View' Aesthetic," in *The Philosophy of Documentary Film: Image, Sound, Fiction, Truth*, ed. David LaRocca (Lanham: Lexington Books of Rowman & Littlefield, 2017a), 159–74.

12 Cavell, *The World Viewed*, 31.

13 See Ibid., 31–32 on genre and medium. I draw from Cavell's discussion for further remarks on genre and idiom in David LaRocca, "From Lectiocentrism to Gramophonology: Listening to Cinema and Writing Sound Criticism," in *The Geschlecht Complex: Addressing Untranslatable Aspects of Gender, Genre, and Ontology*, ed. Oscar Jansson and David LaRocca (New York: Bloomsbury, 2022), 201–67.

14 Stanley Cavell, *Cities of Words: Pedagogical Letters on a Register of the Moral Life* (Cambridge: Harvard University Press, 2004), 70–73.

15 For more on the "green world," see Stanley Cavell, *Pursuits of Happiness: The Hollywood Comedy of Remarriage* (Cambridge: Harvard University Press, 1981), 49, 105, 172.

16 Cavell, *Cities of Words*, 71.

17 For historical reference on the personal lives of these indelible actors, Spencer Tracy never divorced his first and only wife, Louise Treadwell, yet remained with Hepburn from 1941 (when they kindled a romance during the filming of *Woman of the Year*) until his death in 1967. Hepburn herself was only married once (to S. Ogden Ludlow, 1928–34), and never remarried.

18 Patrick McGilligan, *George Cukor: A Double Life; A Biography of the Gentleman Director* (Minneapolis: University of Minnesota Press, 2013); first published by St. Martin's Griffin Press, New York (1997), 200. The breakdown of the familiar onset/offset binary is intriguing, since, as noted, *Adam's Rib* becomes its own species of (Hepburn and Tracy's) home movie. Along similar lines, in correspondence, Byron Davies has shared generative notes on films

that I hope to take up in a future study, including Guy Maddin's *My Winnipeg* (2009) "in which the director uses the film to re-stage his own home, so that the whole film constitutes a kind of home movie." Richard Billingham's *Ray & Liz* (2018) undertakes a similar approach. Though no filming of Hepburn and Tracy was done at Cukor's Hollywood home, "there are examples of movies in which the director has filmed in [his] own home, like in some of Cassavetes' movies." Given these points of reference, we can ponder anew the ways that *Adam's Rib* (perhaps also like *Woman of the Year* and other Hepburn-Tracy collaborations) functions like a home movie for them, and in turn, for us. Haven't we grown to appreciate this documentary aspect of celebrity couples in motion pictures, the way private lives and relationships seem to be uncannily on display for us—as, for example, in Brad Pitt and Angelina Jolie's *Mr. & Mrs. Smith* and *By the Sea*; or Tom Cruise and Nicole Kidman's *Days of Thunder*, *Far and Away*, and *Eyes Wide Shut*; or earlier in Richard Burton and Elizabeth Taylor's *Cleopatra*, *Who's Afraid of Virginia Woolf?* and *Divorce His—Divorce Hers*?

19 Ruth Gordon and Garson Kanin were screenwriting collaborators on not just *Adam's Rib* (1949), and with George Cukor, but also on *A Double Life* (1947, dir. Cukor); *Pat and Mike* (1952, dir. Cukor); *The Marrying Kind* (1952, dir. Cukor); and *The Actress* (1953, dir. Cukor).

20 On the last page of *Pursuits of Happiness*, in the Acknowledgments, we could say that Cavell ratified some of these generative puns and permutations—and their multiple modes of signification—when he wrote: "Amanda's name incorporates a man and an Adam" (278). Such an observation reminds us that hard as it is to see some things, it is often even harder to see them first. We are left to wonder if precedence conveys authority over, even authorship of, what we notice in films (or fail to notice until shown). In this way, precedence forces upon others the citationality of interpretation. If, as Cavell said, "my ignorance and inattentiveness sting me in such a matter," there is no doubt relief in finding another who illuminates the world on my behalf, or in my company, affording "gasps of pleasure in overcoming both." Cavell, *A Pitch of Philosophy*, 181.

21 *Adam's Rib*, 01:28:00.

22 In correspondence about this passage, William Day helpfully notes that "a two-reeler—20–24 minutes—was considered, up to a few years before *The Birth of a Nation*, the maximum length that your typical viewing audience could sit still for. The arrival of films contained on two reels was when the designation 'feature film' was first used. So, to speak of a 'two-reel epic' would have been kind of redundant up to World War I. You might take this as further evidence of *The Mortgage the Merrier*'s (and *Adam's Rib*'s) interest in alluding to the history of film, beyond its allusions to documentary and silent and home movies."

Also, for reference, consider how the duration of a reel changes over time; like the word "film," a "reel" shifts into figurative territory as technologies evolve. A five-reel film from 1918, *Station Content*, starring Gloria Swanson and Lee Hill clocks in at twelve minutes, which means that a reel amounts to about two-and-a-half minutes. If even this duration holds for our example, a "two reel epic" would be a five-minute film, which seems just about the right length for a home movie shared with friends. https://nyti.ms/2IDNogL

23 Henry David Thoreau, "Economy," in *Walden; Or, Life in the Woods* (1845).
24 *Adam's Rib*, 27:32 to 31:32.
25 Cavell, *Pursuits of Happiness*, 192.
26 Ibid., 191.
27 Ibid., 206.
28 Ibid., 207.
29 David LaRocca, "Shooting for the Truth: Amateur Documentary Filmmaking, Affective Optics, and the Ethical Impulse" (2017b).
30 For remarks on the home-movie camera on the war front, see David LaRocca, "Introduction: War Films and the Ineffability of War," e.g., 47–48.
31 Cavell, *Pursuits of Happiness*, 207.
32 The ubiquity of video-equipped smartphones has also given rise to an ethical and political dimension of amateur filmmaking, namely, home movies of violence and brutality. In turn, the capture may be coupled with immediate distribution via the internet. For more on these lines of inquiry, see again LaRocca, "Shooting for the Truth: Amateur Documentary Filmmaking, Affective Optics, and the Ethical Impulse" (2017b).
33 The film frame skips at 00:28:30, and speeds up for a few seconds at 00:29:08; "Censored!" appears on a card at 00:30:51; and the film frame is flipped upside down at 00:31:12.
34 For Adam and Amanda, there is a question of access (viz., what cameras are available at the time?) and class (e.g., what camera would two lawyers likely buy for their home-recording needs?). 16mm was introduced in 1923; the smaller-by-half, Depression-era 8mm did not appear until 1932. But for size and convenience, we know that even today when 4K DSLRs are available, and many have the means to acquire the equipment, most people revert to the camera-in-the-pocket: the home-movie camera default is none other than the smartphone. (With thanks to both William Day and Paul Cronin for input on this matter.)

Indeed, the *use* of the smartphone-as-home-movie-camera is a common element of plotting, not to mention a conspicuous contributor to *mise-en-scène*. Among many recent examples, see *Spider-Man: Homecoming* (2017, dir. John Watts), which opens with "A Film by Peter Parker," a metacinematic trick of a home movie and what is soon-after referred to as a "video diary." Though we see that Peter (Tom Holland) is using an iPhone to create his footage, as in *Adam's Rib*, we are not always sure what is being used to create the footage *we* see. Did Watts, in fact, use an iPhone—like Baker, Soderbergh, Gondry, et al.—to shoot parts of his $175 million feature production?

35 *Adam's Rib*, 00:29:53.
36 All quotations by Chazelle and Sandgren in this paragraph are drawn from Chris O'Falt, "*First Man*: How Damien Chazelle Used Handheld 16mm Cameras to Cut Through the Neal Armstrong Myth," IndieWire.com, November 1, 2018.

37 Thanks to Hugo Clémot for notes on *Minority Report*.
38 For more on Joi's significance as a projection, see Stephen Mulhall, "'The Alphabet of Us': Miracles, Messianism, and the Baseline Test in *Blade Runner 2049*," presented at "Le Pensée du cinéma: en hommage à Stanley Cavell," Université Paris 1 Panthéon Sorbonne, Paris (June 2019), and featured in *Blade Runner 2049: A Philosophical Exploration*, ed. Timothy Shanahan and Paul Smart (New York: Routledge, 2020), 27-47.
39 Cavell, *Pursuits of Happiness*, 207.
40 Ibid., 212–13.
41 Cavell calls Kip's narration "grating" in *Pursuits of Happiness*, 211.
42 Cavell, *Pursuits of Happiness*, 213.
43 *Adam's Rib*, 00:26:35.
44 *Adam's Rib*, 00:27:35.
45 *Adam's Rib*, 00:27:36.
46 *Adam's Rib*, 00:29:18.
47 *Adam's Rib*, 00:29:49.
48 *Adam's Rib*, 00:31:32.
49 Cavell, *Pursuits of Happiness*, 207.
50 Ibid.
51 See David LaRocca, "Object Lessons: What Cyanotypes Teach Us About Digital Media," in *Photography's Materialities: Transatlantic Photographic Practices over the Long Nineteenth Century*, ed. Rasmus Simonsen and Geoff Bender (Leuven: Leuven University Press, 2021), 209–35.
52 Cavell, *Pursuits of Happiness*, 208.
53 As Dennis Lim put the matter: "Jean-Luc Godard once observed that every fictional film is a documentary of its actors. Jacques Rivette finessed the aphorism, proposing that every film is a documentary of its own making, not only a record for posterity of the people in it but also a window into the culture that produced it. In a very literal sense, all films have documentary aspects: once the camera is turned on, whatever is captured, no matter how staged, contains a trace of reality, an element of chance. The inverse is true as well: no documentary, whatever its claims to objective reportage, is ever devoid of manipulation, since a controlling hand is evident in even the most routine matters of camera placement and shot selection." "It's Actual Life. No, It's Drama. No, It's Both," August 20, 2010, *The New York Times*, nytimes.com. https://nyti.ms/2GDdIqk
54 Moreover, the films in this trio are regularly described in terms of their resemblance to Malick's autobiographical experience, which, like *The Tree of Life* before them, can encourage us to reflect on the cinematic translation or transformation of personal history—including its abstraction—much as we would for more standard expressions of the home movie.
55 Cavell, *Pursuits of Happiness*, 207.

56 See LaRocca (2017a), 10, 25; and Jack C. Ellis, *John Grierson, Life, Contributions, Influence* (Carbondale: Southern Illinois University Press, 2000), 347.

57 For more on this line of thought, see Cavell, *The World Viewed*, "The World as Mortal: Absolute Age and Youth," ch. 12, 74–80.

58 *Adam's Rib*, 00:29:33.

59 *Adam's Rib*, 00:29:58.

60 Despite my invocation of *Closed Circuits*, the quotations attributed to Garrett Stewart here are drawn from our correspondence about an earlier draft of this chapter. For more along the lines to which Stewart is directing our attention, consult *Closed Circuits: Screening Narrative Surveillance* (Chicago: The University of Chicago Press, 2015). See also Stewart's *Framed Time: Toward of Postfilmic Cinema* (Chicago: The University of Chicago Press, 2007), 195, 201.

61 Cavell, *Pursuits of Happiness*, 207.

62 Cavell, *The World Viewed*, 90.

63 Ibid., 102.

64 Ibid., 101.

65 Ibid., 95.

66 Ibid., 102.

67 See in this volume, Kyle Stevens, "The World Heard" (chapter 3), and see again, LaRocca, "From Lectiocentrism to Gramophonology: Listening to Cinema and Writing Sound Criticism."

68 Cavell, *Pursuits of Happiness*, 209.

69 Sincere thanks to Paul Cronin for our conversations—and his elucidations—on this point.

70 LaRocca, "Introduction: Representative Qualities and Questions of Documentary Film," 25.

71 See David LaRocca, "Weimar Cognitive Theory: Modernist Narrativity and the Metaphysics of Frame Stories (After *Caligari* and Kracauer)," in *The Fictional Minds of Modernism: Narrative Cognition from Henry James to Christopher Isherwood*, ed. Ricardo Miguel-Alfonso (New York: Bloomsbury, 2020), 179–204.

72 Patricia Erens, "Home Movies in Commercial Narrative Film," *Journal of Film and Video* 38, no. 3/4 (Summer–Fall 1986): 99–101.

73 Ibid., 99.

74 Cavell, *Pursuits of Happiness*, 209.

75 Ibid., 209.

76 In addition to the origin story that finds a young Spielberg equipped with an 8mm camera, we can also see a mature point of reference in his production credit for J. J. Abrams' *Super 8* (2011), a film whose title invokes a specific type of film stock and at that one distinctively associated with the creation of home movies.

77 Vicky opens the hat at 00:42:18 and puts on the white outfit at 00:42:26.
78 *Raging Bull*, 00:41:11.
79 Cavell, *The World Viewed*, 183.
80 For more on *Redacted*, see *The Philosophy of War Films*, 47–48, 144–46, 154–55, 161.
81 For more on *The Final Cut*, see Garrett Stewart, *Framed Time*, 171, 188, 190, 195, 212. For more on Charlie Kaufman and *Eternal Sunshine of the Spotless Mind*, see *The Philosophy of Charlie Kaufman*, ed. David LaRocca (Lexington: The University Press of Kentucky, 2011; paperback with new preface, 2019).
82 LaRocca, "Introduction: Representative Qualities and Questions of Documentary Film," 19.
83 *The Magnificent Ambersons*, 00:03:01.
84 David Bordwell, "Return to Paranormalcy," November 13, 2012, http://www.davidbordwell.net/blog/2012/11/13/return-to-paranormalcy/
85 See David LaRocca, "A Reality Rescinded: The Transformative Effects of Fraud in *I'm Still Here*," in *The Philosophy of Documentary Film: Image, Sound, Fiction, Truth*, ed. David LaRocca (Lanham: Lexington Books of Rowman & Littlefield, 2017a), esp. 551–52 and 562. See also, in the same volume, Karen D. Hoffman, "'Deceiving into the Truth': The Indirect Cinema of *Stories We Tell* and *The Act of Killing*," 517–36.
86 See Hoffman, "Deceiving into the Truth."
87 See LaRocca, "Introduction: Representative Qualities and Questions of Documentary Film," 10, 25.
88 Ibid., 25; and Jack C. Ellis, *John Grierson, Life, Contributions, Influence* (Carbondale: Southern Illinois University Press, 2000), 347.
89 For my development of the notion of hoax *vérité*, see LaRocca, "Introduction: Representative Qualities and Questions of Documentary Film," 40 and "A Reality Rescinded: The Transformative Effects of Fraud in *I'm Still Here*," 537–76.
90 See again Hoffman (in LaRocca 2017a), 517–36.
91 See *Killer Images: Documentary Film, Memory, and the Performance of Violence*, ed. Joram ten Brink and Joshua Oppenheimer (New York: Wallflower Press, 2013) and *Building Bridges: The Cinema of Jean Rouch*, ed. Joram ten Brink (New York: Wallflower Press, 2008).
92 See Noël Carroll, "Fiction, Non-Fiction, and the Film of Presumptive Assertion," in *Philosophy of Film and Motion Pictures: An Anthology*, ed. Noël Carroll and Jinhee Choi (Oxford: Blackwell, 2006). See also LaRocca, "Introduction: Representative Qualities and Questions of Documentary Film," 8, 29, and Gregory Currie, "Documenting Traces and the Content of Photographs" (chapter three) in *The Philosophy of Documentary Film*.
93 Thanks to William Rothman for remarks on Ozu and Wilder at "Le Pensée du cinéma: en hommage à Stanley Cavell," Université Paris 1 Panthéon Sorbonne, Paris, June 2019.

94 Cavell, *The World Viewed*, ix.
95 For more on *Peeping Tom*, see Erens, "Home Movies in Commercial Narrative Film," 100.
96 *Muriel*, 00:52:16.
97 *Muriel*, 00:54:57.
98 See also Erens, "Home Movies in Commercial Narrative Film," 100.
99 This passage comes from a piece of correspondence with Garrett Stewart, who generously shared his remarks. I wish to add a further set of notes from Stewart, sustaining his close reading of *The Way We Were*:

> In the original campus episode, as discreetly filmed (though we wouldn't notice at the time) by one of her fellow undergrads, the leftist firebrand Katie Morosky, after turning the assembled students' jeers to cheers at a campus peace rally with her message, is sabotaged from behind her back. As her voice blares through the microphone to "stand up for world peace now," suddenly up from behind her—on handheld wooden stakes—come five handwritten placards with the block capitals P-E-A-C-E, the first four then mockingly reversed to ANY-PEACE-BUT-KATIE'S, the E cipher left hanging for an extra second—as if it might mean peace on any terms less radical and absolute. But with the target of the ensuing sexual prank unaware of it, indeed still speaking over it, the four letters-turned-words are then followed—after the special syntactic and phonetic pause they induce—with the obviously missing punch-word PIECE. In [Michel] Chion's terms, it is as if the lag-time of phonetic recognition entailed by any on-screen writing is thus visualized, performed twice over, by this dramatic optical pause. No sooner, that is, has the piecemeal nature of alphabetic word formation been spelled out in five isolated graphemes than these are flipped to word forms, one scalar notch up, that depend on the separate temporality of reaction time. Not accidentally, it is something of this cognitive interspace between homonym or homograph (world peace, Katy's peace) and homophone (peace/piece) that wax ontological in [Giorgio] Agamben's recently translated essay on "The Sayable and the Idea" in his return to Aristotle on homonymy.

> For his own part, Stewart has mobilized a remarkable series of claims regarding a select but indelible filmography of Barbra Streisand to the effect that we might wish to claim, as Stewart puts it, and placing his thesis in company with Cavell's own brand of genre-definition/invention: "that the radical innovation of the Streisand persona was to create a genre all its (her) own: the problematic comedy of nonremarriage—*Funny Girl, Funny Lady, The Way We Were, A Star is Born, Prince of Tides*: always the too-known Man That Got Away, with its reincarnation loophole in *On A Clear Day*."

100 Reflections on *My Life* as well as some of the phrasing for describing it developed in correspondence with Paul Cronin.
101 For more on memory and representation, see David LaRocca, "Memory Man: The Constitution of Personal Identity in *Memento*," in *The Philosophy of Christopher Nolan*, ed. Jason T. Eberl and George A. Dunn (Lanham:

Lexington Books of Rowman & Littlefield, 2017); and "Memories: In the End, Is That All There Is?" *Downton Abbey and Philosophy: Thinking in That Manor*, ed. Adam Barkman and Robert Arp (Chicago: Open Court, 2016).

102 Thanks to Hugo Clémot for notes on *Cinema Paradiso* and to Christian Martin for recalling *Falling Down*.

103 For more on *The Family Man*, see LaRocca, "Weimar Cognitive Theory."

104 Manohla Dargis, "*Vox Lux* Review: An Apocalyptic Star is Born," December 6, 2018, *The New York Times* (nytimes.com), https://nyti.ms/2zKiIo8

105 See again, see LaRocca, "Weimar Cognitive Theory."

106 For more on Cavell and nonnarrative, non-Hollywood cinema, see in this volume, Scott MacDonald, "My Troubled Relationship with Stanley Cavell: In Pursuit of a Truly Cinematic Conversation" (chapter 5).

107 Chris Marker, "Letter to Theresa by Chris Marker—Behind the Veils of *Sans Soleil*": chrismarker.org/chris-marker/notes-to-theresa-on-sans-soleil-by-chris-marker/

108 Jonas Mekas, *The Story of Jonas Mekas*, "I make home movies, therefore I live. I live, therefore I make home movies," appears at https://youtu.be/n2sK_EuH_KU?t=21s.

109 Marker, "Letter to Theresa."

110 Among the places Cavell discusses the relationship between the ordinary and the work of film, see Andrew Klevan, "Guessing the Unseen from the Seen: Stanley Cavell and Film Interpretation," *Contending with Stanley Cavell*, ed. Russell Goodman (Oxford: Oxford University Press, 2005), 118–39; and "What Becomes of Thinking on Film?" (Stanley Cavell in conversation with Andrew Klevan), *Film as Philosophy: Essays in Cinema after Wittgenstein and Cavell* (New York: Palgrave Macmillan, 2005), 167–209.

111 Amy Taubin, "The Whole and Its Parts," in the folio accompanying the Criterion DVD#482, *2 ou 3 choses que je sais d'elle* (1967, dir. Jean-Luc Godard).

112 Here we are put in mind of Cavell's remarks in *The World Viewed* on the difference between a painting and a photograph, namely, that the "world of a painting is not continuous with the world of its frame; at its frame, a world finds its limits. We might say: a painting is a world; a photograph is of the world. What happens in a photograph is that it comes to an end" (24). See also Eyal Peretz, *The Off-Screen: An Investigation of the Cinematic Frame* (Stanford: Stanford University Press, 2017).

113 See in this volume, Stewart (chapter 1), 27.

114 See in this volume, ibid., 34.

115 For more on this point, see LaRocca, *The Philosophy of Documentary Film*, 16–17.

ACKNOWLEDGMENTS

A reader arriving at the first line of the first chapter may wonder what Garrett Stewart means when he says, "Celebration—and further spurred celebration—is the business at hand. Little room, or even occasion, for lament." As a quick midrash, the lament is for Stanley Cavell's death at the age of ninety-one on June 19, 2018. Juneteenth. The celebration, well, the *celebration* is in some sense everything before and after that cleave point: the remarkable ninety-one years that led up to it and the now boundless future that awaits his legacy. We, those gathered together in this volume, and those who pick it up to read it, are part of this "other side." We are still here to think about Cavell and so we shall.

Given the timelines for most scholarly books, from pitch to production to publication, it should go without saying that Stanley died during the gestation of this project. So though the collection—its topic, its mandate, what we might hope for it and from it—was conceived while he was still a living companion to our thinking, part of our inheritance of his work (his singular voice, his distinctive philosophical bequest) is to discover how to continue that companionship in his absence. As a result, as editor, I found myself deliberating with contributors about changing the tense of verbs ("Is 'would' less bittersweet now?" asked one attuned reader of a sentence that was written before his death but read after it).

Cavell's writing—with "a voice like no other in philosophy now, or ever" (said Arthur Danto)—is perhaps uniquely gifted with his presence. He is still audible to us, though we may have never met him; this attribute of his prose, surely, owing as much to his uncommon philosophical acumen as his mastery of a life in letters, must be counted as another virtue of his talent. As many contributors to this volume have spent decades reading and responding to Cavell, so, happily, there remains much left to say, to think. As it happened, what was meant to be another intervention into the ongoing reception of Cavell's work has become an inadvertent memorial. Though Cavell will not see this book, we, the contributors, might hope it is a fitting tribute—part of our effort at making our way in the world without him, if ever, gratefully and gratifyingly in the continued company of his prose.

If Cavell's work was the object of our attention in creating these pages, and his memory part of our encounter with it hereafter, it is to the contributors of the volume—to *their* work—that I sincerely offer my most immediate and heartfelt thanks. I have been continually impressed by the force and effect of their ingenuity and am grateful for their generosity in making such findings and innovations available for this occasion.

The four astute (and anonymous) referees for the press were absolutely essential to the final form of the manuscript. They proposed, in one perceptive appraisal after another, probing notes for refinement that made me and the contributors feel very much in good hands. To the referees: thank you for your time, care, and, of course, suffering the particular ache that must come from doing a good job that will (seemingly) remain (forever) unknown to your obliged peers. Though we do not know who you are, our work is better for your labors. At such moments, one feels a true realization of an academic community operating in good faith, with good will.

It is a continual pleasure to thank Haaris Naqvi for his reliable, informed judgment; I so very much appreciate his perspective and his fellowship. And now, at last, with delight, I get to thank Katie Gallof, who so ably shepherded this book to its present incarnation; her savvy reading and incisive responses prompted many delightful innovations for which I am duly grateful. I wish to extend my thanks to her competent colleagues at Bloomsbury who lent their care and skills to the project—especially Erin Duffy and the ever-impressive design team. And lastly, Arub Ahmed, Zoë Jellicoe, and Leela Ulaganathan, who made the final phase of production seamless.

Engagement with colleagues and students at several institutions have been crucial to the development of this and related initiatives, in particular, while I served as Visiting Scholar in the Department of English at Cornell University; Lecturer in the Department of Cinema, Photography, and Media Arts at the Roy H. Park School of Communications at Ithaca College; Visiting Assistant Professor in the Department of Philosophy at the College at Cortland, State University of New York; and Visiting Assistant Professor in the Cinema Department at Binghamton University.

I have enjoyed an unexpected bounty of good summer hours among remarkable visitors to Ithaca, many of them arriving for participation in The School of Criticism and Theory at Cornell University. In recent years, Hent de Vries has presided as an adroit moderator, matched auspiciously by his legendary presentations. I wish to thank him for his rare combination of affability and penetrating reflection. In this same substantive, if temporary, community, I convey my thanks to Emily Apter and members of the "Thinking in Untranslatables" seminar as well as to Philippe Descola, Shoshana Felman, Avishai Margalit, Michael Puett, and Anthony Vidler.

An invitation to the University of Arizona in April 2018, for the New Directions conference, placed me in the company of a receptive and canny audience. Emily Thomas' conscientious hosting and cordial introduction to her community, including student and faculty members of the Department of English, made the occasion a pleasure and propitious. Fielding informed questions about film sound and genre and making relevant forays into experimental and avant-garde cinema were decisive for refinements of thought.

An invitation to Israel, with time spent in the company of gracious hosts Shai Biderman, Dan Geva, and Ohad Landesman proved transformative. The "Docusophia: Documentary Film and Philosophy" conference in May 2018, sponsored by the Steve Tisch School of Film and Television, Tel Aviv University, in collaboration with the Docaviv Film Festival, provided a chance to hear many crucial remarks on the state of documentary film's conjunction with philosophy and to learn from Linda Williams and Thomas Wartenberg, students and scholars based in Israel, among many others. Meeting Avner Faingulernt in Tel Aviv was a highlight (thank you Diana Allan for liaising the connection). For intellectual and cinematic adventuring in Tel Aviv and Jerusalem, I am joyfully indebted to Dan Geva, his family, and their friends and colleagues—including members of the Jerusalem Sam Spiegel Film School. And for unmatched accommodation in Jerusalem, I remain grateful to Amos and Jan Avgar (and Ariel and Christie Avgar back in Ithaca).

In the wake of creating the film *Brunello Cucinelli: A New Philosophy of Clothes*, I have welcomed a continuing relationship with Brunello Cucinelli and Giorgiana Magnolfi, including the sustained hospitality of the Solomeo community. An invitation for a return visit to the Umbrian campus, in September 2018, was fortifying as was a sojourn beyond it—with thanks for arrangements at Abbazia di Monte Oliveto Maggiore under the guidance of Brother Francesco. In Florence, the salutary hours spent with Alessandro Subrizi and the expanded family, along with dear Tekla, Elio, and Katja Wessling, remain conspicuous in my mind and memory.

An invitation to Lund, Sweden, in October 2018 precipitated a generative visit with Oscar Jansson and enabled the continuation of our intellectual collaboration. I am grateful to Oscar and his colleagues at the Centre for Languages and Literatures and the Department of Comparative Literature at Lund University for a warm welcome, fine accommodation, and invigorating discussions of Cavell, cinematic sound, and *Geschlecht*.

"Celebrating the Life and Work of Stanley Cavell," convened in Emerson Hall 105, Harvard University, on November 10, 2018, was the condition for much reflection and remembering within a community of people who share deep feelings about Cavell and steady commitments to his work; it was a privilege to be among them and benefit from their support. Heartfelt good wishes to Charles Bernstein for permission to use, as the book's epigraph, a line he spoke at the memorial event. On that day, he recalled how fifty years had elapsed since he first met Cavell in that same room, when Bernstein was a freshman in the college. The tense of the line—past, not continuous present—also marks a quiet memorial at the opening of the book. It is a claim for Cavell—and for us, in the lines that follow after it—to attempt to make sense of it in *our* continuous present, so long as that lasts.

Richard Eldridge, Paul Cronin, and Sukhdev Sandhu formed the admirable trinity at the "Think Herzog!" event in April 2019, sponsored by the Colloquium for Unpopular Culture and the Deutsches Haus at New York University. Under the auspices of Sara Girner, capable Cultural Program Coordinator of the Deutsches Haus, our conversation was distinctly Herzogian: roving, risky, and full of intellectual surprise. Later, when Thomas Elsaesser said, "meet me at the Marlton," I knew good things were in store. I am grateful to him for supplying, clearly to the advantage of this book, such a characteristically congenial Foreword, which means in this case offering words of welcome that set the tone, and offer a model, for our collective undertaking.

Thank you to Sandra Laugier—and her colleagues and co-organizers, especially Elise Domenach—for the invitation to Paris in June 2019 for "Le Pensée du cinéma: en hommage à Stanley Cavell," convened at Université Paris 1 Panthéon Sorbonne. I benefited from a range of remarks on Cavell's work presented at the conference and was privileged to have the opportunity to share portions of my chapter and receive feedback from a community whose opinion on Cavell and cinema I so much admire and have learned from. A few participants went out of their way to offer constructive comments on this project, including my chapter contribution, that proved amplifying and clarifying, among them Stephen Mulhall, Andrew Klevan, Byron Davies, Hugo Clémot, and Elise Domenach.

A very special thanks to Amir Khan, Sérgio Dias Branco, and the Advisory Board at *Conversations: The Journal of Cavellian Studies*, who entrusted me with the guest editorship of a commemorative issue, "Acknowledging Stanley Cavell," No. 7, which appeared on July 19, 2019. Furthermore, I am grateful to the contributors of the issue for creating new conditions for approaching the inheritance of Cavell's work.

My thanks to the community of supportive people who lent good advice and good cheer during the project's gestation: Steven Affeldt, J. M. Bernstein, Joel Bettridge, Jason and Catherine Blumenkamp, Elisabeth Bronfen, Rebecca M. Brown, Elisabeth Ceppi, Samuel A. Chambers, Alice Crary, Simon Critchley, Julia Cumes, Jigme and Haven S. R. Daniels, Kenneth Dauber, Douglas Drake, Andrew and Jane Fitz-Gibbon, William Flesch, Michael Fried, Tarleton and Jenna Lahmann Gillespie, Larry Gottheim, Timothy Gould, Christopher Grau, Vincent Grenier, Garry Hagberg, David and Stephanie Insley Hershinow, Ann M. Hodge, Katherine Kelley, Richard Moran, John Opera, Joni Papp, Tristan Philip, Laura Quinney, Masha Raskolnikov, Lawrence Rhu, D. N. Rodowick, Kristen Steslow, Andreas Teuber, George Toles, Amy Villarejo, Mario von der Ruhr, Andrew and Sarah Walston, Catherine Wheatley, and the spilling stars of Skootamatta (Etheridge, Fitzgerald, Halverson); in conjunction with the production of the film *New York Photographer: Jill Freedman in the City*, Rita Mullaney, Maxwell Anderson, and, of course, Jill Freedman; members and guests of

The Signet Society of Harvard College; and at Cornell University Library, Fred Muratori, Bibliographer for English-language literature, theater, and film; and Kizer Walker, Director of Collections.

A special note of thanks to Paul Cronin for an extended exchange about my chapter (and much else), supplying compelling cases of the home movie in/as narrative cinema, and expert annotations on selected films by Scorsese, Wenders, and Resnais. And to Paul and Gabrielle Tenzer for your cordial hospitality.

I am especially grateful for the *esprit du corps* exemplified by those who are variously patron saints and *consiglieri* to this and other projects: Robert Pippin, Garrett Stewart, William Day, and William Rothman. They have surprised me, time and again, with the generosity of their discerning observations and good will. On this occasion, I benefited immensely—or better, my chapter did—from Garrett's scintillating commentary on an earlier version of the piece, which, as ever, stimulated and refined what I am trying to say. His capacity to see the best in what I write and make it better is an astonishment to me and a benefaction. Notes from Day, full of a rich prehistory of familiarity with the topics and texts at hand, proved fecund. Earlier, Day was a welcome participant and guide in a Cavell course I taught at Binghamton University, "Love and Conversation in Film," for a session in which we discussed *Adam's Rib*. It is a gesture of the genre, but is said sincerely nevertheless, that despite good advice from others, all remaining errors, blind spots, and infelicities are mine alone; in acknowledging kindness, then, I mean to offer thanks, not to offload responsibility.

I wish to convey my loving gratitude to Sheldon and Lorna K. Hershinow, Ian M. Evans and Luanna H. Meyer, Frances LaRocca and Roselle Sweeney, and David N. and Hi-jin Hodge—representing the families who make so much possible and worthwhile.

As befits the genre, the first shall be last, and so I turn, at the end, to my lovely LaRocca ladies; I marvel at the coincidence of our time on earth. Ruby and Star, you are perpetual gifts; out of the ether, what formidable creatures you have become. I stand in awe and admiration. For me, it is an unaccountable good fortune to share days and nights with the endlessly insightful, knowing, and companionable K. L. Evans, who once again (in Ithaca and for this project also memorably in Paris) became an ideal audience for conjectures and formulations; on this last front, it is something more altogether to discover, and re-discover, that she supplies a standard for criticism that is worthy of aspiration. Admittedly, I despair at falling short of the mark she sets, but I am grateful to her for a vision of what I am aiming for.

CONTRIBUTORS

THOMAS ELSAESSER was Professor Emeritus in the Department of Media and Culture at the University of Amsterdam, Visiting Professor at Yale University (2006-12), and from 2013 until his death in December 2019 taught at Columbia University. Among his recent books are *The Persistence of Hollywood* (2012), *German Cinema: Terror and Trauma: Cultural Memory Since 1945* (2013), *Film Theory: An Introduction through the Senses* (with Malte Hagener, 2015), *Körper, Tod und Technik* (with Michael Wedel, 2016), and *Film History as Media Archaeology* (2016). His final book was *European Cinema and Continental Philosophy: Film as thought Experiment* (2018). A posthumous volume has since appeared, *The Mind-Game Film: Distributed Agency, Time Travel, and Productive Pathology* (2021). He is also the writer-director of *The Sun Island* (2017), a documentary essay film produced for German television ZDF/3sat (https://sunislandfilm.com/).

GARRETT STEWART, author of a dozen volumes of literary and art criticism, is James O. Freedman Professor of Letters at the University of Iowa and was elected to the American Academy of Arts and Sciences in 2010. Both before and since his happy role as press referee for *Pursuits of Happiness*, he has elsewhere been contending with Stanley Cavell—not just in the 2005 collection by that title, in a polemical essay on "The Avoidance of Stanley Cavell" in both literary and film circles—but in four books on cinema over the last two decades from the University of Chicago Press, most recently *Cinemachines: An Essay on Media and Method* (2019).

NOËL CARROLL is Distinguished Professor of Philosophy at the Graduate Center of the City University of New York (CUNY). He is the author or editor of over twenty books including *Beyond Aesthetics: Philosophical Essays* (2001), *On Criticism (Thinking in Action)* (2008), *Living in an Artworld* (2011), *Art in Three Dimensions* (2011), *Minerva's Night Out: Philosophy, Pop Culture, and Moving Pictures* (2013), and *Humour: A Very Short Introduction* (2013). He is the editor of *The Poetics, Aesthetics, and Philosophy of Narrative* (2009) and coeditor with Jinhee Choi of *The Philosophy of Film and Motion Pictures: An Anthology* (2005). He is a Guggenheim recipient, a journalist for *Artforum* and the *Village Voice*, and the author of five documentary films.

KYLE STEVENS is Assistant Professor of Film Studies at Appalachian State University. He is the author of *Mike Nichols: Sex, Language, and the*

Reinvention of Psychological Realism (Oxford University Press, 2015, a book that engages deeply and consistently with Cavell's writings on film), co-editor of the two-volume collection *Close-Up: Great Screen Performances* (Edinburgh University Press, 2018, with Murray Pomerance), and editor of the forthcoming *The Oxford Handbook of Film Theory*. His essays have appeared in *Cinema Journal, Critical Quarterly, Film Criticism, World Picture*, as well as several edited collections. He is also editor- in-chief of *New Review of Film and Television Studies*.

STEPHEN MULHALL is Professor of Philosophy and a Fellow of New College, Oxford University. His research interests include Wittgenstein, Heidegger, and Nietzsche; the relationship between philosophy and religion; and the relationship between philosophy and the arts—especially film and literature. He is the author of *Stanley Cavell: Philosophy's Recounting of the Ordinary* (Oxford, 1994) and editor of *The Cavell Reader* (Wiley-Blackwell, 1996). His recent books include *The Self and Its Shadows: A Book of Essays on Individuality as Negation in Philosophy and the Arts* (Oxford, 2013); *On Film*, third edition (Routledge, 2015); and *The Great Riddle: Wittgenstein and Nonsense, Theology and Philosophy* (Oxford, 2016).

SCOTT MACDONALD is author of the oral history series, *A Critical Cinema: Interviews with Independent Filmmakers*, in five volumes from University of California Press; of four books on institutions that have been crucial for independent cinema: *Cinema 16* (Temple University Press, 2002), *Art in Cinema* (Temple, 2006), *Canyon Cinema* (California, 2008), and *The Flaherty: Decades in the Cause of Independent Cinema* (with Patricia R. Zimmermann, Indiana University Press, 2017); of four books of essays: *Avant-Garde Film/Motion Studies* (Cambridge University Press, 1993), *The Garden in the Machine: A Field Guide to Independent Films about Place* (California, 2001), *Adventures of Perception: Cinema as Exploration* (California, 2009), and *American Ethnographic Film and Personal Documentary: The Cambridge Turn* (California, 2013); and a nonfiction novel, *Binghamton Babylon: Voices from the Cinema Department, 1967-1977* (SUNY Press, 2019). *Avant-Doc: Intersections of Documentary and Avant-Garde Cinema*, a collection of interviews, was published by Oxford University Press in 2014, and *The Sublimity of Document: Cinema as Diorama (Avant-Doc 2)* by Oxford in 2019. He has taught film history and programmed public film events since 1970, most recently, at Bard College, Harvard University, and Hamilton College.

WILLIAM ROTHMAN is Professor of Cinema and Interactive Media at the University of Miami. A student of Stanley Cavell, he received his Ph.D. in philosophy from Harvard University, where he taught for many years at the Carpenter Center for the Visual Arts. His books include *Hitchcock: The Murderous Gaze* (Harvard University Press, 1982; expanded second edition,

State University of New York Press, 2012), *The "I" of the Camera: Essays in Film Criticism, History, and Aesthetics* (Cambridge University Press, 1988; expanded second edition 2004), *Documentary Film Classics* (Cambridge University Press, 1997), *Reading Cavell's* The World Viewed: *A Philosophical Perspective on Film* (with Marian Keane, Wayne State University Press, 2000), *Must We Kill the Thing We Love? Emersonian Perfectionism and the Films of Alfred Hitchcock* (Columbia University Press, 2014), *Tuitions and Intuitions: Essays at the Intersection of Film Criticism and Philosophy* (SUNY, 2019), and the forthcoming *Jean Rouch en tant qu'artiste de cinema* (Jean Rouch Foundation). He is the editor of *Cavell on Film* (SUNY, 2005), *Jean Rouch: A Celebration of Life and Film* (Schena Editore and Presses de l'Université de Paris-Sorbonne, 2007), and *Three Documentary Filmmakers* (SUNY, 2007); co-editor of *Looking with Robert Gardner*; and founding editor of the Harvard Film Studies and Cambridge Studies in Film series.

ROBERT SINNERBRINK is Associate Professor in Philosophy and former Australian Research Council Future Fellow at Macquarie University, Sydney. He is the author of *Terrence Malick: Filmmaker and Philosopher* (Bloomsbury, 2019), *Cinematic Ethics: Exploring Ethical Experience through Film* (Routledge, 2016), *New Philosophies of Film: Thinking Images* (Bloomsbury, 2011), *Understanding Hegelianism* (Acumen, 2007/Routledge 2014), and editor of *Critique Today* (Brill, 2006). He is a member of the editorial board of the journals *Film-Philosophy*, *Film and Philosophy*, and *Projections: The Journal of Movies and Mind*. He has published numerous articles on the relationship between film and philosophy in journals such as the *Australasian Philosophical Review*, *Angelaki*, *Conversations: The Journal of Cavellian Studies*, *Film-Philosophy*, *Necsus: European Journal of Media Studies*, *Projections: The Journal of Movies and Mind*, *Post Script*, *Screen*, *Screening the Past*, and *SubStance*.

THOMAS E. WARTENBERG is Senior Research Fellow in Philosophy at Mount Holyoke College. His main areas of focus are aesthetics, the philosophy of film, and philosophy for children. Among his publications are *Thinking on Screen: Film as Philosophy*, *Big Ideas for Little Kids: Teaching Philosophy Through Children's Literature*, *A Sneetch is a Sneetch and Other Philosophical Discoveries: Finding Wisdom in Children's Literature*, and *Existentialism: A Beginner's Guide*, and *Mel Bochner: Illustrating Philosophy*. He has published numerous papers on the philosophy of film including "Providing Evidence for a Philosophical Claim: *The Act of Killing* and the Banality of Evil," *Necsus: European Journal of Media Studies* (Autumn 2017), "'Not Time's Fool': Marriage as an Ethical Relationship in Michael Haneke's *Amour*," *Film as Philosophy* (2017), and "Dramatizing Philosophy," *Film and Philosophy* (2018). His philosophy for children website, teachingchildrenphilosophy.org, was awarded the 2011 APA/PDC

Prize for Excellence and Innovations in Philosophy Programs. He received the 2013 Merritt Prize for his contributions to the philosophy of education. He served as president of PLATO from 2016–18 and is film editor for *Philosophy Now*. He recently created a website for teaching philosophy through works of art: *Philosophy @ The Virtual Art Museum: Doing Philosophy Through Visual Images* [commons.mtholyoke.edu/philosophyatthemuseum/].

LAWRENCE F. RHU is William Joseph Todd Chair in the Italian Renaissance *Emeritus* at the University of South Carolina, where he taught English and comparative literature. His academic writings focus on the European and American Renaissances and includes *The Genesis of Tasso's Narrative Theory* (Wayne State, 1993) and *Stanley Cavell's American Dream: Shakespeare, Philosophy, and Hollywood Movies* (Fordham, 2006) as well as the Evans Shakespeare edition of *The Winter's Tale* (Cengage, 2011) and many articles. Though he mainly writes poetry now, he is also working on a book, *Plowing the Same Field: The Friendship of Robert Coles and Walker Percy*, which includes their correspondence. His poem "Reading Romance with a Lady Killer" received the 2018 Faulkner-Wisdom Poetry Award from the Pirate's Alley Faulkner Society in New Orleans and his poem "Attachment" received the 2018 John Edward Johnson Award from the Poetry Society of South Carolina.

SHAWN LOHT is the author of *Phenomenology of Film: A Heideggerian Account of the Film Experience* (2017) and co-editor with Noël Carroll and Laura Teresa Di Summa-Knoop of *The Palgrave Handbook for the Philosophy of Film and Motion Pictures* (2019). He has taught in the Philosophy Departments at Tulane University, Mercer University, and Pennsylvania State University and is currently an institutional researcher at Baton Rouge Community College.

SANDRA LAUGIER is Professor of Philosophy at Université Paris 1 Panthéon-Sorbonne, Paris, France, and a senior member of Institut Universitaire de France. She is deputy director of the Institut des sciences juridique et philosophique de la Sorbonne UMR 8103, CNRS Paris 1. A former student of the Ecole Normale Supérieure and Harvard University, she has extensively published on epistemology and philosophy of language; ordinary language philosophy (Wittgenstein, Austin, Cavell); moral philosophy (moral perfectionism, ethics of care); American philosophy (Cavell, Thoreau, Emerson); gender studies; democracy and civil disobedience; and popular culture (film, TV series). She is the translator of Stanley Cavell's work into French and has written extensively on his work. She is a senior member of Institut Universitaire de France (2012, renewed in 2018), member of Academia Europea, and was awarded the Légion d'Honneur. Recent publications include: *Pourquoi désobéir en démocratie?* (coauthored with A. Ogien, 2010); *Why We Need Ordinary Language Philosophy* (The University of Chicago Press, 2013); *Recommencer la philosophie. Stanley Cavell et la philosophie en Amérique* (2015); *Le Principe Démocratie* (coauthored with A. Ogien, 2014); *Etica e politica dell'ordinario* (2015); *Antidémocratie* (coauthored with A. Ogien, 2017); and *Formes de vie* (ed. with Estelle Ferrarese, 2018). She is also a columnist for *Chronique Philosophiques* at the French journal *Libération*: www.liberation.fr/auteur/6377-sandra-laugier.

MATHEW ABBOTT is Senior Lecturer in Philosophy at Federation University, Australia. He is the author of *The Figure of the This World: Agamben and the Question of Political Ontology* (2014) and *Abbas Kiarostami and Film-Philosophy* (2016). More recently, he is the editor of *Michael Fried and Philosophy: Modernism, Intention, and Theatricality* (2018). In late 2018, he joined the Research Center for Analytic German Idealism at the University of Leipzig as Visiting Senior Research Fellow.

DAVID LAROCCA is the author, editor, or coeditor of more than a dozen books. He edited *Movies with Stanley Cavell in Mind* (Bloomsbury, 2021), *Inheriting Stanley Cavell* (Bloomsbury, 2020), and a commemorative issue of *Conversations: The Journal of Cavellian Studies* (2019). Advised by Stanley Cavell during doctoral research, he later edited, annotated, and indexed Stanley Cavell's book *Emerson's Transcendental Etudes* (Stanford University Press, 2003); indexed Cavell's *Cities of Words: Pedagogical Letters on a Register of the Moral Life* (2004) and *Philosophy the Day after Tomorrow* (2005); edited *Estimating Emerson: An Anthology of Criticism from Carlyle to Cavell* (2013); and contributed chapters to *Stanley Cavell, Literature, and Film: The Idea of America* (2013) and *Stanley Cavell and Aesthetic Understanding* (2018), and *Understanding Cavell, Understanding Modernism* (2022). LaRocca is the editor of other books on film and media, including *The Philosophy of Charlie Kaufman* (2011; with a new preface, 2019), *The Philosophy of War Films* (2014), and *The Philosophy of Documentary Film: Image, Sound, Fiction, Truth* (2017), and *Metacinema: The Form and Content of Filmic Reference and Reflexivity* (2021). A recipient of a Teaching Commendation from the Dean of Harvard Extension School and a Teaching Innovation Award from the College at Cortland, he has served as Visiting Assistant Professor in the Cinema Department at Binghamton University; Visiting Assistant Professor in the Department of Philosophy at the State University of New York College at Cortland; Lecturer in Screen Studies in the Department of Cinema, Photography, and Media Arts at the Roy H. Park School of Communications at Ithaca College; and Visiting Scholar in the Department of English at Cornell University. Educated at Buffalo, Berkeley, Vanderbilt, and Harvard, he later became Harvard's Sinclair Kennedy Traveling Fellow in the United Kingdom. His articles have appeared in *Afterimage*, *Epoché*, *Estetica*, *Liminalities*, *Post Script*, *Transactions*, *Film and Philosophy*, *The Senses and Society*, *The Midwest Quarterly*, *Journalism, Media and Cultural Studies*, *Cinema: Journal of Philosophy and the Moving Image*, *The Journal of Aesthetic Education*, and *The Journal of Aesthetics and Art Criticism*. As a documentary filmmaker, he produced and edited six features in *The Intellectual Portrait Series*, directed *Brunello Cucinelli: A New Philosophy of Clothes* and, most recently, codirected *New York Photographer: Jill Freedman in the City*. He has participated in a National Endowment for the Humanities Institute, a workshop with Abbas Kiarostami, Werner Herzog's Rogue Film School, and the School of Criticism and Theory at Cornell University. More details at www.davidlarocca.org Contact: davidlarocca@ post.harvard.edu

INDEX

2 or 3 Things I Know About Her
 (1967)   120 n.13, 280
3D   32, 34–6, 38
5 Broken Cameras (2011)   254
55 Days in Peking (1963)   124
127 Hours (2010)   276

absorption   240, 244 n.52
The Abyss (1989)   193
academic philosophers   7, 137
acting   46, 57, 74, 235, 240,
 262f, 272
The Act of Killing (2012)   271f
*The Act of Seeing with One's Own
 Eyes* (1972)   111–12
actualité   235, 240, 283 n.11
Adam's Rib (1949)   108f, 136, 138,
 ch. 13 (245–90) *passim*
 as allegory of viewing film   252
The Adderall Diaries (2018)   277
Adorno, Theodor   xv
*An Adult's Picture Book View—I Was
 Born, But ...* (1932)   273
aesthetics, sonic   64
 See also sound
aesthetic judgment   97–9, 122, 129
Affleck, Casey   271
Agamben, Giorgio   289 n.99
Agee, James   6
Alien films   192–6, 202–4
Almodovar, Pedro   198–200
amateur filmmaking   60, 235, ch. 13
 (245–90) *passim*
 See also film
America, myths of   100
American academic philosophy   5
American Beauty (1999)   276
American Dream   xv

American movies, nature of   5
The Americans (2013–18)   222
American Transcendentalism
 100, 102
analogy, argument from   168 n.5
Anderson, Wes   198, 277
Anker, Steve   113, 119 n.7, 119 n.9
Anna Karenina (Tolstoy)   242 n.16
Antichrist (2009)   197
Antonioni, Michelangelo   28, 30, 41, 44
Apatow, Judd   219
Arden, Eve   71
Arendt, Hannah   78
Aristotle   136, 198, 289 n.99
Arnold, Martin   117
The Arrival of a Train at La Ciotat
 (Lumière)   ch. 12 (228–44)
 passim
art, therapeutic notion of   79
artificial intelligence (AI)   257
aspect perception/aspect seeing
 ("seeing as")   74f, 157
audience, find and invent   225
audiovisual   8, 64, 72, 75, 77, 79–81,
 82 n.3, 117, 247, 276
augmented reality (AR)   257
Augustine, St.   222
aurality   66, 71, 78
 See also sound
Austin, J. L.   86 n.83, 280
auteur theory   41f, 110, 122, 277
authorship   x, 15, 223, 284 n.20
avant-garde film   8, 14–16, 52, 58,
 246, 278–81
 See also film, experimental;
 nonnarrative film
The Awful Truth (1937)   108, 136,
 138, 171–4, 177, 201, 215

Balázs, Bela 33f
Barn Rushes (1971) 111f
Barry, Philip 175
Barthes, Roland xi, 150 n.39
Bazin, André 25, 34, 36, 43, 45, 54f, 64f, 67, 84 n.38, 121, 131
Bellamy, Ralph 172, 174
Benjamin, Walter 121, 212
Berger, Jr., Harry 177
Bergman, Ingmar 41, 197, 264
Bergman, Ingrid ch. 8 (152–69) *passim*
Bergson, Henri 34, 37, 39 n.20
Bernstein, Charles 1
Bildung 212
Billy Lynn's Long Halftime Walk (2016) 25, 29–38
Binghamton Cinema Department (State University of New York) 110–12, 115, 119 n.6–9
The Birth of a Nation (1915) 250, 284 n.22
Black Mirror (2011) 269
Blade Runner (1982) 193–4
Blade Runner 2049 (2017) 257, 286 n.38
Bodyguard (2018) 262
Bordwell, David 270
Bourdieu, Emmanuel 214, 217f
Boyhood (2014) 271
Brakhage, Stan 59, 111f, 117
Branagh, Kenneth 180
Brief Encounter (1945) 147, 151 n.44
Bright Leaves (2003) 120 n.13
Bringing Up Baby (1938) 108, 138, 249f
Buffy the Vampire Slayer (1997–2003) 217, 219f
Buñuel, Luis 112
The Bureau (*Le Bureau des Légendes*, 2015) 223
Burwell, Carter 146
Butler, Rex 9

The Cabinet of Dr. Caligari (1920) 42, 278
Caché (2005) 262
Cage, John 81

camera, viewpoint of 239
Capra, Frank 108, 138, 216
Capturing the Friedmans (2003) 276
Carol (2015) 142–8
Carroll, Noël 13, 191, 205, 229, 236f, 243 n.35–7, 272
Caruth, Cathy 86 n.80
Casablanca (1942) ch. 8 (152–69) *passim*
 as remarriage film 158–61
Cassin, Barbara 8
Castiglione, Baldassare, *The Book of the Courtier* 183
Castile, Philando 254
Cavell, Benjamin 16, 20 n.42
Cavell, Stanley
 acknowledgment (concept of) 28, 31, 64–5, 83 n.8, 87 n.87, 93, 135f, 138–42, 144–6, 148, 153, 160, 162, 172, 233f, 238f
 "assertions in technique" ch. 1 (23–40 *passim*; *see esp.* 24, 26–9, 31, 35), 49, 51f
 automatism 25–7, 29f, 68f, 72f, 80, 84 n.34, 131, 264
 betterment through repetition 30
 conception of philosophy 201f
 criticism of 153
 Deleuze, Gilles 24, 26
 drama of black and white film 263–8
 "education of grown-ups" 211–13, 223, 225
 Emerson, Ralph Waldo and 3, 6f, 11, 16, 39 n.18, 100, 102, 125f, 129–40, 174, 211–16, 280
 epistemologists and 83 n.24
 film as "moving image of skepticism" 130–2, 234f
 "Film in the University" 107–20, 215
 final paragraph of *The World Viewed* 54, 76, 81
 "genre-as-cycle" 88, 91
 "genre-as-medium" 89, 92f, 96–100
 Judaism and xiv–xv
 legacy in film studies 5, 13f, 191f

"metaphysical memoir" of 15, 123
nature of philosophy for 122, 124, 202
notion of film interpretation as performance 204–6
the ordinary and the work of film 290 n.110
a philosopher of film with no theory of it 24
A Pitch of Philosophy xiv, 284 n.20
possibilities of the medium of film 29, 31, 39 n.15, 47f, 57, 68, 89–91, 100, 216–19, 249f
projection 84 n.38, 91, 267f, 281
readers and students of 225
reassessment of importance 213, 217
seen and unseen 53, 59f, 81, 201, 203, 206, 224f, 234, 264, 290 n.110
The Senses of Walden 2f, 78f, 81 n.2, 85 n.48, 86 n.83
"succession of automatic world projections," 24, 26–8, 30, 32–4, 36, 42, 51, 53, 68, 102, 281
synchronization 72–3, 80f, 85 n.52, 87 n.87
"Thinking of Emerson" 3
Thoreau, Henry David and 6, 79, 86 n.83, 95, 100, 102, 135, 211, 213, 279f
"The Thought of Movies" 3, 5, 201, 216
"threat of skepticism" 79, 83 n.8, 87 n.87, 153f
transparency thesis 55
the unsayable 72–6, 80–1
voice 9, 15, 65, 214
Wittgenstein, Ludwig and xi–xiv, 10, 63, 68–70, 73–5, 82 n.5, 91f, 98, 131, 134, 213–15, 231, 233, 280
Cerisuelo, Marc 216
CGI (computer-generated imagery) 27, 269
Chaplin, Charlie 48, 109, 115
Chardin, Jean-Baptiste-Siméon 237–9

Charleen (1977) 117
Chaucer, Geoffrey, *The Merchant's Tale* 181
Chion, Michel 82 n.3, 84 n.44, 289 n.99
Chopra, Joyce 111
cinema
as audiovisual 64
early ch. 12 (228–44) *passim*
founding myth of 228–30
pedagogical task of 224
spectatorship and 229
See also digital cinema; film; moral education
Cinema Paradiso (1989) 275f
cinematic objecthood 52
citationality of interpretation 284 n.20
Clémot, Hugo 9
cognitive illusionism 229, 241 n.9
cognitivists 229, 231f
Cohen, Sacha Baron 244 n.53
Colbert, Stephen 118
color 49f, 143, 146, 256, 263f, 266–9
See also Cavell, drama of black and white film
comedy
new 138
old 138
Roman 171
romantic comedy 93, 109, 116f, 138, 149 n.22, 171, 219
screwball xi, 28, 30, 48, 72, 88
Shakespearean 174, 181
See also remarriage, comedy of
Conant, James 25–7, 34, 36, 38 n.5, 238–40
conversation 137–8
"meet and happy" 11, 93, 98f, 103, 138f, 171f, 194
Corinthians 177, 183
Cousins (1989) 275
Critical Mass (1971) 112–17, 119 n.7–9
Cukor, George 28, 30, 108–9, 114, 138, 175, ch. 13 (245–90) *passim*
See also Adam's Rib; *Gaslight*; *The Philadelphia Story*

Cunningham, Cecil   172
Currie, Gregory   229, 232, 241 n.7, 241 n.9, 242 n.16, 243 n.35, 272

Danto, Arthur C.   9, 201, 291
Dassin, Jules   80
Day, William   284 n.22
Dear Zachary (2008)   276
Deleuze, Gilles   xi, xv, 24–6, 30, 33–4, 37f, 64, 198
  affection-image   34
  time-image   24f
Demand, Thomas   243 n.40
de-marriage, comedy of   116
  See also marriage; nonremarriage; remarriage, comedy of
DeMille, William   87 n.90
democracy   101, 212
  American   175
  of cinema   214–16
De Niro, Robert   49, 266, 268
Deren, Maya   117
Derrida, Jacques   xi, xv
Descartes, René (and Cartesian) 53, 70, 72, 79, 131, 152, 159, 194f, 198, 233, 279
  post-Cartesian   152f
Dewey, John   221
Diaries (1971–1976) (1981)   117
Dictionary of Untranslatables (Cassin)   8
digital cinema   3f, 10, ch.1 (1–20) *passim*, 212, 222, 257, 260, 271
  surveillance and   268
divorce   116, 143, 145, 172, 177, 219
  threat of   93, 96, 113, 138, 171
  See also de-marriage, comedy of; Milton; nonremarriage; remarriage, comedy of
Doane, Mary Ann   82 n.3
documentary (film)   6, 111, 236, ch. 12 (228–44) and ch. 13 (245–90) *passim*
  creative treatment of actuality and   261, 271
  hoax *verité* and   271, 288 n.89
  makers of   240
  newsreels and   43, 157, 249f
  ontology of   244 n.53
  subgenres of   243 n.38
  theory of   243 n.35
A Doll's House (Ibsen)   93, 141
Down and Out in Beverly Hills (1986)   275
Dragonfly Eyes (2017)   262
Dunne, Irene   172, 201
duration (temporal)   25, 31, 34f, 71f, 198, 220
durée   37

Eclipse (1962)   28
Eden, Garden of   94, 177
Eighth Grade (2018)   278
Eisenstein, Sergei   33, 43, 52, 82 n.3
Eliot, T. S.   138, 179, 185f, 224
Elsaesser, Thomas   141
Emerson, Ralph Waldo   xii, 3, 6f, 16, 39 n.18, 125, 133–40, 174, 211, 213–16, 280
Emersonian
  friend   102, 137
  moral perfectionism   11, 100f, 129f, 132–40
  philosophy   126
  See also moral perfectionism
Empire (1964)   59
Epicureanism   183–4
Epstein, Jean   24, 26, 30, 33f, 36–8
Erens, Patricia   266
Eternal Sunshine of the Spotless Mind (2004)   269
ethics   7, 129–37, 142, 148, 157, 199, 225, 248
  in academic philosophy   133
  cinematic   129f, 134, 199
  meta-   220

Falling Down (1993)   276
The Family Man (2000)   277
Family Portrait Sittings (1975)   117, 120 n.13
Fassbender, Michael   194
Fauda (2015)   223
feminism   xi, xiv, 24, 87 n.88, 114, 153, 221
F for Fake (1975)   271
film
  aesthetics of   122

as art 42f, 46, 48, 50–3, 64, 89–91, 121, 213, 222, 261, 279
avant-garde 8, 14–16, 52, 58, 246, 278–81
criticism 15, 17, 41, 47f, 98, 121–3, 196–200, 203, 205f, 213, 220, 224, 248–9
democratic nature of 220
dialogue xii, xiv, 10f, 71, 114–19, 137, 147, 172
dimensionality of 253
drama of black and white 263–8
experimental 6, 14, 52, 246, 275, 278–81, 292–3
film-philosophy (and film-as-philosophy) 1–17
flashback 27, 32–6, 156–63, 266, 274
found footage 247, 270
genre. *See* genre
indexicality of 14, 236
medium's origin 27, 29, 91, 228f
medium specificity of 13, 47, 243 n.36, 250, 260, 263, 271
modernism and 8, 43, 50–2, 58f, 68, 84 n.38
ontology of 2f, 7f, 14, Part I (21–104) *passim*, 131, 191, 214, 244 n.53, 245f, 258, 260, 276, 278, 281, 289 n.99
ordinary aesthetics of 215, 290 n.110
as "philosophy in action" 192, 195–7, 202
poetry of 122, 126, 203, 224
of presumption assertion 236, 272
pretense and 235, 240
reality and 27, 37, 42, 45–9, 51, 53, 55f, 63–5, 68f, 91, 129, 131, ch. 12 (228–44) *passim*, 246–8, 263–5, 269, 286 n.53
relationship of philosophy and 10f, 14, 16f, 103, 125, 129f
in a state of philosophy ch. 10 (191–209) *passim*
teaching ch. 5 (107–20) *passim*, 211
trace theory and 272

what is 42, 61 n.6
See also documentary (film); nonnarrative film; painting; photographs; realism
film studies ix–xi, 5, 7–9, 13f, 23f, 89, 95, ch. 5 (107–20) *passim*
The Final Cut (2004) 269
Fincher, David 193
First Man (2018) 256
Fishburne, Laurence 185
Flaherty, Robert 261, 271
Foucault, Michel 136, 263
Frampton, Hollis 59, 112–17, 119 n.9
Frankfurt School x–xi
Freeland, Cynthia 9
French pre-modernism 238f, 244 n.55
Freud, Sigmund xi, xiii–xiv, 94
See also psychoanalysis (and the psychoanalytic)
Fried, Michael 50, 59, 61 n.15, 237–9, 243 n.40, 244 n.52, 244 n.55
Frye, Northrop 138, 170f, 174, 177

Gabler, Neal xiv–xv
Garden of Eden 94, 177
Gaslight (1944) xi, 18 n.14, 136, 139
Gaut, Berys 229
Gehr, Ernie 58, 111f
gender xiv, 114f, 140–2, 163f, 194, 203
class and 142
stereotypes 164
genre 3f, 7, 13–15, 48f, 57f, ch. 4 (88–104) *passim*, 108f, 130, 137–40, 144, 152, 170, 179, 204, 215, 217–20, 249f, 259, 265, 267
conception of 204
creation of 201
expressive grammar of 200
family resemblance and 91f, 98, 223
idiom and 137, 249, 254, 283 n.13
mixing of 217
See also melodrama, genre of; remarriage, comedy of

Geschlecht und Charakter (Weininger) xiv
Godard, Jean-Luc 17, 260, 280, 286 n.53
Gondry, Michel 255, 269, 285 n.34, 288 n.81
Goodenough, Jerry 9
Gordon, Ruth 251–6, 284 n.19
Gottheim, Larry 107f, 111f, 119 n.5
Grant, Cary 102, 115, 123, 172, 175, 201, 215, 250
Gravity (2013) 204
Greaves, William 117
green world, Shakespearean 93f, 139, 170, 174f, 177f, 203f, 249f, 252, 283 n.15
Grierson, John 261, 271
Groundhog Day (1993) 25, 30–2, 39 n.18
Gunning, Tom 241 n.6, 244 n.55, 283 n.11
Guzzetti, Alfred 117, 120 n.13

Halliday, John 176
Haneke, Michael 262
Happy Mother's Day (1963) 111
Haynes, Todd 15, 130, 142–8, 150 n.37, 150 n.39, 151 n.42
Hays Code (Motion Picture Production Code) 163, 251
Heidegger, Martin xi, 76, 131, 133f, 149 n.6, 153, 201–3, 205–6
   Dasein 202f
   disclosure 203
   discourse 205f
Henry VIII 171f
Hepburn, Katharine xv, 47f, 108, 115f, 175, ch. 13 (245–90, incl. 283 n.17f) *passim*
Herzogenrath, Bernd 9
Highsmith, Patricia 143f
Hiroshima, Mon Amour (1959) 77–80, 86 n.80
His Girl Friday (1940) 108f, 138, 172, 174, 219f
Hitchcock, Alfred x, 5, 8, 47, 80f, 125
hoax *vérité* 271f, 288f

The Holiday (2007) 219f
holographic (imagery) 257
Home for the Holidays (1995) 274
home movies 60, 61 n.6, ch. 13 (245–90) *passim*
   See also film
Horkheimer, Max xv
Howard, John 175
How I Met Your Mother (2005–14) 219f
humanities, crisis in the x
Humphrey Bogart 48, ch. 8 (152–69) *passim*
Hurt, John 193
Hussey, Ruth 176
hyperbolic discounting 167

Ibsen, Henrik xii, 93, 138, 141
IMAX 256
The Immediate Experience (Warshow) 6, 13, 210, 212f, 222, 224f
I'm Still Here (2010) 271
intention (and intentionality) 45, 53, 60, 223, 237, 240, 243 n.40, 244 n.55, 276
iPhone 255, 278, 285 n.34
It Happened One Night (1934) 96, 108, 136, 138, 152f, 163, 216

Jacobs, Ken 111f, 119 n.5
James, Henry 224
Jefferson, Thomas (and the pursuit of happiness) 11, 99, 115f, 142, 225, 251
Jeunet, Jean-Pierre 193
Johnson, Samuel 184
Jones, Duncan 31f, 204

Kanin, Garson 251–6, 284 n.19
Kant, Immanuel xi, 54, 101, 133–6, 216
Kaufman, Charlie 269, 288 n.81
Keane, Marian 2, 4, 9, 16, 85 n.52, 123
   See also Rothman
Kenny, Anthony 6
Kierkegaard, Søren 6

Kleist, Heinrich von   xii
Knocked Up (2007)   219
Koehler, Marlene   238
Kracauer, Siegfried   47f, 57, 287 n.71
Krazy Kat (Herriman)   224
Kubrick, Stanley   204
Kurosawa, Akira   27, 30, 41, 112

Lacan, Jacques   xiii, xv
Lachman, Ed   146
The Lady Eve (1941)   94, 108, 174, 219f
Lady in the Lake (1946)   238f
Lamont, Molly   172
Land, Owen   59
Langer, Suzanne K.   70
Laugier, Sandra   9
Leacock, Richard   111f, 119 n.5
Lean, David   147
Leavis, F. R.   179, 185
Lee, Ang. *See Billy Lynn's Long Halftime Walk*
Léger, Ferdinand   58
lesbian romance   143–8, 151 n.41
Lessing, G. E.   47
Letter from an Unknown Woman (1948)   xi, xiii–xiv, 139
The Life Aquatic with Steve Zissou (2004)   277
listening   13, 66, 70, 74, 78f
  See also sound
Livingston, Paisley   191
Logan (2017)   266
Loiperdinger, Martin   ch. 12 (228–44) *passim*
The Look of Silence (2014)   272
Lubitsch, Ernst   15, 109f, 113f
Lucretius, *On the Nature of Things*   183
Lumière brothers   ch. 12 (228–44) *passim*
Luther, Martin   171

Macarthur, David   242 n.21
McCarey, Leo   108, 138, 172, 201, 215
McElwee, Ross   117, 120 n.13

The Magnificent Ambersons (1942)   269
Malick, Terrence   197, 207 n.19, 260f, 286 n.54
The Man in the High Castle (2015)   256
Marker, Chris   279f
marriage   xv, 27, 93–5, 98, 100, 109, 113, 115–17, 125, 139
  of film and philosophy   13, 103, 129, 138–48, 165, 170–7, 181f, 201, 249, 251–3, 259f, 266f
  See also de-marriage; divorce; nonremarriage; and remarriage, comedy of
masculinity   160, 162, 164
mass media   x–xi, xv
Maynard, Patrick   55
Maysles brothers   236
medium. *See* film, medium's origin; film, medium specificity of
Mekas, Jonas   112, 279f, 290 n.108
Méliès, Georges   47, 57, 61 n.13
melodrama
  genre of   xi–xiii, 88, 97, 130, 135, 137f, 140–4, 152, 219, 248
  maternal   143–8
  moral   199
  queer   142–8
melodrama of the unknown woman
  xi–xiv, 15, 88, 97, 100, ch. 7 and ch. 8 (152–69) *passim*
  possibilities and limits of   148
memory   34, 206, 215, 222, 225, 248, 266, 268f, 273, 275f, 282 n.7, 289 n.101
Meshes of the Afternoon (1943)   117
meta-art   273
metacinema   5, 32, 36, 58f, 245f, 250, 259, 269, 272, 274, 276f, 279, 281, 285 n.34
  a film projecting a film it contains   258
  film staging an awareness of itself as art and   260
meta-ethics   220
metafiction   273
meta-history, of cinema   118

meta-metacinema 277
metamorphosis xii, 139, 143, 182f
metaphor
  conversation as 172
  film-within-the-film as 199
  mystical 76
  narrative and 154
  Platonic 42
  political 79
  silence as 72
  sound as 65
  visual 70
metatheatre 273
Metz, Christian 230–2, 241 n.9
Meyers, Nancy 219f
Mildred Pierce (1945) xi
Mill, John Stuart 136
Miller, Max ix, xv
Milton, John 93, 138f, 171f
  See also conversation, "meet and happy"
Minority Report (2002) 257
Mission Impossible—Fallout (2018) 269
modernism x, 8, 43, 50–2, 58f, 68, 84 n.38
modernist
  aesthetics 68
  art 50–3, 61 n.15
  cinema 63, 68f, 77, 79
  filmmaking 58f
  ideals 70
  impulse 260
  metacinema 58
  mission 75
  reflexivity 51f
  task 71
Moon (2009) 204
moral education ch. 11 (210–27) *passim*
  grammar of 200
  television and 221
moral imperfectionism 142–8
moralism 137, 176
moral perfectionism 11, 99–102, ch. 7 (129–51) *passim*, 152, ch. 11 (210–27) *passim*
  moral paradox and 137

negative version of 143
revised 142f
See also Emersonian moral perfectionism
Moran, Richard 79, 84 n.31, 87 n.87
Moriarty, Cathy 266f
Mottola, Greg 219
Mr. Blandings Builds His Dream House (1948) 250
Mulhall, Stephen 10, ch. 10 (191–209 *passim*; *see esp.* 192–6, 202–5), 209 n.50
The Murderous Gaze (Rothman) 125
Muriel (1963) 273f
My Architect (2003) 276
My Life (1993) 275

Nagy, Phyllis 143
Nancy, Jean-Luc 70
Nanook of the North (1922) 271
newsreels 43, 157, 249f
New Wave/Nouvelle Vague 41, 273
The New World (2005) 197
Nichols, Bill 243 n.38
Nichols, Mike 87 n.88
Nietzsche, Friedrich xii, 6, 133f, 136f, 138, 149 n.22
nonnarrative film ch. 5 (107–20) *passim*, 235, 246, 278f
  See also avant-garde film; film, experimental
nonremarriage, comedy of 289 n.99
  See also divorce; marriage; remarriage, comedy of
North by Northwest (1959) 5
(nostalgia) (1971) 59, 112f, 139
Now, Voyager (1942) xi
Nussbaum, Martha 133f

Oedipus xiii, 94, 210
Olivier, Laurence 46, 86 n.82, 179, 185, 210
ontology of film (*see* film, ontology of)
Ophüls, Max xi, xiv, 139
Oppenheimer, Joshua 271f
ordinary
  importance of the 43, 137, 213f, 220–5

language philosophy xii, 65–7, 213, 280
  poetry of the 224
other minds, problem of xii, 65, 83 n.8, 87 n.87, 152f, 231
Ovid, *Metamorphoses* 182f
Ozu, Yasujiro 41, 198, 273

painting 43–7, 50f, 56, 59, 63–5, 68–70, 91, 124, 198, 237–9, 244 n.55, 290 n.112
  photography and 43–7, 51, 56, 59, 63–5, 68f, 91, 198, 237, 243 n.40, 290 n.112
Paisan (1946) 47
Panofsky, Erwin 29, 43, 64f, 131, 212, 216f, 249
panopticon 263
Paris, Texas (1984) 266, 274
Parker, Oliver 185
Patton, Paul 149 n.22
Paul, St. 177, 183f
pedagogy (and teaching) 14, 25
  cinema and ch. 5 (107–20) *passim*, 211, 216, 220, 224f
Peeping Tom (1960) 269, 273
perceptual illusionism 241 n.9
Perkins, Victor 15, 26, 38 n.5, ch. 6 (121–26) *passim*, 218f
Persona (1966) 197
The Philadelphia Story (1940) 28, 39 n.12, 102, 108f, 114–17, 138, 175–7, 273
Phoenix, Joaquin 271
photogenesis 214, 223
photographs (and photography) 25–7, 34, 38, 39 n.12, ch. 2 (41–62) *passim*, 63–77, 84 n.31, 84 n.38, 112, 122, 131, 237, 238, 243 n.40, 290 n.112
  indexicality and 236
  projection and 90f
  trace theory and 27, 77, 243 n.35, 243 n.37, 272
  See also painting
Pièce Touchée (1989) 117
Pincus, Ed 117
Pippin, Robert B. 3, 8, 25f, 29

Plantinga, Carl 236f, 243 n.38
Plato 1, 4, 18 n.11, 42, 51, 78f, 98, 103, 135f, 182, 198
  Parmenides 173
  Republic 133
Poe, Edgar Allan 37
Poetic Justice (1972) 112f
Polley, Sarah 117, 271f
popular culture xiv–xv, 6, 95, 103, 173, 176, ch. 11 (210–27) *passim*
Powell, Michael 269, 273
pre-modernism, French 238f, 244 n.55
projection *vs.* recording 27, 42, 68, 84 n.38, 84 n.40, 268f, 281, 286 n.38
Prometheus (2012) 193f
Proust, Marcel 210
Psycho (1960) 124f
psychoanalysis (and the psychoanalytic) xi–xiii, 32, 94, 99
  cinema and xii, 24, 95, 229
Pudovkin, V. I. 46, 82 n.3
Pygmalion 182f

queer
  Carol (2015) and 142–8
  Eve Arden and 71
  melodrama 130, 143
Quine, Willard Van Orman 5f, 83 n.24

radio 73f, 84 n.39
  See also sound
Raging Bull (1980) 247, 266–8, 278
Random Harvest (1942) xi–xii
rape
  Alien films and 194
  Talk to Her (2002) and 198f
Ray, Nicolas 57, 111, 113f, 123–6
Read, Rupert 9
Ready Player One (2018) 38
realism 51, 68–70, 76, 80
  Bazin and 36, 67
  Bourdieu and 214

classical 10
indexical 63
"irrealism" and 37f
ontology of film and 131
painting and 239
synchronization and 73
television series and 223
See also film
recording *vs.* projection 27, 42, 68, 84 n.38, 84 n.40, 268f, 281, 286 n.38
Redacted (2007) 269
Rede (discourse) 205
reflexivity
  cinematic 50–2, 58f, 103
  television and 223
  See also metacinema
remarriage 11, 93, 102, 160–3
  comedy of xi–xii, 13, 94, 138–40, 211–15, 245f, 265, ch. 5 (107–20) and ch. 9 (170–88) *passim*
  document of 260
  gendered nature of 163f
  genre, myth of 91–100
  motif of 139f
  See also de-marriage, comedy of; genre; nonremarriage, comedy of; romantic comedy
Reminiscences of a Journey to Lithuania (1972) 112
Renoir, Jean 45
repetition xi, xiii, xv, 30, 141
  of dialogue 114
  the everyday and 215
  of film 215
Resnais, Alain 77, 273f
Reynolds, Diamond 254
Rhu, Lawrence F. 4, 9
Rififi (1955) 80
Rivette, Jacques 260, 286 n.53
Robeson, Paul 46, 185
Rodowick, D. N. 4, 8, 129
Rogin, Michael xiv–xv
Rohmer, Eric xii
romance, lesbian 142–8
romantic comedy 93, 109, 116f, 138, 149 n.22, 171, 219

Rorty, Richard xv, 5, 9, 18 n.18
Rossellini, Roberto 47
Rothman William 2, 4f, 8f, 16, 85 n.52, 120 n.13, 123, 273
Rouch, Jean 123
The Rules of the Games (1939) 123

Salih, Tayeb 185
Sandgren, Linus 257
Sans Soleil (1983) 279
Sarris, Andrew 110
Scenes from a Marriage (1974) 197
Schneemann, Carolee 117
Schumacher, Joel 275f
science fiction (films) 192–6, 202–4
Scorsese, Martin 257
Scott, Ridley 193f
  See also Alien films
screenwriters
  function of 221, 223
  married 251f, 255, 261, 270, 284 n.19
"seeing as." *See* aspect perception/aspect seeing
Seely, William 229
self, conceptions of the 100f, 134–6
selfhood, myths of 102f
self-reliance 135, 139f
self-transformation ch. 7 (129–51) *passim,* 210–13, 245
Senex iratus 171
Serene Velocity (1970) 111f, 209 n.54
sex (and sexuality) 94f, 100, 124f, 164f, 177f, 194, 203
  same- 142–8
sexes, relationship between 138f
sexism 153, 164
sexual
  identity 142
  politics 250f
  revolution 87 n.88, 289 n.99
Shakespeare, William
  As You Like It 174f, 203f
  Hamlet xiii, 46, 54, 76, 86 n.82, 180, 186
  King Lear xii, 177f, 231

The Merchant of Venice   174f
A Midsummer Night's Dream   174–7
  movies and   ch. 9 (170–88 *passim*; see esp. 177–86), 203f
Much Ado about Nothing   175, 179–83
Othello   xii, 46, 177–86, 187 n.10
The Tempest   138, 203f
The Winter's Tale   xii, 138, 179–86
Shakespearean green world   93f, 139, 170, 174f, 177f, 203f, 249f, 252, 283 n.15
Shaw, Daniel   9
Show Boat (1936)   172
silence   63, 71–5, 80f
  acknowledgment of   42
  expressivity of   84 n.31
  meta-   81
  Perkins and   124
  in *The Senses of Walden*   85 n.48
  in *The World Viewed*   87 n.88
  See also aurality; silent film; sound
silent film   48, 58, 64, 73, ch. 5 (107–20), ch. 12 (228–44), and ch. 13 (245–90) *passim*
Sinnerbrink, Robert   ch. 10 (191–209 *passim*; see esp. 192, 196–200, 204f, 207)
Sirk, Douglas   147
skepticism   ch. 7 (129–51), ch. 8 (152–69), ch. 9 (170–88), and ch. 12 (228–44) *passim*
  Cartesian   53, 152f, 159f
  feminization of   xiii
  overcome   162
  passive   79, 87 n.87
  See also Descartes
Smith, Murray   191
Snow, Michael   58f
Soft Rain (1968)   111
Solaris (1972)   204
Sophocles   94
  See also Oedipus
sound   44, 58, ch. 3 (63–87) *passim*, 89, 108f, 237, 248, 250, 256, 260, 264f, 270, 274, 282 n.7
  countrapuntal   82

Critical Mass (1971) and   112–17, 119 n.8
  See also aurality; silence; silent film
Source Code (2011)   31f
Spider-Man: Homecoming (2017)   285 n.34
Spielberg, Steven   38, 257, 267, 287 n.76
Stella Dallas (1937)   xi, 136, 139–42, 152
Sternberg, Josef von   xii
Stewart, Garrett   3, 262, 274, 281, 289 n.99
Stewart, James   11, 47, 176
Stoicism   186
Stories We Tell (2013)   117, 271f
Streisand, Barbra   274, 289 n.99
structural film   58f, 203
structuralist   229
  post-   xii
Sturges, Preston   49, 108, 174
subjectivation   213, 224
sublime, humanistic   11, 19 n.33
Sunset Boulevard (1950)   273
Super 8 (2011)   287 n.76
Superbad (2007)   219
surveillance
  digital   39 n.21, 268, 287 n.60
  footage   60, 254, 262f, 269, 275
Symbiopsychotaxiplasm: Take One (1971)   117
Symbiopsychotaxiplasm: Take 2 ½ (2005)   117

talkie   64, 71–5, 81, 87 n.88, 108, 138, 172, 255
  See also aurality; silence; sound
Talk to Her (2002)   198–200
Tangerine (2015)   255
Tarkovsky, Andrei   198, 204
teaching. *See* film, teaching; pedagogy
television   16, 43, 67, ch. 11 (210–27) *passim*, 269
  before   ix
  series, ch. 11 (210–27) *passim*
Terminator films   193f
The Text of Light (1974)   59

The Theory of Everything (2014) 256, 277f
therapeutic
  aspect of moral experience 136
  dimension of modern philosophy 134
  notion of art 79
The Thin Red Line (1998) 197
  See also Malick
Thoreau, Henry David 6, 79, 86 n.83, 95, 100, 102, 135, 211, 213, 252, 279f
Three Identical Strangers (2018) 276
Tolstoy, Leo 42, 242 n.16, 280
trace, theory of the photographic 27, 77, 243 n.35, 243 n.37, 272
  See also painting; photographs (and photography)
Tracy, Spencer xv, 115, ch. 13 (245–90) *passim*, 283 n.17–18
Transcendentalism (American) 100
transfiguration 93, 98f, 100, 103, 134, 201f
translation 8, 16
  cinematic 286
  studies 14
  untranslatability and 16
Travers, P. L., *Mary Poppins* 183
Trier, Lars von 197
Truffaut, François 27, 30

Unsane (2018) 255
utilitarianism 133, 135, 136f
utopia 136, 138f

Vertigo (1958) 49, 80f
Vice (2018) 277
virtual reality (VR) 34, 257
voice 67, 71, 76, 78–80, 86 n.82–3, 123, 172f, 215
  arrogation of 12, 17, 265
  cinematic 87 n.88
  in film 82 n.4, 84 n.44
  of impersonal rationality 124
  See also aurality; Cavell, voice; silence; sound

voice-over 197, 199, 236, 259–61, 265, 268f, 273f, 277, 279
Vox Lux (2018) 277

Walden (1969, dir. Mekas) 279f
Walden (Thoreau) 252
  See also Cavell, *The Senses of Walden*; Thoreau
Walton, Kendall 55, 242 n.16
Warhol, Andy 58f
Warshow, Robert 6, 13, 210, 212f, 221, 224f
Wartenberg, Thomas E. 3, 9
The Way We Were (1973) 274, 289 n.99
Weaver, Sigourney 193
Wedlock House: An Intercourse (1959) 117
Weidler, Virginia 176
Weininger, Otto xiv
Welles, Orson 46, 71, 112, 269, 271f
Weltbild (world-picture) 131
Wheatley, Catherine 9
Whedon, Joss 221
Williams, Linda 142
Wiseman, Frederick 236
Wittgenstein, Ludwig xi–xiv, 4, 6f, 9, 75, 91f, 231, 233
  Philosophical Investigations xi, 18 n.11, 86 n.81, 91, 133, 222, 231
  See also Cavell, Wittgenstein
The Wizard of Oz (1939) 49, 263
The Wolfpack (2015) 276
World War Z (2013) 269
WR: Mysteries of the Organism (1971) 120 n.13

Young, Roland 176

Zapruder, Abraham 254, 259
Žižek, Slavoj, interface effect 35f
Zweig, Stefan xiv

www.ingramcontent.com/pod-product-compliance
Lightning Source LLC
Chambersburg PA
CBHW070808300426
44111CB00014B/2456